775 A

Guiding Language Learning

Guiding Language Learning

Learning SECOND EDITION

MILDRED A. DAWSON
Sacramento State College

MARIAN ZOLLINGER
Portland Public Schools

ARDELL ELWELL
Paterson State College

Harcourt, Brace & World, Inc.

New York · Chicago · Burlingame

PHOTO CREDITS

PAGE 21, Carl Purcell from NEA. PAGE 37, Hays from Monkmeyer. PAGE 49, Hays from Monkmeyer. PAGE 65, Carl Purcell from NEA. PAGE 67, Hays from Monkmeyer. PAGE 75, Michael F. Logerfo. PAGE 87, Nancy Rudolph. PAGE 91, Hays from Monkmeyer. PAGE 101, Max Tharpe from Monkmeyer. PAGE 111, Hays from Monkmeyer. PAGE 131, Hays from Monkmeyer. PAGE 132, Carl Purcell from NEA. PAGE 157, Ewing Galloway. PAGE 165, Standard Oil of New Jersey. PAGE 167, Hays from Monkmeyer. PAGE 175, Aigner from Monkmeyer. PAGE 183, van der Meid from Monkmeyer. PAGE 189, Ewing Galloway. PAGE 193, Merrim from Monkmeyer. PAGE 207, Landwehr from Monkmeyer. PAGE 213, Stantis. PAGE 227, Howard Knaus. PAGE 229, Aigner from Monkmeyer. PAGE 231, Hays from Monkmeyer. PAGE 239, Hays from Monkmeyer. PAGE 241, Hays from Monkmeyer. PAGE 249, Scholastic Magazine. PAGE 259, Bloom from Monkmeyer. PAGE 261, Hays from Monkmeyer. PAGE 281, Max Tharpe from Monkmeyer. PAGE 311, Carl Purcell from NEA. PAGE 325, Ewing Galloway. PAGE 329, Hays from Monkmeyer. PAGE 337, Hays from Monkmeyer. PAGE 339, Hays from Monkmeyer. PAGE 371, Lew Merrim from Monkmeyer. PAGE 373, Hays from Monkmeyer.

© 1957, 1963 BY HARCOURT, BRACE & WORLD, INC.

Library of Congress Catalog Card Number: 63–15121

PRINTED IN THE UNITED STATES OF AMERICA

Preface

THE TEACHER of language arts in the elementary school is beset by difficult questions. What is each child's potential best? How can he be helped to achieve it? What should he know about language? What attitudes are desirable? What skills should he have mastered? What abilities should he be developing?

This book is designed to aid the thoughtful teacher in seeking the answers to these questions. It is intended for practical everyday use in enlivening and enlightening instruction in language. Its purpose is to provide methods for promoting the development of good language habits in the early school years. The text begins with a discussion of the basic concepts of language teaching and learning and proceeds to a consideration of all the language arts—listening, speaking, reading, and writing—as they are practiced in the kindergarten, the primary grades (1–3), the intermediate grades (4–6), and the upper grades (7–8). It reviews the nature of language, the facts of child development, and the principles of learning. While the authors acknowledge research findings on general growth patterns in children, they recognize that teaching techniques and materials must be flexible to allow for individual differences among pupils. The procedures offered are constructed to afford the necessary adaptability and to align with whatever curricular program prevails, and the emphasis throughout is on intake-outgo: in other words, expression results when enough ideas and experiences have been received.

The entire text of the earlier edition has been revised and updated, with two new chapters added—one on "Basic Concepts for the English Teacher" and one on "Developing Pupil Interest in English"—and others combined or deleted. The first edition, published in 1957, was based in part on *Teaching Language in the Grades*, published in 1951. Both they and this edition relate very closely to *Language for Daily Use*, an elementary series. Teachers can rely on the new edition for the most modern and effective methods of presenting the subject matter in this and other series.

It is the sincere hope of the authors that those who read this book may discover in it something that meets their own particular needs—that college students and beginning teachers may get a clearer picture of what they will teach and how and why; that experienced teachers may gain suggestions for improved teaching; and that principals and other supervisory personnel may find help in curriculum-planning and in referring teachers to ideas that may enhance instruction.

MILDRED A. DAWSON
MARIAN ZOLLINGER
ARDELL ELWELL

February, 1963

Contents

Guiding Language Learning

1

Basic Concepts for the English Teacher

Chapter 1 is based on the premise that a teacher of English must have accurate and recent information about language, must understand the principles upon which the English language functions, and must exemplify high standards in the use of English in both speech and writing. Eight concepts are presented, each significant in shaping the teacher's approach to language instruction.

NOTHING is more frequently assumed to be part of the teacher's training and equipment than competence in English. School administrators and teachers sometimes reason that one whose education has been acquired through the medium of English and whose daily communication with others is carried on in English has all the understanding about the language which an English teacher must have. The assumption and conclusion are often faulty. Using language and understanding language sufficiently to teach it are two different things.

Understanding Language

KNOWLEDGE about the language is not enough in itself. It should be accompanied by an understanding of values, of what is right and good in the use of language. The teaching profession calls for high standards of competence in many fields, and the English language is among the most important. In the daily use of language, a teacher must adjust to many different situations, addressing various groups, from little children to adults. The choice of expression must be appropriately adapted to each situation, but, in all, the basic values must be observed. The teacher should speak and write English well, according to reasoned standards of goodness and badness, correctness and incorrectness of language. A basic purpose of English instruction is to help boys and girls to develop these reasoned standards and to learn to apply them. Such instruction, by both precept and example, must be based upon the teacher's own awareness and consistent use of good English.

The modern teacher of English needs to be conversant with the extensive developments in linguistics that have taken place during the last few decades. Through study and research, scholars have contributed abundantly to man's knowledge of language, shedding light on both old and new facets of the subject. As with science, the subject is broad, the advance of scholarship rapid, and the student is hard put to keep up with progress. Nevertheless, the English teacher should be informed and able to provide facts and explanations about the language that are consistent with recent findings. How much, if any, organized instruction in language is presented in the classroom depends on the grade level of the teaching assignment, but the teacher's training will serve a useful purpose at all grade levels in establishing an interest in language and a regard for its use without undue restrictions. Probably the teacher's full resources are seldom sounded by elementary pupils, but the existence of such knowledge and understanding constantly serves as the rudder in directing instruction.

The teacher should be acquainted with the English language from both the scientific and historic viewpoints. The perspective of the historian is important since English is today a product of its past. The teacher also needs to look at the language of today with the objective view of the scientist; only a willingness to observe the facts of language and accept them can free the teacher from certain common misunderstandings about English and permit the use and enjoyment of its remarkable flexibility. Since use of language is very largely a matter of selection—of words, phrases, and sentence patterns—one who seeks to guide the young in such selection should be well grounded in the subject.

To one uninitiated in language study, the characteristics of his own language may not be well defined even though he uses it well. This seeming paradox occurs because language is learned imitatively, usually without analysis. Many people use the language without knowing much about it, just as many drive high-powered cars without knowing the principles of internal combustion. But this ignorance of language fundamentals is unacceptable if one is to teach English. A knowledge of the working principles of the language is as important to one who works with language as the knowledge of machinery is to the scientists and mechanics who work with autos.

Concepts About Language and Language Teaching

THE following pages of this chapter introduce a few important concepts about language and the teaching of language, which every English teacher should have as a basis for instruction. Inevitably, the first concept deals with the nature of the subject we are studying. It arises from the elementary question, What is language?

Language is an arbitrary system of vocal symbols. Communication is carried on in several ways. The lower animals seemingly have their own expressive sounds; and man sometimes speaks by gesture, sign, or facial expression, which is sometimes described as a kind of language. But here the word is used in a more limited sense. *Language,* in this book, refers to communication by human speech. Speech, in this sense, includes both oral and written expression.

The spoken word comes first. Communication of ideas rests upon agreement that certain facts or experiences shall be represented by certain vocal sounds. Then, when the sound is uttered, it brings to mind whatever the members of the group have agreed it shall represent. For most words such agreements took place in the dim past, no one knows when. Yet within the memory of all, some words have been added to the vocabulary by use and common consent. The process is still operating. When new inventions create the need for a word to describe them, our language develops a word—*helicopter, television, electronics,* for example. The spoken word becomes the symbol for the object or the idea, and before long, it seems, the new word is on the lips of children, as well as adults, and the meaning well established.

Words so easily created are not necessarily used by all who speak the same language. Geographical and social differences in usage occur. Examples from England and America point up this fact. Americans speak of elevators, movies, TV, the hood of a car, and gas to make the car go. The British, on the other hand, ride on lifts, see the cinema, watch telly, open the car bonnet, and buy the necessary petrol.

For most practical purposes the word is the smallest unit of the language; yet it is obvious that words are composed of smaller units of sound. Though different languages have many sounds in common, each language has some particular characteristic of its own. Its system of sounds and words helps to make it unique.

The written language is one more step removed from fact and experience. It is a secondary system of signs and symbols formed to represent the vocal symbols of speech. The hieroglyphics of ancient Egypt expressed the thoughts of the Egyptian priests on stone. That system used conventionalized pictures for ideas, often for whole groups of words. With the invention of an alphabet, man was able to represent each word separately, the letters of the alphabet corresponding directly, though somewhat inaccurately, to each unit of vocal sound.

Not every society enjoys the benefits of such a writing system. Even today some primitive groups possess no written language at all. Needless to say, where writing exists it is of utmost importance, allowing man to use the thoughts of individuals recorded from the distant past or the faraway parts of the world and to record his own thoughts for the future. In the cultural history of mankind, the written language, symbol of symbols, is of untold value.

That people in various parts of the world use different symbols for speech and writing is a reminder that language is man-made, not heaven-sent. As such, it is subject to change through error or individual preference. The Chinese child refers to his mother as *mu-chin;* the Russian, as *mat';* the Spanish, as *madre.* The relationship is the same in all, only the symbol varies. And the symbol is effective for communication because each society has arbitrarily designated its meaning. Almost three thousand different languages are spoken in the world today, each with its own symbols understood by its own group. A recognition of the human source and the arbitrary selection of the symbols used for communication is important to understanding the nature of language.

What is true about the sounds and the words of a language is true also of other characteristics. The changing forms of words and the system by which arrangements of words in a sentence bear certain implications vary from one language to another. To understand a language one must know how it operates—what its sounds and words symbolize and how they change in form and sentence pattern to effect a change in meaning. From this fact a second principle holds true.

A language must be described in terms of its system. The major divisions of a linguistic system include its phonology, its morphology, and its syntax. The meaning of each will be briefly explained, with illustrations taken largely from the English language.

Phonology is the science of the sound system of a language. Though different languages may have many sounds in common, each has distinctive sounds not easily acquired by one who has grown up without them. Thus foreigners are likely to mispronounce the English *th,* and Americans have difficulty with the German umlauted *u* or the vowel sound in the French word *oeuf.* A study of the phonology of the Hawaiian language reveals an abundance of vowel sounds that make the speech melodious. Some languages, on the contrary, are heavy with consonants or guttural sounds. In certain African languages the sound system includes various clicks that seem strange to English ears. In Chinese the tone in which a word is expressed is an integral part of the word so that a change in pitch may mean a change in meaning.

To record the sounds of any language, even the most exotic, linguists have developed an International Phonetic Alphabet (IPA), designed to provide a separate written symbol for every vocal sound. The IPA enables them to make a record of what they hear, noting the variations in vowels and consonants—the articulated sounds—as well as their duration, the stress placed upon syllables or phrases, the pitch or tone of voice, and the juncture or separation of speech units. It is possible for linguists, trained in the use of the IPA, to enter a region and obtain an accurate description of the language used by the people, whether or not the language has a writing system.

Even in the United States, to describe accurately the sounds of English as spoken by different people, a linguist needs a more accurate system than the alphabet. Some linguists, rather than force the exact distinction of the IPA in describing a familiar language, use a simplified form to describe English sounds for English-speaking people. One form is the phonemic transcription of Trager and Smith(6).

Though the spelling system in English serves its purpose remarkably well in providing an understandable writing system, it cannot be considered an accurate index to pronunciation. Inaccuracies in representing articulated speech sounds are evident to anyone studying the phonology of the language. One reason is that there are only twenty-six letters in the alphabet, but more than that number of separate vowel and consonant sounds, in addition to a number of diphthongs.

Of the twenty-six letters in the alphabet, three are insignificant in describing the pronunciation of English: the *c* represents two sounds which are accurately represented by other letters, *s* and *k*; and *x* and *q* are really not representative of single sounds but of combinations of two—*ks* for *x*, *kw* for *q*. The alphabet fails to provide separate symbols for six single consonant sounds in the English language. As a consequence, five of them are symbolized by a combination of two letters, as follows:

> *sh* for the first consonant sound in *shell*
> *ch* for the first and last consonant sound in *church*
> *ng* for the last consonant sound in *sing*
> *th* for the first consonant sound in *think*
> *th* for the first consonant sound in *then*

The last two in the list differ in that one is voiced, the other voiceless; yet the alphabetical symbol, *th*, is the same. Dictionaries, in showing pronunciation, use various devices to distinguish the voiced sound of *th*: the use of italics in one dictionary, the "bar th" (th) in another, and a different form of "bar th" (th) in still another. The sixth consonant sound that lacks a symbol of its own is illustrated by the medial consonant sound in *leisure* and the final consonant sound in *garage*. Dictionaries show the pronunciation with *zh*.

Regional differences are likely to occur in the pronunciation of vowels. Certainly the five vowels in the alphabet are inadequate for an accurate description of the vowel sounds. A list of words like the following indicates more than five vowel sounds:

bit, bet, bat, cut, cot, cook, cone, caught

Some vowel sounds are actually diphthongs. More than one sound can be heard in the diphthongs *a* in *day, i* in *lie,* and *u* in *cue.* A number of other diphthongs, like *oi* in *boy* and *ou* in *about,* increase the total number of English sounds.

The phonology of a language includes the study of more than vowel and consonant sounds. Meaning and feeling are also expressed by the pitch of the voice, the stress given by extra force or volume, and the juncture of point at which syllables, words, phrases, and sentences are joined. A true description of the phonology of a language must also include these variations in sound.

The classroom teacher should be able to recognize the different sounds of English and should know how they are formed. Such knowledge can be useful in recognizing problems of pronunciation and, in some cases, of spelling. It can enable the teacher to use judgment in dealing with such problems or, if serious, in referring them to others.

Morphology is the study of words and their meaningful parts. In many languages a strong tendency is to combine more than one idea into one word. English uses this system to enlarge its vocabulary many times over. To a base word a prefix or suffix is added, making a derived form of the word. Thus *-ation* or *-ition* is frequently used to make a noun from a verb or another noun, as in *sense, sensation,* and *rend, rendition.* Or *-able* or *-ible* is combined with a noun or verb to make an adjective, as in *sense, sensible,* and *pass, passable.* Or *-er* is commonly added to a noun or verb to make a noun suggesting a person and his work, as *hat, hatter,* and *farm, farmer.* A wide range of prefixes can be applied to a stem or base word, multiplying its uses and varying its meanings, as in *receive, conceive, deceive,* and *perceive,* or, as another example, *amoral, immoral,* and *unmoral.* The addition of two prefixes is not uncommon, as *non-* and *re-* in *nonrestrictive,* or *in-* and *sub-* in *insubordinate,* or *co-* and *ef-* in *coefficient,* or *dis-* and *en-* in *disentangle.* A somewhat ridiculous example of combining stem and affixes in English is the record-breaking word *antidisestablishmentarianism.* One other way in which derived forms are constructed is through the combination of two independent words to form a single new word. Examples of such compounds are *grandmother, wholesale, play-*

ground, and *cockleshell.* All the prefixes and suffixes shown in this paragraph produce derivational changes.

Another kind of change in word forms is called inflectional, which has to do with grammatical relationships and occurs in English only with the addition of suffixes. Some languages are highly inflective, investing in a single word signals that indicate complex relationships of number, person, mood, tense, and the like. Other languages, on the contrary, tend to express many of these relationships by using separate words or phrases. To some extent, both methods are used in English. One can speak of *the city's wealth* or *the wealth of the city.* In the former case, the *'s* is an inflectional ending showing a relationship commonly called possessive. Since the inflective nature of English has been subject to considerable change, further examples will be noted later in the discussion of that topic.

It is possible for a trained linguist to communicate with a person whose language he has never heard before and learn from him many morphological characteristics of his language. The method he pursues involves steps similar to these: first he holds up an object, such as a stick, indicating by gesture that he wishes to know the word; the native gives him the word; then the linguist records it in the accurate symbols of the IPA. Next, the linguist holds up two of the same objects; the native gives the word for two sticks. Now the linguist not only has a record of the phonetic symbol for the word, but he has discovered at least one way in which the system expresses plurality. By further probing, he can discover any number of words, thus increasing his vocabulary of nouns in the new language. By inducing the native to describe his own or the linguist's actions, he can get at verbs. He records in IPA such expressions as "You are sitting," "I am standing," and "He is standing." In addition to the vocabulary, he discovers the system for expressing first, second, and third persons and the accompanying changes that may be made to show grammatical relationships between different parts of the sentence. So he goes on to the discovery of further systematic changes in the inflection of words.

Syntax is the study of words or word groups (phrases, clauses, and independent elements) and their interrelationships within the sentence. The syntax of the English language places great significance upon the order or arrangement of words within the sentence. In our language, syntactic structure involves four major relationships: the subject and predicate; the word and its modifier; coordinate patterns of words, phrases, and clauses; and subordinate patterns of the same.

Word arrangement is well established for a relatively small number of sentence patterns. When the order of words in a sentence varies from these patterns, the result is awkwardness or loss of meaning. The normal English sentence pattern calls for subject first, then verb. *There he goes* is a normal pattern. A shift to *There goes he* is permissible, but is so unusual that it attracts immediate attention. The transposition may be useful for the purpose of emphasis. In the sentence *He eats cabbage,* a transposition cannot even be allowed for emphasis as its result would be nonsensical.

In some languages the syntactic structure is so arranged that even the slightest variation in word order alters the meaning; the English language is not so severely restricted. In a sentence such as *Tomorrow we eat fish,* English syntax does not permit interchange of subject and object (*we* and *fish*). Latin would permit such transposition for the inflectional endings on the nouns would always distinguish subject from the object. English does, however, allow the transfer of the adverb (*tomorrow*) from the beginning to the end of the sentence without alteration in the meaning.

Since every language has its phonological, morphological, and syntactical structure, the description of the language must point up these characteristic features. The traditional study of English grammar grew out of analogies thought to exist between English and Latin. Much of the terminology used in the early grammar schools came directly from Latin grammar. Yet English grammar cannot be described in terms of Latin grammar since its system is not the same. While Latin is highly inflective, English has dropped most of its inflective changes; and while Latin makes no use of word order to express relationships, the meaning of an English sentence is dependent upon it.

That English grammar was well analyzed by some early grammarians is rather remarkable, but inaccuracies and false statements existed which could not be corrected as long as the language was described in terms of Latin. English has its own systematic grammar, discovered by direct analysis of its own sounds, words, and sentences. It must then be described in terms of that system.

It might be appropriate here to mention that the study of grammar now, as pursued by the scholars, involves extremely complex matters. Much that is known comes from the great grammarians of the past as well as the present, and no grammar is capable of explaining by principle all the intricate relationships used in human speech. As the linguist Edward Sapir(17, p. 38) said, "Unfortunately, or luckily, no language is tyrannically consistent. All grammars leak."

Being an arbitrary system, language is subject to change. The history of a language shows an interesting succession of changes. The reasons are sometimes evident, sometimes not. It is understandable that since language is learned by imitation, the learning is limited by human imperfection. The phonological structure of a word may change because of careless slurring or omission of syllables. Thus *an* comes from an earlier form of *one,* and *curtsy* appears to be a slurring pronunciation from the word *courtesy. Gas* from *gasoline* and *bus* from *omnibus* illustrate the cutting off of syllables. By cutting, *taxi* has derived from *taxicab*, perhaps because of the hurry of today's world; but yesterday's *taxicab* was originally *taximeter cab*, suggesting that hasty short cuts were used even in the more leisurely days when automobiles were a luxury.

Word meanings also change. In changing environments and in the light of new experiences and increased knowledge, new interpretations are attached to the old symbols. Here, too, human failure to understand another's meaning has sometimes been responsible. Certainly in the days of the Norman invasion, the Saxons missed both meaning and sound of some phrases the French-speaking conquerors used. A famous error was the application of the term *Rotten Row* in London to the *route de roi*, where the king exercised himself on horseback. Words run their courses, sometimes changing in meaning so radically that the original meaning is actually reversed. An example is the word *nice*, from Latin *ne-*, *not*, plus *scire, to know*. It is noted in the *Oxford English Dictionary*, in an entry marked 1290 A.D., as meaning "foolish or stupid"; but since the latter part of the eighteenth century it has been used commonly as a general term of commendation, meaning "well-mannered or agreeable." Another example is the word *crafty*, from Anglo-Saxon *craefte*, meaning "strength or power." It is noted in the O.E.D. as meaning "skilled or ingenious" in a passage written in 971 A.D., but by Chaucer's day (1386 A.D.) it meant "skillful in deceiving." These two illustrations indicate that changes may work both ways, toward increasing or decreasing the respectability of the meaning.

The greatest changes are observed when today's language is compared with its earliest form. Certainly the words of the Angles, Saxons, and Jutes, who came from northern Germany in the fifth century A.D. to their island home now known as England, show little resemblance to present-day English. Even the forms of Middle English, in a period roughly estimated between 1100 and 1400 A.D., are very strange to an untrained reader. Yet by the end of that period, drastic changes had already taken place. Chaucer's *Canterbury Tales*, from the literature of that period, resembles modern English closely enough that high school seniors can read the Prologue with enjoyment in the original form.

Perhaps the most significant change of all was the drift away from inflection. Anglo-Saxon was a highly inflected language. The forms of its nouns and verbs, like those of Latin or Modern German, changed internally or at the end to indicate complex relationships. In the West Saxon dialect of Old English, a speaker might have had to adapt a given noun to singular or plural form in any of four cases in the declension and know to which of a half dozen different declensions the noun belonged, since each declension had characteristic endings(18). Modifiers, too, were inflected; adjectives even had two declensions, differing according to whether they were "strong" or "weak."

The trend away from such extensive inflection had already begun by the time Middle English was developed. Now the English language bears only a few traces of the old inflective style: for example, in the plurality of nouns (usually with *s* or *es*) or possession (with apostrophe and *s*); person, number, gender, and case of personal pronouns; person, number, and tense in verbs (with *s* or *es* added for third person singular and *ed* for past); and comparative degrees in many one- or two-syllable adjectives or adverbs (with *er* and *est*).

Important syntactic changes have occurred, too, in the passage of time. Otto Jespersen(9) cites a number of examples. The expression of tense has been greatly enriched with the expansion in use and meaning of *have* and *had* as auxiliaries for the perfect and pluperfect. Not until Middle English was *have* used in the imperfect of intransitive verbs, and *I have been* apparently did not occur before 1200 A.D. For many centuries *am* was used in the perfect, as in *I am come* or *I am returned*. Another significant expansion has been in the use of the present participle with the infinitive. Until the end of the eighteenth century passive constructions like *the house is being built* were not used; *the house is building* was used instead. The modern trend seems to be toward increasing the number of tenses, with new forms developing in the use of *can, must, may, do,* but diminishing the number of moods, the subjunctive having less use than formerly.

Changes in the structure of English have been paralleled by growth in vocabulary, particularly during certain periods of history. The first noteworthy influence upon the Anglo-Saxon language came from missionaries, both Roman and Irish, who established schools and served as teachers. The Danish invasions followed, after which the Danes and other Scandinavians settled down to live in England, contributing many of their words to the speech of the people. The most extensive additions came with the Norman invaders, whose French language, used socially in court life and in formal communication in school and government, was frequently adopted by the English with their own peculiar shift in pronunciation.

In the Renaissance period, renewed interest in Latin drew a great many Latin words or derivatives into the vocabulary; and travel, education, and the world outlook that followed stopped nowhere, it seemed, in bringing to the English new ideas from foreign lands and new words to express them. The vocabulary of the English language continues to grow. Currently, new adventures into the realm of science bring new words, frequently coined with prefixes or roots of Greek origin, such as *psychiatry, bathysphere,* and *astronaut*. Increased travel, whether for war, commerce, or pleasure, is continually bringing new terms to English from remote corners of the earth. The current changes in vocabulary lead to discussion of another kind of change indicated in the following principle.

Variety in today's English is observed in social and regional dialects. Anyone who knows people of different social levels is aware that they use the language in characteristically different ways. The dialects of the educated and the uneducated frequently display sharp differences. Vulgar American, as H. L. Mencken noted in *The American Language*(13), exhibits its peculiarities almost entirely in pronunciation and vocabulary. Verb forms, particularly the past and past participle, account for the majority of differences. Any teacher whose class represents a cross section of the people will recognize common usages that differ from acceptable standards for the formal speech or writing of educated persons. They include *He come, run, seen,* or *done; I woulda give, I knowed he coulda took it;* and such picturesque expressions as *He snuck away, His ankle swole.* Pronoun usage similarly varies, with vulgar American including such expressions as *Me and her was late; them guys; hisn, hern,* and *ourn.* The double negative is especially noticeable: *I don't see nobody, I couldn't hardly walk;* or triple negative, at times: *He ain't never coming back no more, I ain't scarcely got practically nothing.* This is English as spoken by a large number of persons from a specific socio-economic background. It is the language with which they are completely familiar, one accepted without criticism or self-consciousness among their friends, and, therefore, one that permits them the greatest freedom of expression.

That American English could have social dialects of such great variance at the extremes of education is an interesting fact. Yet such dialects exist in other languages today and have in the past. An interesting example is the Cockney dialect of London, about which Simeon Potter, in *Our Language*(14, p. 134), makes this observation: "Slang and dialect meet and mingle in London Cockney, that racy, spontaneous, picturesque, witty, and friendly English spoken not only by Londoners 'born within the sound of Bow Bells' (the bells of St. Mary-le-Bow Church in Cheapside) but also by millions of other Londoners living within a forty-mile radius of the 'mother of cities.' As a dialect, London Cockney is both regional and social." Mencken(13, p. 473) concludes, "The plain people, hereafter as in the past, will continue to make their own language and the best that grammarians can do is to follow after it." This is recognition of its existence, even its eventual influence; but it is not an acceptance in the schools where usage of another social dialect is taught.

Regional dialects, like social dialects, are most likely to appear where some degree of isolation preserves the peculiarities of a group and prevents them from learning other forms by imitation. Regional dialects should not be confused with dialects growing from social and educational differences. The kinds of individual expressions used in both regional and social dialects, however, have one interesting thing in common. The differences between standard educated English in various regions, like those between social dialects, are virtually all to be found in pronunciation and vocabulary. Syntactic structures are only slightly affected. Sentence patterns do not vary; word order remains the same; modification follows the same arrangement; coordination and subordination are expressed alike in various regional and social groups.

The study of regional dialects, or linguistic geography, has been conducted in the United States over a period of years under the leadership of Hans Kurath, Raven McDavid, Jr., Carroll Reed, and others. Teams of linguists, trained in hearing and recording the language of the people, have accumulated data illustrating the variation in vocabulary and pronunciation. *The New England Atlas of Linguistic Geography* holds fascination for the browser as well as the scholar as it maps deviations for common terms, such as *tree toad, peeper, March peeper, marsh peeper, peewink, peepwink,* and *pinkletink.* One can surmise the influence of careless pronunciation (from *peepwink* to *peewink*) and of logical association (*March* to *marsh*).

Pronunciation is often sharply differentiated in various regions of the country. Linguists identify three general areas in which characteristic differences are likely to occur—North, Midland, and South. For example, they can show on a map the boundaries within which the word *greasy* is pronounced with a sound of *z*, and beyond which, with a sound of *s*. Each pronunciation is "right" among educated people in the region. At present, regional dialects are declining rather rapidly. School, radio, television, and motion picture films tend to establish general standards of pronunciation and word forms. Easy methods of transportation leave fewer remote areas in the country, but even in remote areas people now hear the same programs and are influenced by the same characteristics of speech as those who live in cultural centers.

The dialect of standard English varies to suit the occasion. It is reasonable to think of standard English, such as that taught in the schools, as a dialect—the dialect of educated people. Within the dialect of standard English, the language of educated individuals is also subject to change under the varied circumstances of their lives. The occasion may demand either formal or informal speech or writing; the subject under discussion determines the use of technical or general terms; those for whom the message is intended must be addressed appropriately for their age, their vocabulary, and their general experience or acquaintance with the subject. Other determinants of linguistic choice include the character of the speaker or writer, his own purpose in communication, and, in the case of the writer, his choice of literary form.

Differences in language occur between speech and writing. A person dares take more liberties in the spoken language than in writing, depending upon gesture, tone of voice, or facial expression to fit the words to the situation. Speech is frequently uninhibited. When the expression of an idea is rather lengthy in conversation, the speaker is likely to be interrupted, or to interrupt himself, or sometimes to leave the sentence dangling and skip to something else. Even when the situation stimulates the speaker to more than ordinary care, and when he is expressing himself upon a topic in which he is well informed, the spoken words are likely to include some examples of diction which he would not use in writing. The very permanence of written English enables standards to be maintained. Whereas the spoken word, once uttered, vanishes, the written word remains on the page to be scanned, interpreted, and criticized. Teachers recognize that pupils must learn to be even more careful of conventional standards of usage and diction when they write than when they speak. Formal speeches represent a different kind of spoken English, frequently a learned repetition or variation of a written speech. In any formal speaking the same standards required of the writer hold for the speaker.

It has not been unusual for a teacher to encourage a child whose empty sheet of paper lies before him by saying, "Just write as you would talk. Put down on paper what you can tell me about the events we have discussed." To a certain extent, the advice may be good. The teacher, in this case, is striving to induce some spontaneity in the pupil. But if the child responds literally, he must revise his paper to conform to the standards expected of writers, before considering it readable. In the process of educating an individual, spontaneity may need to be encouraged at an early period even at the expense of standard form; but as soon as a child is mature enough, he can learn to accept the fact that the first draft, written to get the thought on paper, is the first stage of writing only; the second stage, involving the necessary working over, must follow.

The schools are responsible for teaching standard English. In our society it is agreed that the schools should teach young people the dialect known as standard English. The informed teacher who knows something of the history and characteristics of language will recognize the inevitability of dialectal differences. The approach to the teaching of the dialect used by educated people, then, will not be made by condemnation of other dialects. Nor will the standard usage of American English be held up as absolute right opposed to absolute wrong. The teacher, recognizing the superior effectiveness of standard English in most relationships conducted in the business and social world of the educated, will undertake the development of language habits which young people will need in dealing with others whose dialect is that of educated English. These usage forms may plainly be acknowledged as those required in school.

In the elementary school, with little children who are not yet mature or experienced enough to recognize the reasons, the teacher simply begins habit-forming practice in standard usage. As noted before, the differences will be concerned with word forms and pronunciation. Capitalizing on the ability of young children to learn by imitation, the primary teacher will provide practice of standard forms in a positive approach. As children advance, guidance can be offered by teachers who are wise in a knowledge both of language and of children. Young people whose language usage is substandard need not be ashamed of the language they have learned at home, need not develop fears that prevent them from freedom of expression, need not resentfully scorn the efforts of a teacher whose language is different. Instead, they can be led gradually toward the broader view of language which their teacher possesses. As they come to understand the differences in dialects and the effects of language usage in their own lives, they can begin to develop reasoned standards of their own. When their own will propels them to use the most effective language forms, even when they differ from those commonly used in their own social group, they will learn rapidly.

While the approach to the teaching of standard English usage must be made with kindness and wisdom, there is no suggestion that it cannot or should not be made with firmness. If the pupils' attitudes are receptive the teacher can offer planned and continuous guidance in the standard English forms which they need to learn. Gross differences can be handled first, minor points later; and wisdom will dictate frequent help on a few changes until the language habits begin to take form, rather than scattered work on a great many.

English is an important language and teaching English is important. Less than four centuries ago, in Shakespeare's day, only five million people spoke English as their mother tongue. Then, beginning in the reign of the first Queen Elizabeth, with the period of colonization, and later in the building of an empire, the aggressive British spirit led English-speaking people to spread all over the world. The United States, with its millions relying on English for common communication, contributed most to the remarkable increase in the use of the English language. People from strange lands, speaking foreign tongues, learned English or saw to it that their children did. As the United States became one of the great world powers, English was still more firmly established. And in far corners of the world, Britain's former colonies, including Canada, Australia, and New Zealand, bear the legacy of the empire and its educational systems in their distinctive English dialects and literature. Today over two hundred million people use English as their first language, and millions more read and understand it as their second language.

Schools in Europe and South America commonly require English as a foreign language; students in Russia, Turkey, and Japan are among those who study it. It has been asserted that "over half of the world's newspapers are printed in English. English is the language of over three fifths of the world's radio stations." Around the world, in commercial enterprises, in schools, in government and international affairs, English is one of the great languages. To know the language and to speak it well is a truly great privilege. Many in our own country are born to it, and many others can learn to use it well with the guidance and inspiration of a teacher. The teacher of English may frequently be burdened with difficult details, but the spirit rises when the goals are viewed: to teach an impressively important language to human beings whose individual worth is held supreme in both the philosophy and the law of their land. The work of the English teacher must be considered a great privilege and a great responsibility.

The study and teaching of language can be useful and pleasant. The study of English requires some understanding of the nature of language and its history, but it also involves a scientific curiosity about the English of today. From infancy on through early childhood, most individuals find that sounds and words are endlessly interesting. A very small girl heard the word *zephyr* used. "Zephyr, zephyr," she repeated. "I like the sound of *zephyr*. I like *zephyr* better than *breeze* or *wind*." She was finding joy in words, and why shouldn't she? In the whole world of adventure that lay ahead of her, a very large and important part was to be inextricably linked with words. If a teacher can help a child to keep his delight in language, an important step in his education has been accomplished.

It cannot be denied that some individuals lose their love for language in the very classroom where it should be further developed. Could it be possible that in such cases an attitude of fear develops from a too strict application of standards which are unrealistic or for which the individuals are not yet ready? Or has an attitude of boredom grown out of endless drill on parts of speech to which little real value seems to be attached? Or could it be that some teachers, products of schooldays when grammar-by-rule was inherited from the eighteenth-century formal grammarians, have kept their noses buried in the rule book and forgotten to examine the language itself as it is presented daily around them?

English teachers must approach language with an explorer's view. They need to have an open eye and ear, ready to achieve linguistic learning inductively by current examples of good English, carefully observed and noted. Two common bugaboos for those uncertain of their grammar are the split infinitive and the preposition at the end of the sentence. Instead of repeating a questionable rule, scientifically inclined teachers will observe the speech habits of their educated friends and watch the written English in periodicals and books of good taste. Almost certainly they will observe that infinitives are sometimes split by irreproachable authors, not out of ignorance or eccentricity, but because in those instances the sense is expressed more clearly that way. The preposition at the end of the sentence may also be found quite legitimately used in both the speech and writing of the educated. The moral of such observation is not that standards are unimportant, but that the "rules" of usage may sometimes need to be checked against the evidence.

A mother of a child in the upper grades made the remark, "Why do English teachers have to be so old fashioned?" A denial of the accusation was promptly voiced. Then the mother explained the reasons for her conclusion. Her child's teacher had marked as a misspelling the word *sulfur* (the dictionary gives two acceptable spellings). Later an assignment called for a formal invitation. Since the family had recently received an engraved invitation to the governor's ball, the child modeled hers on the one received. It was returned for correction because the form differed from the one in the textbook. Still later a composition was assigned. Having written it with due care, the child gave it to her father to criticize. A successful writer himself, he felt obliged to have his daughter remove more than half of the commas. When her revised copy was submitted and eventually returned, there, in red, were all the commas which had been so carefully removed. No wonder the mother assumed that the teacher was living in a world of the past. The text by which the classroom rules were formed seemed not to be built upon the usage of educated persons in the modern world. Perhaps it rested securely (or so it seemed) on the rules expressed in the grammars of preceding generations.

Because English continues to change and must meet the needs of many peoples, neither its teaching nor its use can be governed by narrowly restrictive rules. Children should be taught that there are many ways to express a thought and that they need to look critically at their own expression and think of its effect upon the reader or listener. Having opened the eyes and mind of a child to the interesting and infinite number of ways of expressing an idea, the English teacher can help him to explore and choose the best.

Many characteristics of language can be discovered by young people for themselves. The rules they learn can be made as generalizations of their own discoveries. In addition, new wonders about language can be unfolded—the stories of words, the making of the alphabet, the history of writing, the treasures of dictionaries, the sounds of language, and the sense and nonsense of English spelling. If teachers can keep alive and develop the natural interest of children in language, if they can excite in them the exploring instinct by requiring them to look for answers to their own questions, if they can explain correctly and clearly the puzzling questions—then they will find most children ready and willing to receive instruction in their own mother tongue.

SUGGESTIONS FOR STUDY AND DISCUSSION

1. There are many new words in the English language today. List a few of them and tell how they must have been formed.

2. What are the three major divisions of a linguistic system? Explain the meaning of each one.

3. Explain how a trained linguist can communicate with a person whose language he has never heard before.

4. Are regional dialects increasing or decreasing? Give reasons for your answer.

5. In your classroom find the pupils whose parents can speak a language other than English. Have each pupil ask the parent how to say a simple sentence such as "I went to bed early yesterday evening." Notice the word arrangement in each of the languages. Find out whether "yesterday evening" can be transferred to another place in the sentence, such as the beginning, as it can be in English.

FOR FURTHER READING

1. ALLEN, HAROLD B., ed., *Readings in Applied English Linguistics.* New York, Appleton-Century-Crofts, 1958. Paper.

2. BAUGH, ALBERT C., *A History of the English Language,* 2nd ed. New York, Appleton-Century-Crofts, 1957.

3. CURME, GEORGE O., *English Grammar.* New York, Barnes & Noble, 1947. Paper.

4. DAVIES, HUGH SYKES, *Grammar Without Tears.* New York, Day, 1953.

5. DEAN, LEONARD F., and KENNETH G. WILSON, *Essays on Language and Usage.* New York, Oxford U. Press, 1959. Paper.

6. FRANCIS, W. NELSON, *The Structure of American English.* New York, Ronald, 1958.

7. FRIES, CHARLES C., *The Structure of English.* New York, Harcourt, Brace & World, 1952.

8. GLEASON, HENRY A., JR., *Introduction to Descriptive Linguistics,* rev. ed. New York, Holt, Rinehart and Winston, 1961.

9. JESPERSEN, OTTO, *Growth and Structure of the English Language.* Garden City, N. Y., Doubleday (Anchor), 1956. Paper.

10. LAIRD, CHARLTON, *The Miracle of Language.* New York, World, 1953. Paper.

11. LLOYD, DONALD J., and HARRY R. WARFEL, *American English in Its Cultural Setting.* New York, Knopf, 1956.

12. MARCKWARDT, ALBERT H., *American English.* New York, Oxford U. Press, 1958.

13. MENCKEN, H. L., *The American Language*, 4th ed. New York, Knopf, 1936.
14. POTTER, SIMEON, *Our Language*. Baltimore, Penguin, 1957. Paper.
15. ROBERTS, PAUL, *Patterns of English*. New York, Harcourt, Brace & World, 1956.
16. ROBERTSON, STUART, and FREDERIC G. CASSIDY, *The Development of Modern English*. Englewood Cliffs, N. J., Prentice-Hall, 1954.
17. SAPIR, EDWARD, *Language*. New York, Harcourt, Brace & World (Harvest), 1949. Paper.
18. SCHLAUCH, MARGARET, *The Gift of Language*. New York, Dover, 1955. Paper.
19. SLEDD, JAMES, *A Short Introduction to English Grammar*. Chicago, Scott, Foresman, 1959.

2

Language as Communication

Chapter 2 is an introduction to the language arts background for the teacher of elementary school pupils. It
tells the part that language plays in both formal and informal learning and shows the intimate relationship between language and thought. The chapter explains how
necessary it is that children have a rich intake of ideas, as
through actual experience or reading and listening, if they
are to speak and write well. It also explains the purposes
of communication through language.

THE language arts are a way of communicating through words
by speaking, listening, reading, and writing. The teacher of language is
concerned with stimulating thought in pupils, enriching their ideas, giving
them an opportunity to express their reactions to their own experiences and
to the thinking of others, and developing in them the skills that facilitate
communication.

In earlier times teachers were concerned with grammar, rhetoric, and
usage. Emphasis was on definitions, rules, drill on isolated items, memorization, some speaking fashioned to the teacher's assignment, and prescribed writing in formal fashion.

Oral language was a relatively minor phase of the curriculum. The
model pupil listened as his teacher gave assignments and made explanations or as classmates took their turns in the question-and-answer recita-
tions; he answered when the teacher called on him. His written language
was rarely for the purpose of communicating or exchanging ideas. Rather,
it was a formalized writing of answers to questions or the preparation of
compositions on prescribed topics.

The standards for the school of today are far different. The classroom
is a busy place where pupils observe, raise questions, then investigate and

experiment so that they may later be able to explain and share their information. All through the day pupils talk and listen, write and read in order to promote their learning activities and achieve their social purposes. For instance, they may use a map or a globe, explain an experiment, search for facts, enjoy a story, or discuss a problem. Such activities may be repeated daily, but the situations change. However, the ways of handling the situations, through the effective use of language, remain a constant challenge.

Another common incident leads to varied learning activities in which language plays an important role. A child may have moved away. His fellow pupils discuss ways in which they may show their good wishes and help him to adjust to his new home. So the pupils write letters—probably after discussing suitable topics—and they prepare materials to accompany the letters. They draw pictures and puzzles; they make surprise packets, one to be opened each hour of the day; they put together a booklet of original stories and poems. Here, as the children plan together and display what they have prepared, their learnings are social as well as linguistic.

The pupils will intersperse reading with the phrasing and listing of questions, planning for committee work, taking notes, telling stories, and possibly using some dramatization. They occasionally make a trip, as to a nearby art gallery. Before going, they will discuss the types of information to be sought, the division of responsibilities for recording pertinent facts, and personal behavior for safety and courteous conduct. During and after the visit to the art gallery, they will have further need for asking questions, offering information, clearing up inaccurate impressions, supplementing partially learned facts, and systematizing the learnings through a group-planned outline or series of summaries. Throughout such an enterprise, language is a constant aid to learning.

Thus, in the modern classroom, language is interwoven with all phases of the learning process. Although young children learn best through direct observation and actual sensory experience, they need the teacher's help in developing the vocabulary with which to describe and interpret their experiences. Language supplements observed facts and sharpens children's powers of observation and discrimination. By informal exchange of ideas, children develop the social skills required for carrying on group enterprises.

Today a prescribed curriculum might well be one in which the power to think and to live democratically is stifled. A classroom in which pupils listen and study quietly on occasion is desirable; but also desirable is a classroom in which children spend much of their time in conversation, discussion, storytelling, explanations, reporting, and other oral communicative activities—all cooperatively planned—that will motivate, extend, clarify, and deepen learnings.

On a trip to an art gallery, the teacher adds to the pupils' intake through her explanations.

General Considerations

IN PLANNING a language arts program, curriculum makers must recognize the function of language in everyday living and understand the intimate relationship between thinking and verbal expression. While all teachers are concerned with pupils' skills and accuracy in their speaking and writing, the chief concern is still the quality of ideas to be expressed.

THE FUNCTION OF LANGUAGE

The child's every waking hour is devoted to language in one form or another, whether he is in school or out. It is his vehicle of thought and communication. He thinks in words, for the most part; he expresses his ideas in words; he builds up his vicarious experiences as he listens to or reads words. They are indispensable to self-revelation, for it is through speech and writing that he is able to convey to others his bits of information and advice, his viewpoints, his attitudes, and his more articulate feelings and desires. His urge to communicate with others is irrepressible; he desires not only to speak or write his own thoughts, but to listen to, or read, the ideas communicated by others. As he hears the information, viewpoints, and interpretations that his companions express, his firsthand learnings are extended and modified by his secondhand information. Reading the printed page, too, makes a contribution to his knowledge and to his appreciation of conditions and situations, current and near at hand or distant in time and place.

As with adults, much of the speaking, listening, and writing in which a child engages seems quite casual—almost without purpose. With his playmates he chats at random about this and that. Yet, even in these most informal types of communication the underlying purpose—even though usually unconscious—is being part of a social group, achieving social adjustment with another individual or with a group of individuals his own age.

On innumerable occasions a child does employ language in a deliberate, planned attempt to establish new or improved relationships with others. He may be trying to make up after a quarrel; he may want to play on the ball team; he may try to persuade his father to increase his allowance. Frequently a child discusses issues and plans, advances arguments, explains a seeming laxity in his behavior, appeals to someone's good nature, and otherwise aims to fashion relationships in conformity with his own viewpoints and desires.

Language, then, is the human being's instrument for thinking and carrying on social intercourse. Words are his medium of exchange as he trades ideas with his associates through speaking, listening, and writing.

He thus takes in the viewpoints and information that others have to give and, in his turn, gives out facts, preferences, and opinions. In so doing he fulfills his inborn social nature and attempts to work out comfortable social relationships.

RELATION OF THOUGHT AND LANGUAGE

We tend to think in words. It is difficult to determine how much of our thinking can be done without words, through imagery. The more closely connected are our mental processes with direct sensory experiences, the greater is the probability of using imagery and the less our necessity to think altogether in verbal terms. A city child who has seen but one cow and viewed no pictures of others is likely to envision this particular black-and-white Holstein in a flashlike recalled image when the idea "cow" comes to mind. Later, after he has acquired a knowledge of cows through pictures, films, and perhaps a trip to see the real thing, and after he has heard and read stories that have broadened his concept of a cow, there is less chance that he will keep in his mind the picture of any particular cow.

In the beginning children probably have much mental imagery of specific objects and situations. "Being good" may mean being quiet when Mother is at the telephone. "Being punctual" may mean being at school before the final bell, but it may not include getting dressed on time or being prompt in reaching the table at mealtime. It is only when these concepts of goodness and punctuality have been broadened to mean general qualities through a many-angled series of experiences that verbalized generalizations almost completely replace imagery.

Do we think before we can speak; are thinking and speaking simultaneous; or do our thoughts clear up as we endeavor to put them into words? A. F. Watts(18, pp. 20–22, 26) explains the relation of thought to language in the following way:

> It is clear that both the infant and the unsophisticated adult have to try out their thoughts by uttering them aloud before they can feel sure that they know what they are. . . . On the other hand, it is also clear that to educated persons a great many thoughts occur with unmistakable identity in advance of their expression in words, so that they can truthfully say that many ideas come to mind before passing into speech.
>
> It would appear that our more familiar thoughts become matched sooner or later with words sufficiently adequate for their effective expression, so that whenever the occasion occurs for their "release" they are apt to become expressed time after time in the same forms. This being so, our having an idea may in many cases be no more than experiencing a feeling that the appropriate verbal response is about to follow. . . .
>
> When, however, thought is tentatively following new tracks and break-

ing fresh ground it is another matter. In this case we must give our thoughts words to make them known. Then we find out what we think by expressing it. . . .

The difficulty, as children encounter it, is that the language required for general discussion comes easily only to those accustomed to comparing freely with one another ideas which they have separately experienced, so that when experience is scanty and discussion rare this kind of language is not readily acquired. As long as children need language merely for telling what they have seen or heard or done, without attempting to summarize it briefly or to express any judgment about it, they will have little or no need of words other than those which call up pictorial images of concrete things and events.

The first steps in their progress to a greater mastery of language may well follow upon their having to talk about properties which a number of things have in common. Some of these properties they will have observed, no doubt, before they learn the words by which they are named; others they may not observe until their attention is drawn to them in reading or in conversation. . . .

Children need a rich variety of experience of all kinds if they are to make the most of their capacities, but to become fruitful in the highest sense their experience must be ordered and systematized, and here language is able to play an indispensable part with its apparatus for expressing differences—gross, moderate, and fine—in genera and species, in number, tense, direction, etc. Needless to say, this ordering and systematizing can best be effected through free and full discussion of all that has been seen, heard, suffered, and done. Only in this way will ideas become interwoven into patterns of greater power and complexity.

It appears, then, that these conclusions are justified: Experiences must provide the food for thought; mental processes that center on initial experiences tend to feature concrete and graphic images rather than words; unsophisticated persons tend to think along with their talking, with little disposition to think matters out before speaking; children acquire the ability to think verbally as they are led to compare, judge, or evaluate such sensory impressions and then to express the results of their thinking in systematized oral (or possibly written) form. The teacher must see that the pupils become familiar with the vocabulary that enables them to express exactly their increasingly abstract thoughts. Therefore, as they learn to verbalize their impressions and their thinking about such impressions, they grow in power both to think and to express their thoughts.

THE DUAL NATURE OF LANGUAGE

There are two distinct, yet interrelated, phases of language: the *intake* and the *outgo,* or reception (impression) and expression. The child takes in ideas through direct experience and observation, through viewing pictorial representations (flat pictures, films, and television, for instance) and three-dimensional models, and through listening and reading. By such means he gathers materials that will give him something to talk and write about.

The more a child (or an adult) knows about an object or a process, the greater his readiness to speak or write about it and the more fluent and clear-cut his expression of ideas. A person who is never at a loss for something to say if the conversation begins to lag is often an inveterate reader. He converses well because he has read so widely. Another interesting conversationalist is the person whose life is full of adventure, whether the circumstances of his life are unusually exciting or not. Because he savors each experience for its full human interest, he can use its details to entertain an audience.

Many teachers of language neglect the intake side of their instruction and concern themselves only with teaching the skills of speech and writing. This neglect results in a barren, poorly motivated program of language instruction—because children must have something worth saying and a genuine reason for communicating it if they are to improve their ability to express themselves clearly and interestingly. Ruth Strickland(15, pp. 321–22) comments that "the art of writing as of speaking consists in having something to say and knowing how to say it." She goes on to state that teachers should

> turn their attention first to what the child wishes to say and his purpose in saying it, and last to an appraisal of the form in which the ideas are set forth. . . . It is impossible to correct or improve a pupil's expression until he proffers enough of it to work with. When it is flowing as freely as he is capable of at the time, he is ready for help with form and correctness.

Oral and Written Communication

RELIABLE sources suggest that ninety-five per cent of our language needs in today's world are in the oral area. Oral communication is more frequent and generally more valuable for social needs than written communication. It is also through speaking and listening that most everyday domestic, business, and public affairs are arranged and carried out.

Speaking and listening skills are essential to stimulate others to thought and action and, in turn, to receive the thoughts and feelings of those with whom one communicates.

Speech must be recognized as part of a two-way process in the oral-communication cycle. The speaker must be aware of what he says and how he says it. He must also be aware of the listener and the resultant response to the spoken message. The speaker seeks to have the meaning and feeling he has expressed interpreted correctly by his listeners. The speaking-listening cycle, which is oral communication, is the chief mode for exchanging ideas, thoughts, feelings, and experiences.

Written communication is principally an instrument for recording ideas and events. It usually involves the communication of information, opinions, attitudes, and feelings to people not immediately present. While a person may write creatively for personal reasons or may keep private records, such as a diary or file of notes, most written communication involves an exchange of ideas among individuals and groups just as does oral communication. Usually the objective in written communication lies in the audience situation, with the writer looking forward to having his production read (or heard) by some other person or persons.

Man speaks and writes in response to two deep-rooted social and biological tendencies: self-expression and social communication. He speaks in an attempt to persuade or influence his hearers, to entertain them, to get aid or give help in making decisions, to report on past activities, to spread the news, to work out his social relations, or to transact his business. In all such talking there is purpose. Likewise, when a person writes, there is direct motivation in any communication that actually transmits interesting or needed information, spreads the news to someone at a distance, reaches out to a wider audience than a person's immediate companions, helps to organize and make definite critical statements that are to be given orally, makes notes of information to be shared with a group, or records events that will be of later interest and value.

PURPOSES OF COMMUNICATION

The language activities of elementary school pupils, in school and out of school, could probably be classified under the following purposes: *to inform, to convince, to maintain rapport, to move to action, to entertain.* The pupil who makes a report, or explains, instructs, or directs does it to inform. If he takes part in a debate, he is trying to convince. When he indulges in casual conversation, seemingly with no specific purpose in mind, he is attempting to maintain rapport—that is, showing politeness and consideration for the person to whom he is talking. In a pep talk he tries to persuade or cause to move to action. Here he would very likely have other purposes in mind, such as to maintain rapport, to inform, and to convince. When he tells a joke or a story, he is trying to entertain. For language instruction to be effective, however, it is important that children in school should talk and write for the same purposes and in the same type of situations that prevail in everyday living outside of school. The teacher must see that the proper kinds of opportunities for expression are developed and utilized in the classroom and that the children are helped wherever their speech and writing skills are deficient.

Expert teachers in our modern schools have found out that the best way to motivate children to an effort to master language skills as such is not to drill on these skills, but to emphasize communication. When children have ideas they want to impress on others, they will welcome suggestions for clearing up their organization, developing fully each phase of a subject, using vocabulary precisely in a pleasingly varied way, and maintaining a poised manner.

Interrelationships Among the Language Arts

T HE language arts curriculum has four facets: *listening, speaking, reading,* and *writing*. Each is closely related to the other three in various ways; and instruction that facilitates improvement in one facet is likely to benefit the others. Teachers should take advantage of the fact, for instance, that a child's ability to hear the sounds in a word precisely (auditory discrimination) is an advantage in learning to speak and write this same word correctly and in learning to analyze it for independent recognition when reading (phonics). Auditory discrimination, therefore, is an important factor in each of the language arts, and instruction to build up auditory skills should benefit all four of the language arts.

This section of Chapter 2 outlines certain important interrelationships among the language arts. These interrelationships should influence the way of teaching language skills.

SEQUENTIAL RELATIONSHIPS

The order in which children acquire the language arts is a very familiar one: first, in infancy, children learn to *listen* to language, eventually to *speak*, much later still to *read* and *write*. Before entering school, girls and boys have progressed far in mastering the skills involved in listening and speaking, but they learn to read and write in school. Listening, of course, is basic since children imitate the speech of those around them—pronunciation and enunciation, inflections and quality of voice, word choice, and sentence patterns. In turn, speech habits that children acquire are factors in developing reading readiness and in making progress in reading—favorable if the speech patterns are good, unfavorable if they are not.

This sequential relationship continues to be important throughout the elementary school years. Impression should precede expression—*intake* before *outgo*—and pupils should not be expected to talk or write fluently and effectively before they are full of ideas. They need to observe and experience before they read or discuss what they have read. Before pupils read a particular selection, they should be prepared, or motivated, for the reading.

A discussion is, of course, a good way to introduce the reading of a selection. It will help the children to recall facts and ideas already familiar to them, and it will also help them to relate these old facts and ideas to the new concepts contained in the selection. Again, before children write about new and relatively abstract learnings, they should observe and listen, read and talk over these learnings. Speaking, listening, and reading in abundance should precede writing unless much direct experience has made ideas completely familiar. Therefore, at all levels, children should observe the typical sequence of *listening, speaking, reading*, and—last of all—*writing*.

COMMON ELEMENTS

Progress in each of the language arts depends upon the others largely because of the elements common to all. One such element is vocabulary. The words that a child hears and understands are the words he is likely to adopt in his own speech, to read with comparative ease and adequate comprehension, and to use in his informal writing. The correlation of vocabulary with each and all of the language arts is relatively high. Anything that a teacher can do to build meaning vocabulary in one facet of the language arts (listening, speaking, reading, or writing) is likely to improve vocabulary in the other three facets.

Auditory discrimination is a common element found in the four language arts. The child's ear must be able to discriminate between such words as *pin* and *pen* and *been, ask* and *asked, lamb* and *land, drain* and *train, wail* and *whale*. Unless a child hears the differences in similar words, he is unlikely to speak these words correctly and to spell them accurately later on. His word recognition will similarly be affected.

Another common element is the organization of ideas. The listening child hears words strung meaningfully into sentences and gradually learns to speak in sentences patterned on those he hears. The typical six-year-old has progressed to the stage where, in his speech, he utilizes all the common sentence patterns in various degrees of complexity. The child's sentence patterns are modified to some extent as he listens to stories and later learns to read selections independently. As a result, his sentences come to have greater variety, better balance, and more discriminating emphasis. His listening and reading influence him constantly in his use of oral and written sentence patterns.

At a still more advanced stage of learning, the child comes to use the more complex organization demanded to make his sentence order conform to his pattern of thinking. In his listening, speaking, reading, or writing, he gains a sensitivity to a good sequence of ideas (telling the episodes in a story in order), relevance and selection of ideas (sticking to the point), and the clustering of details about the main point they support (proving the point with detailed evidence).

Each of the language arts correlates closely with the thought processes underlying language. Thinking is largely in words; it is sequential, with details clustering about the respective points they support. The child's language reflects this thinking. Teachers of the language arts, therefore, should focus on the ideas of their pupils rather than on the mechanical techniques for their listening, speaking, reading, and writing.

RELATIONSHIPS BETWEEN SPEAKING AND LISTENING

Research(1, 2) has brought out certain facts about the relationships between listening and speaking: (1) Speech is learned through listening and imitation. The model which the child hears and copies is, therefore, most important in speech proficiency. Plenty of practice in social situations is very necessary to the learning of correct speech habits. (2) The words children will learn to use is determined by the stimuli they meet (rural versus urban life, for instance) and the words they find of greatest service in conveying their ideas. From radio and television programs they will be more likely to adopt the words they hear if the teacher (or parent) provides both a preliminary and follow-up discussion that utilizes and clarifies the new words involved in each program. (3) A child's speech reflects language usage in the home and community—articulation and voice intonations, vocabulary, word usage, and sentence patterns. (4) The young child can understand sentences that are much longer and much more complicated than the sentences he can speak. (5) Improved listening skills help to improve the quality of speaking. (6) Sound is a potent factor in the improvement of usage. Thus, a child is helped when he listens to the cultured speech of his teacher, to recordings, and to stories expertly told, or to the broadcasts and the telecasts of well-trained announcers. He is helped, in addition, by a playback of his own speech from a tape recording, since the playback enables him to identify mispronunciations, faulty enunciation, and other poor speech habits. (7) Speaking that is reinforced by visual aids produces better recall of information on the part of listeners. In general, the child speaks the language he hears.

RELATIONSHIPS BETWEEN LISTENING AND READING

Skills in listening are also basic to success in learning to read effectively. Research work has revealed several important interrelationships between reading and listening: (1) Instruction in reading is given by a teacher through her oral language, and the pupil's ability to listen comprehendingly is crucial. (2) Listening is the chief mode for verbalized learning during the primary years. Retarded readers in the upper grades continue to learn more through listening than through reading. (3) Even though listening comprehension is superior to reading comprehension, children do fail to comprehend and retain many of the facts they hear. (4) Pupils, therefore, need guidance in learning to listen more effectively. (5) A narrow listening vocabulary is associated with difficulties in learning to read well. (6) For older pupils, the correlation between reading vocabulary and listening vocabulary runs high—possibly eighty per cent or higher. (7) Poor auditory discrimination is frequently associated with ineffective reading and may be a contributing factor in poor reading. (8) Listening helps children to get main ideas, rather than details; for older pupils, reading is superior to listening for immediate recall and for comprehending detailed information.

Since listening and reading skills are closely related, improvement in one should result in improvement in the other. Both are *intake* processes. Reading should be accompanied by discussion (before, during, and after the reading) if children's vocabulary, general comprehension, and retention of ideas are to be promoted.

RELATIONSHIPS BETWEEN SPEAKING AND READING

Numerous research projects have demonstrated the close relationship between the development of oral-language proficiency and reading readiness. Studies show that general oral-language abilities provide a favorable background of experiences and skills for the teaching of reading. These abilities include clear, fluent speech, a wide and varied vocabulary, the use of complete sentences when warranted, accurate auditory discrimination, and the ability to follow sequential development of a story or to relate an incident in sequential order.

Relationships between the oral area and reading have been identified in some research studies. These studies seem to show these relationships: (1) Reading performance varies significantly with oral-language proficiency. (2) Illiterate speech patterns may interfere with the child's learning to read. (3) While, in the early school years, speech forms a base for learning to read, the reading of older children helps to improve their oral language; for instance, their linguistic awareness of new terms, effective and pleasing sentence structure, and correct use of words. (4) The special vocabulary of the content subjects should be taught directly. As new words appear in the children's textbooks and their other reading, the teacher should discuss these words with the children and make sure the words have meaning before they start to read informational materials.

RELATIONSHIPS BETWEEN ORAL AND WRITTEN EXPRESSION

It is natural that oral and written communication should be very closely related because they have much in common: (1) The child learns to speak long before he can write; and the vocabulary, sentence patterns, and organization of ideas characterizing his speech are the foundation for subsequent written expression. (2) The child who has learned to write with ease can usually write down his firsthand experiences adequately without preliminary oral discussion, but he still needs to talk over complex ideas that he has secured secondhand. When a child is to write a description, explain a process, or report on a historic event (and he has not personally experienced the situation of which he is writing), he profits from a preliminary group discussion. He thus can clear up his thinking, fill in gaps, correct wrong impressions, and organize his ideas before he attempts to do any writing. Of course, a teacher may on occasion let a child write of familiar situations without talking them over first; but the ideas that a child gleans from his reading and from other vicarious means will need to be discussed before he begins writing—at least, if the ideas are quite complex and not too well understood. (3) There are differences in oral and written communication. Oral expression tends to be less structured, more fluid, but usually more incoherent than written communication. Most speaking is informal, and often the sentences of the person who is speaking do not hang together. The speaker thinks through his ideas as he goes along, and he often forgets how a sentence began long before he has finished it. Because of these problems in oral expression, instruction in the skills of speaking and listening needs to be emphasized. Experience has shown that to improve the oral expression of individuals is to improve the thinking of those individuals. Eradicate the habits of slovenly, sloppy speech, run-on sentences, incomplete and inconsistent thoughts in oral expression, and much has been done to guide the individual in precise and logical thinking habits. Written communication, on the other hand, tends to be superior both in thought content and sentence structure—more formal in style, and much better organized as to ideas. The writer usually has to think through each sentence before he writes his rough draft; he often checks and revises his sentences several times before he finishes his writing. (4) Taking notes and making an outline of the ideas to be presented in a talk will help a pupil to impress these ideas upon his audience. Pupils should learn to talk from notes, and they need much practice in talking from notes if their presentation is not to be indirect and halting. Usually the outline to guide the speaking will be adequate except in the case of formal and detailed reports which may need to be written out beforehand.

All in all, the teacher of language must see her instruction in proper context. She must see that the teaching of listening, speaking, and writing must be interrelated and tied in with the fourth language art, reading. Anything done to improve one of these facets of language is likely to affect the other three facets favorably; and neglect of any one of them may lead to gaps in the others. Learning is an integrated thing.

SUGGESTIONS FOR STUDY AND DISCUSSION

1. Try to analyze your purposes for each time you speak and write during an entire out-of-school day.

2. Which of the categories of oral and written communication were prevalent in your speaking and writing?

3. What intake experiences contributed to your oral and written communication? How?

4. Observe in a classroom and adapt the preceding questions to the situations you observe.

5. How do sectional differences (deep South, New England, and Middle West, for example) prove that listening and oral language are closely related?

6. To what degree do your experiences in speaking and writing validate the statements in the section that deals with the interrelationships of oral and written communication?

7. Which of the common elements seem particularly significant in the elementary school? Why?

FOR FURTHER READING

1. ARTLEY, A. STERL, "Research Concerning Interrelationships Among the Language Arts." *Elementary English* (December 1950), 527–37.

2. —— and others, *Interrelationships Among the Language Arts.* Champaign, Ill., National Council of Teachers of English, 1954.

3. DAWSON, MILDRED A., and FRIEDA HAYES DINGEE, *Children Learn the Language Arts.* Minneapolis, Burgess, 1959.

4. *The English Language Arts* (Chapters 5, 6, 9), Commission on the English Curriculum of the National Council of Teachers of English. New York, Appleton-Century-Crofts, 1952.

5. EVERHART, RODNEY W., "The School as a Communication Laboratory." *Elementary English* (February 1962), 129–31.

6. —— "Teaching Language in the Elementary School." *Elementary School Journal* (March 1959), 336–39.

7. GREENE, HARRY A., and WALTER T. PETTY, *Developing Language Skills in the Elementary School* (Part III). Boston, Allyn and Bacon, 1959.

8. HAIMBACH, DAVID, "Organizing Thinking." *Elementary English* (February 1962). 114–18, 143.

9. HAMPLEMAN, RICHARD S., "Comparison of Listening and Reading Comprehension Ability of Fourth and Sixth Grade Pupils." *Elementary English* (January 1958), 49–53.

10. JENKINS, WILLIAM A., "Time That Is Intolerant." *Elementary English* (February 1962), 84–90.

11. *Language Arts for Today's Children* (Chapters 8, 9, 10), Commission on the English Curriculum of the National Council of Teachers of English. New York, Appleton-Century-Crofts, 1954.
12. LOBAN, WALTER, MARGARET RYAN, and JAMES R. SQUIRE, *Teaching Language and Literature* (Part 4). New York, Harcourt, Brace & World, 1961.
13. POOLEY, ROBERT C., *Teaching English Usage* (Chapter 4). New York, Appleton-Century-Crofts, 1946.
14. SINGLETON, CARLTON M., "Needed Research in the Language Arts." *Elementary English* (May 1962), 495–96.
15. STRICKLAND, RUTH G., "Evaluating Children's Composition." *Elementary English* (May 1960), 321–30.
16. ——— *The Language Arts in the Elementary School* (Chapter 2). Boston, Heath, 1957.
17. TIDYMAN, WILLARD, and MARGUERITE BUTTERFIELD, *Teaching the Language Arts* (Chapter 1). New York, McGraw-Hill, 1959.
18. WATTS, A. F., *The Language and Mental Development of Children* (Chapters 1, 3, 6). London, Harrap; Boston, Heath, 1947.
19. WINTER, CLOTILDA, "Interrelationships Among Language Variables in Children of the First and Second Grades." *Elementary English* (February 1957), 108–13.

3

The Language Program in the Total Curriculum

Chapter 3 establishes the principles upon which an effec-
tive language program can be based. It outlines objec-
tives for kindergarten through the upper grades in terms
of child behavior. It also gives consideration to both cur-
ricular and administrative problems that affect language
instruction and offers some suggestions toward their
solution.

ANY effective language program in the elementary school has two basic aspects: the *ideas* that the children wish to express, and the *techniques* and *skills* that facilitate expression of those ideas—the *what* and the *how* of communication. Such a program provides for the *intake,* or observing, experiencing, listening, reading, and thinking through which the child acquires ideas; and the *outgo,* or the speech and writing by means of which he communicates ideas.

Language instruction, then, depends heavily upon provision for wide and varied experiences both direct and indirect in nature. Children gain facts and ideas by observation of the world around them, by their own efforts in construction and their experimentation to see what happens under given circumstances, by contacts with other people, and by study of books and pictures. The value of such experiences can be greatly enhanced as the teacher uses them to develop powers of verbal expression: to increase vocabulary and add depth to the meaning of words; to help children think about and discuss facts and ideas with greater clarity and objectivity; to broaden their understanding; and to foster imagination and creativity. In a classroom abounding with learning experiences of interest and value, the teacher builds upon the children's natural desire and need to share impressions and exchange thoughts through speech and writing. Much unobtrusive guidance in language usage can be given incidentally; but many class periods must also be devoted to learning and improving the needed language skills. In providing for constant reception and expression of ideas, the curriculum places an emphasis upon language as a tool to be used in effectuating all phases of learning.

In addition to meeting this practical and essential need for instruction in the use of language, teachers can, even in the elementary school, lay the groundwork for an appreciation of language and a respect for its powers. They can lead young children to enjoy words and to notice their variations in meaning and sound. Through the elementary years, they can tell the pupils something of the story of the English language, explain some of its characteristics, and point to its importance in the world today. They can find appropriate occasions and suitable material for introducing the study of language as a fascinating and significant aspect of the history of man's development.

Principles Underlying a Basic Language Program

THE language curriculum in any particular school must be flexible enough to adjust to local, current needs and interests of the pupils. Topics and situations that make up language lessons will vary from school to school, and from time to time in the same school, as will occasions that call for corrective teaching and for developing new skills. The variations, however, should be planned within the framework of established principles which serve as guidelines in selection of materials and procedures. Here are principles that underlie every adequate language program:

The language program should be developed from the interests and experiences of the children. In the early primary grades vocabulary growth and skills in expressing ideas develop largely from firsthand experiences in school and at home. As children grow older their environment expands in ever increasing circles from the immediate neighborhood to distant times and places. Experience then includes not only what they do and see but what they read and hear. Only in a curriculum that provides rich learning experiences, a wealth of ideas, and opportunity to express them can a good language program develop.

The program should incorporate all modes of language expression necessary to the interchange of thoughts and ideas in the course of normal daily living. As the school day proceeds, the interests and experiences of the class are likely to call for a sharing of experiences and ideas: discussion of plans and procedures, reporting on the outcomes of individual or small-group observation and research, listening to others, making records, writing letters, telling stories, exchanging social courtesies, and the like. These forms of expression are complex techniques, each involving a galaxy of skills. Gradually, as the children progress through school, need for each individual skill will emerge. The teacher is responsible for noting the needs that successively appear and for providing instruction in a timely, meaningful, appropriate, and thorough manner to those pupils who are ready for the skill.

Language skills are most readily learned and mastered in connection with interest and occasions that demand their use. Psychological experiments have proved the close relationship between interest and learning. Children who sense a need for instruction in a specific language skill or who expect to apply it shortly are highly motivated. The young child who seeks information about the frog's eggs that have been brought in, for example, finds that learning to use an index to gain the information he wants is comparatively easy. His satisfaction in achievement further strengthens his learning. In like matter an older child can learn to outline more easily as he recognizes how the outline aids in mastery of the major facts in his social studies lesson. Skills should be taught when they can be put to immediate use in the learning activities of the school day. Any teacher alert to the ever recurring needs for language skills will have no difficulty in planning instruction that has immediate, practical value.

Language teaching is a daylong activity, contributing to and drawing from other subjects. Efforts toward improving accuracy and clarity of expression are basically related to training in clear thinking. Since the elementary teacher is usually responsible for instruction in many subject fields, the opportunity for developing effective expression is multiplied by the attention that can be given to it through the school day regardless of the subject matter. The values of keeping a close relationship between language instruction and other subject fields can be felt in both directions: language learnings should increase proficiency in other subjects wherever they are carefully applied; and other subjects can provide some of the vital content for the various language activities.

The program should provide a few definite standards each year. In some schools the language curriculum is overcrowded, and so many skills are assigned for instruction each year that children learn little or nothing. The language teacher's slogan should be "A few language items each year, and those learned well." If a few standards appropriate to each grade level are set and attained year by year, if a limited number of skills are thoroughly mastered year by year (usually introduced two or three years before mastery can be expected), the children will emerge from the elementary school with greater power to express themselves clearly and correctly than if they have half-learned a multitude of things.

Grade placement of skills should take account of child maturation, as

The questions raised by observation of these specimens motivates research in books.

well as of demands for the use of these skills in normal situations that confront children at successive age and grade levels. If language techniques and skills are introduced prematurely, children are only confused. They learn to make mistakes or they acquire a dislike for any situation in which the uncomprehended skill is involved. Furthermore, they fail to find genuine cause for using and applying the skill. The teacher should avoid having younger children engage in forms of expression suitable only for older pupils. In these early years, for example, oral reports and stories should be brief and simple. It is equally undesirable to delay the presentation of language techniques and skills with the result that pupils fail to receive guidance just when they need it. Such delay leads to frustrations, carelessness, or indifference. Independence in written communication is gradually acquired through careful guidance that is in step with maturity.

The program should stimulate interest in language and, as maturation permits, an understanding of the nature of the English language. Children very early indicate an interest in words; they play with sounds, chant rhythms, and enjoy strange words, whether they be sense or nonsense. The wonder of words should not be lost as age increases experience. In addition, every child should know stories about his language, including such information as how it has changed through the centuries, how it is related to other languages, how it started in a small way and has spread over the world, how the alphabet developed, how the making of books has changed. Study of the language leads ultimately to a consideration of its forms, functions, and structures, but this is a relatively mature phase of language study suited only to advanced students. The elementary grades seem an appropriate time to interest children in language, to acquaint them with some of the basic terminology needed in discussing language, and to help them to observe some of its characteristics.

The language program should make definite provision for individual differences in the interests, capacity, and achievement of children. The gifted child should be encouraged to undertake tasks that challenge his ability. At the same time the slow learner should be given opportunities to achieve success at his own level.

Language teaching should employ a positive approach whenever possible, making use of children's tendency to imitate. In his earliest years the child learned to talk by contagion, through hearing and imitating the speech of his family and friends. In later years imitation is still a strong factor in the improvement of expression. A teacher who speaks correctly in a pleasing voice, enunciates distinctly, has a rich vocabulary, and speaks in clear-cut and orderly sentences does much to develop good habits of speech in pupils. A pleasant manner in communication also contributes to their poise and stability.

Similarly, in the field of written expression, the study of correct models, projected on the screen or in printed form, is an excellent way to teach the mechanics of written communication. The practice of displaying a few papers that are neatly written and attractively arranged, with correct headings, legible handwriting, and proper margins is likely to induce all the children to prepare manuscripts carefully.

In addition to learning through direct instruction, the child learns from the milieu in which he lives. If his world includes much reading from good books, the thoughts and language on the printed page will influence his own. A positive approach to better language includes a program rich in children's literature.

Oral expression should be considered fundamental to development of both speech and writing. Pupils will develop fluency and effectiveness in oral communication if they have abundant opportunities to speak and listen, if they have real purposes for doing so, and if careful attention and guidance is given toward improvement of the speaking-listening skills. Most classrooms provide a wide variety of speaking-listening activities, but in few classrooms will the observer find a planned program with definite speaking-listening goals being carried out. In the oral area teachers should remember that "practice may make permanent" applies as forcibly to ineffective as to effective use of spoken English.

The child should acquire the tendency and ability to appraise his own work. The very young child is necessarily quite dependent on the teacher; but, as he progresses through school, he should learn definite standards for performance and should be encouraged and directed to evaluate his own efforts and to make necessary improvements. Only when the habit of self-checking and self-appraisal becomes firmly established will language teaching carry over into out-of-school life, where the individual has little or no direction in his language expression.

Objectives for Language Learning

TO SOME degree objectives for language teaching may be the same from school to school. However, the following differences will require adjustments: influences and experiences provided by each individual community and family, the particular school with its varied instructional equipment and its policies, and the individual differences among the pupils in any group. To the degree that there are common elements within communities, families, and schools, and also among children, similar objectives may be established, and *vice versa*. Over the period of the elementary school years, the objectives should be so devised as to provide continuity and a cumulative effect.

Although language instruction in the kindergarten is completely informal, there are improvements to be sought, attitudes to be fostered, and interests to be developed. Some typical objectives described in terms of child behavior are listed here:

Expression: content

1. Engage in play and work experiences that will help to interpret and enrich background.
2. Use increasingly enriched vocabulary gained by listening to stories and verse, sharing in conversation and discussion, and participating in activities suited to children of this age.
3. Talk naturally and spontaneously with classroom associates.

Expression: mechanics

1. Through imitation and practice, learn the correct formation and intonation of the various sounds of speech.
2. Speak naturally, rhythmically, and distinctly.

Social aspects

1. Adjust happily and easily to social situations in school living: learning to share, taking turns, feeling secure, planning and working smoothly with a small group of children of the same age.
2. Overcome shyness or excessive aggressiveness.
3. Be an increasingly attentive, courteous, and responsive listener.

THE LOWER PRIMARY GRADES

Children who have had kindergarten experience will have made a good start toward achieving the objectives for first and second grades. Otherwise, the first-grade teacher will have to start with the objectives suggested for the kindergarten.

Expression: content

1. Talk freely, happily, and easily about experiences in school and out.
2. Increase the fund of ideas through alert and accurate observation of, and participation in, everyday experiences and through familiarity with suitable literature, pictures, processes, and objects.
3. Think straight in the process of assimilating and reporting on this fund of ideas.
4. Develop a sense of sequence of ideas when listening to, or giving, reports and when telling and acting out stories.
5. Speak, dictate, or write in sentences (not sentence fragments) when

the situation naturally demands them, as in reporting or developing experience stories for reading.

6. Continue to extend the vocabulary by means similar to those used in kindergarten, but with a constant reaching out into a broadening environment.

7. Write own name and address and the name of the school.

8. Write single words, such as labels, for some definite purpose.

9. Copy accurately sentences from the chalkboard when there is a valid pupil purpose for doing so.

10. Dictate to the teacher (a) labels of original pictures, (b) a simple note or letter asking or thanking someone for a favor, (c) a chart story of recent experiences, (d) announcements and memoranda.

11. (For pupils of suitable advancement and ability) Write simple sentences without difficulty and plan and write stories independently.

Expression: mechanics

1. Use a natural speaking voice and appropriate intonation, with clear articulation and correct pronunciation. Speak rhythmically in connected speech and with good voice tone which can be heard and understood by all.

2. Assume a natural, easy manner and posture when speaking before a group.

3. Learn to use simple capitalization and end punctuation by noting usage when working with reading charts, reading stories in readers and on the board, and copying stories that have been dictated to the teacher.

4. Read orally to a group, interpreting the thought on the printed page and using a conversational style for reading.

Social aspects

1. Form habits of courteous verbal and bodily responses to simple social situations.

2. Listen with increasing absorption and responsiveness and with habitual courtesy.

Correct usage

1. Imitate the correct usage of others in trying to eliminate certain gross errors.

2. Heed incidental correction when given by teachers, parents, and friends.

THE UPPER PRIMARY GRADES

The objectives itemized below apply to advanced second graders, most third graders, and to the less mature pupils in fourth grade. Continuity and articulation of the language program from year to year, and cumulative treatment that builds on what has gone before, characterize the objectives for the upper primary group.

Expression: content

1. Build on the various phases of power acquired in earlier years.

a. Talk with greater fluency and confidence in connection with projects and other school activities, as well as various interests outside of school.

b. Continue the enrichment of experiences through alert and accurate observation and active participation, and through contacts with suitable literature, pictures, processes, and objects.

c. Show increased facility in acquiring (observing, listening, reading, and having actual experiences) and assimilating ideas independently, in reporting them clearly and accurately, and in putting them into effect.

d. Continue to use good sentences, leaving out unnecessary *and's, then's,* and *so's.*

e. Continue to add to the vocabulary words made necessary through growing interests; acquire facility in putting to use the various forms of expression that have been gleaned from reading, listening, and dramatization.

f. Make labels and signs neatly and accurately as the occasion demands.

2. Enhance basic sentence sense by listening, reading orally, and taking occasional training exercises, as needed. In more structured responses, think sentences through carefully before speaking or writing them.

3. Select for discussion or reporting a single episode or phase of a subject; stick to the point; observe the sequence of ideas. Develop the idea of a simple outline (beginning sentence sequence of ideas, ending sentence).

4. (Second year) In the latter part of the year write stories and reports independently, usually not to exceed three or four sentences.

5. (Third year) Begin to acquire a paragraph sense; develop through cooperative composition the ability to organize a paragraph with the following parts: (a) an interesting opening sentence; (b) sentences in orderly sequence; (c) a closing sentence that concludes the account.

6. (Third year) Write original stories, news accounts, and informal notes of three to five sentences in paragraph form.

Expression: mechanics

1. Establish the habit of speaking in a natural, distinct tone, with clear articulation, careful pronunciation, and natural intonations.

2. Retain a natural, easy manner and posture whenever speaking before a group.

3. From the beginning, write all papers neatly in good form.

4. Spell correctly the common words needed in expressing ideas. Keep an individual word list of all troublesome words of appropriate difficulty, and study the words until they are no longer troublesome. Consult a convenient source for hard and unfamiliar words.

5. Inspect and correct all written work habitually before handing it in.

6. Read orally to a group whenever such reading will give enjoyment, add to appreciation, or clear up a disputed point.

Social aspects

1. Continue to develop the cooperative, responsible attitude and the habits of courtesy, attentiveness, and responsiveness that were cultivated in preceding years.

2. Write legibly as a matter of pride and courtesy.

3. Listen with interest to increasingly varied topics of greater depth, and with increasing discrimination and a proneness to evaluate what is heard.

4. Give and accept constructive and positively framed criticism as a form of helpfulness.

Correct usage

1. Eradicate completely the common errors of usage that have been treated in previous years.

2. Overcome several other common errors by means of careful listening to correct usage in oral-reading selections, heeding incidental correction, working simple practice exercises, and applying appropriate usage in all situations.

3. (Second year) Learn to correct all mistakes in a composition under the teacher's direction or by applying standards that have been developed.

4. (Third year) Correct mistakes by increasingly independent use of standards with less dependence on the teacher's direction.

5. Make a sincere attempt to be effective in expression.

THE INTERMEDIATE GRADES

These aims reflect the increasing independence of the pupils and their ability to use more and more detailed skills. There is also a growing power of self-evaluation and self-correction.

Expression: content

1. In all informal expression, use simple, direct, conversational language.

2. Express the speaker's and writer's meaning clearly, pointedly, forcefully, and fluently.

3. Employ consciously the words learned in other subjects and in independent reading.

4. Collect and arrange effectively needed materials for reports, class discussions, and assembly talks and performances.

5. Make and use simple outlines; arrange in orderly sequence the sentences that develop a particular phase of a subject.

6. Begin a discourse simply and directly with a significant first sentence.

7. Use clear-cut sentences; avoid choppy sentences and sentence fragments; employ variety in sentence structure by understanding and consciously using, in different positions, the various structural elements of sentences.

8. Write fluently informal notes and friendly letters.

9. Write simple, clear-cut, courteous business letters in correct form.

10. Draw up or fill out business forms.

11. Make attractive and definite the announcements required in intermediate school activities.

12. Learn gradually to take meaningful and selective running notes on a talk or interview and on reading materials.

Expression: mechanics

1. Develop poise and ease of manner.

2. Maintain good posture.

3. Use a natural, conversational tone in all oral work.

4. Pronounce words properly, articulate distinctly, and use natural intonations.

5. Capitalize, spell, and punctuate accurately and speedily.

6. Follow definite standards in arranging written work on the page.

7. As maturity warrants, understand and learn to apply the simplest grammatical concepts in the use of effective sentence patterns and in the selection of the most graphic and precise words for expressing ideas clearly.

8. Read orally to a group for these reasons: when a genuine audience situation develops in the silent-reading lesson and when a training lesson can give practice on a specific skill.

Social aspects

1. Listen thoughtfully and responsively when being addressed.

2. Cooperate in kindly and helpful group criticism.

3. Participate actively and thoughtfully in the language activities of such groups as clubs and assemblies.

4. Continue to practice common social amenities in speaking and listening at school and in public places.

Correct usage

1. Recognize and avoid the common gross errors of careless speech and writing.

2. Overcome individual gross language errors.

THE UPPER GRADES

As adolescence approaches children develop a strong interest in social activities. Upper-grade boys and girls are aware of themselves as members of a class or group, a particular school, a club, a team, or even a gang. This fact is a major consideration in the development of a language program for them. Social life and the development of group interests depend upon communication. The major objectives, therefore, are these:

Expression: content

1. Acquire fluency, skill, even artistry in oral and written expression.

2. Speak forcefully, accurately, and clearly in discussing, reporting, explaining, and expressing planned arguments on pupil-recognized issues.

3. Translate ideas and sensory impressions into vivid, meaningful, and creative language.

4. Acquire a constantly enriched, varied, and precisely selected vocabulary on the basis of listening, reading informational and literary materials, and referring to a dictionary or a thesaurus.

5. Learn the value of exact, accurate, authenticated information. Know how to locate and select pertinent facts and how to organize information and individual interpretations for a logical and convincing presentation.

6. Think critically, but objectively, while listening, reading, and discussing.

7. Use an economical and orderly system of taking memoranda gained through listening and reading.

8. Work consciously for effectiveness through a lively and graphic beginning, varied sentence patterns, a brisk and orderly movement of episodes, colorful words, and sustained suspense.

9. Write business letters and reports clearly, correctly, and economically.

10. Use sentences that are pleasingly varied, forceful, complete, and structurally correct.

11. Develop an appreciation of the richness and flexibility of the English language and some understanding of its grammatical characteristics. Acquire critical judgment concerning literature and the other arts.

Expression: mechanics

1. Build up group standards for technical performance in all the major forms of listening and oral and written expression.

2. Seek group approval through conformity with these standards.

3. Be sincere, direct, and poised in manner.

4. Use a natural tone when speaking or reading aloud. Adjust voice, attitude, vocabulary, and method of presenting material to the audience and to the purposes of the presentation.

5. Articulate clearly and distinctly; pronounce correctly.

6. Be correct in spelling, capitalization, and punctuation.

7. Write neatly and legibly. Arrange written work so that it will be attractive in appearance and effective in conveying leading ideas.

8. Learn the skills and technicalities, including a restricted number of helpful grammatical principles, that will function in improving the various forms of expression.

9. Read orally when, in an audience situation, fresh and interesting material can be presented; and when training lessons can develop proficiency in conveying meanings and moods.

Social aspects

1. Cooperate with the group (class, committee, club) in planning and meeting language situations. Engage effectively and responsibly in club and other organizational activities.

2. Learn the social proprieties and observe them on all occasions when courtesy in listening, speaking, or writing is involved: listening to oral reading and reports, writing courtesy notes, acknowledging favors, making introductions, and the like.

3. Learn to listen for specific purposes, with evaluative alertness and objectivity.

Correct usage

1. Expect to use acceptable English without any hesitation or doubt.

2. Help to build up group standards and make class lists of items where usage needs improvement.

3. Participate as needed in group study and practice on a specific item of instruction.

4. Keep a record of individual personal needs in correct usage.

A study of the foregoing aims for the upper grades reveals an emphasis upon language learnings in group participation, whenever appropriate, in accordance with the social characteristics of adolescents. Both individual and group needs can be met most effectively in many cases when motivation is based upon learning language skills for use in groups. When a pupil recognizes a need for improving his language for a more effective contribution to the group, he is more willing to learn. Such recognition requires a program of evaluation and individual analysis with a rapport that encourages acceptance of thoughtful criticism. It underscores the need for review and reteaching of individuals or small groups and for offering adequate opportunities for practice.

The content of the language arts program at the upper-grade level, as elsewhere in the curriculum, must provide for the intake of ideas that pupils find interesting and helpful. Meaningless drill has little value; the language program is lifted to a higher level when members of the group have ideas worth communicating.

Curricular Organization for Language Instruction

THE organization of the language program holds its own particular difficulties, many of which are not easily resolved. Among them are grade placement and sequence of language learnings from kindergarten through the grades, the correlation and integration of language with other subjects in the curriculum, administrative arrangements and daily schedules for instruction, individualized and group instruction, and articulation from grade to grade for the benefit of the best possible learning experiences.

GRADE PLACEMENT AND SEQUENCE OF LANGUAGE LEARNINGS

If the group of teachers in a school system can agree upon pupils' behavioral objectives for language instruction at different levels, such as those recorded in previous pages of this chapter, they can use them as a basis for planning the content of language work at each grade level. Most often, the sequence is established by the adopted textbooks. This fact emphasizes the importance of selecting textbooks that conform to carefully conceived objectives. Analysis of textbooks and courses of study, over a long period of years, has shown that school systems vary widely in their grade placement of the items in the English curriculum. This disparity can be explained: (1) If language skills are to be mastered, practice in each skill must be repeated from year to year. (2) Since items like the comma have many uses, a few uses should be allocated for direct teaching each successive year. (3) A truly functional program is based on the exact status of the pupils in each class and should therefore vary from school to school and from year to year. (4) Views of language authorities differ on the bases for deciding placement. While certain authorities favor organization on the basis of the "logic of English itself," others argue for a psychological basis that is concerned with the learner's maturity, his interests, and his aptitudes. There are also strong proponents for a sociological basis that considers the demands of adult living, rather than the changing status of children. Perhaps all of these bases are necessary, and grade placement should be determined by a balanced consideration of the logic of English, child development, and adult needs.

Currently, the trend points toward determining desirable learning sequences for each of the specific items in the language curriculum. Teachers should recognize what is expected in the performance of children with normal ability at successive grade levels, introducing important facts and concepts at one grade, giving extensive experience in the next, and demanding mastery when and if it is possible after adequate instruction and practice. For children who are not achieving at grade level, instruction should begin wherever learning is possible and proceed in sequence at the child's own rate. Any grade placement of specific items must be considered flexible enough to meet the changing needs and interests as well as abilities of the individuals in a class.

VARIED APPROACHES TO INSTRUCTION

When the teaching of language is paralleled with lessons in other subjects, language is said to be *correlated* with these subjects. For instance, the anniversary of the Wright brothers' flight at Kitty Hawk on December 17 may motivate a correlated treatment of man's attempts to fly as told in mythology and history. Through history and geography, the pupils will gain their factual background. Reading, literature, and art will deepen their understanding and develop appreciation of the man-into-space story; arithmetic will provide an opportunity to compare space flight of the present time with air travel in the time of the Wright brothers and to study the distance of the earth from the sun, moon, and other celestial bodies; language lessons will involve storytelling, reports, discussion, note taking, spelling, preparation and staging of an original play, and making plans for an assembly in which these various activities culminate.

In correlation, school subjects still retain their identity and are taught more or less separately. There are values to be gained through the correlated teaching of language. From the other subjects, the pupils garner ideas to be communicated through speech and writing; they utilize occasions for sharing these ideas through storytelling, reports, discussion, and dramatization. Because their speaking and writing call for certain language skills that are as yet unmastered, they are receptive to language lessons that will help to develop mastery of such skills. Too, materials and occasions that will tend to stimulate creative writing may be found in the correlated treatment of the various subjects.

In *integration,* there is a more nearly complete breakdown of subject-matter lines. The speaking, listening, and writing that occur throughout the school day are seen as a part of the language curriculum; much learning of the language skills takes place through their use in any and all of the curricular areas.

Integration is often planned through unit instruction. A question or problem is presented to a class. For example, pupils may be led to ask,

Discussion, reporting, and storytelling are outgrowths as children accumulate facts in content subjects.

"How does our city get its water supply?" In pursuing an answer, the class considers certain governmental procedures commonly included in social studies; some natural science having to do with water supply; health problems and the necessity for water purification; even some arithmetic related to measurement and cost. Language activities are an integral part of the entire unit, including the first steps in planning, the letter writing and interviews, the explanations, oral reports, and written summaries, and at last, a concluding presentation of what has been learned.

When unit instruction like this draws the various curriculum areas together to serve the larger interests of the children, language activities assume a genuine and impelling purpose. The unit provides for ample practice in almost all types of communication. But it should not be overlooked that an important part of unit teaching is the instruction necessary for mastery of skills. Only when the teacher provides direct help for improved skill in the kinds of communication required will the unit work be adequate in language instruction. It is also important in over-all planning for the year's work in unit development that the teacher has the objectives of language instruction in mind in order to make effective use of the occasions when new skills should be introduced or old ones strengthened.

Aside from individual corrective teaching of speech skills, most primary teachers integrate their language instruction with all the daily learning activities, even though teachers of upper primary grades may depend upon a textbook for much of their instructional material. The correlated program is practical for many intermediate teachers because they instruct the same group of pupils in all subjects. Correlation is made easier in systems where the junior high school combines English and social studies under one teacher. If English is a separate class, correlation may occur with teacher planning.

In the intermediate and upper grades, many teachers have a separate language period and depend on a textbook for their material. They may have a handwriting manual and a speller to give additional aid in planning these special phases of the language program. Such separate instruction facilitates a sequential development of language skills which are introduced as children develop readiness to learn them. In practice, teachers under such a program frequently rely on the textbook to suggest the order and the time for introducing the skills. Under such circumstances, there may be relatively complete coverage, not a hit-and-miss program that might be the result of an integrated program. However, to keep the work from becoming stereotyped and uninteresting, the resourceful teacher, oriented to children's natural interests at each grade level, can frequently plan practical application of language skills to correlate with other studies and activities. Parts of the textbook are selected for instruction as they apply to the current needs.

Under any of the approaches to language instruction discussed in the foregoing section, adequate time for direct instruction must be planned. Practice in the use of language must be preceded by careful instruction. The pupils' progress will come through purposeful effort toward goals which they understand. An incidental reference to needed skills is rarely adequate. Children need to focus their attention on the new learning. The focus can be given at the moment of need, as in an integrated program, or at a time closely correlated with the use of the skill.

For example, an occasion for using certain capital letters and punctuation marks will grow out of activities in social studies or elementary science. Then the teacher sets aside a definite period for teaching pupils how and when to use capital letters or items of punctuation and provides additional time for practice if the pupils do not easily master such technicalities.

Similarly, some children will need help in improving speech skills, in mastering sentence construction, in improving spelling and penmanship, and in organizing ideas. Any skill—whether it is pitching a ball, analyzing unfamiliar words in reading, or enunciating clearly—must be practiced after getting a clear notion of how to perform the act correctly; then it should be used in connection with real-life activities.

Techniques required in note-taking, preparing and giving a report, telling a story interestingly in proper sequence, and writing a precisely worded business letter need direct teaching in a specific period, but always in response to a need that has arisen in connection with daylong school activities. The teacher must be alert to the pupils' emerging needs for language instruction and must constantly take careful inventories of their growth as well as their need for direct teaching as indicated by weaknesses in certain language skills and techniques.

GROUP AND INDIVIDUAL INSTRUCTION

Language is essentially social, not individual, in nature. It is an interchange of ideas between a speaker and his audience, or a writer and those who will read or hear what he has written. The expressional aspects of language instruction are, therefore, usually part of a group situation. An outstanding exception may be individual creative writing, when a child is responding to his own inner feelings and to his personal reactions to a moving experience. Even here, some children are stimulated by the prospect of an appreciative audience for their creative results. Creative writing may be personal, not intended for the eyes or ears of others; or it may be entirely original and yet be intended for sharing.

It is in the area of skills that individual language instruction is most often necessary. Decades ago, Lyman's *Summary of Investigations Relat-*

ing to Grammar, Language, and Composition(17) made clear the fact that individualized instruction in correct usage is essential if the errors are to be eliminated. If the entire class is given instruction on items that are incorrectly used by only a few pupils, the lessons are poorly motivated and pointless. Teachers should give instruction on only those items of usage that are actually misused and to only those pupils who make the respective mistakes. In this way, language instruction can be made pointed, purposeful, and effective.

Some schools provide for individualized instruction in written expression through the establishment of a writing laboratory period. This consists of a daily period in which each pupil carries on any writing activities that are required in his different lessons. Thus, some pupils will be working on a committee report while others are writing news stories or creative compositions for a class magazine, and still others are taking notes on outside reading. During this laboratory period, the teacher acts as consultant, giving such help as individuals need.

Valuable experience in correcting technical errors results when a teacher and his pupils join in working out a set of standards which lists the technical skills that the children will try to employ, whether in oral expression or in written work. The teacher can then assist the pupils in keeping their individual charts as they evaluate their products. After the pupils have tallied their mistakes or weaknesses against the list of standards, the teacher will read the list to the class, asking for a show of hands to see how many have marked each item. The number of hands gives a quick indication of the type of instruction needed: general instruction when the whole class requires further teaching; concentrated work with a small group that needs special help; or specific instruction to meet different needs of each of several individuals.

Ideally, every pupil should become aware of his own particular needs for skill development and should evaluate his personal progress as he tries to overcome his weaknesses. A plan for setting up goals and then carrying on continuous measurement of relative success in mastering the items listed in the goals is described in later chapters of this book.

Certain enterprising teachers have reported spectacular success in guiding individual pupils to high levels of achievement by a conference method. Here the teacher talks over each pupil's writing individually— sometimes in helping the less resourceful to plan their productions, sometimes by giving a comment as he notes some need or some evidence of progress during the child's act of writing down his ideas, often in a conference that follows his writing. By keeping a record of his conferences, the teacher can make sure that he is properly distributing his attention and giving help where it is most needed. Pupils will, of course, be encouraged to check their papers before coming for a final evaluative conference.

Administrative Arrangements

THE pattern of a school's organization profoundly affects the type and quality of its language activities. The way in which language activities are scheduled, the policies that determine whether the respective language arts are taught separately or are interrelated, the departmentalized teaching or the lack of it, and any measures that are taken by school authorities in articulating the language program from one school year to the next are very powerful factors in determining the nature of the whole English language program.

SCHEDULING LANGUAGE INSTRUCTION

Not too many years ago the prevailing practice was to teach language in a separate period, with little or no relation to lessons in other subjects. Investigators who concerned themselves with the then moot question of time allotments per subject determined such facts as these: (1) Language ranked next to reading and arithmetic in the amount of time given in the typical daily program. (2) There was little or no variation in the minutes per day allotted language in the intermediate and the upper grades. (3) Wide variations in time allotments were found within and between school systems.

Probably the majority of elementary schools still maintain a separate period for language instruction, but not necessarily a daily one. This practice is, of course, less prevalent in the primary grades where an integrated program prevails. For teachers who are expected to schedule periods for language instruction, the following example of a daily program may offer some help. Variations could be made to adjust it to different age levels and local requirements.

8:50	Introductory activities
9:00	Reading (developmental) and literature
10:00	Spelling
10:15	Intermission
10:30	Social studies
11:15	Language, including handwriting
12:00	Lunch
1:00	Arithmetic
1:40	Science
2:20	Physical education and health
2:45	Music
3:05	Art
3:25	Evaluation
3:30	Dismissal

The more modern type of program where language instruction is scheduled daily is organized in blocks of time devoted to related subjects. All of the language arts are grouped together. The pupils devote time to these subjects in flexible fashion varying the time according to the needs.

In the period for social studies, for example, they may take three or four days to find information on a topic by reading in the library, with some note-taking required. They may then need to use the language arts period for several days to talk over the information and to get it organized for writing, to learn the spelling of required words, and to write organized reports. Later, they will need only short periods for checking and correction, and thus they will be able to spend more time in reading instruction. A typical blocked program follows:

8:50 Introductory activities, pupil-teacher planning
9:10 Social studies, science, health
    Unit or correlated studies
    Observation, experimentation
    Reading, discussion
    Related music, art, literature
    Creative expression, critical evaluation
10:40 Physical education and intermission
11:00 Language
    Training lessons to improve language skills
    Oral and written expression
    Spelling and handwriting
    Learning about language, usage and grammar
12:00 Lunch
1:00 Reading
    Developmental skills
    Study-type reading
    Literature study and appreciation
2:00 Arithmetic
2:40 Intermission
2:50 Music and art
3:30 Dismissal

In general, a blocked program provides the necessary flexibility to meet the immediate demands of classwork. However, the teacher whose objectives for the year are clearly aimed toward a developmental program will find it necessary to provide a regular study time for reading, writing, speech, language study, spelling, and handwriting for all who need it. The content of much of the work during the language period will be an intrinsic part of the daylong learning experiences of the children, but the separate study time gives them a chance to understand their language and learn to use it effectively.

TEACHING ASSIGNMENTS IN THE ELEMENTARY SCHOOL

The practice of departmentalizing instruction in the elementary school seemed well on the way out a decade ago; but there are still scattered school systems that have departmentalized teaching in grades five and six, and many that do so in the junior high school years. In extreme cases, where there is a separate teacher for each major area of the curriculum, subjects as closely related as language, handwriting, and spelling may be completely divorced. Thus, the values that reside in functional, integrated instruction are lost.

Fortunately many elementary schools have moved away from departmentalization through the intermediate grades, enabling their teachers to be with the students for all or most of the day. Primary teachers and most teachers of intermediate grades have self-contained classrooms. Because of the greater demand on the teacher's knowledge by upper-grade pupils, teaching assignments at that grade level often make use of special competencies among members of the staff. In some places one teacher handles language arts and social studies in a half-day program, while specially trained teachers take the class in other subjects.

Team teaching is another method by which some schools overcome the handicap of unequal teacher training in the various subjects to be taught. By careful staff planning, several classes may be prepared for group sessions where one of the teachers presents basic material to all the pupils in a given grade (or possibly more than one grade). Follow-up sessions are conducted separately in the classrooms. In the course of the year, each teacher may be responsible for instructing the large group in his own specialized ability.

GROUPING PRACTICES OF ELEMENTARY ADMINISTRATORS

One perplexing problem of classroom management is how to handle the individual needs and interests of pupils. At one time, homogeneous grouping based on standardized test results seemed to be the answer; but such grouping was found to reduce the range in achievement and ability levels but little, and teachers still had to meet the problem of adjusting to individual differences. Aubrey Haan(12) gives this suggestion:*

> What is needed is a kind of flexible grouping that allows schools to work for the broad range of objectives in which they believe. In teaching social skills, interpersonal relations, a heterogeneous group has obvious advantages. For specific instruction in reading skills some homogeneity seems

* *Elementary School Curriculum: Theory and Research*, p. 117. Copyright 1961 by Allyn and Bacon, Inc., Boston. Reprinted by permission of the publisher.

best. Let us use groups according to our purpose. Total categorization of a child as inferior, which is implied by a complete homogeneous grouping is intolerable in its effects on the person's self-contempt; temporary categorization according to need that one can recognize is an experience all individuals learn to accept.

At the present time, teachers are becoming quite adept in handling small-group instruction where pupils are placed in groups according to interests or current needs for instruction. Such grouping is flexible. For successful handling of small-group instruction, teachers require a diversity of materials so that they can provide for a variety of ability and achievement levels as well as greatly differentiated interests. Gradually the market is providing self-instructional materials, with self-inventory and keyed practice exercises which a pupil may use independently in meeting his current needs.

There seems, however, to be a growing tendency for large systems to make special provision for the mentally handicapped (those with IQ's below 75, for example) and for the gifted. School systems are providing specially trained teachers, special equipment, and an adjusted curriculum so that both the extremely low-ability and the highly gifted pupils can learn to their optimum. For the former, there is likely to be a special room in a school where "normal" children also attend; for the latter, there may be interest groups meeting separately a few periods each week. There they have the advantage of group work in fields of special interest and aptitude where teachers of special competence are provided.

As teachers work with their pupils in small groups, they become aware of significant individual differences. Because of these differences teachers must provide a measure of individualized instruction. At the present time, there is a trend toward individualized teaching, not only for the gifted and slow-learning but for average pupils as well.

Some schools employ a part-time staff member either to supply specialized kinds of instruction or to release, for a short time, a regular staff member who can teach special areas like creative dramatics, creative arts, creative rhythms and dance, creative writing, foreign languages, or advanced science activities. In other cases a specialized teacher is called in for two or three periods a week to provide advanced training for small groups of students, all interested and all skilled in the work of a certain area.

ARTICULATION IN THE LANGUAGE ARTS PROGRAM

Another problem in language teaching is removing gaps between the primary and intermediate grades, and more especially the intermediate and upper grades. Not only do instructional methods and curricular organization tend to be different at these respective levels in the school program, but the teachers' objectives for language instruction may be utterly divergent. Consequently pupils are confused and frustrated as they move from level to level in the school.

Primary teachers usually work for fluency and spontaneity and are less concerned with details of correctness; they integrate language with all the learning experiences of the school day. Teachers in the intermediate grades often have a separate language period devoted to drill on details of correct usage and the mechanics of written expression, though some teachers do have a program as integrated and functional as that at the primary level. All too often the upper-grade teacher spends an undue amount of time on grammar. To achieve a satisfactory articulation in the language arts program from kindergarten through high school, the teachers at all grade levels must clarify and unify their goals.

When objectives are set, most of them can best be expressed in terms of general competence of pupils. Progress can be measured in operational terms by showing how well the pupils put to use the skills they have studied and practiced. At the same time, teachers can also recognize as one objective an increased knowledge about the language, with better understanding and appreciation resulting. Such goals need to be established by teachers of all grade levels as a basis for planning sequential instruction and grade placement of specific instructional matters.

Superintendents and supervisory personnel who realize the need for achieving articulation in their schools have tried out various means. Some have set up in-service study groups in which their teachers have outlined their objectives of language instruction, year by year. They have then built up a system of beginning each school year with a check-up to determine to what extent the pupils have actually attained the objectives that have been outlined for the preceding grades.

The danger here is either that the teachers will overemphasize the mechanics of speaking and writing (correct usage, capitalization, and punctuation, for instance) and neglect the ideational and creative sides of language expression, or that the teachers will expect all the children to master the same skills at the same time, thus neglecting individual differences. Nevertheless, teachers come to a better understanding of their mutual problems by working together. Their most important problem is that of learning about individual differences and how to care for them.

Other school systems organize teachers into curriculum committees which continuously plan learning experiences in alignment with the local environmental resources, socio-economic conditions, and the known facts of child development. In order to attain continuity in the program, each committee is drawn from the various levels of the school, or separate committees at each level are coordinated by a steering committee with representatives from each of the grade-level committees. For example, there may be a committee on creative writing, whose members represent the kindergarten, primary, intermediate, and upper grades, and possibly the high school. Or there may be separate committees for each grade level, each of which is almost solely concerned with language growth at a single grade level, and also a central committee made up of one representative selected from each of the grade committees. This central committee is concerned with working out a continuous, smoothly transitional curriculum for the school system as a whole. It is possible under a system of interlocking curriculum committees to consider any and all phases of a language program and to work out articulation between the successive levels in the school system.

Essential in attaining articulation in an all-school language program is the keeping of cumulative records. A teacher who is interested in the continuous progress of his pupils will begin the year with an inspection of the cumulative card that contains systematic records of an individual pupil's school history: health, physical growth, school attendance, results of achievement and psychological tests, marks (if condoned by local school policy), and teachers' remarks on the child's effort and general behavior in previous years.

This card offers useful information; but even more valuable are other materials that the teacher should have available in individual pupil folders. For instance, he should have sociometric diagrams that show a pupil's past relationships with children of his own age; and he should have dated samples of the pupil's school work from each previous year so that future teachers may determine his progress in work habits, interests, linguistic competence, and his emerging needs for instruction.

Anecdotal records, brief reports on conferences with parents or with the child himself, and an annual summary that represents each teacher's evaluation of his personality, behavior, achievements, and future needs should also be among the materials that the teacher will study in trying to understand and provide for the continuous optimal growth of the child. Staff meetings, in which the teachers discuss individual children, may be needed if the teachers are to evaluate such records adequately.

If articulation is to be achieved, a teacher should have available an entirely different kind of information. That is the annual end-of-year progress report that gives a brief outline of the major curricular experiences of the group during the school year just completed: the units, centers of interest, and learning activities, along with an accounting of the information, skills, and understandings that the pupils will presumably have attained through these curricular experiences. Thus the teacher can avoid duplication, can plan to fill in gaps, and can provide for an extension and a deepening of learnings that could be only partially mastered by the immature pupils in their earlier school years.

Administrative procedures merely clear the way for making curricular adjustments to encourage continuous learning by the pupils. These procedures are significant only if they are tied in with curricular adjustments.

SUGGESTIONS FOR STUDY AND DISCUSSION

1. For one week, keep a log that shows the intake and the outgo of ideas in your own experience. Analyze your log. Which was prevalent: intake or outgo? Of the fundamental types of communication, which were most used? In which type do you recognize need for improved skill? Explain.

2. For each of the principles that underlie a basic language program, suggest ways of applying them in the classroom. (Later chapters will present major ways. Now, use your past experiences and knowledge of children in thinking out answers.)

3. Which of the objectives do you consider to be most significant in a functional language arts program? Defend your choices.

4. From kindergarten through the grades, trace each specific kind of objective; for instance, fluency, organization, vocabulary. How are continuity and articulation shown?

5. Suggest possible improvements in the elementary language program on the basis of weaknesses you recognize in high school and college students.

6. In what ways should the curriculum be organized to care for individual differences? Give pros and cons for each.

7. Should there be a separate daily language period? (Consider various grade levels.) If not, should there be an occasional separate period? Defend your answer.

8. Discuss the effects of departmentalization on language learning.

FOR FURTHER READING

1. BAKER, ZELMA W., *The Language Arts, the Child, and the Teacher* (Chapter 1). San Francisco, Fearon, 1955.
2. BECK, ROBERT H., WALTER W. COOK, and NOLAN C. KEARNEY, *Curriculum in the Modern Elementary School* (Chapter 14). Englewood Cliffs, N. J., Prentice-Hall, 1960.
3. BENNETT, ROBERT A., "Unit Ideas for the New School Year." *English Journal* (September 1960), 400–08, 430.
4. *A Curriculum for English: Grades K–12*, Nebraska Council of Teachers of English. Lincoln, Nebr., Woods' Charitable Fund Workshop, 1961.
5. DAWSON, MILDRED A., *Outline for Teaching the Language Arts*. New York, Harcourt, Brace & World, 1959. Pamphlet.

6. *The English Language Arts*, Commission on the English Curriculum of the National Council of Teachers of English. New York, Appleton-Century-Crofts, 1952.

7. GOODYKOONTZ, BESS, "The Organization of the Language Arts Program," in Virgil E. Herrick and Leland B. Jacobs, eds., *Children and the Language Arts*. Englewood Cliffs, N. J., Prentice-Hall, 1955.

8. GREENE, HARRY A., and WALTER T. PETTY, *Developing Language Skills in the Elementary School* (Part II). Boston, Allyn and Bacon, 1959.

9. *Guide for Language Arts in the Elementary School: Grades K–3*. Evansville, Ind., Evansville School Corporation, 1959.

10. *Guide for Language Arts in the Elementary School: Grades 4–6*. Evansville, Ind., Evansville School Corporation, 1959.

11. *Guideposts to the English Language Arts: Grades K–12*. Seattle, Wash., Seattle Public Schools, 1962.

12. HAAN, AUBREY, *Elementary School Curriculum: Theory and Research* (117). Boston, Allyn and Bacon, 1961.

13. HATCHETT, ETHEL, and DONALD HUGHES, *Teaching Language Arts in Elementary Schools* (Chapters 2, 3). New York, Ronald, 1956.

14. HERRICK, VIRGIL E., and LELAND B. JACOBS, eds., *Children and the Language Arts* (Chapters 3, 5). Englewood Cliffs, N. J., Prentice-Hall, 1955.

15. HOLLIDAY, LARRY, "Enriching the Curriculum in Language Arts." *Elementary English* (March 1958), 188–90.

16. *Language Arts for Today's Children*, Commission on the English Curriculum of the National Council of Teachers of English. New York, Appleton-Century-Crofts, 1954.

17. LYMAN, ROLLO LaVERNE, *Supplementary Education Monograph No. 36*. Chicago, U. of Chicago Press, 1929.

18. MACKINTOSH, HELEN K., "Language Arts in the Elementary School." *Educational Leadership* (February 1962), 290–93.

19. MARCUS, MARIE, "A Functional Program in Sixth Grade." *Elementary English* (October 1960), 389–91.

20. MERSAND, JOSEPH, "English Meets the Challenge." *Elementary English* (February 1960), 69–80.

21. PRONOVOST, WILBERT, and LOUISE KINGMAN, *The Teaching of Speaking and Listening* (Chapter 1). New York, Longmans, Green, 1959.

22. STAHL, STANLEY S., JR., "The Language Arts in Today's World." *Elementary English* (December 1961), 556–60, 565.

23. STRICKLAND, RUTH G., *Language Arts in the Elementary School* (Chapters 3, 9). Boston, Heath, 1957.

24. TIDYMAN, WILLARD, and MARGUERITE BUTTERFIELD, *Teaching the Language Arts* (Chapters 2, 3). New York, McGraw-Hill, 1959.

4

Promoting Vocabulary Growth

*Chapter 4 discusses the various types of vocabularies—
listening, speaking, reading, writing, and potential or
marginal. It shows how these vocabularies grow, and it
indicates the estimated and relative sizes they attain.
Word meanings are shown to be important in each type
of vocabulary. The chapter suggests the more valid methods of inducing sound vocabulary growth.*

BEFORE the child enters school, he has already acquired a considerable vocabulary along two lines: his *listening* vocabulary—words he can understand when he hears them used by others; and his *speaking* vocabulary—words he uses in his own speech.

Because the size of vocabulary varies with the ability and experiences of individual children, various investigations have sought to determine the range in size of vocabulary and an acceptable average for children at various age levels. The results of these investigations vary considerably because different measures get different results, and the conditions under which a child's vocabulary is sampled will affect his choice of words in speech.

How Vocabularies Grow

FOR several years, 2500 words were considered an average *speaking* vocabulary for a six-year-old child. The earlier studies had indicated an annual increment averaging over 2000 words, so that an eleven-year-old had acquired a vocabulary of almost 14,000 words. More recent studies tend to show that the child's speaking vocabulary is considerably larger than these figures indicate.

When research centers on the words a child knows (his *listening* or meaning vocabulary), much larger figures result. R. H. Seashore accepts the research of Mary K. Smith, who found that first-grade children, on the average, know almost 17,000 basic words and about 7000 derivatives, or 24,000 words in all. Smith's numbers for sixth grade (about the eleventh year in chronological age) are 31,500 basic words and 18,000 derivatives, or a total of 49,500. This indicates an average annual increment of nearly 5000 words when the totals are the basis for comparison. These data seem to show quite reliably that the typical child at each grade level has accumulated a very considerable meaning vocabulary which tends to increase at a rapid rate; but Smith's figures do not measure the speaking vocabulary, which is certainly much smaller.

Upon entering school, a child gradually acquires two other kinds of vocabulary: *reading* and *writing* vocabularies. In the beginning these are limited; but they grow apace. For the most part, these four vocabularies overlap; but there are more informal, possibly slangy words in the speaking vocabulary than in those for reading and writing. Because of the increasing span and variety of children's actual and vicarious experiencing (the latter includes reading), the listening vocabulary grows constantly throughout the elementary school period. Meanwhile, the reading vocabulary expands to the extent that, for the more able readers, it may surpass the speaking vocabulary whose growth tends to parallel the listening vocabulary. For slow-learning pupils, the speaking and listening vocabularies are likely to exceed that in reading. The writing vocabulary, for most elementary school pupils, is far less than the other three types.

J. Conrad Seegers(10) identifies a fifth type of vocabulary, the potential or marginal, which includes completely unfamiliar words that the child would be able to figure out and interpret on the basis of their form or through the use of contextual clues. There can hardly be an estimate of the size or usefulness of this vocabulary.

FACTORS THAT AFFECT MEANING

A child's sensory experiences affect meaning, not only in early childhood, but throughout life. In the beginning, all meanings are derived from the child's direct experiences. He touches, manipulates, tastes, smells, watches, hears, throws, and strikes the objects in his immediate environment and thus, through his own senses, builds up meanings. By imitating the speech of his elders, he acquires words to express those meanings. It is only as words take on meaning that they are useful.

The first meanings are specific and limited in scope. "Chair" will at first mean a particular chair in the child's own home, and it is only after the child has been in contact with many kinds of chairs, seen many pictures and heard stories in which chairs appear, and otherwise learned to know chairs through many actual and vicarious experiences, that he has a well-rounded notion of what "chair" means. So must each single word in the child's vocabulary take on full and accurate meaning.

The diversity of the English language affects a child's progress in mastering vocabulary. There are words that have varied, diverse meanings. *Hard* may refer to *solid* coal, *diligent* study, *harsh* words, an *unfeeling* heart, a *close* bargain, *distressing* times, *difficult* to manage, *metallic* money, or *vigorous* work. Over a period of years, the child hears the word in many contexts and gradually gains an understanding of its varied meanings; but in the beginning he is likely to be quite confused.

There are also a multitude of words that are abstract and relatively meaningless to the immature child or the child with narrow experience. *Latitude* and *longitude* are terms that gain significant meaning slowly and gradually. Just what a *galvanized* pail is or how a house is *insulated* or what parts of a car are involved in the *ignition* may be very vague concepts for even a bright older child, because very concrete terms are actually abstract until real or vicarious experiences bring meaning. Sensory experiences in themselves do little toward direct learning of words such as *law* or *truth*. Understanding, however, does come through the interpretation of concrete experiences and situations that intrinsically represent *truth* or *law*. Such words usually involve rather complicated, intermeshed ideas and feelings which it is almost impossible to express concretely.

The farther from direct personal experience, or the more indirect vicarious experience through the mass media, a concept is, the greater must be the speaker's reliance upon language as a conveyor of meaning. The teacher must, therefore, delve into the previous experiences of pupils. He must decide which information is unfamiliar to them and what explanations he will need to give them a clear understanding of the concept. Too, he must remember that the pupils will acquire general and abstract terms gradually through repeated contacts. He cannot expect understanding to come quickly or fully through any single experience.

GROWTH IN THE MEANING OF WORDS

Children compare, summarize, and evaluate experiences; and as they do these things, they extend their meanings of words beyond anything that would be possible through direct experience only. A famous and modern-thinking educator recently stated that school trips and excursions are sometimes almost valueless. This is true when the teacher has not prepared the children for the trip by planning with them the particular questions to be answered while they are on the trip; they do not know what to look for, and thus they fail to observe essential facts. All too often the teacher does not use an evaluative follow-up discussion for organizing the children's thinking.

Similarly, before and after viewing slide films or a movie, the children should have both preliminary and subsequent discussion to make their observations keen and meaningful. Language must supplement experience if children's concepts are to be clear, accurate, and meaningful. Abstractions develop in children's thinking over a period of time as they use language in interpreting their experiences.

Growth in meaning vocabulary is full of variations. Some words easily take on rich meanings, especially those that refer to concrete objects and activities; others are difficult to understand because of a variety of diverse meanings and because of their abstractness. Also children vary in the rates at which they acquire vocabulary: some are quicker to learn than others; certain children have a much richer environment and more favorable conditions for acquiring wide experiences and a correspondingly wide vocabulary. Some pupils will need clarification and correction of the meanings of relatively simple words, while other pupils need help only in the areas of abstruse and advanced meanings.

The teacher should take advantage of children's vicarious experiences that will add new words to their vocabulary or extend and enrich the meanings of partially familiar words. The modern school can take advantage of mass media in this connection—newspapers, radio, recordings, television, still pictures, filmstrips, slides, and films. Those media to which a school does not have access may be available in the home. One of the jobs of the teacher today is to take an inventory of both home and school opportunities for vicarious experiencing by the pupils, then to carry on discussions of the more promising of these experiences. These discussions will ensure the pupils' more complete understanding of what they have seen or heard and will fix in their vocabulary any new words that may be useful in the future. Too often children do not have a chance to talk over their vicarious experiences and their observations (as on a vacation trip), and thus they fail to garner the benefits that they might otherwise reap.

FACTORS THAT INFLUENCE GROWTH IN VOCABULARY

A factor in determining the character and amount of a child's vocabulary is the type of environment in which he lives. If poverty and ignorance prevail and his experiences are limited, his fund of words will be relatively low grade and scanty. On the other hand, the child whose parents provide a wealth of experiences with toys, books, pictures, playmates, trips, and manifold opportunities to talk them over will probably acquire a rich vocabulary. Socio-economic conditions strongly affect a child's vocabulary.

What the child gains from his environment is conditioned by his capacity to learn. The richest of experiencing in an excellent environment cannot guarantee a wide vocabulary for the child who is unobservant and slow to learn. On the other hand, the alert child will pick up a multitude

This child will learn many new words as she pursues her interest in classifying leaves.

of meanings and concepts, along with the words to match. Intelligence is a major factor in the acquisition of vocabulary.

Another contributory factor in vocabulary growth is the interest the child has developed. If he is interested in mechanical things, he may be able to talk fluently about mechanical toys or the workings of television and movie projectors, even at a tender age; or if he likes the outdoors, he may talk fluently about fishes and birds, flowers and trees. A child tends to notice the objects and activities that interest him and to ignore even the obvious when it has little or no appeal for him.

A fourth factor consists of the instruction and guidance the child receives in the use of words. His parents may or may not take pains to explain unfamiliar processes and articles and to encourage him to learn the related vocabulary. They may frequently converse with him and, if he shows some misconception or confusion, they are careful to straighten him out; or they may fail to do so. The teacher should deliberately work to widen and deepen meanings in what the child observes and discusses, especially for those children seriously deficient in their stock of words. Such guidance brings enrichment and refinement in the use of words; the lack of it may cause gaps and inaccuracies in a child's vocabulary.

Specific Methods of Inducing Growth in Vocabulary

EXPERIENTIAL ENRICHMENT

The prime method of promoting growth in children's vocabularies is, of course, the enrichment of experience, both actual and vicarious. Big new words have special appeal for young children, and they quickly begin to use any words they hear in connection with their various learning activities. Take, for instance, the third-grade child who got confused in a classroom dramatization and went to the last character in the play prematurely so that two steps in the play were omitted. The teacher said, "Now, you *are* in a predicament, Sammy. What will you do about it?" Sammy responded quickly, "Yes, I *am* in a predicament. Will I get myself out of the predicament by starting over?" He had picked up the word *predicament* and used it correctly. Whether pupils are in the midst of developing an aquarium, preparing an exhibit of pioneer relics, making an insectarium, weaving a basket, or building a spacecraft from hollow blocks, they will be gaining new concepts and adding words to their vocabulary. These words are made meaningful through imitating the talking and oral reading by the teacher and other informed people.

Vicarious experiences, too, extend and deepen the children's understanding as they listen to stories and explanations, watch television or films or slide projections, listen to the radio or recordings, study pictures

This boy's mastery of newly learned words is assured through his use of them in a report.

in their books, and read verse and stories. Although such experiences are a source of additional ideas and of words for expressing them, the pupils derive full benefit only as they have an opportunity to discuss these ideas and thus are able to clarify and correct the impressions they have received. Through talking over these secondhand experiences, they also take into their active vocabulary many of the words they have just met for the first time.

One kindergarten class was listening intently to an informational story about the robin. (One was nesting in a tree just outside the classroom window.) When the teacher came to the word *beak*, he stopped to explain that a bird's bill is also called the beak. Then from lip to lip all through the class went "beak," "beak," "beak"! The children were enchanted with their new word. Learning a new word from firsthand experience is a thrilling experience for young children.

DIRECT AND INDIRECT TEACHING

Intrinsic in experiential situations where the teacher uses discussion to prepare the children for an experience and later to interpret it, is the opportunity for the children to imitate the teacher's use of words. That teacher who is ever on the alert to note new elements of experience in the children's ongoing activities and then to bring such elements to the children's attention through an apt use of words is doing much to extend their vocabulary. It is through the imitation of the teacher's word-rich vocabulary that children grow in their own.

Research has shown that incidental teaching of new words is not so effective as direct teaching; that is, the children should not be left to their own devices in the acquisition of new words. It is not enough, then, for a teacher to use in her own speech the words that will express the unfamiliar concepts the pupils are beginning to acquire. He will give additional direct attention to the new words in the following ways:

1. Take time to discuss unfamiliar words.
2. Phrase questions in such a way that new words are called for in the child's answer.
3. List key vocabulary on the chalkboard in summarizing main ideas in a situation.
4. Display and label pictures that will clarify and enrich the meaning of critical terms.
5. Provide activities that will require the use of new words as children plan, carry through, report on, and evaluate them.
6. Teach children to use contextual clues and reference books that explain words.
7. Generally impress upon pupils the meaning and usefulness of new terms.

Not only are unfamiliar words to be the concern of the teacher, but she should be alert to notice the misconceptions and incomplete understandings that the children manifest in their ordinary conversation, discussion, and other types of language activity. Since words gain full meaning only after years of varied experiences and consistent use of references, such as the dictionary, the learning child can be expected to have only partial and often faulty understanding of many terms in his vocabulary. For this reason, the teacher has a heavy responsibility for seeing that children constantly deepen and extend their understanding of the terms already in their working vocabulary. Teaching words and the concepts they represent should be a part of lessons in every subject almost every day of the school year.

Vocabulary of Curricular Areas

PARTICULARLY in the various subject areas will the pupils encounter important, unfamiliar words. "Product" in arithmetic and "product" in geography are entirely different concepts; so are "capital" and "capitol" in the social studies, the former also having a special meaning in arithmetic and still another in the language arts. "Diet" in civics may be confused with the more familiar and identical term in the area of health. Until children have learned to use the dictionary and other reference books, the teacher should help them to learn the special vocabulary of each curricular area.

In a single day one teacher taught several technical terms. In arithmetic he explained *commission* in relation to some local real estate sales. Here he wrote the term on the chalkboard, worked several illustrative examples, and had the pupils label the commission in each one. By chance, the children's discussion of the news of the day brought out the work of a United Nations *commission*. Again the teacher listed and explained the term. On inquiry, the teacher learned that a pupil was absent because of a fractured lower arm, and he proceeded to clear up the difference between a clean *break* and a *fracture*.

Later in a science class the pupils learned to read a meter showing the amount of electric current that had been used up to the end of the past month. In so doing several electrical terms took on meaning. The teacher took advantage of every likely occasion to make new words meaningful and to clarify terms that pupils might not understand.

REFERENCE MATERIALS

It has already been implied that children should learn to use the dictionary to check on the exact meaning and use of words, as well as to discriminate among shades of meaning for synonyms or to confirm the correct pronunciation of an unfamiliar word. However, dictionary definitions often provide little enlightenment to the beginner in using a dictionary since a particular definition may be fully as unfamiliar or perplexing as the word that is being looked up. Just because a child knows the techniques of finding words and using various aids provided in the dictionary, the teacher cannot slough off responsibility for guiding pupils in their search for a precise and appropriate vocabulary.

The teacher, then, throughout the intermediate grades should train the pupils gradually in the successive steps involved in using the dictionary, encyclopedia, atlas, and other reference materials. The upper-grade teacher should supplement and extend these learnings so that library skills and efficient use of all reference materials are thoroughly learned. Through frequent, purposeful, and well-directed use of these different study helps, pupils can gain the ability to widen, refine, and correct their vocabulary usage.

CONTEXT AND STRUCTURE

Even before children learn to use such reference materials, they can and should use reading activities as a means of extending their vocabulary. Through the careful guidance of the teacher, they should learn to infer the meaning of unfamiliar words through the use of contextual clues as provided by surrounding words in the sentence or by the story's illustrations. Contextual clues are a valuable means of interpreting meanings while reading. Another aid during reading instruction comes through the pupils' growing ability to figure out new words for themselves through structural, visual, and phonetic analysis. Often a word that the child does not appear to recognize will become familiar in meaning as soon as he has determined how to pronounce it. As children master the techniques of recognizing words through context or structure, they are well on the way to independence in building up a proper vocabulary.

In the intermediate and upper grades, word analysis can go further as pupils work with a restricted number of prefixes, suffixes, and root words of major usefulness. They really like to determine the meaning of unfamiliar words by breaking them up into their component parts; for instance, such a word as "inconsequential" in the upper grades. Pupils also enjoy looking up the original meaning of familiar words such as "peninsula" or "taxicab"; the comparison of the derivatives with the original words is a valuable and most interesting learning activity.

The selected list that follows contains twenty-five each of the common prefixes, suffixes, and roots.

Common Prefixes

PREFIX	MEANING	EXAMPLE
ab, a	away from, off from	absent, avert
ad, a	to, toward	adjoin, aspect

PREFIX	MEANING	EXAMPLE
ante	before, preceding	anteroom
anti	against	antitoxin
auto	self	autograph
bi, di	two	bilateral
circum	around	circumnavigate
com, con, col	together with	compile, congenial
contra	against	contradiction
de	down, away	depart
dis	apart from, reversing	disappear
en, in	in	enclose, include
ex, ec	out of	export
fore	in front of	foreground
im, in, il	not	illegal, inactive
mis	wrong, wrongly	misunderstand
peri	around	perimeter
post	after	postscript
pre	before	preview
pro	forward	promotion
re	back, again	return
semi, hemi	half	semicircle, hemisphere
sub, suf, sup	under	subway, suppress
super	over, above	superman
trans	across, beyond	transatlantic
un	not	unwelcome

Common Roots

ROOT	MEANING	EXAMPLE
biblio	book	bibliography
dem, demo	people	democracy
dic, dict	say	contradict
fer	carry	transfer
geo	earth	geology
graph	write	biography
lect, let	read, choose	lecture, election
legis, leg	law	illegal, legislature
log, logy	word, study	monologue, astrology
micro	small	microscope
mit, miss	send	mission, transmitter
mov, mot	set in motion	movable, motor
pend, pens	hang	pendulum
phon	sound	microphone
photo	light	photograph
sci	know	science
scop	see	telescope
scrib, script	write	manuscript, scribble
sent, sens	feel	sensation

ROOT	MEANING	EXAMPLE
tele	far	telephone
tend, tens	stretch	tension, extend
tract	draw	traction
vent, ven	come	convention
vert, vers	turn	reversal
voc	call	convocation

Common Suffixes

SUFFIX	MEANING	EXAMPLE
able, ible, ble	capable of	reasonable
al	pertaining to	comical
ant, ent	one who acts	president
ar, ary	pertaining to	singular
dom	state, condition	wisdom, kingdom
er, ar, or	one who acts	lecturer
ful	full, full of	spoonful, zestful
fy, efy, ify	to make	rarefy, beautify
ic, ical	pertaining to	geographic
ice	act, quality, state	justice
ion	state, act of	election
ish	acting like	womanish
ism	philosophy of, art of	witticism, liberalism
ist	one who is skilled in	humorist
itude	state, quality	exactitude
ive	having the nature of	imaginative
ize, ise	to make like	sterilize
less	without	helpless
ly	similar in manner	happily
ment	state, act of	movement
ness	state	preparedness
ous, ose	full of	joyous
ship	state, skill, act	friendship, partnership
try	art, profession of	forestry
ure	act, process	pressure

VARIETY AND PRECISION IN VOCABULARY

The natural interest in new and big words that young children manifest can be continued through the school years if the teacher will follow the suggested procedures and if he will see that the children, during their day-long learning activities, put their increasing vocabulary to use. The teacher should do all he can to encourage variety in the children's use of words as they communicate through speech or writing. Zelma W. Baker(2, p. 146) gives an excellent example of a class discussion where graphic and varied use of words developed:

The morning after a terrific storm, third graders were discussing the fury of the night.

TEACHER: How did you feel last night when the storm was raging? Let's see how many words we can think of that would describe a person's feeling during that storm. I'll write them on the board.

JANET: Scared.
MARY: Frightened.
JIMMY: Afraid.
JOHN: Alarmed.
MILLY: Terrified.

The teacher added *awed*. To the question, "What did you do?" the group answered: *shuddered, shivered, laughed, cried, quaked*. To the question, "What did the wind do?" the group answered: *howled, moaned, shrieked, groaned, raged, wailed, roared*.

Shortly after, a new poem appeared on the bulletin board. It read

THE STORM
The wind wailed, howled, shrieked and groaned,
It raged, laughed, roared and moaned
While I shivered, shuddered, quaked—then said,
"Keep on blowing. I'm going to bed."

BOB AND JAKE

Increasingly children should be precise in their use of synonyms so as to give exact meanings; variety, then, should be tempered with precision in vocabulary usage. Older children often like to list unfamiliar words they have encountered so that they can recall them and use them in appropriate ways. These they may employ as they rewrite commonplace paragraphs or stories.

Rodney W. Everhart(7, pp. 549–50) goes even further in suggesting that children need to sense the more elusive connotations of words and the shifts in meanings of the words they hear and read: *

I recently asked a group of sixth graders what the word "good" meant to them. As anticipated, many definitions were offered by the pupils who chose to respond. Some of the typical statements were: "carrots are good"; "ministers are good"; and "some people make a good impression." In a few minutes of discussion, I found that the commonplace word "good" can have many interpretations ranging from emphasis on taste or nutritional value, behavior, aesthetic appreciation, and physical fitness to social adequacy. Both the classroom teacher and I felt that many of the children held only a nebulous conception of the word "good." Obviously, this

* Reprinted with the permission of the National Council of Teachers of English and Rodney W. Everhart.

simple configuration which many of us take for granted is not understood on common grounds.

Without doubt, other words such as "wonderful," "bad," "truth," and "lovely" would have produced similar results. Apparently there is need for a more thorough study of word meanings. This is especially important if we accept the thesis that language is the principal instrument by which we can achieve better personal associations and status with our fellow men.

It would seem that some provision should be made in the classroom to help pupils to habitually look for the best meaning of a word as it is used in a specific sentence. This could assist children to scrutinize their own language usage. At the same time, it might help them to understand the total meaning of the verbal, or written expressions of others.

Looking up words in a dictionary is desirable, but not sufficient in itself. Verbatim knowledge is frequently inadequate. To be effective, the definitions found in the dictionary have to be correlated with words as they are used in context. How might this be done?

Critical listening to platform, television, radio, and classroom speakers could be employed with the goal of analyzing meaning in terms of word content. The words which carried the significant meaning might be examined, in regard to determining what definitions would be most appropriate as they were used in the total thought pattern. Class time could be allotted for ascertaining what other words might have been more acceptable, when there seems to be some doubt of valid usage. The use of a tape recorder is suggested, as it would be possible to repeat certain passages of a speech for more discriminate listening. A similar approach could be used for examining written material, with the exception of the tape recorder.

FAULTY METHODS OF INDUCING VOCABULARY GROWTH

Some teachers make the mistake of encouraging children to learn new words without due attention to their meaning and use. The pupils make long lists of new words and even use them incorrectly or in inappropriate contexts in an obscure or vague way. Children should list and look up words that promise to be useful to them in their current or near-future communication.

Other teachers lay too much emphasis upon building vocabulary by analyzing words into prefixes, roots, and suffixes to determine the meaning of unfamiliar words. When they require children to learn many word-parts of little functional value, the time is not well spent. Besides, the literal translation of words through such analysis rarely reveals the modern meanings of, and ways of using, words. Word study requires teaching guidance to keep it interesting and helpful. A limited amount of word analysis, in connection with currently useful words, can be helpful in making words meaningful to children; for instance *anti* in *antiseptic, antitoxin,* and *antivenom.*

Vocabulary games such as scrabble and crossword puzzles tend to increase vocabulary.

No one method of teaching vocabulary can be used in a rigid, unvarying way. Children need to acquire vocabulary through dozens of procedures applied throughout the day in every curricular area. Some of their learning will be incidental, but the teacher should always be ready with guidance when the children have difficulty with word meanings or assume an inaccurate understanding of some words. Vocabulary growth thrives best in an integrated program in which children learn through activities that bring concrete, interrelated learnings.

Specific Aids in Developing Vocabulary

FROM their early years, children have a natural interest in words, an interest that can be kept alive if teachers and their pupils will revel in the apt use of words in the stories, poems, talks, reports, and descriptions that are part of the ongoing learning activities of each school year. The pupils will also enjoy activities that are immediately concerned with words as such. Several valuable and intriguing activities are listed below.

1. Have word games at hand for indoor play at intermissions on stormy days; commercial games like anagrams, or games made by pupils or teacher will prove useful.

2. Discuss the meaning of new words related to any vivid experience, such as a field trip, a film, a school game, or an assembly. Then see that the pupils put these words to use in their own speaking or writing. Some of the more unusual words may be listed on the chalkboard to facilitate correct spelling.

3. After the pupils have viewed a film of special appeal, have them write a paragraph or some original verse that describes a favorite part or expresses personal reactions and ideas inspired by the film. Encourage them to select words that will be likely to create the same feeling in their readers or listeners.

4. Ask the pupils to select the most vivid verbs in an account of a football game by a sports writer or a newspaper article on a lively exciting event.

5. Have them list the words that a magazine or news writer has used figuratively.

6. Give the class a synopsis of a well-written paragraph taken from a book. Ask the pupils to write these ideas in their own words as effectively as they possibly can. Then let them compare their products with the author's original paragraph. Which words did the pupils use better? Which words did the author use more effectively?

7. Let each good oral reader select a vividly worded poem to be read to the class.

8. Select a sentence or two from a pupil's composition. Let the class or a small group rewrite the excerpt for greater liveliness and interest.

9. List words appropriate in describing something strongly associated with one of the five senses; for example, for smell—carnations, lilacs, the kitchen on a baking day, earth after a shower; for sound—jet airplanes, the brakes of swift-rolling tires, a kitten's cry; for taste—a green persimmon, heavily peppered vegetables, lemon meringue pie; for feeling—a raw oyster, a cat's fur, a mountain brook.

10. Develop charts that list homonyms and illustrate the different meanings with pictures; for example, *reign* (a crown) and *rain* (an umbrella).

11. Work to increase vividness in sentences through the choice of verbs rather than a heavy dependence on adjectives.

12. Analyze individual writing by copying it on the chalkboard or reflecting with an opaque projector and then asking the class to consider the choice of words and expressions. Try to improve the exactness, accuracy, and interest of the paragraph.

13. Play with puns. Let the pupils listen for puns or find them in print; then let them make puns. Show that puns are clever only when both meanings of the word make sense as used in the expression.

14. Encourage the pupils to find out the origin of words or phrases.

15. Let a committee determine where the English language comes from: the old Anglo-Saxon, the invading Romans and French, or modern inventions, as *gyroscope*.

16. Examine a new dictionary to find a section devoted to words that have recently been added to the listed vocabulary.

The preceding aids have been arranged in order of roughly increasing difficulty. Those that follow can be used anywhere in the middle and upper grades since the difficulty can be controlled in terms of the words that are selected for attention.

17. Play with words for the fun of so doing.

   a. Make a list of words that begin and end with the same letter; for instance, *bib, civic, deed.*

   b. Make a list of words that have three uses of the same letter; for instance, *babble, giggle, stress.*

   c. Play "teakettle" with homonyms. Make a sentence for each of two or three homonyms; but use the word "teakettle" instead of the homonyms. One child will say sentences such as the following while the class tries to guess the homonyms.

   "I teakettle what I say." (mean)

   "The Puritan had a severe teakettle." (mien)

   d. Play with rhyming words in which the leader has more guessing to do than do the members of the class. In the example that follows, the leader is thinking of *glee,* and says, "I am thinking of a word that rhymes with *she."*

JOE: Is it something that stings?

LEADER: No, it is not *bee.*

MAY: Is it something to drink?

LEADER: No, it is not *tea.*

DORA: Is it what you pay the doctor?

LEADER: No, it is not *fee.* (and so on until *glee* is guessed)

SUGGESTIONS FOR STUDY AND DISCUSSION

1. List five words you have learned in the past few months. (They may have been completely unfamiliar, or a known word may have taken on an entirely novel meaning for you.) For each word, indicate the different ways by which it took on meaning.

2. Make an outline of this chapter that will give an organized view of how vocabulary grows. Divide teaching procedures into two classifications: direct teaching and incidental teaching.

3. Classify the procedures according to your evaluation of them into "most valuable," "good," and "fair."

FOR FURTHER READING

1. ARCHER, MARGUERITE P., "Building Vocabulary with a Fourth-Grade Class." *Elementary English* (November 1960), 447–48.

2. BAKER, ZELMA W., *The Language Arts, the Child, and the Teacher.* San Francisco, Fearon, 1955.

3. CROSBY, MURIEL, "Words Can Make the Difference." *Elementary English* (February 1960), 81–85.

4. DEIGHTON, LEE C., "Developing Vocabulary: Another Look at the Problem." *English Journal* (February 1960), 82–88.

5. —— *Vocabulary Development in the Classrooms.* New York, Bureau of Publication, Teachers College, Columbia U., 1959.

6. DOLCH, E. W., "Needed Vocabulary." *Elementary English* (December 1960), 530–34.

7. EVERHART, RODNEY W., "Why Not Teach Children Semantics?" *Elementary English* (December 1957), 548–51.

8. FRY, EDWARD, "Teaching a Basic Reading Vocabulary." *Elementary English* (January 1960), 38–42.

9. GREEN, IVAH, "All Words Belong to First Graders." *Elementary English* (October 1959), 380–84.

10. SEEGERS, J. CONRAD, "Children's Experiences in Vocabulary Development," in Virgil E. Herrick and Leland B. Jacobs, eds., *Children and the Language Arts.* Englewood Cliffs, N. J., Prentice-Hall, 1955.

11. SHIBLES, BURLEIGH H., "How Many Words Does a First-Grade Child Know?" *Elementary English* (January 1959), 42–47.
12. STRICKLAND, RUTH G., *The Language Arts in the Elementary School* (Chapter 10). Boston, Heath, 1957.
13. TIDYMAN, WILLARD F., and MARGUERITE BUTTERFIELD, *Teaching the Language Arts* (Chapter 10). New York, McGraw-Hill, 1959.
14. WATTS, A. F., *The Language and Mental Development of Children* (Chapter 2). London, Harrap; Boston, Heath, 1947.

5

Gaining Ideas Through Reading

Chapter 5 emphasizes the principle that a rich intake of ideas is the basis for communication, that children tend to speak and write well when they are full of ideas. The chapter relates reading to the other language arts by pointing out that reading is one of the basic sources of information. This is not a methods chapter; it deals only with informational reading in textbooks, parallel readings, and reference books and presents some of the more fundamental steps in teaching pupils to study.

THROUGHOUT life, much information is gained through reading. For many people the newspaper and periodicals are the source. Other persons read pocket books that they buy at the corner drugstore or the supermarket. Still others join a club that sends one or more books each month, or they keep in touch with best sellers in other ways. The public and circulating libraries are meccas for a considerable group of people. All these reading materials supply a rich source of topics for discussion, conversation, storytelling, explanations, reporting, and other oral and written activities. Intake for later communication is a major function of reading.

Along with information comes pleasure in reading, for literature provides a rich source of enjoyment and escape. Dramatization and storytelling depend heavily on the stories that children read and hear. Literature puts the child in touch with new words graphically used, with sentences characterized by variety and balance; and frequently the child unconsciously absorbs these fine qualities into his own expression. His creative tendencies are also encouraged by the literature he reads and to which he listens. Since the contributions of literature to language are stated in other chapters, this one deals with reading for information.

Textbooks and Parallel Reading

TEXTBOOKS constitute an important source of information for pupils in elementary schools, and, if pupils are to discuss with understanding, they must read with efficiency. Effective reading of materials so extremely condensed as the typical textbook calls for a number of basic procedures, several of which are discussed in this division of the chapter.

PREPARATION FOR STUDY READING

One phase of reading readiness in the upper primary and intermediate grades consists of preparing the pupils for a lesson by giving a forward look into their printed materials. First the teacher will allow them *to discuss already familiar topics* that provide a basis for new information which they are about to read. For instance, if a chapter in a fifth-grade textbook is entitled "Using Language in Study," the pupils will recall and discuss such study skills from third and fourth grades as using an index and table of contents, using a dictionary, using an encyclopedia, outlining, making a report, and so on. Then the teacher will encourage them *to raise questions* they hope to have answered or, if they cannot think of any, to consider thoughtfully questions that the teacher raises such as the following: What is study? Would you read a book of fiction the same way you would a textbook? How can you make a report interesting?

If the textbook lesson contains totally unfamiliar words or some with unaccustomed meanings, the teacher will ask the pupils *to consider these words* before they begin the reading—unless the author of the book has carefully suggested the meaning through contextual clues so that the pupils can independently interpret the meaning. Words that do need preliminary attention may be incorporated in the discussion, listed on the board, presented in a preliminary phrase drill, and—if need be—carefully explained.

Still another helpful procedure in preparing pupils for their reading is for the teacher to instruct the pupils *to make a preliminary survey of the topical headings* which the textbook provides. In fact, the chapter title should itself give a strong hint as to the main idea that is to be presented. As the pupils survey the topical headings—half titles, boldface, italics, and the like—covered in a lesson, they will be surprised to find that they can get a good idea of the nature and the sequential organization of the information they will be reading. This survey may suggest further questions to guide their thinking as they read. Often the textbook provides excellent illustrative pictures, a survey of which will likewise aid in comprehension of important ideas.

Children should always read informational materials with questions in mind, since questions serve to guide their thinking and to assist them in selecting the most important facts. These questions may grow out of a discussion of previously learned information which is still incomplete or inadequately understood, or out of a preliminary survey of pictures and topical headings. Whenever there is the possibility that the children will not understand the new words on the basis of their use in context, the teacher should consider the crucial vocabulary before the pupils begin reading. Such procedures give a forward look into a textbook lesson and thus build in the children readiness to read with comprehension and interest.

SELECTED READING

Pupils cannot be expected to retain all the details in the materials they read; rather they should read to get major points and attempt to retain only the details related to their purposes for reading. They should be trained to read for a definite purpose; for instance, to find the answer to definite questions already in mind, to find facts to supplement what is already known, to find evidence for or against a tentative conclusion, sometimes specifically to find details (as in cases when the pupils need to know exactly how a colonial lady dressed so that a mural may be correct in its details). Reading in textbooks should always be preceded by a discussion that helps to define a purpose for reading. Only in this way can the pupils read discriminatingly and select the information that will be useful to them in accomplishing their purposes. Selective reading is encouraged by *the preliminary raising of questions, a forward look at topical headings, a careful consideration of each such heading at the time it comes up in reading,* along with *a definite statement of purpose* before the reading begins.

PRELIMINARY SKIMMING

A textbook sometimes has no topical heading, or the headings it does have may be barren and non-suggestive of the main ideas they cover in the text. In that case the pupils can learn to make a preliminary hop-skip-and-jump over the materials they are to read so as to get a helpful idea of the materials; that is, they may learn *to skim.* Such skimming should, at first, be done under the teacher's close supervision and used to help the pupils raise questions in discriminative reading; eventually they should learn to skim by themselves.

A FEELING OF RESPONSIBILITY FOR UNDERSTANDING

Pupils should come *to feel responsible for getting satisfactory results* in their reading for information (*if* the teacher has made sure that the materials are suitable in difficulty and treatment). For instance, a pupil should not feel satisfied to start nor continue his reading if he does not understand the assignment or the particular purpose for his reading. An understanding teacher will encourage a pupil *to inquire about a question or passage* that he does not understand. More than that the teacher will try to induce him to feel responsible for asking questions to clarify what he is reading. Too, the pupil should feel it is his responsibility *to reread any section* that he believes he has not fully understood. One of the finest characteristics that a teacher can cultivate in pupils is a feeling of responsibility for mastering the ideas they read. In this way they can learn to work well when they are later engaged in independent, individually selected reading.

BASIC READING SKILLS TO BE DEVELOPED

During and after the act of reading, various procedures are helpful. The pupil should first learn how *paragraphing* is an aid in following the thought of an author. Each paragraph deals with but one major topic; and pupils need to learn to alert themselves to the central idea of each successive paragraph. There may be a *topic sentence* that sums up the main idea; and the pupils should be given experience in identifying it. If the topic sentence is not specifically stated, the pupils should get practice in formulating one. Such practice may be given in reading class, or it may come in the language period as part of the training for writing well-organized paragraphs. At any rate pupils should have so much experience with thinking through the central idea of individual paragraphs that such thinking becomes automatic and helpful in comprehensive reading.

Another skill involves identifying the two, three, or four *main ideas in a selection.* Young children do this when they dramatize a story because each scene represents a division of the story, or when they take turns telling parts of a story in order. Some of the exercises that will help pupils locate the main divisions of a selection are these:

1. The teacher lists the two, three, or four main steps in the story; the pupils find where on a page each step in the story starts and ends.

2. The teacher tells how many main steps the story has; the pupils read silently and try to decide just what each step is; they work with the teacher to name each step after discussion has revealed what the steps truly are. These are listed as they are identified.

3. The teacher lists the first step on the chalkboard and uses Roman

numerals to indicate each additional step in the story; the pupils read and list independently their conception of what the remaining steps are. In the earlier stages of learning to outline, each step should be written in a short, complete sentence.

4. Each pupil decides the number and identity of the steps in an independently written list. Then follows a discussion in which the outlines of the pupils are compared, and a final form is decided on.

The teacher should follow much the same stages when he shows the children how to make an outline of their reading by using supporting *subtopics*. Children need to have direct and specific instruction in the art of outlining if they are to read with a sense of organization, of the relative importance of topics, and of the interrelationships among them.

A much more advanced skill that pupils should acquire is that of *summarizing*. After they have learned to outline well, they can progress to the art of stating the main points of the outline in a paragraph-form summary. Upper-grade pupils of average and high ability can learn to write summaries after they know how to outline.

INTERPRETATIVE READING

Children should learn *to pause briefly from time to time* as they read textbook materials, so as to organize their thinking and assimilate ideas. Especially should they stop to recall a personal experience or to associate previously learned information that will lend meaning to the unfamiliar facts they are encountering. That is, they should pause to think, to interrelate ideas, and to consider the relative significance of the information they have just read. A teacher can promote such thinking by suggesting ahead of time that a certain preliminary question will relate to a particular point in their reading materials. He may say, "You will recall that Mary was puzzled by the flare she saw in the sky last night. You will find an answer to her question as you read the topic on page 117." Too, the teacher may from time to time discuss the values of stopping to think over what is being read and may suggest different places where such pauses will help in the lesson of the day.

To give further impetus to the pupils' tendency to think interpretatively during the act of reading the teacher should encourage the pupils *to take part in a follow-up discussion* of the lesson. Sometimes the teacher will refer the pupils back to a certain portion of the textbook and say, "This part of the lesson explained how to use a lever in raising a weight. What experiences of yours illustrate this principle? You would have been helped to understand levers if you had paused and tried to remember where you have seen a lever used in this way." If the teacher will encourage the pupils to recall illustrations from their experience, to think of ways that certain facts may help them in the future, or to explain how certain events may affect the course of history, he will advance interpretative reading.

In connection with the reading of both textbooks and other references, pupils have occasion to search for information. In first grade most teachers teach the pupils *to use a table of contents* by asking them to find the page on which a certain primer or first-reader story begins. Teachers also help the children learn how *to open a book to a page as near the desired one as possible.*

Often in third grade, pupils begin *to use the index.* In using the index pupils find a genuine need *to know the alphabet in order.* In many instances they may already have learned alphabetical order through their use of the picture dictionary and a telephone directory.

If the pupils are not yet adept in finding words arranged in alphabetical order, the teacher can give them practice in locating words found in the index of some textbook. At the same time, the pupils can get experience in turning to one or more of the pages mentioned for each topic which they locate in the index. They will enjoy a contest (after preliminary and initial instruction) in which each row or team tries to be the first to find an item in the index, to find the actual page in the book, and eventually to find the sentence that gives the exact information for which the group is searching.

Increasingly the pupil should be able *to locate materials for himself* as he seeks information in his parallel reading. In connection with social studies or science lessons he may have found a need for using the table of contents or the index at the back of the book. Whenever the need for using such locational skills arises, the teacher should take several minutes to guide the pupils in their use of such aids as the table of contents or the index. He must do direct teaching if each pupil is to acquire the skills essential to his independent use of parallel references.

A final skill in locating information is for the pupils *to skim to find the exact information which is being sought.* In regular reading lessons, as well as in the use of textbooks in various content subjects, pupils need much experience in looking quickly down a page to find the sentence that tells the desired fact. Practice brings facility and speed. The pupil should understand, however, that skimming is only the preliminary to the next step, which involves study at a slower, more thoughtful rate.

Often individual pupils are given different references so that each may report supplementary information. In the late primary and early intermediate grades, careful guidance is necessary. The teacher should usually prepare a slip of paper for each pupil and indicate on it the exact pages and the precise questions to be answered. A sample follows:

1. Read pages 25 and 26 in Gray's *American Pioneers*.
2. Find answers to these questions:
   a. How did pioneers use animal and Indian trails?
   b. How did men like Boone travel?
   c. What made it hard for their families to follow these trails?

In locating information through their parallel reading, the pupils may find occasion *to consult a bibliography* at the end of a chapter or at the end of the book. A knowledge of alphabetical order is necessary here so that, if a pupil wants to find a book by Maury, he will know that he should look beyond names that begin with letters A to L. In the higher grades pupils also need to learn how to make a bibliography for themselves; that is, a mechanically correct notation of the author's name and the title of the book, followed by accurate page citations. The more advanced pupils may learn to annotate each bibliographical reference with a brief statement of the key ideas in it.

In addition to locational skills the reading of parallel references often calls for a pupil *to take running notes*. The questions that either he or his teacher has posed before the reading starts will act as a guide in selecting the noteworthy facts. Usually the facts may be described in topical form or in elliptical sentences, such as "first crossed mountains in 1775." At the beginning the teacher should select simple informational passages and use the chalkboard to work out appropriate running notes that the pupils dictate under her guidance. Then the pupils will learn how to select ideas of major importance and how to phrase their notes. When gathering exact evidence from a truly authoritative statement, the pupil may find it necessary to copy verbatim some of the statements. In that case he should note the exact page on which the statements appear, as well as the title and author of the book.

Reference Books

IN THE course of seeking definite information, pupils need to go to various sources, such as the dictionary, encyclopedias, the atlas, *Who's Who*, the *World Almanac*, and *Readers' Guide*. While learning to use such references should come mostly through the pupil's individual experience (with individual guidance in the early stages), the teacher can include some group instruction on the nature of each of these references and general practices in using the references. Some basic suggestions follow.

This girl's work will be a source of pride because she is checking the accuracy of her facts in authoritative reference books and the precision of her word usage in a dictionary.

USING THE DICTIONARY

Some reading manuals for first and second grades give suggestions that tell how the pupils may build a picture dictionary of their own. There is a separate page for each letter in initial position. The A page, for instance, may contain a pupil-drawn picture that illustrates some sight word that begins with that letter. Each pupil selects a word from a class list of words like *airplane, apple, animal;* he writes the word in manuscript letters and draws his illustrative picture. Also available are commercially prepared picture dictionaries that pupils find very helpful when they need to look up the spelling of a word as they write down their original stories.

As a rule, the use of a regular dictionary begins in late third or in fourth grade. The following outline indicates the preparatory experiences that pupils should have had in the primary grades.

I. Informal learning of the letters in alphabetical order
    A. Making picture dictionaries that combine practice on sight words and manuscript writing
    B. Using a commercial picture dictionary
    C. Using the index at the back of a textbook
    D. Using the telephone directory
    E. Making of alphabetized lists: pupils' names; titles of books
    F. Filing of individual spelling words
    G. Indexing for pupils' booklets
II. Syllabication of longer words
    A. Analyzing simple polysyllabic words in spelling
    B. Improving pronunciation of parts of longer words, as *library*
    C. Dividing a word at the end of a line
III. Division of compound words, as *milkman*

In the following outline are four phases of elementary dictionary training. Many pupils learn the tasks listed here in fourth grade. Even slow-learning pupils can do some of the simpler tasks under close teacher supervision.

I. Practice in alphabetizing lists of words
    A. Listing of words, all of which begin with a different letter
    B. Listing of words, several beginning with the same letter
        1. Grouping in terms of initial letter without regard to the second letter
        2. Arranging in terms of both the first and second letters
        3. Arranging in terms of first, second, and third letters
            a. All words having the same first and second letter

  b. No more than three different initial letters represented

  c. Listing words miscellaneously, but using several words for each of several initial letters

II. Location of specific parts of dictionary; specific words

 A. Opening the dictionary by estimate

  1. Halfway, one fourth, three fourths, and so on, to see what letters are initial to words there

  2. At any page with a specific initial letter, such as *l, f, s*

 B. Using key words at the head of each page

  1. Recognizing that the first key word shows the first word, and the second word the last word on the page

  2. Listing of key words on the chalkboard (or study sheet)

   a. Attempting to turn to the part of the dictionary where the words begin with the same letter as each of the key words

   b. Looking for the exact key words

  3. Finding on what page each word in a brief list begins by seeing whether it belongs between the two key words on a page (close supervision necessary)

   a. Making a board list of paired key words; locating words in another list, most of which belong between one pair or other of the key words

   b. Using the dictionary for a list of single words

III. Pronunciation of unfamiliar words

 A. Making a systematic study of diacritical markings

 B. Using pronunciation key

 C. Learning syllabication

 D. Accenting syllables

IV. Selection of a meaning to fit the context of the word in the sentence in which it is embedded

 A. Listing various meanings for the same word, as *present, fly, run*

 B. Making a list of sentences, each of which contains the same word but with a different meaning

 C. Finding unfamiliar words in context and trying to "guess" their meanings

 D. Selecting the dictionary meaning of an unknown word, found during reading, in terms of the meaning suggested by its sentence context

At the beginning of each school year, a teacher should take inventory of the dictionary skills of his pupils. Some will be ready to go ahead with more advanced learnings; others will need review or reteaching. The abler pupils will probably need only a suggestion for learning the advanced skills; the slower pupils will need much supervision on even the simpler aspects. An outline of some of the more advanced dictionary skills follows:

I. Refinement of skills already in use
  A. Words commonly mispronounced
    1. Listing words the pupils commonly mispronounce
    2. Using diacritical markings
    3. Noting difference in accent in a different part of speech: *defer, deference*
  B. Greater precision in use of words through building up lists of synonyms; avoiding crude misuse of words, as *awful, nice*
    1. Matching synonyms
    2. Replacing a word with a synonym that is more suitable or precise or colorful
    3. Studying dictionary lists of synonyms to determine their nice distinctions
    4. Doing multiple-choice exercises in which the pupil selects the best of several synonyms
    5. Making a class list of monotonous and crudely misused expressions, and finding in the dictionary ways of expressing meaning pleasingly and exactly
II. Formal word study, especially in the upper grades
  A. Prefixes and suffixes
  B. Frequently used roots of words
  C. Some etymology
    (See suggestions in Chapter 4, "Promoting Vocabulary Growth.")

USING OTHER REFERENCE BOOKS

Initially, many of the pupils' learnings in the area of dictionary skills can come through class or small-group instruction, although the follow-up use and practice on the skills are individual. Most of the skills in using other types of reference materials should probably be individual as each pupil finds a need for any particular skill.

Encyclopedias are an important source of information and will first be used by the abler pupils as they seek supplementary information for individual and group enterprises. The teacher may instruct individuals or a small group of pupils by demonstrating how to locate topics—alphabetical arrangement, key words on the back of each book, and the like—and showing how to skim until the desired items of information have been located. On the basis of previous learnings in the effective way to read parallel materials and use the dictionary, most bright pupils can quite easily learn to use encyclopedias with only this introductory demonstration. Slow learners later on will need much guidance from the teacher or a skilled classmate.

Most of the skills involved in using an *atlas* are usually learned in connection with the use of maps in textbooks and parallel reading, reference to road maps, and the viewing of weather maps on television. The same

Advanced pupils solicit the help of their teacher or librarian in using new types of reference books that furnish specialized information.

materials will often afford the pupils some experience in reading tables that report figures on areas, population, and value of products. Mainly the new learnings involve knowing what information the atlas provides and understanding how to locate each type of information.

The teacher may hold the atlas before his group and, as he displays the various sections, tell the kind of information that is provided in each section. Finally he may turn to the table of contents, index, and other locational aids and explain their use. Subsequently each pupil will work with the atlas on his own, with assistance when needed from the teacher or a classmate who is familiar with its use.

Upper-grade pupils will have occasion to use *The World Almanac* and *Who's Who*. In each group, it will be the advanced pupils who first turn to these references. Either the classroom teacher or the elementary school librarian will give instruction to each individual as he needs to learn how to use one of the references. It is wise for the instructor to encourage such pupils to inspect each new reference for the purpose of determining what locational aids are provided and what the scheme of organization is. Then an advanced pupil who is using new types of reference on his own will gain the ability to learn its use independently. Average and slow-learning pupils will eventually need to use some such references. Their already tutored classmates may assist the teacher or the librarian in teaching these pupils how to use these informational sources.

The *Readers' Guide* and *Children's Catalog* are other references of use to older pupils. The librarian or teacher may take small groups of pupils to the library and give them instruction on such points as the kind of information available in the reference, the parts into which the volume is divided, and effective ways to look for the facts they are seeking. Subsequently each of the instructed pupils should work by himself in an effort to find some information that he really wants, and he should feel free to ask assistance whenever he is unable to find exactly what he wants. Particularly perplexing is a decision on what topics to look for; for instance, if a pupil wants to find out how much livestock is raised in Argentina, what should he look for—"livestock," "cattle and hogs," "agriculture," "Argentina," or what?

USE OF THE LIBRARY

Many of the references previously mentioned are normally found in a library. Pupils need instruction in such matters as: What is the Dewey Decimal System? Where are the books on recreation located? How are they arranged? Where are the encyclopedias and other special reference books? How can I use the card catalog? Pupils need direct instruction on the many phases of library usage, but it is not within the province of this book to explain such instruction. However, the last section of this chapter's bibliography offers suggestions for library instruction to elementary school children.

SUGGESTIONS FOR STUDY AND DISCUSSION

1. Secure all the textbooks (and several parallel references) that are used in any grade. List all the types of study and reading guidance which these books provide.

2. Interview several teachers representing, among them, each of these levels: primary, intermediate, and upper grade. Find out what they do to assist pupils to use books independently and to read selectively and understandingly.

3. Observe the language activities in a selected grade on several occasions. To what degree are the children's ideas drawn from the reading of either the teacher or the pupils?

4. Consult several references on the use of the library. Make a summary of the chief learnings in library usage that children should achieve.

FOR FURTHER READING

1. BAKER, ZELMA W., *The Language Arts, the Child, and the Teacher* (Chapter 8). San Francisco, Fearon, 1955.
2. COLE, TOM J., "A Ladder of Library Skills." *The Elementary School Journal* (May 1961), 427–30.
3. DAWSON, MILDRED A., and HENRY A. BAMMAN, *Fundamentals of Basic Reading Instruction* (Chapter 12). New York, Longmans, Green, 1959.
4. DEBOER, JOHN J., and MARTHA DALLMANN, *The Teaching of Reading* (Chapter 9B). New York, Holt, Rinehart and Winston, 1960.
5. GRAY, WILLIAM S., *Improving Reading in Content Fields* (111–201) and *Improving Reading in All Curriculum Areas* (125–38, 150–63, 170–82, 242–46). Chicago, U. of Chicago Press, 1952.
6. HATCHETT, ETHEL, and DONALD HUGHES, *Teaching Language Arts in Elementary Schools* (129–39). New York, Ronald, 1956.
7. HERRICK, VIRGIL E., and LELAND B. JACOBS, eds., *Children and the Language Arts* (Chapter 14). Englewood Cliffs, N. J., Prentice-Hall, 1955.
8. HILL, JERALDINE, "Teaching Critical Reading in the Middle Grades." *Elementary English* (March 1962), 239–43.
9. KELLEY, VICTOR H., and HARRY A. GREENE, *Better Reading and Study Habits*. New York, Harcourt, Brace & World, 1960. Pamphlet.
10. LARRICK, NANCY, *A Parent's Guide to Children's Reading* (Chapter 9). Garden City, N. Y., Doubleday, 1958.
11. MACCARTHY, JOSEPHINE I., "When Elementary Children Use Reference Books." *Elementary English* (April 1959), 240–43.
12. MCKIM, MARGARET G., *Guiding Growth in Reading in the Modern Elementary School* (Chapters 8, 11, 12). New York, Macmillan, 1955.

13. SHAW, PHILLIP, "Study Activities: A Checklist." *Elementary English* (October 1959), 390–94.
14. SHORES, J. HARLAN, "Reading Science Materials for Two Distinct Purposes." *Elementary English* (December 1960), 546–52, 565.
15. SMITH, NILA BANTON, "Teaching Study Skills in Reading." *Elementary School Journal* (December 1959), 158–62.
16. STRANG, RUTH, and others, *Problems in the Improvement of Reading* (127–207). New York, McGraw-Hill, 1959.
17. STRICKLAND, RUTH G., *The Language Arts in the Elementary School.* Boston, Heath, 1957.
18. TIDYMAN, WILLARD, and MARGUERITE BUTTERFIELD, *Teaching the Language Arts.* New York, McGraw-Hill, 1959.
19. WATNUF, WALTER A., "Notetaking in Outline Form." *Elementary English* (April 1959), 244–47.
20. WOLFE, DON, *Language Arts and Life Patterns* (Chapters 22, 23). New York, Odyssey, 1961.

LIBRARY INSTRUCTION

21. BOYD, JESSIE E., and others, *Books, Libraries and You.* New York, Scribner's, 1949.
22. CAMPBELL, LEILA, and LOUISE KNIGHT, *A Student's Guide on How to Use a Library.* Chicago, Follett, 1948.
23. COLONIUS, LILLIAN, and GLENN W. SCHROEDER, *At the Library.* Los Angeles, Melmont, 1954. For Primary Grades.
24. FENNER, PHYLLIS, *The Library in the Elementary School.* New York, Hinds, Hayden & Eldredge, 1945. Pamphlet.
25. GARDINER, JEWEL, and L. B. BAISDEN, *Administering Library Service in the Elementary School* (Chapters 11, 14, 15). Chicago, American Library Association, 1954.
26. LARRICK, NANCY, *A Teacher's Guide to Children's Books.* Columbus, Ohio, Merrill, 1960.
27. MOTT, CAROLYN, and L. B. BAISDEN, *The Children's Book on How to Use Books and Libraries.* New York, Scribner's, 1948.
28. SANTA, BEAVEL, and LOIS HARDY, *How to Use the Library.* Palo Alto, Calif., Pacific, 1955.

6

Literature as Part of the Language Program

Chapter 6 offers suggestions for developing reading tastes and interests and explains the several values to be derived from an appreciation of literature. Included in the descriptions of methods for increasing children's enjoyment of prose and poetry are suggestions for pleasurable memorization of individually selected verse. Simple and effective ways of teaching choral speaking are presented. Also included are suggestions for setting up a program. The chapter concludes with lists of materials suitable for choral speaking at the various grade levels.

THE influence of literature on the speech and writing of children is undeniably important. Long before they come to school, many children begin their experience with literature by learning nursery rhymes and fairy tales. So adept do they become as listeners that a reader who misplaces a word or intentionally skips a section is immediately corrected. Those who enter school without such experience in childhood's traditional lore need to have provision made for it, for every person has a right to the wonderful heritage of folk literature. Through the school years, other classics, both old and new, belong in the curriculum as surely as the most "practical" subjects. The child's pleasure in story and rhyme will lead to a lifetime of enjoyment in good reading.

Language Learnings from Literature

SURELY not least among the pleasures of good literature is the joy one finds in an author's word choice. Children respond to the unusual and readily enter into the spirit of play when long, difficult, or humorous words are introduced. They may find charm in rolling heavy words over the tongue, like *galoshes* or *befuddled* or *blunderbuss*, as suggested by Alastair Reid in *Ounce, Dice, Trice*(25). They may like the nonsense of Lewis Carroll's

> 'Twas brillig, and the slithy toves
> Did gyre and gimble in the wabe.

As they mature, they can appreciate the beauty and power in the exact choice of the right word in any selection they are reading.

Well-written books, even though selected approximately for the child's reading level, are likely to make use of new and interesting words that will extend the vocabulary. If the teacher is reading to the class, a word of explanation may be made with scarcely an interruption; but if the child is reading independently, the word in context begins to take on meaning and other occurrences thereafter tend to make the meaning more precise.

Pleasure in rhythmical phrasing is another result of familiarity with good literature. The repeated chants of folk literature serve as examples. Because children like the sound and rhythm, they repeat over and over phrases like those of the old giant, "Fee-fi-fo-fum, I smell the blood of an Englishman." But rhymed verse is not the only source of rhythm. The well-phrased prose of literary masters has its own kind of rhythm that binds the listener in a magic spell. The opening lines of Ruskin's "King of the Golden River" serve as an example:

> In a secluded and mountainous part of Stiria, there was, in old times, a valley of the most surprising and luxuriant fertility. It was surrounded, on all sides, by steep and rocky mountains, rising into peaks, and from which a number of torrents descended in constant cataracts. One of these fell westward, over the face of a crag so high, that, when the sun had set to everything else, and all below was darkness, his beams still shone full upon this waterful, so that it looked like a shower of gold. It was, therefore, called by the people of the neighborhood the Golden River.

Literature also acquaints children with the endless variety of expression of which the English language is capable. Because their own conversational speech tends to flow in limited patterns and their textbooks aim for simple explanation, often at the expense of freshness in style, the curriculum must depend on literature to introduce the elements of beauty and charm in language. Without reference to technical structure, the examples alone exert influence, as follows:

Strangeness from another age

"Nay," quoth Little John testily, at the same time rising carefully, as though his bones had been made of glass, "I can help myself, good fellow, without thy aid."*

Emphasis through parallel phrasing

The heavens declare the glory of God
And the firmament sheweth his handywork. (Psalms 19:1)

Beauty in metaphor

The Lord is my shepherd; I shall not want. (Psalms 23:1)

Unconsciously, the child picks up the language and the style of what he reads. With a mind well stocked with prose and poetry of literary worth, the child is better able to express himself with true dignity and beauty when the occasion calls for it. In creative writing and dramatics he will reflect his literary experiences. For the experiences to be of real merit and lasting influence, the teacher must take the initiative in bringing to the pupils the best in children's literature.

Bringing Books to Children

Every classroom should afford a rich and varied sampling of books for children—sometimes housed there, sometimes drawn from the school's central library or a nearby public library, and perhaps brought from home by the children themselves. From one source or another the teacher should collect a large supply of books, enough to offer each child several volumes, that are peculiarly suited to his level of reading achievement and to his range of interests.

There should be books that he can read with relative ease and genuine enjoyment so that he will be induced to read widely and to develop his personal repertory of book friends. Whenever he is seeking data to help in answering some question of genuine interest, he will welcome informational books somewhat harder to read. He should have, therefore, a daily or weekly allotment of time for enjoying old book friends and for getting acquainted with friends-to-be. Therein lie rich opportunities for the intake of ideas which pupils may later communicate to others through speech and writing.

* Howard Pyle, *The Merry Adventures of Robin Hood,* Garden City, N. Y., Doubleday, 1954.

GUIDING LANGUAGE LEARNING

DEVELOPING TASTES AND INTERESTS

Children's interests and tastes naturally are immature and subject to developmental change. New interests can be aroused and old ones modified so that tastes are elevated and diversified. At the start of each school year the teacher should ascertain the reading proficiency and the prevalent interests of his group and of the individuals within the group. With such information as a background, he can then guide and stimulate reading activities that will open new vistas and reveal increasingly high and more intriguing planes of reading achievement.

One fourth-gráde teacher got good results early in the school year by the following procedures. After taking an informal interest inventory by administering standardized and simple teacher-made tests to his class, he encouraged his pupils to bring in their favorite books of the year before, and he set about the work of pulling out reading materials likely to appeal to individual pupils in the first weeks of school.

For the devotees of comic books, he secured classics put up in "funny-book" style; for the more prosaic, fact-loving pupils, he laid out intriguing science and travel books at different levels of difficulty; for the many lovers of fantasy, he supplied an abundance of fairy stories and tales of giants, gnomes, and legendary heroes. In areas of general interest, such as stories of children and animals in real-life situations, he sampled generously in both easy-to-read and harder books so that all the children might enjoy such popular types of books.

Then he gave the last half hour of each school day to a free-reading period. Each child had the privilege of gathering with a group of classmates in a corner for a quiet sharing of a story through the showing of pictures or the telling and oral reading of favorite passages. And how his children did read! As the year progressed, the teacher took advantage of the children's growing interests and increased ability. Comics disappeared; fact lovers began to enjoy science fiction and lovers of fantasy began to seek facts.

This teacher's procedures exemplify the following facts: Every teacher should, of course, start where the pupils are. He should provide materials related to their present interests and suited to their abilities; he should lead them on to new interests and discriminating and refined tastes. In view of the fact that newsstands, bookshops, and even libraries make available some undesirable books, it is incumbent on the school and the teacher of language arts to provide a rich offering of desirable books and magazines. Through these reading materials children may cultivate wide interests and develop improved tastes for literature that will enrich their living even as it affords enjoyment. Stories and plays take on special appeal when presented through well-selected recordings, radio and television programs, movies and filmstrips.

To awaken new interests, to enhance the desirable old ones, and to influence children's choices in reading materials, certain considerations must be kept in mind: (1) The reading proficiency and general maturity of the individual children to be served should govern the reading program. In any one class there will be a considerable spread in maturity, which will necessitate a wide variety of materials. (2) The number, kind, and quality of the books available will largely determine the tastes and interests of young readers. (3) The conditions under which reading takes place should be favorable. The children should be comfortably seated, the lighting good, the general atmosphere happy and informal. (4) Materials in books should be partially familiar; that is, the child should already have a background of experiences, actual and vicarious, that will enable him to interpret and enjoy the books made available to him. (5) Books characterized by dramatic, swift-moving action and suspense are likely to attract real interest.

Preferences change as children grow older. Children of five and six prefer stories of the here and now, especially those that are true to life and relate to children of their age. They like obviously ridiculous fantasy, as portrayed by rhymsters like Dr. Seuss. Young children, too, will accept tales of animals that talk, dress, and behave like human beings because the tales are lively and, besides, these children know enough about animals to know which ideas are make-believe and which are true.

The liking for talking-beast tales by the younger boys and girls is, in two or three years, replaced by a preference for scientific but dramatically told animal stories. Seven- and eight-year-olds revel in fairy tales and fanciful stories; children a few years older, especially boys, prefer hero tales and adventure stories. Tall tales are also popular.

At the upper-grade level, adventure stories continue to be popular. History, biography, travel, science, and animal stories are well liked; and nonsense, realism, and graphically written informational books all have a steady appeal. Adolescent girls enjoy romance and fiction bearing on home life and school days; they also like the same kinds of literature that boys enjoy except that the girls want less violence in the adventure tales. However, the less mature types of stories, preferred by younger children, have been replaced by materials better suited to the tastes of the preadolescent and the adolescent.

Increasingly, as the child masters the art of reading for himself, he delves into the literary world on his own. Much of his reading, then, is silent. Even so, he is glad to share his enjoyment by telling excerpts from a story, discussing his reactions to it, dramatizing a lively scene, and reading orally. In everyday vernacular, he is "advertising" what he likes in order to induce his friends to read what he has enjoyed. There can and should be much sharing through telling parts of books (but not enough to betray the endings), reading selected bits orally, making illustrations to be posted and explained, or writing out a brief recommendation such as the following report on Fred Gipson's *Old Yeller* given by an upper-grade pupil:

OLD YELLER

WHEN Travis found that a big, ugly, yellow dog had stolen and eaten the last side of pork from the winter's hog butchering, he started to chase the dog away. Little Arliss had other ideas, however, and he promptly went into one of his tantrums. Mama decided they had better keep the dog. Before many weeks had passed, Travis thought so much of him that he "couldn't do enough for Old Yeller."

It was during the late 1860's. Papa left Texas on a cattle drive, and fourteen-year-old Travis stayed behind with two big responsibilities on his shoulders. He had to do a man's share of the work on the place and also protect Mama and Little Arliss from the dangers of frontier life.

During the months Papa was gone, the family had many exciting adventures. If you would like to know whether Travis was successful in his two jobs and what part a brave dog played in the family's adventures, you must read *Old Yeller* by Fred Gipson. You will never read a better boy-and-dog book.

For very young children, the teacher should do much oral reading and much storytelling. Daily he will find occasion to tell a story or to pick up a picture book and read the brief text as he displays the pictures to the children gathered in a semicircle about him; or he will read a more extensive treatment with fewer pictures. Preferably he should tell stories rather than read them. Storytelling has a vitality, freshness, and directness that may be lacking in the reading. Some stories, however, are so well written that the beauty of the language should be preserved through the interpretive reading of the teacher or pupil skilled in oral reading. The world of books opens to children as the teacher or pupil shares stories and poems through reading and telling.

All too often the teacher of older pupils abandons the practice of reading aloud to his pupils. This should not be. At all levels girls and boys should have the opportunity of listening to fanciful, realistic, and factual materials that will enrich their thinking and induce an interest in reading further for themselves. The teacher may introduce new books in these

As pupils make informal comments about their reading, they communicate their interests to others.

ways: (1) by reading brief excerpts of special interest, (2) by displaying pictures, (3) by relating exciting and stimulating facts about the author, (4) by letting the children guess the story that might well go with such a title as "The Lonesome Island."

There is a place, too, at all levels for the teacher to read entire books to the children. These should be books of quality, books that the children are not yet able to read easily for themselves but which are suited to their maturity in theme and action. Mary Norton's *The Borrowers*, for instance, is a favorite of fourth graders. They enjoy listening to this amusing fantasy which few nine-year-olds can read for themselves. The teacher should familiarize himself with the book he is to read; only then can he read fluently, with due response to the mood and movement of the story. He should get pleasure from the experience so that his feelings will unconsciously carry over into the pupils' own positive emotions.

Abundant contact with literature will induce creativity in boys and girls. They will make up stories; they will dramatize. (Chapter 19 discusses children's creative expression.)

Enjoying Poetry

CHILDREN like the musical cadences of poetry as well as its vivid imagery. The melody and swing of the lines appeal to the ear, the graphic word pictures to the mind's eye. Even the three-year-old will snuggle down to listen for long minutes to nursery rhymes with their marked rhythm, boldly apparent rhyme, and rapidly dramatic action. The very young child derives great pleasure from chiming in as the more familiar nursery rhymes are repeated. Children continue to revel in the singing qualities of poetry into and through the high school years *if* some adult has not already ruined their pleasure in poetry by poor selection, compulsory memorization, or overanalytic treatment.

Poems, like jewels, concentrate beauty in small compass. Where prose would take many words to describe or relate, good verse will in a few words portray or suggest a whole scene or experience, as in the sounds and sights described by Carl Sandburg in "Niagara."*

NIAGARA

The tumblers of the rapids go white, go green,
go changing over the gray, the brown, the rocks.
The fight of the water, the stones,
the fight makes a foam laughter
before the last look over the long slide
down the spread of a sheen in the straight fall.

* Carl Sandburg, *The People, Yes*, New York, Harcourt, Brace & World, 1936.

> Then the growl, the chutter,
> down under the boom and the muffle,
> the hoo hoi deep,
> the hoo hoi down,
>   this is Niagara.

Walter de la Mare describes the moonlight vividly in his poem "Silver":*

> Slowly, silently, now the moon
> Walks the night in her silver shoon;
> This way, and that, she peers, and sees
> Silver fruit upon silver trees. . . .

These bits of verse illustrate several of the qualities that give poetry its appeal. The word pictures are vivid; there is sensory appeal in these instances to the eye and ear. Words such as the *growl* and *chutter* of the falls suggest the sounds they represent (they are onomatopoeic). There is alliteration as in the *s* beginnings of the words in "Silver." The style suits the mood of the verse; note the vigor of the thunderstorm and the stillness of the moonlit night. Particularly appealing are the rhyme, rhythm, and tone color of the poems these excerpts represent. May Hill Arbuthnot(3) sets up these criteria for judging poetry:†

> When we choose a new poem for children we may well test it by asking ourselves these questions: First, does it sing—with good rhythm, true unforced rhymes, and a happy compatibility of sound and subject—whether it is nonsense verse or narrative or lyric poetry? Second, is the diction distinguished—with words that are rich in sensory and associative meanings, words that are unhackneyed, precise, and memorable? Third, does the subject matter of the poem invest the strange or the everyday experiences of life with new importance and richer meaning? When a poem does these three things, it is indeed good poetry—it may add to the child's day one brief moment of laughter, or give him a new dream to dream over in solitude, or leave him with a sharpened awareness of life. . . .

When the poetry is within the children's experiences, they can find the meaning and feel the mood. Children delight in rhyme, rhythm, meter, onomatopoeic words, alliteration, tone color, cadence, all that goes into melody of verse. Poetry should be read aloud for the appreciation of these elements. But the reader must never allow rhyme and meter to dominate meaning and mood. A singsong pattern in the reading of poetry (with the

* From *Collected Poems 1901–1918* by Walter de la Mare. Copyright, 1920, by Henry Holt and Company. Copyright, 1948, by Walter de la Mare. By permission of the publishers.

† *Children and Books*, pp. 160–61. Copyright, 1947, Scott, Foresman and Company, Chicago.

exception of jingles) is poor reading. Teachers must like poetry, understand its meaning, interpret its mood, and be sincere in their reading, and
then children will like poetry, too.

Good poetry has other charms for children. If it is narrative—and children prefer narrative to descriptive poetry—the action must be brisk.
Younger girls and boys like humor of the more obvious types—the incon-
gruous, the unexpected. The subjects that appeal to them are varied: for
example, animals, children and grownups, play and games, weather. While
young children care little for nature poems of a descriptive type, their older
brothers and sisters do enjoy artistic, graphic description. Ballads and the
longer narrative poems are also popular.

Types of Poems That Appeal

As HAS been indicated, the variety, rhythm and rhyme, and brisk action
of Mother Goose make the nursery rhymes favorites with young children.
Children of all ages enjoy storytelling poems. Consider the appeal of "A
Visit from St. Nicholas" and "The Pied Piper of Hamelin," which younger
girls and boys like so well; equally popular with these children are "A
Visit from Mr. Fox" and Eliza Lee Follen's "The Three Little Kittens,"
Laura E. Richards' "The Monkeys and the Crocodile," and Eugene Field's
"The Duel." In the early middle grades narrative poems suitable for choral
speaking are popular as, for instance, Beatrice Curtis Brown's "Jonathan
Bing," Mildred Plew Meigs' "The Pirate Don Durk of Dowdee" (note the
alliteration), and Walter de la Mare's "The Lost Shoe." Traditional and
adventure poems like "The Highwayman," by Alfred Noyes, appeal to the
children in the upper grades.

Nonsense verse, too, has appeal. Edward Lear, Eugene Field, Laura E.
Richards, and Lewis Carroll are writers in the nonsense vein. Less obvious
but pleasurable humor is to be found in the verse of Eleanor Farjeon and
Rose Fyleman, Vachel Lindsay and Carl Sandburg (their simpler verse),
James Whitcomb Riley, and—above all—A. A. Milne. Really humorous
verse has an easy swing and dexterous phrasing.

Among the moderns who write on a child's level, one favorite is Elizabeth Madox Roberts. With this poet, one can climb under the butterbean
tent, listen to the ruffling feathers and "little asking words" of the hens, or
watch "a little bug all lit and made to go on wings." Even an adult reader
can shed years while reading and can become a child again, peering into
the old stone henhouse where sleepy hens clucked a quietly startled greeting. Others who can interpret the world in childlike terms are John Farrar,
Rachel Field, Eleanor Farjeon, Walter de la Mare, Elizabeth Coatsworth,
Rose Fyleman, and Robert Louis Stevenson.

The melody and imagination in lyrical poetry appeal strongly to children. Christina Rossetti's *Sing Song*, the nature pictures of Elizabeth Coatsworth and Sara Teasdale, the adventures of Rose Fyleman's fairies, and the simpler verse of Walter de la Mare sing their way into high favor with girls and boys. Children with finer sensibilities will revel in the lilt, the fancy, the delicacy of those lyrics that are not too elusive for the immature mind.

Every elementary school teacher should possess two or more anthologies of children's verse (see pages 124–25 for a list of them) and should also make his own collection to supplement such books, with due care that this verse should have real merit.

Procedures in Teaching Poetry

THE key to children's appreciation and continued enjoyment of poetry is much listening to verse, read by a person who likes poetry, reads it well, and revels in an opportunity to share his enjoyment with others. A friend once confided,

> When I was in junior high school, I despised poetry. The teacher was always gushing over poems and trying to force us to like and memorize poems she read to us. I felt that her remarks were an affectation, that she didn't really like poetry.
>
> One day she was absent, and a substitute teacher came in. This teacher was direct and sincere in manner. She told us she could not teach the regular lesson and that she would like to share with us some things that she liked. So she started reading poetry to us, even some of the same poems that we had heard before; but this teacher was genuine in her liking. She didn't say much about the poems, but her reading brought out the mood, the meaning, the words that suggested pictures to our minds. And I have liked poetry ever since. Today the first thing I read in my new magazines is the poems I find in them.

Appreciation is caught, not taught. If a teacher gets a deep-down pleasure out of reading poetry, if he reacts sensitively to the mood and the meaning, his love of poetry is likely to be conveyed to those who listen to him. A simple and sincere manner, a natural voice, and his genuine response to the situation portrayed in the poem will help the children to share his enjoyment.

The reading of poetry should not be restricted to any single period in the school day. It should come in whenever the occasion warrants. Perhaps Jimmy has told the other children about the little calf he saw at his grandfather's farm. The teacher could choose this time to read to Jimmy's group Robert Frost's "The Pasture." Or a bird suddenly perches on the limb of a tree just outside the schoolroom window. Then the teacher of the second graders may share with them a favorite poem, Emily Dickinson's "The Bird."

A story in the *American Junior Red Cross Magazine* has interested the third-grade children in knowing more about the Netherlands; so a project on life in that country has begun. Dinah Mulock Craik's "A Little Dutch Garden" will be enjoyed. Or the younger children may be tired. Some nonsense verse will revive them, so the teacher reads "The Owl and the Pussy Cat" to them.

These illustrations are given to show that poems may be read at any time of day, in connection with any subject or learning activity, to children of any age. The one prerequisite is that the poem be a suitable one— to the occasion, and to the maturity and experiences of the children.

That poetry should be read aloud has already been stressed. It should be read by an accomplished oral reader, often an adult. Only in this way can the singing qualities be enjoyed and the intrinsic mood be transmitted. Inverted order, which is found in many poems, confuses the immature child so that he is unable to read smoothly, to stress the more important meanings in the poem, or to give proper inflections to his voice. Children can understand, enjoy, and appreciate poetry far beyond their capacity to read well. The teacher or some other mature reader, who loves poetry and can read with sincerity and genuine pleasure, should present such hard-to-read poems so that the children can listen with the utmost pleasure. Only when a child is thoroughly familiar with a favorite poem and can read it competently, or when he is engaging in the preliminary stages of choral speaking, should he do the reading. The skills of oral reading are different from those of silent reading. They are the interpretative skills and go beyond the thought-getting processes of silent reading.

And what of memorization? Some courses of study still require the memorization of a certain number of poems in each grade of school and may even specify which ones are to be memorized. All too often traditional selections that are about children, not for them, are really adult reactions that only adults can understand and appreciate. "The Barefoot Boy" and "A Boy's Song" are cases in point. Required memorization almost surely dulls the zest for even the most appealing of poems. What memorization there is should be voluntary, should come at the child's own suggestion. Since some children will like one poem while their classmates prefer others, the teacher should not expect all the pupils in a class to memorize any one poem. Let the choice be made by the individual.

Memorization should come without conscious effort on the part of the pupils. As the teacher reads poem after poem during the weeks of school, the children will request certain best-liked ones again and again. To one group, "Some One" and "Tired Tim" by Walter de la Mare were especially appealing. They requested these many times, gradually beginning to

chime in, in choric effect. Without intending to do so, the children memorized these two poems. From time to time, small groups and individuals
requested the opportunity to say one or the other of them to the group
during a free period; and the interesting thing is that they recited both
poems with proper inflections, meaningful pauses, and due response to the
meaning and mood. There was no singsong, no rattling off, as would probably have been the case in routine memorization.

There will be times, of course, when one or more children will want to
memorize a certain poem. The teacher should encourage them to do so,
but he should feel responsible for suggestions on the best way to memorize. For instance, the teacher should encourage the *whole method;* that
is, the child should read the entire poem again and again and thus memorize it as a whole.

One teacher had the privilege of sharing John G. McGee's "High
Flight" with an eighth-grade group engaged in a unit on advances in
transportation. He was deeply stirred by it, but endeavored to read with
due restraint. The pupils liked it, and several asked for the privilege of
copying it. Next morning it was the hard-boiled street gamin in the group
who came to him and said, "I'd like to say 'High Flight' in the upper-grade
assembly next week. Do you think the class will let me? Last night as I
was helping Dad load the truck, I said it over and over, and now I know
it by heart. I've never liked any poem so well before." He did say it, and
well. He had caught the mood of the pilot, his exaltation and reverence,
and was able to convey these to the audience.

As children progress through school, they will tend to memorize voluntarily one poem after another. They enjoy repeating their favorites from
time to time. In one school the pupils have for many years held a weekly
Recall Hour in which they take turns saying entire shorter poems and
excerpts of longer ones. The Recall Hour is perhaps the most enjoyable
time of the week.

And what if the teacher is assigned a specific list of poems for memorization? If he must conform, it is his responsibility to make the poems as
palatable as possible. He should introduce a poem like Rachel Field's
"Gypsy Children" in such a way as to suggest the fun of living outdoors;
for instance, he might take from his file of clipped pictures one that shows
a gypsy cooking over an open fire, or some similar theme. The children
may discuss the picture briefly and relate similar experiences of their own.
The teacher may then read the poem to see if their feelings agree with
those shown in the poem.

One teacher was required to have a fourth-grade group learn James
Russell Lowell's "And what is so rare as a day in June?" An especially
bad feature was that the poem had to be memorized within three lessons—
in time for the Friday assembly. The day before the teaching was to start,

he asked a gifted boy to make a drawing of the scene that Lowell portrays. It was done beautifully in colored chalk. The next day the whole
class listened with pleasure as they heard the words that suggested the
scene that was pictured before their eyes.

The teacher found several good "reasons" for rereading the poem; for
instance, which words suggest sounds and which ones suggest things to
be seen, which aspects of the June day would individual pupils enjoy
most, which parts of the stanza would they like to repeat with the teacher,
and so on. Next, the group worked out the two or three key words for
each line; the teacher listed these phrases on the board. By following this
list, the children were able to chime in as the teacher read. Mimeographed copies of the poem made it possible for the pupils to consult the
words of the poem at will.

At the end of the third lesson most of the pupils had memorized the
line of Lowell's description of June, and without too much pain. Note
that the children had been given as many reasons for listening as there
were rereadings, that they had been encouraged to chime in as favorite
and familiar parts were being read, and that key words had been used to
give them clues. Boys and girls vied in the effort to learn quickly and to
speak with due response to the feelings conveyed by the poet. Only in an
emergency or after a group request should an entire group be expected to
memorize in this manner.

Should children be expected to copy poems? They should certainly not
be required to do so. However, many children like to collect poems they
particularly enjoy, and teachers should encourage them to do so. Almost
any child occasionally will find a poem that has special appeal for him,
and he will gladly copy it, especially if he is allowed to draw colored
border illustrations. Some attractive bulletin board exhibits can be made
up of travel poems (boat, airplane, prairie schooner, train, taxi, and the
like) that individual pupils have selected for copying and illustrating.
When a poem has been copied, the poet's name should always be given.
Older children should be taught to include other bibliographical data:
name of book, publisher, date, and page number.

Many narrative poems are suited to pantomime and dramatization.
Nursery rhymes like "Jack Be Nimble" and "Little Jack Horner" are especially good for smaller children. They may skip to "Hippity-Hop to the
Barber Shop," march to the rhythm of "The Grand Old Duke of York,"
and dawdle along to "A Dillar, a Dollar." Pupils in the middle grades
enjoy dramatizing such poems as Florence Page Jaques's "A Goblinade"
or Robert Browning's "The Pied Piper of Hamelin." More mature children, too, will find verse that lends itself to being acted out, for instance,
the pantomiming of Langston Hughes's "African Dance."

Abundant listening to good poetry is conducive to creative writing of verse. Pupils with great facility in the use of words and a predisposition to rhythmic writing will burst forth in poetic expression. A child with a flair for writing needs only the hint that such writing is possible and the opportunity to write as, for instance, the child who wrote the following poem:

He Let Me Ride

Horses
Went galloping, galloping around the corral
    With hoofs beating fast,
    Kathump! Kathump!
But soon one horse slowed down
Trot-trot; trot-trot—
He came nearer—slower still—
    Walk .   .   .   . Walk.
He came
Right close to me
And stopped
And muzzled his tickling nose
    Against my hand.

So they put the saddle on his back,
And a bridle on his head
    With reins
    For a rider to hold
    When he sat
    Way up high—astride
Across the horse;
And then he let
    Me ride.

BONITA TAGUDING

The remarkable poem quoted above was written under circumstances such as these: An eighth-grade girl had formerly attended a traditional school in another area where her writing had been confined to exercises on correct usage, sentences using each word in a weekly spelling list, and answers to test questions. In the departmentalized program, her eighth-grade English teacher was a young man just out of college. He introduced choral speaking to the class and encouraged the pupils to add a stanza to a nonsense poem they had enjoyed. This particular girl responded with enthusiasm and, in the library period that followed, asked if she might try to make up a poem all her own. "He Let Me Ride" was the result. She continued to write several high-quality poems each week during the remainder of the school year—poems varied in style and theme but uniformly excellent in quality. The fact that this girl was full of ideas and had a high writing potential was discovered almost accidentally. She needed only to realize this writing potential and then to take her pen in hand.

For a full discussion of creative writing, see Chapter 19.

Choral Speaking

CHORIC speech is the interpretation of verse or rhythmic prose as several or many voices speak in perfect unison. It may involve speech by an entire group, by subgroups in turn, or by single persons whose parts alternate with those spoken by groups. There is often an antiphonal effect as groups respond to one another in turn. Usually the individual's voice is lost as it blends with the voices of his companions, yet each child is conscious and proud of the contribution he is making to the total harmonious effect. Thus, choral speaking has both personal and social values.

Choric speech is an activity that is new, yet old. It is estimated that groups spoke with antiphonal effects as early as the fifth century B.C. The psalms from the Old Testament, which constitute some of our best choral-speaking materials today, were probably first used in King David's day when priests and their congregations worshiped their Creator with antiphonal repetition of the Songs of David. The Greeks, in the natural amphitheaters of their hills, were likewise accustomed to antiphonal responses similar to the most finished voice-choir productions of today. Even so, choral speaking is a relative newcomer to American schools. As late as 1922 Marjorie Gullan organized the first speaking choir in Glasgow, Scotland. From that time the movement spread and eventually reached America.

VALUES OF CHORAL SPEAKING

Of all the experiences children may have with poetry, that of speaking chorally is possibly the most rewarding. The joy of making oral response to the lilt and melody of verse, a growing sensitivity to the beauty and emotional appeal of literature, the pleasure of making an individual and unself-conscious contribution to a group enterprise, the resultant feeling of group solidarity and rapport, perceptibly improved control over voice and related speech skills—such are the benefits and rewards of engaging in choral speaking.

Any classroom teacher who likes poetry and understands children can lead his pupils fruitfully and pleasurably in choric speech. While special training is beneficial, the teacher inexperienced in directing choral speaking may do a creditable piece of work if he heeds the principles that underlie such activity.

The timid child, when engaged in choral speaking, tends to lose his

Older pupils regain a love for poetry as they interpret it through choral reading.

self-consciousness and to be increasingly ready with suggestions for arranging poems for group work. On the other hand the exhibitionist learns to find pleasure in group endeavors in which he has no chance to be conspicuous and to show off. He becomes one with his classmates. Democratization of the classroom atmosphere, socialization of the pupils, and cooperation are promoted. There are, besides, values gained through the pupils' growing appreciation of literature, the widening range of literary experience, enrichment of vocabulary, a developing flexibility of voice, rhythm in speech, and improved articulation and enunciation. In fact, many upper-grade teachers, whose pupils had learned to dislike poetry because of earlier inept teaching, have made poetry popular again by introducing choral speaking. Properly handled, choral speaking is indeed worthwhile.

DANGERS TO BE AVOIDED

Valuable as experiences in choral speaking may be, it is quite possible to derive harm rather than good if the program is unwisely planned and carried out. In the first place, teachers who do not understand the rich educational values to be gained may achieve only a monotonous, *verbatim* recitation of poetry. Authentic choral speaking is the *interpretation* of poems and rhythmic prose, each performer actively sensing the meaning and swing of the words and trying to convey his individual conception and appreciation as he speaks in unison with his group or perhaps takes over a solo part. The wise teacher of choral speaking will never try to arouse an exhibitionary aim in his pupils. They should share with their listeners a pleasure they genuinely feel.

A second danger to be avoided is the selection of mediocre verse. In seeking a satisfactory arrangement for any one poem, the teacher and his pupils often try one scheme after another, the suggestions coming largely from the pupils themselves. Only really meritorious verse can be enjoyed and appreciated after such long-continued attention.

The writer has often divided a class into five groups, each of which was to plan and practice a choric rendition of "Oh, Susan Blue." What fun the groups have had as they listened to one another's presentation! Almost never has any one of the groups duplicated exactly the rendition of another group in the way the lines have been divided for antiphonal effects or the style of voice inflection. Often a group has substituted a locally appropriate line for the closing "Out in the meadow where the cowslips grow." There is a thrill in working out the most suitable renditions for worthy verse because of the sense of accomplishment that arises when the "best way of all" has been achieved through group effort. Appreciation is enhanced; there is no monotony.

A third danger arises because of the children's tendency to singsong their verse. In the early stages of learning to do choral speaking, the children's efforts are likely to be crude in various ways, including this singsong effect. To combat this, they need to work with the teacher to get at the deeper meaning of the poem, to decide which words contribute most to this meaning, and to try to speak in such a way as to make the meaning clear. The method of speaking even in verse should be like that of conversational speech. The meaning must cut across the rhythm, or the singsong pattern of the poem's meter will be so strong that the poem will be meaningless to the readers and to the listeners. With some groups of children the teacher will need to convey the thoughts in the poem with the correct vocal emphasis until the pupils become accustomed to reading verse with meaning.

A fourth danger lies in the children's use of their voices, which may be strained and frequently too loud. As in singing, it is the well-modulated tones that give pleasing effect. The teacher should help the children to realize this.

Words must be articulated clearly in identical intonations from the very beginning, or the effect will be muddled. Children readily see the need for this precaution. However, some pupils may need separate remedial training on certain sounds which are especially troublesome for them. Special practice sentences, words or groups of words should prove helpful.

As children work together to get at the fundamental meaning in a poem on which they are working, and as they attain a feeling for its significance and mood, they may become overenthusiastic and speak in an overly dramatic way. This is a serious danger which the teacher should try to avoid. The teacher should always treat poems simply, with genuine but restrained feeling.

Poetry is real, not overdramatic. Robert Frost remarked, "I say my poems." The teacher's mood and manner set an example for the children who tend to match his genuineness and simplicity. Neither the teacher nor his pupils should strain for effect; he should never set a rigid formula for the saying of any poem, but let the treatment of the poem grow out of the poem itself. The pupil-shared search for its meaning, mood, and rhythm (not singsong pattern) will produce genuine interpretation.

INITIATING A CHORAL-SPEAKING PROGRAM

There is no one way to begin a program of choral speaking with children. A natural method with the younger children is to let them chime in as the teacher reads again and again bits of verse that are high favorites. In this unison work their voices should be light and their articulation precise so that the whole effect is not a blurred one. The poems should be short, for then it is easier for all to keep together. Although unison speaking is a difficult phase of choral speaking, Harry A. Greene and Walter T. Petty(52) show that, in simple form, unison speech has value for young and untrained children:*

> Young children enjoy repeating poetry in unison. Group reading or choral speaking helps to improve voice quality and clear speech. It also provides opportunities for the shy to participate without embarrassment. A teacher has to read or repeat a poem to primary children only once or twice, allowing them to say as much as they can after each reading, and they will know it.

Some experienced teachers advise a start through oral reading. As the children engage in dramatic reading, with each reader assuming the part of one of the characters and reading what this character says, he learns to respond to the said personality and to the situation; in other words he reads in an interpretative manner. As a pupil reads orally he should be encouraged to ask other good readers to read a passage with him. As children read parts together the teacher may find a good opportunity to initiate choral reading.

The teacher can control tempo and rhythm by directing the choral speaking with motions of his hand, as if directing the singing of a melody. In fact, the children may learn to follow the motions of the right hand for these purposes while watching the teacher's left hand to determine changes in volume—again, just as in music. Some experts in choral speaking suggest that children in kindergarten and early primary grades recite a simple verse in unison, and then repeat, clapping their hands to match its rhythm. This would be particularly fitting for verse suited to marching or skipping: for instance, A. A. Milne's "Hoppity" or the old rhyme "The Grand Old Duke of York." These experts, too, indicate the importance of stressing the meaning to avoid a singsong production.

As suggested above, a good approach may be through the children's making bodily responses to appropriately selected rhymes. They may "hippity-hop to the barber shop," "jump over the candle stick," or go galloping with Keery in Rose Fyleman's "Husky Hi."

SELECTION OF VERSE FOR CHORAL SPEAKING

It has already been pointed out that the quality of the verse should be high so that pleasure of working with it will endure. Its mood may be light and gay, dramatic, or humorous; still it should be of superior quality.

For choral speaking, a teacher should select passages with decided

---

* *Developing Language Skills in the Secondary Schools*, p. 209. Copyright 1959 by Allyn and Bacon, Inc. Reprinted by permission of the publisher.

rhythm and possibly a refrain—poetry that resembles simple musical compositions. The theme should be so clearly stated that the audience can follow it with ease and interest. Also, there should be true artistry—a colorful and graphic portrayal of life, with imagery so vivid that it will appeal to the imagination of the listeners.

Preferably there should also be contrast so as to permit telling effects in the rendition of the verse. No matter how lively the rhythm, a change of tempo helps to bring out meaning. This variation in tempo may reflect a change in mood. There may also be variety through the portrayal of different personalities or a contrast in ideas. Without contrast of some sort, choral speech may sound monotonous.

At the end of this chapter are lists of poems recommended for choral speaking. Although the lists are roughly graded, many of those recommended for younger children may be used for older ones just beginning verse speaking.

INSTRUCTIONAL PROCEDURES

Several of the fundamental procedures in teaching choral speaking were suggested earlier in this chapter. These are briefly reviewed here.

Select poems of real merit that are suited to the maturity and literary appreciation of the children. Before reading a poem to them for the first time, acquaint yourself thoroughly with it so that you respond to its mood and meaning and make the most of its rhythm and sound patterns. Be sincere, vital, intelligent in your oral reading. After clearing up any significant unfamiliar or vague meanings, read the poem a second time. Let the pupils share with you the work of arranging it for choral presentation by them. Work over any rough spots by identifying the words in which articulation and enunciation have been poor and by searching out the poem's meaning in the effort to eradicate singsong effects and to get proper inflections of the voice. Conduct the speaking much as if you were teaching a song, by using one hand to indicate tempo and the other to control volume; or allow the pupils to beat time for themselves.

As children gain experience in choral speaking, they will develop the ability to emphasize the key ideas in a selection. This they will do through changes of pace to suit the mood of the poem, through shifting inflections in voice, and particularly through the tendency to pause or linger on the more significant words and phrases. The teacher will respond in similar fashion when he first reads a poem—in response to meaning, of course, not in an artificial way. In the long run the optimal effects will be decided after the pupils have worked with the teacher in trying out various interpretations.

Young children are able to engage in the simpler aspects of four types of choral speaking: *unison, refrain, antiphonal,* and *line-a-child.* Although unison is the most difficult of the types because of the precision required in rate of speaking, phrasing, simultaneous pauses, emphasis, inflections, and pronunciation, the children like joining in with the teacher as he reads and rereads favorite bits of verse. They like to say the nursery rhymes together. One second-grade group asked again and again for Christopher Morley's "Animal Crackers" and Vachel Lindsay's "The Moon's the North Wind's Cooky." Not only did they have fun while they softly joined in as the teacher read, but they also profited from the experience of fitting their rate and rhythm of speech, their voice quality and inflections, to a pattern suited to each poem's meaning and mood.

The refrain is the simplest of all the types, and well suited for use with young children. Here the teacher or a capable child may repeat, as a solo, the main body of the poem while the entire group repeats the refrain whenever it comes in. "Hot-Cross Buns" and "Hickory, Dickory, Dock" are two nursery rhymes good for this purpose. Older children in the middle and upper grades, with little or no previous training in this art, may begin with the repeating of refrains as in Van Dyke's "America for Me" or Beatrice Curtis Brown's "Jonathan Bing."

When rather brief poems contain considerable contrast or when there is much conversation, antiphonal choral speaking is called for. "What Are Little Boys Made Of?" and "Pussy Cat, Pussy Cat" are suitable for such use. The class may be divided into two groups, such as boys and girls, or the left and right halves of the room. To get good antiphonal effects, the children must be keenly aware of the situation or story in back of the poem and be in a responsive mood. Then their voice quality and inflections, the pauses they make for emphasis, and their rate of speaking will be suited to the part of the poem they are interpreting. They will get fun out of varying their responses to suit different situations; for instance, Pussy Cat may have been a wee kitten, a timid Mother Cat, or great big bold Father Cat. Changing their voices to suit these occasions will give good practice in vocal control.

When older pupils are inexperienced in choral speaking, the antiphonal type of choral speaking is suitable. Poems that have much conversation, particularly of the question-and-answer type, and very strong contrast may be used in this way. Usually the heavier voices (often the boys') will ask the questions or speak the lines with strong effects, such as those having many long-voweled words or vigorous action. Elizabeth Coatsworth's "The Storm Snapped Its Fingers" or the Mother Goose rhyme "Where Are You Going, My Pretty Maid?" illustrate poems of the question-and-answer type. The following poem illustrates antiphonal effects when there is strong voice contrast. Heavier voices will speak the italicized lines.

There are big waves and little waves,
   Green waves and blue,
Waves you can jump over,
   Waves you dive through.
Waves that rise up
   Like a great water wall, (Gradual crescendo)
Waves that rise softly
   And don't break at all,
Waves that can whisper,
   Waves that can roar,
And tiny waves that run at you
   Running on the shore.

UNKNOWN

"One, Two, Buckle My Shoe" makes an easy beginning for the line-a-child type of choral speech because there is no special continuity to be maintained from line to line. Even so, the children will sense the need for each child's being ready to speak in his turn. " 'Bow, Wow,' Says the Dog" is equally easy to repeat. In older pupils' rendition of "For Want of a Nail" and "Mice," there is need for much more continuity in treatment. It is necessary for the participants to have heard the entire poem several times, to have the total development in mind, and to sense the mood of the poem. Then, each child will be able to pick up where the preceding speaker leaves off and not lose unity in treatment.

The lists of choral selections that conclude this chapter contain names of various selections for use by older children who are to participate in these simpler types of choral speaking. It is advisable that they follow these simpler techniques in the beginning; then they may progress to the more complex and finished productions of the advanced phases of verse speaking.

The voices of older children may be classified into *light* and *dark,* or *high* and *low,* if two-part speaking is to be done. If three groups are to participate, a third or *middle* group may be selected from pupils whose voices are among neither the highest nor the lowest in range. The classification of voice is not the most difficult aspect of *part speaking;* rather, difficulty lies in dividing the poem into parts the various pupil groups are to speak. In respect to arranging the poem, Louise Abney(49, pp. 19–20) says:

> In arranging the poem into parts, *thought mastery must come first,* since meaning is fundamental in all interpretation and appreciation. The meaningless recital of little "memory gems" with accompanying gestures is fortunately almost a thing of the past. Communication is the first and basic principle of speech, and Choral Speech is concerned with the communica-

tion to an audience of the thought and feeling of the author. Content is always more important than technique, and literary values are perverted if ever tonal exhibitionism takes precedence over thought-mastery.

Tonal quality should be considered in Part Arrangement, however. Obviously such words as "singing," "swish," "swing," "skipping," "clicking," "dancing" are soprano words because the short and light vowels predominate; while such words as "blow," "cold," "old," "gold," "moon," "gloom" are alto words because of the predominance of the darker vowels. "I," with its forward placement, is a soprano word; "you," alto. . . .

Pitch and mood also condition arrangements in Part Speaking. A fairy poem would probably require a high pitch, and a light and dancing mood. A dirge, on the other hand, would be more effectively voiced in a low pitch and somber mood. A lullaby would lend itself to a medium-low pitch, with soothing mood. Rare beauty and feeling may be developed within the choir through sensitivity to mood changes, and expression of feeling in pitch. *Thought analysis must* come first, however. Never break the sweep of a thought for the sake of tonal interpretation. . . .

In the reading list at the end of this chapter are the titles of several books that contain poems already arranged for part speaking. Beginners in teaching this type of choric speech may do well to consult these ready-made arrangements and to study the reasons for assigning certain lines to low- or high-register voices. Eventually, the teacher should gain ability to make his own arrangements and, better still, to work with his pupils in cooperative planning.

The most difficult aspect of choral speaking is unison. Here each pupil must fit his voice quality and inflections, phrasing, and pauses to the pattern set for the group. Precision is the rule. Unison groups should be quite small. Possibly an upper-grade class could be divided into two or three groups, each of which will work out a different selection. Only the teacher who has had special training in choral speaking should engage in unison work; expert leadership and guidance are necessary for precision.

SUGGESTED LIST OF POEMS

A list of poems and poetic prose suitable for use in the primary, intermediate, and upper grades follows.

Lower primary

RHYMES THAT SUGGEST DRAMATIC ACTION

A Dillar, a Dollar
Hippity-Hop to the Barber Shop
Bye, Baby Bunting
Sleep, Baby, Sleep
Hush-a-Bye, Baby

Ride a Cock-Horse
Wee Willie Winkie
Buckingham Palace

REFRAINS

The Wind (STEVENSON)
The Mitten Song (MARIE ALLEN)
A Farmer Went Trotting
Hickory, Dickory, Dock
Hot-Cross Buns

DIALOGUE AND ANTIPHONAL

There Was an Old Woman Tossed Up in a Basket
What Are Little Boys Made Of?
Susan Blue (GREENAWAY)
Bow-Wow-Wow
Pussy Cat, Pussy Cat
The North Wind Doth Blow
Ding, Dong, Bell

LINE-A-CHILD

Mice (FYLEMAN)
Little Wind (GREENAWAY)
One, Two, Buckle My Shoe
"Bow, Wow," Says the Dog
For Want of a Nail

SOLOS INTERSPERSED WITH GROUP WORK

Merry-Go-Round (BARUCH)
Puppy and I (MILNE)
Stop—Go (BARUCH)
Where Go the Boats? (STEVENSON)
Choosing Shoes (FFRIDA WOLFE)
I Had a Little Pony
Christmas Is Coming
Girls and Boys, Come Out to Play
The Squirrel
Three Little Kittens

UNISON

I Had a Little Nut Tree
There Was a Man in Our Town
Polly, Put the Kettle On
There Was a Crooked Man
One Misty, Moisty Morning
Daffy-Down-Dilly
Hoppity (MILNE)

The Woodpecker (ROBERTS)
The Rabbit (EDITH KING)
Windy Nights (STEVENSON)
Some One (DE LA MARE)

Upper primary; intermediate

REFRAINS AND CHORUSES

Shoes and Stockings (MILNE)
Popcorn Song (DIXIE WILLSON)
The Owl and the Pussy Cat (LEAR)
The Lamb (BLAKE)
A Swing Song (ALLINGHAM)
The Fairies (ALLINGHAM)
The Umbrella Brigade (RICHARDS)
The Light-Hearted Fairy
This Is the House That Jack Built
Kindness to Animals (RICHARDS)

DIALOGUE AND ANTIPHONAL

The Grasshoppers (ALDIS)
Godfrey Gordon Gustavus Gore (RANDS)
Who Has Seen the Wind? (ROSSETTI)
What Is Pink? (ROSSETTI)
The Duel (FIELD)
The Waterfall (SHERMAN)
Psalms 24, 100
The Little Fox (EDEY and GRIDER)

LINE-A-CHILD OR LINE-A-GROUP

Noise (POPE)
Doorbells (RACHEL FIELD)
Laughing Song (BLAKE)
Boys' Names (FARJEON)
Girls' Names (FARJEON)
Bunches of Grapes (DE LA MARE)
Amy Elizabeth Ermyntrude Annie (SCOTT-HOPPER)
The People (ROBERTS)
Little Charlie Chipmunk (LE CRON)

SOLOS INTERSPERSED WITH GROUP WORK

The Monkeys and the Crocodile (RICHARDS)
Little John Bottlejohn (RICHARDS)
The Pirate Don Durk of Dowdee (MEIGS)
The King's Breakfast (MILNE)
The Goblin (FYLEMAN)

The Rock-a-By Lady (EUGENE FIELD)
Jonathan Bing (BROWN)

UNISON

Seal Lullaby (KIPLING)
A Kitten (FARJEON)
Indian Cradle Song
Mrs. Peck-Pigeon (FARJEON)
Night (TEASDALE)
Wynken, Blynken, and Nod
Strange Tree (ROBERTS)

Upper grades
(Most poems should use two or more techniques.)

REFRAINS AND CHORUSES

The Raggle, Taggle Gypsies
O Captain! My Captain! (WHITMAN)
For Snow (FARJEON)
In the Week When Christmas Comes (FARJEON)
Here We Come A-Caroling
Psalms 24, 67

DIALOGUE AND ANTIPHONAL

Where's Mary? (EASTWICK)
Dogs and Weather (WELLES)
City Streets and Country Roads (FARJEON)
Wander-Thirst (GOULD)
Washington (TURNER)
Winter Night (BUTTS)
Carol, Brothers, Carol (MUHLENBERG)
Psalms 46, 47

LINE-A-CHILD OR LINE-A-GROUP

Hie Away (SCOTT)
Travel (STEVENSON)
April Rain Song (HUGHES)
Afternoon on a Hill (MILLAY)
Evening Hymn (ROBERTS)
Silver (DE LA MARE)
The City of Falling Leaves (LOWELL)
Abraham Lincoln (MEIGS)
Psalm 150

SOLOS INTERSPERSED WITH GROUP WORK

Skating (ASQUITH)
Old Ellen Sullivan (WELLES)

A Piper (O'SULLIVAN)
The Cowboy's Life (ADAMS)
Lone Dog (McLEOD)
High Flight (McGEE)
Phizzog (SANDBURG)
In Time of Silver Rain (HUGHES)
Stopping by Woods on a Snowy Evening (FROST)
The Day Will Bring Some Lovely Thing (CROWELL)
Psalm 100

UNISON

The Mysterious Cat (LINDSAY)
The Potatoes' Dance (LINDSAY)
I Hear America Singing (WHITMAN)
Sea-Fever (MASEFIELD)
I Meant to Do My Work Today (LE GALLIENNE)
Hard from the Southeast Blows the Wind (COATESWORTH)
Snow Toward Evening (CANE)
Splinter (SANDBURG)
First Snow (EASTWICK)
Velvet Shoes (WYLIE)
Psalm 103

SUGGESTIONS FOR STUDY AND DISCUSSION

1. Discuss the following topics:

    a. Probable differences between a classroom in which little literature is used and one in which literature is used abundantly, so far as the nature and quality of language expression are concerned
    b. How literature can be used to get optimum benefits in language growth
    c. How and why the literary offering should be differentiated in difficulty, theme, and treatment within each classroom.

    2. For each of three grades, list ten books you would select for purchase as the beginning of a classroom library. Use the ACEI bibliography, reviews in *Elementary English,* and other references that recommend books for specific ages or grade levels.
    3. In what respects is good literature conducive to desirable mental hygiene?
    4. How well do you like poetry? What factors do you believe have helped to determine your attitude?
    5. Arrange to read two or three poems to a group of children. Select those you think will be especially appropriate and appealing; prepare so that you read your very best. Determine just how much

or how little you should discuss the poems before reading them and after reading them.

6. Begin to make a collection of poems useful in teaching. Select only those of merit. Star those suitable for choral speaking.

7. Form committees, each of which will prepare to present a different form of choral speaking to the other committees. Select appropriate poems or psalms so as to demonstrate the proper accommodation of the form of choral speaking to the nature of the poem.

FOR FURTHER READING

1. ADAMS, BESS PORTER, *About Children and Books.* New York, Holt, 1953.
2. *Adult Books That Have Been Recommended for Young People.* New York, Harcourt, Brace & World. Pamphlet.
3. ARBUTHNOT, MAY HILL, *Children and Books.* Chicago, Scott, Foresman, 1957.
4. ———— "Books That Open Windows." *Childhood Education* (February 1960), 263–66.
5. *Bibliography of Books for Children,* Association for Childhood Education International, 1956 ed. Washington, D. C., The Association.
6. BONE, ROBERT, "Using Literature to Extend Children's Experiences," *Elementary English* (May 1959), 314–18.
7. BURROWS, ALVINA TREUT, "Life, Liberty and the Pursuit of Literature." *Elementary English* (April 1962), 321–23, 335.
8. BURTON, DWIGHT, L., and NANCY LARRICK, "Literature for Children and Youth." *Development in and Through Reading,* Sixtieth Yearbook of the National Society for the Study of Education (Part I, Chapter 11). Chicago, U. of Chicago Press, 1961.
9. DEES, MARGARET, "Easy to Read for Beginning Independent Readers." *Elementary English* (May 1962), 418–20.
10. FENNER, PHYLLIS, *The Proof of the Pudding.* New York, Day, 1957.
11. *A Graded List of Books for School Libraries.* New York, Harcourt, Brace & World. Pamphlet, published biennially.
12. HEFFERMAN, HELEN, and V. E. TODD, *The Kindergarten Teacher* (Chapter 12). Boston, Heath, 1960.
13. HUCK, CHARLOTTE S., "Planning the Literature Program for the Elementary School." *Elementary English* (April 1962), 307–13.
14. JACOBS, LELAND B., "More than Words." *Childhood Education* (December 1960), 160–62.
15. JOHNSTON, A. MONTGOMERY, "The Classics of Children's Literature." *Elementary English* (May 1962), 412–14.
16. LARRICK, NANCY, *A Teacher's Guide to Children's Books.* Columbus, Ohio, Merrill, 1960.
17. ———— "Making Books Come Alive for Children." *Childhood Education* (March 1962), 311–15.
18. *Literature Guides, Grades 4–8.* Portland, Oregon, Portland Public Schools, 1962. Reading lists and teaching suggestions.

19. LOHRER, ALICE, "Guideposts to Children's Books." *Elementary English* (April 1958), 215–20.
20. MADDOCK, LAWRENCE H., "What Is Good Literature for Children?" *Elementary English* (May 1957), 298–300.
21. MAIB, FRANCES, "Improving Children's Literary Tastes." *Elementary English* (March 1959), 180–84, 204.
22. ——— "A Suggested List of Literature Books." *Elementary English* (April 1959), 253–65.
23. MCCREARY, ANNE PHILLIPS, "A Reconsideration of Classics for Children." *Elementary English* (April 1962), 330–35.
24. REEVES, JAMES, *Teaching Poetry.* London, Heinemann, 1958.
25. REID, ALASTAIR, *Ounce, Dice, Trice.* Boston, Little, Brown, 1958.
26. SMITH, DORA V., "Children's Books Around the World." *Elementary English* (February 1958), 81–92.
27. STRICKLAND, RUTH G., "Children, Reading, and Creativity." *Elementary English* (April 1957), 234–41.

ANTHOLOGIES

28. ARBUTHNOT, MAY HILL, ed., *The Arbuthnot Anthology of Children's Literature.* Chicago, Scott, Foresman, 1953.
29. ——— *Time for Poetry.* Chicago, Scott, Foresman, 1952.
30. BARROWS, MARJORIE, ed., *Two Hundred Best Poems for Boys and Girls.* New York, Grosset & Dunlap, 1942.
31. BREWTON, JOHN E., ed., *Gaily We Parade.* New York, Macmillan, 1952.
32. BREWTON, SARA and JOHN E., eds., *Bridled with Rainbows.* New York, Macmillan, 1950.
33. ——— *Sing a Song of Seasons.* New York, Macmillan, 1955.
34. COLE, WILLIAM, ed., *Story Poems New and Old.* Cleveland, World, 1957.
35. DE LA MARE, WALTER, ed., *Come Hither.* New York, Knopf, 1960.
36. HAZELTINE, ALICE I., and ELVA S. SMITH, eds., *The Year Around.* New York, Abingdon, 1956.
37. HUBER, MIRIAM BLANTON, ed., *Story and Verse for Children.* New York, Macmillan, 1955.
38. JOHNSON, EDNA, and others, *An Anthology of Children's Literature.* Boston, Houghton Mifflin, 1959.
39. LEACH, MACEDWARD, *The Ballad Book.* New York, Harper, 1955.
40. MCEWEN, CATHERINE SCHAEFER, ed., *Away We Go.* New York, Crowell, 1956.
41. OPIE, IONA and PETER, eds., *The Oxford Nursery Rhyme Book.* New York, Oxford U. Press, 1955.
42. PARKER, ELINOR, ed., *100 Poems About People.* New York, Crowell, 1955.
43. READ, HERBERT, and JULIET KEPES, eds., *This Way, Delight.* New York, Pantheon, 1956.
44. REEVES, JAMES, ed., *The Merry-Go-Round.* Melbourne, Australia, Heinemann, 1955.
45. SECHRIST, ELIZABETH H., ed., *One Thousand Poems for Children.* Philadelphia, Macrae Smith, 1946.

46. UNTERMEYER, LOUIS, ed., *Rainbow in the Sky*. New York, Harcourt, Brace & World, 1935.

47. —— *The Magic Circle*. New York, Harcourt, Brace & World, 1952.

CHORAL SPEAKING

48. ABNEY, LOUISE, *Choral Speaking Arrangements for the Junior High*, rev. ed. Magnolia, Mass., Expression, 1959.

49. —— *Choral Speaking Arrangements for the Upper Grades*, rev. ed. Magnolia, Mass., Expression, 1952.

50. —— and GRACE ROWE, *Choral Speaking Arrangements for the Lower Grades*, rev. ed. Magnolia, Mass., Expression, 1953.

51. BROWN, HELEN, and HARRY HELTMAN, eds., *Let's-Read-Together Poems*. Evanston, Ill., Row, Peterson, 1949.

52. GREENE, HARRY A., and WALTER T. PETTY, *Developing Language Skills in the Elementary School*. Boston, Allyn and Bacon, 1959.

53. GULLEN, MARJORIE, *Choral Speaking*. London, England, Methuen, 1957.

54. —— *The Speech Choir*. New York, Harper, 1937.

55. JONES, MORRIS VAL, "Choral Speaking in the Elementary School." *Elementary English* (December 1958), 535–37.

56. NEUMANN, M. A., "Choral Reading with Pantomime." *Instructor* (December 1957), 39.

57. PLACE, C. S., "Choral Reading with Music." *Grade Teacher* (September 1960), 71, 121–22.

58. RASMUSSEN, CARRIE, *Choral Speaking for Speech Improvement*. Magnolia, Mass., Expression, 1953.

59. —— "Choral Reading in the Elementary School." *NEA Journal* (November 1960), 26.

60. SCOTT, LOUISE BINDER, "Choral Speaking Is Teamwork." *Instructor* (May 1958), 82.

7

Developing Basic Speech Skills

---

*Chapter 7 considers the importance of speech education
and the need for teachers to understand some basic concepts underlying speech training. The chapter stresses the
part that the classroom teacher must play in the speech-
improvement program and the speech-correction program.*

EVERYONE encounters daily situations that demand clear
thinking, attentive critical listening, good speech, and careful use of language. Whether the group is social, business, or political, the power of the
effective speaker and the advantage of the good listener are apparent to
any observer.

Today, as never before, teachers are beginning to realize the tremen-
dous impact and powerful force of the spoken word upon the world, the
nation, and the individual. Probably ninety-five per cent of our language needs for the present state of civilization is oral. Consider the
present-day use of the telephone, telegraph, radio, and television along
with the usual face-to-face speech activities of every person. Consider
also the problems of social, interpersonal, and intergroup relationships
faced by children and adults at home and abroad. To learn and to teach
a set of skills for speaking which may be used throughout a lifetime is,
therefore, a challenge and a necessity for pupils and teachers at all educational levels.

Importance of Speech

UNDERLYING a well-conceived speech-education program are two basic
factors which every classroom teacher recognizes. In the first place, *speech
is our chief means of communication.* Speech is the method by which we

orally transmit our ideas, thoughts, and feelings. In speech, we include verbal expression and any outward manifestations, such as gestures and facial expressions. In our fast-moving world other forms of communication seem plodding, slow, and time-consuming. We talk far more than we write; we listen more than we read. The spoken word is, indeed, the prevalent avenue of communication.

The second basic factor that emerges is that *speech is of the utmost social significance*. Through conversation and discussion, we express our thoughts and reveal our feelings; we seek and get cooperation from our companions; we inform, inspire, and persuade our listeners; we adjust differences and inconsistencies in purpose and viewpoint; and we bring our social environment under control. Moreover, our listeners tend to evaluate us on the basis of our speech and language patterns and accordingly decide what kind of person we are.

Responsibility of the School System

How does the elementary school take care of the needs in the speech area? A broad speech-education program which includes (1) speech improvement for all children, (2) speech arts in the classroom, and (3) speech correction for the handicapped has long been envisioned by many administrators, classroom teachers, speech consultants, and curriculum coordinators. Many school systems have provided for the school children in all three areas of speech instruction; other school systems have children with needs and abilities yet to be aided. Most educators are now agreed that speech is, indeed, an integral part of most activities and experiences throughout a lifetime and, therefore, should be a part of the curriculum for all children.

Basic Concepts of Speech Training

THE classroom teacher does not need to be a speech major to undertake a developmental speech program. He does, however, need to understand certain principles underlying speech teaching.

In the first place, *speech is learned*. To the teacher this means that in place of poor voice and articulation habits the child, with practice, time, and patience, may learn to use better voice production and more distinct articulation. The final goal should be effective and efficient voice and speech in terms of the audience, the situation, and the speaker's purpose for speaking. Educators believe that it is possible to cultivate in the typical educated American, a pleasing voice, clear and precise articulation, rhythmic and conversational speech, an appropriate rate of speaking, and effective phrasing with proper emphasis. These are the dividends an adequate speech program can bring.

Second, the classroom teacher recognizes that *the speech education program must be a cooperative one.* The child imitates those about him, wherever he may be. Hence, the home, the school, and the playground are involved. It is not enough for teachers to set good examples and to encourage good speech habits in the classroom. The child spends many hours on the playground and at home. Many parents and teachers have been appalled because six-year-olds have adopted their playmates' ungrammatical expressions. An effective speech and oral-language program is and must be a cooperative one. The home, school, and community must unite to back a developmental speech program which builds an appreciation for the way people speak and what they say.

Related to the preceding consideration is a third one: *speech education is considered an integral part of the pupil's daylong school living.* Speech is rarely considered as a separate subject for study in the elementary curriculum. It is, rather, a set of skills which may be developed in a variety of settings and through the use of subject matter drawn from wide areas. Speech may also be considered in any social setting, including life at school, at home, or in the community. It is, therefore, necessary for the classroom teacher to develop with his pupils definite goals in speech. Speech will improve only when the pupil recognizes the problem or error to be corrected, knows how to correct it, and has the interest and initiative to practice until the improved pattern of speaking is habitual.

The fourth consideration is that *speaking and listening are best taught together.* While the teacher may have specific lessons for emphasizing the separate skills, speaking and listening are inevitably linked in the communication cycle. The speaker must always be aware of his listeners and their reactions. The listeners are affected by the skills of the speaker. One set of skills provides the outgo; the other set provides the intake. Both are linked because of the time element in oral communication. Teaching the two sets of skills together will make sense to any classroom teacher after a careful study of the nature of listening, the nature of speech, and the act of oral communication.

The fifth and final consideration is that *improvement of the oral skills may affect the learning of other skills, attitudes, and appreciations within the total language program.*

Although research is inadequate concerning the interrelationships among the language arts and skills, most authorities conclude that there is positive evidence of such interrelationships. Much work needs to be done before definite statements of specific interrelationships can be made. As Nila Banton Smith(16, p. 4) says:

While differentiation studies in regard to separate strands of the language arts are needed . . . . there is also a very urgent need for studies of the child's general language development. No doubt some significant relationships are evading our recognition because the preponderance of studies in the past have been concerned with isolated strands rather than with a constellation.

Virgil E. Herrick and Bernice E. Leary(7, p. 47) comment on the same problem:

The organization and patterning of language development [have] not been emphasized to the same degree as have the differences in beginning and end points and in rate of development; yet this concept has importance in understanding some of the major instructional problems of the language arts.

The language arts area is rich in the possibilities of the existence of interrelations, and an emphasis upon the oral area may be rewarding. For example, the very nature of speech might lead one to predict that vocabulary development and precise thinking would improve with instruction in the skills of speech. We know that until school age the child uses his speaking-listening skills to very good advantage in the development of vocabulary and in the communication of thinking and feeling. The teacher or researcher may then question why the developmental processes in speaking and listening should be neglected upon entrance to formal education. Classroom teachers in their daily teaching of the language arts are in a good position to carry on pilot studies and action projects in the search for possible relationships among the arts and skills of language.

The Speech-Improvement Program

THE classroom teacher is responsible for a speech-improvement program for all children in his classes. He must provide opportunities for pupils to develop acceptable voice and speech patterns and to enjoy various speech activities. He must also provide opportunities for pupils with special talents in dramatics to extend their experiences.

The teacher must provide the setting and the speech activities which form the basis for speech improvement. One third-grade teacher made a lesson plan for Monday's classes. He listed the following oral activities: (1) news reporting, (2) group discussion, (3) appreciation of poetry, and (4) oral reading. He then used these activities for the content and enjoyment of the activity and also for teaching the skills of speech. For example, the teacher may emphasize organization of subject matter and clear articulation in news reporting and then re-emphasize the necessity for clearness of speech in the oral-reading lesson. He may emphasize the communication cycle and the need for good listening during the group discussion period. In the poetry lesson he may ask his pupils to listen for meaning and then lead them to see, hear, and feel what the author has written in poetic form.

In a good speech program the teacher will emphasize listening skills because speaking and listening form the cycle of communication. Listening to good speech will help pupils to improve voice and speech skills and to acquire facility in the use of the language. The speech of all children will improve as they listen to careful articulation in connected conversational speech and as they practice for good volume, acceptable rate, and easy rhythmical flow of speech in informal speaking situations, in oral reading, and in sentences and rhymes.

Improvement in speech often requires oral lessons which have specific objectives for speech improvement and are based on group and individual needs. Oral activities, such as show and tell, oral reading, reporting, choral speaking, dramatics, and discussion, may all be used for direct practice of speech skills. In general a good speech program, especially in the early grades, means teaching the sounds of English. It means utilizing the arts of storytelling, reading, and dramatics. It means guiding children to say what they want to say and to say it in the best possible manner of speaking. It means developing an appreciation and knowledge of words and their meanings and some understanding of English rhythm, intonation, and articulation. It means all these and more, but the teacher knows that whatever the future holds for his pupils they will need proficiency in the oral skills.

USING CHECK SHEETS

The teacher may find a check sheet (see p. 133) very helpful in planning speech-improvement lessons for the whole class, for groups of children, or for individuals. The competences as listed may be restated and used as objectives for specific lessons. For example, item number 8, "speaks at a rate acceptable for subject, situation, and group," may be a needed objective for any grade level. A lesson with this objective would become meaningful if pupils were giving oral reports, telling stories, or reading orally to others.

The check sheet may be used at the beginning of the school year to identify the strengths and weaknesses of a given group of pupils. From such a survey, the teacher then plans his speech program which should include sufficient practice periods for the needed skills. Many times, however, the teacher must individualize the help given his pupils, and this can be done with almost any oral-speech activity. Needless to say, the teacher

Making tape recordings is an invaluable means of assessing the strengths and weaknesses of speech.

must know his pupils and must thoroughly understand the aims and objectives of a comprehensive speech-improvement program.

In the middle and upper grades, the pupils often enjoy having a record of individual improvement. Marking a check sheet at the beginning, the middle, and the end of the school year may serve as an evaluation of progress. Once the pupils have established their own goals in speech, they need successful practice sessions followed by an abundance of speaking situations in which to practice the new skills.

Teachers may like to use the check sheet as a guide for their own listening. It is as necessary for teachers to know what they are listening for as it is for their pupils to have specific purposes for listening. The three columns on the check sheet are self-explanatory. In the first column the teacher checks the pupil as acceptable in the skill if the performance is good; he need not necessarily perform to perfection. The second column is checked when the teacher finds a need for improvement and knows that the correction and improvement can be undertaken in the classroom situation. The teacher checks the third column for any severe speech problem. These problems and questions should be referred to the speech correctionist for diagnosis and therapy when necessary. Sometimes the teacher may be uncertain about the severity of a speech difficulty, or the child may think his problem more severe than it appears to be to the teacher. In all such cases the teacher should call upon the speech correctionist for consultation and help.

IMPROVEMENT IN ARTICULATION

Teachers recognize sloppy, slovenly, and indistinct speech as a problem in many classrooms. Even the students who have so-called good speech may profit by attention to the skills of articulation. Clear and distinct speech depends greatly on the manner in which consonant sounds are articulated. Probably one pupil out of ten has severe or persistent difficulties in articulation and should be referred to the correctionist. Some studies report one out of five pupils should be referred. This is a problem for the classroom teacher and a difficult one because the availability of speech specialists is usually limited. However, the teacher must not overlook the fact that *improvement in articulation is needed by most pupils*. He can accept this responsibility in the classroom situation if he acquires an understanding of the consonant sounds of English and how they relate to speech improvement.

In the improvement of speech patterns in articulation, every teacher should be aware that letters and sounds of English may or may not be synonymous. There are approximately forty spoken sound units in English. Phoneticians list these as twenty-three to twenty-five consonants, nine

SPEECH CHECK SHEET

Areas	Is Acceptable	Needs Work	Should Be Referred	Competences
				THE PUPIL
A. Communication				1. listens to and understands the communication of others.
				2. communicates orally his thoughts and feelings to others.
				3. is able to speak to a group without mannerisms, poor posture, or habits which attract attention to himself.
				4. is able to talk to individuals and to groups with ease, directness, and enthusiasm.
B. Voice				5. controls volume (not too loud nor too soft).
				6. produces clear, strong, resonant voice tone (normal pitch).
				7. speaks with a voice* that is free from: nasality denasality hoarseness other*
C. Speech				8. speaks at a rate acceptable for subject, situation, and group.
				9. has distinct, clear articulation.†
				10. does not hesitate or break thought units in speaking.
				11. does not hesitate or break thought units in reading.
				12. has little substandard usage (words or expressions).
				13. uses words exactly and precisely for age.
				14. uses acceptable pronunciation.

* See description of voice problems, page 141.
† If articulation is poor, see Consonant Chart, page 137.

vowels, and the remainder as diphthongs. The English alphabet has only twenty-six letters. The letter *c*, for example, has no sound of its own. In general, the *k* or *s* sound is made for the letter *c*. The letters *ng* as in *sing* may have only one sound, expressed by the symbol ŋ by those who know the symbols of the International Phonetics Alphabet. In most dictionaries the one sound is represented by the letters *ng*. The teacher needs to be aware of these inconsistencies in English spelling and in English sounds. For example, in a word like *finger*, the letters *ng* are pronounced ŋ, with the addition of the *g* sound (*fing ger*), but in a word like *singer* the *g* sound is not produced (*sing er*). The teacher must constantly be aware that the sounds of English as picked up by the ear and the spelling of English as written for the eye are often different.

Variances in regional speech may confuse the teacher as he studies and listens to the sounds of English. The important fact to remember at this point is that *consonant sounds should be made precisely and should sound the same* whether the child lives in the West, the South, New England, or the Midwest. A second important fact to remember is that *clearness of speech depends primarily upon correct articulation of these consonant sounds.* For these reasons the classroom teacher should emphasize in the speech-improvement program for all children the correct articulation of the consonant sounds. For the vowel and diphthong sounds the classroom teacher may use his own speech as the model for his pupils to hear and to copy acceptable pronunciation patterns.

What are the consonant sounds and how are they made? A consonant sound is a speech sound made by the stoppage or hindrance of voiced or voiceless breath. Consonants may first be classified according to whether or not the vocal cords have been set into vibration as the air passes through them. If the vocal cords are vibrating, the consonant sounds are called voiced consonants. All other consonants are called breathed or voiceless consonants.

The chart is so arranged that the voiced and breathed consonants

CHART I
Voiced and Breathed Consonants

VOICED CONSONANTS	b	d	g	m	n	ŋ	l	w	y	v	z	th	r	zh	j*
BREATHED CONSONANTS	p	t	k					wh		f	s	th		sh	ch*	h

* The sounds of *j* and *ch* are considered with the consonant sounds in this chapter Actually there are two sounds involved in the production of *j* and of *ch*. (See footnote to Chart III.)

similarly produced are grouped vertically. Example: *z* and *s*. The sounds are produced in like manner except that *z* is voiced and *s* is breathed.

Consonants may also be classified according to the manner in which the air is impeded. The consonants (*p, b, t, d, k, g*) are called plosives. This group is so named because the outgoing breath is checked and then released through the mouth with a slight explosion.

Another group of consonants is called continuants (nasals, laterals, fricatives). If the air, instead of being stopped, is merely impeded in its outward passage through the mouth or diverted and sent through the nose, the sound is called a continuant. The nasals (*m, n, ŋ*) are the chief continuants in English and are made by stopping the air and directing it through the nasal passage. The only lateral (*l*) is made by pressing the tip of the tongue against the upper teeth ridge and emitting the air at the sides of the tongue. The fricatives (*wh, w, f, v, th, th, s, z, sh, zh, y, r, h, j, ch*) are made by impeding, but not stopping, the passage of outgoing air.

CHART II
Plosives and Continuants

PLOSIVES	p b		t d		k g	
NASALS	m		n		ŋ	
LATERAL			l			
FRICATIVES	(wh w)	(f v)	(th th)	(s z)	(sh zh)	(ch j) r y h

The plosives, nasals, and the lateral sounds have been grouped vertically for use by the teacher. The *place* of articulation is the same for the plosives, nasals, and lateral sounds found in a vertical column. The fricatives are grouped in pairs for teaching purposes.

The teacher may find Chart II helpful in planning speech lessons. For example, the three nasal sounds are the only English sounds made through the nasal passage. A lesson emphasizing these sounds as final sounds will help voice resonance.

In every class pupils have some trouble with the production of the lateral *l*. The teacher will see by Chart II that there is only one lateral in English and will wonder how to help the child, beyond describing and demonstrating the production of the *l* sound. The teacher should then look in the vertical column and find another sound made with the same articulators. The first one above the lateral is the nasal *n*. If the *n* is placed in a group of words like this

ten little Indians

directly before the *l* sound, the child will be using the correct articulators for the *n* and may carry the correct position over to the *l* sound. Of course, the teacher must teach him to hold the *n* sound over to the *l* sound by giving the pattern to follow.

The third method of classifying consonants is by place of articulation. For example, the sounds *p, b, m, w, wh* are all made with the lips. In the chart below, the teacher will find the names of the organs of articulation and the use of the organs listed on the left. The consonants are listed in a horizontal line opposite the place of articulation.

CHART III
Consonants and Place of Articulation*

	Plosives	Nasal	Lateral	Fricatives
LIPS	p b	m		wh w
LOWER LIP TO UPPER TEETH				f v
TIP OF TONGUE TO TEETH				th th
TIP OF TONGUE TO TEETH RIDGE	t d	n	l	s z r
BLADE OF TONGUE TO TEETH RIDGE				sh zh
MIDDLE OF TONGUE TO HARD PALATE				y
BACK OF TONGUE TO SOFT PALATE	k g	ŋ		
GLOTTIS				h

* The *j* sound is made by a quick glide from the position of *d* to *zh*. The *ch* sound is made by a quick glide from the position of *t* to *sh*.

One of the teacher's greatest problems is to be able to identify the consonant sound or sounds needing improvement. Most teachers find this step difficult because they do not know what they are listening for. It may help the teacher to know certain common faults in articulation. In general pupils will be found to make the following mistakes: (1) substitute one consonant sound for another (*wed* for *red*), (2) omit one or more sounds (*-ittle* for *little*), (3) add a sound (*acrost* for *across*), (4) distort one or more sounds.

Teachers have found that one simple way to train their own ears and to identify poor articulation habits at the same time is to ask the child to say,

"My name is (*Mary Smith*)."

| | | | | | |

CHECK: m n z r s th

Teacher says, "Count to six."

CONSONANT CHART

Name of Pupil

SOUNDS	INITIAL	MEDIAL	FINAL	COMMENTS
p				
b				
t			✓	omitted or distorted
d				
k				
g				
m				
n				
ŋ			✓	substitutes <u>n</u> ("runnin")
l				
wh				
w				
f				
v				
th	✓	✓	✓	omitted
~~th~~	✓	✓	✓	omitted
s			✓	substituted or distorted
z			✓	usually omitted
r				
sh				
ch				
j				
h				
y				

GENERAL COMMENT: *Ending sounds are clipped or blurred. Too rapid rate.*

"One, two, three, four, five, six."

CHECK: w   t   th   f   v   ks

Notice that twelve different consonant sounds out of the total twenty-five consonants on the preceding charts may be tested by this simple method. If the child is in the primary grade, a Mother Goose rhyme or other well-known poems may be used to check other sounds. If the child is older and reads easily, the teacher may wish to check the consonant sounds by using a paragraph from a story. The tape recorder is a very valuable instrument to use at this time. Both teacher and pupil may profit by listening.

To do a complete job of pretesting for all consonant sounds in all positions in the flow of speech, the teacher may wish to make a chart (see page 137) for an individual child. For example, one teacher's third-grade boys seemed to have several articulatory difficulties. He has marked the chart as he listened to the boys' speaking and reading.

Under general comment, the teacher may be as detailed as he wishes. This teacher has merely added the comments which seem relevant to the articulation problem. He knows, however, that the chart is incomplete, and he will add to it as he identifies other sounds needing improvement. He plans to draw a red line through the check mark as soon as his pupil has learned to use the sound correctly in conversational speech.

Improvement of speech is both a group and an individual process. The classroom teacher must identify the speech skills most needed by the majority of his pupils. He then selects oral activities through which he may teach the skills effectively. For example, the nasal sounds *m, n, ŋ* are good resonant sounds if produced well—especially if they are well sustained as ending sounds. Most pupils do not hold these sounds at the end of words and thought units. The teacher who decides to use this group of sounds for a lesson might choose a choral-speaking selection so that the entire class would receive practice for improving the ending nasal sounds. During the lesson he should also give individual help to those who continue to clip or muffle these nasal sounds. Many other ways of grouping consonant sounds for class practice are possible (see Charts I, II, and III).

In correcting poor sound production with an individual pupil, the teacher needs to remember that speech is a very personal thing. The pupil is usually faced with two major problems in correcting defective sounds. First, he may not hear his mistake. He will often say, after the teacher has corrected the sound *r* in the word *red*, "Yes that's what I said—*wed!*" His second problem is that he is using the wrong speech organs to produce the sound. It may help the pupil to watch the teacher's lips for the sounds *p, b, m, w.* A looking glass may also aid him in practicing for coordination

Pupils with poor sound production or more severe speech handicaps need individualized instruction.

of visible speech organs. To improve listening, pupils and teachers find the tape recorder an invaluable aid.

The following general procedure is suggested for correcting and improving sounds:

1. Teacher says *sentence* containing the corrected sound. Pupil repeats the *sentence*.
2. (If sound is still incorrect) Teacher says *phrase* containing the corrected sound. Pupil repeats *phrase*.
3. (If sound is still incorrect) Teacher says the *word* with corrected sound emphasized. Pupil repeats the *word*.
4. (If sound is still incorrect) Teacher says *single* sound. Pupil makes *single* sound several times.
5. Teacher puts sound back into word. Pupil repeats word.
6. Teacher puts sound back into phrase. Pupil repeats phrase.
7. Teacher puts sound into sentence. Pupil repeats sentence.

In this teaching procedure the teacher may stop at any step and reverse direction until the corrected sound is again in the complete sentence. For example, if the pupil produces the sound correctly in the phrase (Step 2), the teacher need only repeat the entire sentence again. To learn a single sound and repeat it (*s-s-s-s*) is not correcting the sound in connected speech. The pupil must reach the place where he will be able to produce the sound correctly in the normal flow of speech, in oral reading, and in conversation.

The wise teacher will give the pupil practice words and sentences with the corrected sound in three positions: initial, medial, final. For example, the phrase *see me* has an initial *s*; in the phrase *I see*, the *s* is medial; in the sentence, *I see the books*, there is a medial and final *s*. Practice in some activity, such as a game, dramatization, choral speaking, conversation, or oral reading, is excellent. Through continued practice, the pupil may bring his corrected speech skill to the point of automatic response. When this happens, the teacher may rightly say, "He has corrected his articulatory problem."

In conclusion, to correct consonant sounds the teacher needs to know what organs of articulation are involved, how the sound is produced, and what methods and activities to use for improvement and correction. Above all he must produce the sounds of English correctly and precisely in his own flow of speech so that he may give good patterns for his pupils to imitate. Improvement in the speech of all pupils and pride in their speaking ability will be the outcome of an effective speech program. Additional methods for teaching speech in selected oral activities are given in other related chapters.

The Speech-Correction Program

IN THE speech-correction program, the role of the classroom teacher is to cooperate with the speech specialist in identifying the children with severe problems. The teacher and the speech specialist must see that these children are referred to the proper persons for further diagnosis if necessary. If no speech correctionist is employed by the school system, the teacher needs to know how to initiate action and obtain help elsewhere. In this circumstance administrative personnel along with health and medical officers are the most available sources of assistance. Under the best conditions the teacher and the speech therapist, with advice and reports of other specialists, work together to help the children improve their speech to the maximum of their ability.

VOICE PROBLEMS

The teacher may locate voice problems by identifying those voices (1) with unusual pitch (too high, too low, monotonous), (2) with poor volume (too loud, too soft, monotonous), and (3) with unpleasant quality (hoarse, nasal). Causes of voice problems fall into three categories: physical, psychological, and functional. In recent studies authorities seem to agree that approximately one per cent of the population is afflicted with some serious voice disorder. Many voice problems which become apparent in adult years may have been developing in childhood through misuse of the vocal apparatus. It is possible that many problems are caused by "straining the voice," which is a result of poor tone production. In many cases the person could have learned to produce voice easily and correctly at an early age.

While teachers should refer severe voice problems to a specialist, lack of volume or poor control of volume may usually be improved in the classroom situation. Children, like adults, do not "hear" their own voices. They need to learn to adjust volume to the situation, to the purpose for speaking, and to the listeners. Good tone is produced by *energy, vibration, and resonation*. The ear must be trained to regulate the volume. Problems of voice may involve mental attitude, emotional response, or physical condition. Those with defective hearing must partially or wholly rely upon "feeling" the volume necessary, and they must also watch for cues from listeners. In the classroom, teachers should emphasize a well-supported conversational tone of voice. The best way to get pupils to use good voice production is again by the teacher's constant use of voice that serves as a model for them to copy.

RATE AND RHYTHM PROBLEMS

Teachers may find that some pupils have such poor rate and faulty rhythm that thought units are broken and speech is cluttered. With these pupils, careful teaching of word grouping for thought, correct emphasis in blended speech, and much oral reading that emphasizes these skills will greatly improve speech patterns. If the problem is severe, it is usually labeled stuttering or stammering. This problem, if persistent, should receive a specialist's help as soon as possible.

Suggestions to guide the procedures and interpersonal relationships of the teacher with the stuttering child follow; the Dos and Don'ts may be helpful with rate and rhythm problems.

Don't

call attention to his mannerisms, blocks, or prolongations
ask him to stop and repeat
react emotionally to any phase of his difficulty
say words for him
interfere with native handedness
place him in awkward or tense situations
ignore him

Do

establish a free and relaxed classroom atmosphere
use a calm, conversational, pleasant voice and speech
encourage him to participate in singing, in choral speaking, and
    in all non-speaking activities in and out of the classroom
in most cases encourage him to *volunteer* in all kinds of oral work
    (but do *not* usually call on him to recite)
help him to develop an objective attitude toward his speech and
    speech problem
encourage rest and good physical condition
discover and help him develop special interests
ask him to practice reading poetry aloud (and later prose)

POOR VOCABULARY

Retarded speech development usually is correlated with meager vocabulary. Pupils who have poor vocabularies and who lack fluency in the use of English, however, may or may not be retarded in speech. Pupils develop speech and language to a great degree before entering school. Speech development follows certain rather well-defined steps. The pupil who has been ill during one of these periods, or for some reason has failed to acquire certain skills in his development, may come to school with defective speech. The teacher should remember that a pupil with retarded speech is not necessarily a retarded child. This pupil needs help from the speech correctionist and from the teacher. He must in some cases retrace the developmental process.

CLEFT PALATE

Cleft palate speech is generally identified by its nasal quality. Modern surgery has done much to correct the cleft palate and cleft lip. Most children with cleft palates need the help of a speech correctionist. Parents should be urged to give their children this help early so that normal speech may be encouraged from infancy. Children of school age with repaired cleft palates may still be having a difficult time coordinating the muscles of the speech organs so that the palate will make a satisfactory closure against the back wall of the pharynx. Much tenseness and some improper positions of the muscles may be noted. Children with this problem may try too hard and actually use too much air which, in turn, pushes its way out through the nostrils, thus causing a nasal tone to be emitted.

CEREBRAL PALSY

Cerebral palsy is defined as a disturbance of the motor area due to brain damage. When the muscles of the articulatory and respiratory organs are not affected, speech is normal. When these muscles are affected, the speech is usually slow, labored, and arhythmic. The voice quality may be weak and unnatural. Breath, rate, and pitch control may be poor. Since the tongue is a very active organ in the production of many consonant sounds, the clearness of speech is affected when the coordination of the muscles is affected.

Since the cerebral palsied child often has more than one handicap, he may not be able to attend the regular classes. Centers for these severely handicapped children, both public and private, have been established in ever increasing number. Most authorities think that the less severely handicapped should attend the regular classroom. Probably one of the important suggestions to the classroom teacher who has a cerebral palsied child in the regular classroom is to remember that many such children are in the normal group, intellectually. Studies indicate that from twenty-five to fifty per cent may be considered mentally retarded. Some cerebral palsied children with speech and other muscular involvements may give outward manifestations of lower ability which should not be interpreted as low intelligence. The children who have speech difficulties and who are in the regular classroom should, of course, receive therapy from a speech therapist.

IMPAIRED HEARING

The child with impaired hearing may be discovered by the teacher through observations and hearing tests. Symptoms of hearing loss may be indicated by (1) loss, substitution, or distortion of sounds; (2) monotonous voice pitch; (3) too loud or too soft speech; (4) inability to copy the teacher's speech pattern or pronunciation; (5) inattentiveness and poor work; (6) habit of turning one ear toward the speaker; and (7) frequent requests for repetition.

Upon identification of a hearing problem, the teacher should see that the child has a seat toward the front and center of the room. If the hearing loss is severe (check test records), the teacher must remember to face the pupil when speaking so that he may read lips to reinforce the hearing. Many children today who have a hearing loss wear hearing aids. The problem with some of these children is to get them to accept and use the hearing aid just as other children accept and use eyeglasses. The speech teacher may teach lip or speech reading to some children with impaired hearing along with, or in addition to, regular speech lessons.

The Teacher's Voice and Speech

WHATEVER the method, activity, or material, the most important element of speech teaching is the model voice and speech which the children hear and imitate. Speech is an indispensable tool of the teacher, and the voice is his most used instrument. Teaching is communication, and the teacher at all levels of instruction uses his voice and speech to communicate facts, thoughts, feelings, and moods. It is through speech that the teacher arouses in his pupils the desire and the interest that spark learning. It is through speech that he sets the climate of the classroom and encourages or discourages those interpersonal relationships which may make or break the effectiveness of individuals, both teacher and pupils. It is also through speech that the teacher meets his social as well as professional obligations. How the teacher sounds may overshadow what the teacher says. It may well be noted here that the teacher is often judged by pupils, parents, and acquaintances, as friendly or unfriendly, cooperative or uncooperative, angry or calm, peaceful or quarrelsome, by the sound of his voice as well as by what he says.

The teacher of the early elementary grades must be especially aware of the sensitiveness of small children. He must realize that the tone of his voice also communicates. A poet has expressed it in this manner:

TONE OF VOICE

It is not so much what you say,
As the manner in which you say it;
It is not so much the language you use,
As the tones in which you convey it.

"Come here," I sharply said,
And the baby cowered and wept;

"Come here," I cooed and he looked and smiled,
    And straight to my lap he crept.

The words may be mild and fair,
    And the tones may pierce like a dart;
The words may be soft as the summer air,
    And the tones may break the heart.

For *words* but come from the mind,
    And grow by study and art;
But the tones leap forth from the inner self,
    And reveal the state of the heart.

Whether you know it or not—
    Whether you mean or care,
Gentleness, kindness, love, and hate,
    Envy and anger are there.

Then would you quarrels avoid,
    And in peace and love rejoice,
Keep anger not only out of your words,
    But keep it out of your voice.

SARA EDWARDS HENSHAW

Much more work is being done now than previously in preservice speech preparation for teachers. Some teachers, however, still have such faulty speech that they serve as bad models for their pupils. Not only do the pupils tend to imitate the high-pitched, thin, nasal, or flat voices of such teachers and to assume the same habits of careless articulation, but these pupils often react unconsciously to unpleasant voices by highstrung, excitable, or inattentive behavior. A good voice and excellent diction are personal and professional assets and may be acquired by any teacher.

SUGGESTIONS FOR STUDY AND DISCUSSION

1. Observe a kindergarten, primary, and intermediate grade. Notice which speech difficulties are most and least common.

2. List some activities that will help to improve these speech difficulties.

3. Make sets of cards for testing deficiencies in articulation.

4. Make sets of cards for providing practice on certain sounds.

5. Hold a panel discussion on the importance of speech in the elementary school program.

6. To what extent is the regular classroom teacher responsible for testing and improving speech patterns of her pupils?

FOR FURTHER READING

1. BAKER, ELMER E., JR., "Ten Ways for the Classroom Teacher to Aid the Speech Correctionist." *Elementary English* (November 1957), 479–80.
2. BAKER, ZELMA W., *The Language Arts, the Child, and the Teacher* (Chapter 7). San Francisco, Fearon, 1955.
3. EISENON, JON, and MARDEL OGILVIE, *Speech Correction in the Schools.* New York, Macmillan, 1957.
4. FRENCH, RUTH E., "Planning Speech Training for All Youth." *English Journal* (September 1956), 328–33, 340.
5. GOLDEN, RUTH I., *Improving Patterns of Language Usage* (Chapter 9). Detroit, Wayne State U. Press, 1960.
6. GREENE, HARRY A., and WALTER T. PETTY, *Developing Language Skills in the Elementary School.* Boston, Allyn and Bacon, 1959.
7. HERRICK, VIRGIL E., and BERNICE E. LEARY, "Putting What We Know About Children's Language Development into Home and School Practice," in *Child Development and the Language Arts,* Research Bulletin of the National Conference on Research in English. Urbana, Ill., National Council of Teachers of English, 1952–53.
8. HINZE, HELEN K., "Speech Improvement: An Overview." *Elementary School Journal* (November 1960), 91–96.
9. *Language Arts for Today's Children* (133–41), Commission on the English Curriculum of the National Council of Teachers of English. New York, Appleton-Century-Crofts, 1954.
10. LLOYD, M. PEARL, *Our First Speech Book.* Chicago, King, 1954.
11. LOGAN, LILLIAN M., *Teaching the Young Child* (221–34). Boston, Houghton Mifflin, 1960.
12. OGILVIE, MARDEL, *Speech in the Elementary School.* New York, McGraw-Hill, 1954.
13. RASMUSSEN, CARRIE, "Children Enjoy Choral Reading." *Curriculum Letter No. 14,* Middletown, Conn., Department of School Services, Wesleyan University.
14. —— *Choral Speaking for Speech Improvement.* Magnolia, Mass., Expression, 1953.
15. —— *Fun-Time Puppets.* Chicago, Children's, 1952.
16. SMITH, NILA BANTON, *Areas of Research Interest in the Language Arts,* Research Bulletin of the National Conference on Research in English. Urbana, Ill., National Council of Teachers of English, 1952.
17. TIDYMAN, WILLARD, and MARGUERITE BUTTERFIELD, *Teaching the Language Arts* (Chapter 12). New York, McGraw-Hill, 1959.
18. WOLFE, DON, *Language Arts and Life Patterns* (Chapter 24). New York, Odyssey, 1961.

8

Helping Children to Listen Effectively

Chapter 8 presents listening as a specific area in the lan-
guage program, an area involving activities that are sel-
dom passive and skills that must be taught just as surely
as any other language skills. Suggestions are offered for
developing the skill of listening in the everyday ongoing
school activities of children. This chapter stresses that
learning to listen, like all other language skills, must have
purpose and meaning for the child before it can become
effective.

SINCE far more time is spent by the pupil or adult in listening than in speaking, reading, or writing, the need for examining how well this art is taught seems advisable. No more important lesson can be learned than that of undivided attention to and concentration on what is being said. This is but one element in the cycle of communication that includes speech, response, and recognition of that response. The ability to listen well must be taught. It will not, like Topsy, "just grow." The teacher needs every skill and teaching device available to promote situations conducive to the development of this silent, but active, partner in speech activities.

While teachers have always realized how important it is for children to listen with interest and concentration if learning is to take place, only recently has the school's responsibility for *teaching* children to listen effectively been realized. In 1945 the keynote speech at the annual convention of the National Council of Teachers of English highlighted listening; there a nationwide committee was set up to promote listening as an integral part of the language arts program. Since that time the teaching of listening has highlighted many conferences, has been emphasized by means of research, by experimental classroom procedures, and by publicizing the need for teaching this skill. More and more teachers are attempting to improve their pupils' ability to listen thoughtfully and appreciatively.

Teachers think that the reason many children and adults do not listen is that they have never learned how. With the many audio inventions in the modern world thousands of words are pounded out upon the air waves hourly. Teachers know that listening is increasing in importance as one of the two major avenues to learning. Teachers are constantly seeking more information about listening itself, how children learn to listen, and what aids, methods, and activities help develop skills for effective listening. Teachers realize with Mark A. Neville (11, pp. 226–27) that:

> Listening is an art, and must be practiced as an art; therefore, the techniques and skills of the art must be understood and practiced before the speaker-listener experience can be fully realized. We must not take for granted that a person can listen because he can hear.
>
> It is axiomatic that a poor teacher makes a captive audience endure; a good teacher compels a class to listen. No parent, elementary or high school teacher, or college professor who cannot hold the attention of children, youths, and adults can teach pupils to listen intelligently. The reason is that listening involves disciplined attention. . . .
>
> One striking defect of education all along the line, from kindergarten through college, is the failure to set up techniques and skills that will result in disciplined listening. In the main, students listen without direction. That the ability to listen has been emphasized through the ages is undoubtedly true; that, like the weather, nothing much has been done about it is, I believe, also true.
>
> Students listen to recitations, conversations, teacher-lectures, student floor talks, and readings; they listen to textbooks, newspapers, magazines, and encyclopedias; they listen to short stories, one-act plays, narrative poems, essays, memoirs; they listen to novels, full-length drama, and biography; they listen to radio, recordings, and television. They need to develop techniques and skills for the many purposes for which they listen.

Miriam Wilt (18) has found that elementary school children average two and a half hours of listening in a typical school day. Since so much of the teacher's motivation and direction are given orally, the child's ability to listen comprehendingly is a major factor in effective learning. To ensure effective learning, the teacher must guide and train his pupils to listen attentively, selectively, critically, or appreciatively, in turn, as he gives directions, explains parts of a process, gives the pros and cons of controversial issues, or shares with them entertaining stories and poetry. Indeed, the same qualities of listening are demanded as the children themselves exchange ideas through discussion, report on individual reading or other activities, explain some novel procedure, or relate their personal experiences. Careful, thoughtful listening is fundamental in children's learning, whether they are in kindergarten or eighth grade.

Listening is, perhaps, even more important in out-of-school living. With senses alert the child takes in the world about him. He looks, touches, manipulates, tastes, listens. This sensory experience is basic; yet it takes on full meaning and significance only as, through language, it is explained. So the child listens as Father explains about the coming out of the stars, the rising elevator, the fire engine, the sharp knife, the danger of running into the street, the wrongness of taking Joan's ball away from her. "Why . . . why . . . why . . . how . . . how . . . how?" the child asks; and he learns as he listens. Much of his fund of information, many of his understandings, most of his ethical and moral standards come through his listening and observing in the family circle and among his friends.

And the significance of listening does not decrease in later life. Family problems are dealt with as its members alternately speak and listen to one another. Listening is involved as citizens and their appointed representatives debate the community's issues; the business of men and of nations is done as men sit around a conference table and come to terms through an interchange of ideas in which listening is fully as important as speech. Over television and radio and at forums come the persuasive speeches of politicians and civic leaders; and citizens formulate their views in response to what they hear and how they interpret what they hear.

What Listening Is Like

WHAT is the psychological nature of listening? What skills are involved? Does the nature of listening vary with the situations in which it is involved, with the varying purposes of a listener? This section of Chapter 8 will attempt to help the teacher to find out what listening is like by discussing questions such as these.

THE NATURE OF LISTENING

According to Althea Beery in *Language Arts for Today's Children* (8, p. 77),

> listening is more than hearing. It involves following attentively the thread of a conversation, the development of an idea, the points of an argument. Like reading, it requires comprehension in terms of the past experience of the listener and often involves critical examination of what is heard. Whenever attention wanders, a portion of what is being presented is lost.

Intrinsically, reading and listening are much alike. They represent the *intake* aspects of the language arts program. In both situations, the child is following the discourse of another in order to gain information, to achieve understanding, to locate and get a many-sided view of issues, to select the main points in the development of a theme, or merely to be entertained. Knowledge gained through both reading and listening is secondhand; yet each is active, not passive. The reader and the listener must think; they must react in some way to the printed and the spoken word.

Even though reading and listening are basically similar, there are important differences. These are well defined by Paul A. Witty and Robert A. Sizemore(19, pp. 297–98), who recognize the unique characteristics of listening:

> The argument concerning whether listening is superior to reading as a way of learning is in some respects a futile one. It has become clear that reading will never be replaced by listening since reading enables us to achieve certain goals that cannot be realized through listening. Reading materials provide records which can be studied, reviewed, and reexamined—acts that are essential in acquiring some complex skills or understandings. Moreover, both silent and oral reading have other values which are not only distinctive but also rewarding to the student.
>
> Listening too has some unique characteristics. Through listening the student may experience satisfactions in hearing beautiful phrases and artistic expression; he may enhance his appreciation of poetry, drama, and various forms of literature; he may grow increasingly discriminating in evaluating the language he hears and thereby extend and improve his own usage; he may become better able to recall information and ideas which are reinforced by listening as part of a multisensory approach; he may learn to react critically and thereby become increasingly selective as he learns. Since the foregoing acquisitions are in large part products of skillful teaching, it is clear that most pupils should receive systematic instruction in listening.

It is, then, apparent that listening makes greater demands on the critical thinking of the listener than reading does on the peruser of the printed page. A demagogue, in particular, depends on emotional appeal of gestures, facial expressions, inflections, and intensity of voice as means of influencing his listeners and reducing their critical examination of the address.

There are more obvious, but not less important, differences between listening and reading. In reading, the child can proceed at his own rate; he may go back as many times as he likes to re-examine what he has been reading; he may even stop to reflect or to daydream, and the page is still before him when he is ready to resume reading; ideas that appear in print are likely to be expressed in a clean-cut, well-organized style and, if not, the reader has time and opportunity to search out the kernel of the thoughts.

Listening is different. The listener has no control over the rate at which he must listen; the speaker determines that. The words are spoken but once; the listener hears them then, or not at all. If his mind lags or goes woolgathering, the loss is likely to be permanent unless the speaker is careful to draw his ideas together in a subsequent summary or the entire speech appears later on a recording or in print. A listener, therefore, has little time for reflection as the speaker proceeds. A further difficulty in listening lies in the fact that few speakers are as precise and well organized as they would be if they were writing down their ideas.

It would seem, then, that listening is in some ways a more difficult process than reading, especially when critical and sequential thinking is demanded of the listener. Admittedly, the child who enters school has already acquired considerable facility in listening although he has little or none in reading. Teachers, however, have always felt a deep responsibility for teaching the child to read well, but have done little to train him to be an effective listener. This fact is important because the research that is now barely beginning in the area of listening has already revealed that curricular needs for listening grow in number and intensity as the child proceeds through school and that specific training is needed. The mere opportunity to listen does not teach a child to listen effectively. He must have carefully planned instruction.

FACTORS THAT INFLUENCE LISTENING

Several factors help to determine the effectiveness and quality of listening. These may be physical, psychological, or experiential.

Physical conditions within the listener himself may be factors. For instance, he may be hard of hearing. Under such circumstances, he may be annoyed and distracted by the effort he has to make in order to hear, or he may entirely miss key ideas. Too, he may be physically below par from malnutrition, fatigue, or some bodily ailment so that his attention is superficial or flighty. Physical well-being is a decided asset to any listener.

The physical environment, too, may be responsible for ineffective listening. The room may be too warm, humid, or chilly; there may be distracting noises from a nearby street, an adjoining room, or some part of the room where the listener is; other persons in the audience may be moving about in an annoying way. The pupil may have before him distracting articles, such as those that fill boys' pockets, and he may be playing with these and giving but half of his attention to the speaker, oral reader, or recording. The speaker himself, in fact, may be responsible for poor listening conditions as he makes ungainly gestures, speaks in a guttural or extremely loud voice, looks over the heads of his audience, or otherwise distracts attention from his message.

In school the teacher should meticulously provide a classroom environment conducive to easy and uninterrupted listening. So far as possible he should try to shut out noises from hallways and playgrounds. He should see that the pupils' desks are free of attention-distracting materials, and he should be careful not to distract or repel his listeners by unseemly gestures, lack of poise, a grating or shrill voice. Furthermore, he should help his pupils to acquire a pleasing and interesting manner of presentation.

The *psychological* factors in listening, which involve attitudes and personality traits, are often difficult to handle. Prejudice and lack of sympathy for the speaker or his cause; egocentricity and preoccupation with personal interests and problems; boredom and complete lack of interest in the subject; narrow-mindedness; an improper attitude toward school, the teacher, the subject, or the speaker—any or all of these may affect listening adversely and lead to partial and distorted learning. Here the teacher must perform his guidance function and try to correct the conditions. He should also cultivate fair-mindedness and unselfishness and try to provide an interest-provoking background that will serve as a setting favorable to responsive listening. On the other hand the psychological factors may be most favorable to attentive listening. For instance, previous pleasant experiences, already established interests and preferences, versatility—these, when related to an area of discussion, are influences favorable to engrossed listening.

Attitudes are the outgrowth of experience, of course. Lack of interest is likely to be the result of meager experience or none at all in the area in which listening is to take place. Antagonistic attitudes grow out of unhappy experiences. Thus the *experiential* background is a factor in listening. The listening vocabulary also affects the quality of listening. Meanings couched in unfamiliar words tend to evade the pupils' minds. Children do not "hear" ideas that are beyond their understanding.

An early experience illustrates this: A six-year-old child tried for weeks to write a "penmanship paper" that her teacher would accept for a proposed exhibit. The child had learned "printing" at home. Again and again the teacher told her to leave a margin, and the child did her best to write an acceptable paper; but she left no margin because she did not know what a margin was. Finally, by accident, the teacher demonstrated a margin, and the next paper was acceptable. "Margin" was not in the child's listening vocabulary, and until the teacher made the meaning clear to her, there was no hope of getting the required results.

Listening vocabulary tends to lag behind the pupils' needs as they progress through the elementary school. So many unfamiliar technical and abstract terms are introduced in the expanding curriculum that children are left with vague and incomplete understanding of the words they hear used in their lessons. Just as the children need training and guidance in mastering a sight vocabulary in reading, so do they need thoughtful instruction that will build up a wide and meaningful listening vocabulary. Otherwise, much of the oral instruction goes over their heads.

KINDS OF LISTENING

The young child has little reason to listen intently. Rather, his is a random kind of listening as he chats with his playmates in the course of play activities or with his family in an effort to be sociable. Too, he listens casually, though with marked interest, to the stories his mother reads or tells him. Such casual listening is important throughout life and may be said to have several phases: *conversational* and *courteous* listening in social situations in which people chat about matters of mutual interest and listen to one another in order to make appropriate responses, to follow up interesting details, and to show considerate interest in what a companion is saying; *secondary* listening, as to music that accompanies rhythm exercises or folk dances in school and to radio programs dimly heard while writing friendly letters at home; and *aesthetic* or *appreciational* listening to good music, choral reading, or drama.

Creative listening results in a child's reconstructing imaginatively the pleasures of sound, vision, motion, and kinesthetic feelings suggested by what he is hearing. Elizabeth Madox Roberts is a child's poet who recreates authentic childhood observations and feelings, and young listeners cannot but listen creatively as they relive moments under "The Butterbean Tent," recall the ruffled sounds of "The Hens," and observe the bulging eyes of "The Rabbit" hiding under the grapevine. Such poets encourage creative listening, as do writers like Dr. Seuss who portrays graphically Bartholomew's too replaceable hats, and Charles Dickens with his Scrooge and Tiny Tim.

Somewhat more narrowly purposeful and intent is *exploratory* listening, in which the listener alerts his mind to find matters of new interest, additional information on a topic, or perhaps a juicy bit of gossip. He is at ease and puts forth little effort, inasmuch as his search is relatively incidental, not specific. As a rule, *interrogative* listening, which follows the asking of questions, requires more concentration and selectivity. Here the listener narrows and points his attention toward getting information or help along a specific line.

Although none of these types of listening is passive, *intent* listening requires greater effort. One phase of intent listening is the *concentrative* type, in which there is definite purpose as the listener tries to elicit specific items of information, to attain understanding, to follow carefully the sequence of ideas, to perceive the speaker's organization of ideas, and to settle on his main premise. Closely related is *critical* listening, in which a lack of authenticity or the presence of bias and inaccuracies is being watched for. It is an exceptional listener who can listen objectively and appraisingly to an emotion-charged appeal or dissertation and come out with a factual and defensible conclusion. Yet in our democracy we constantly meet situations in which demagogues spout forth half-truths, distorted facts, and their prejudiced opinions, making it necessary for listeners to evaluate carefully what the speaker has said in an attempt to determine whether his information and viewpoints are reliable. Children need to learn to listen critically to get at the truth.

LEVELS OF LISTENING

According to Ruth Strickland(15) there are nine successive levels of listening that range from the altogether desultory to the very intent. These levels may be described as follows: (1) occasional conscious listening only at those times when the child feels an immediate concern in the talking about him, (2) frequent distractions as he listens intentionally but superficially, (3) half listening while waiting for an opportunity to express what is on his mind, (4) apparent absorption during actually passive reception, (5) off-and-on listening in which close attention alternates with preoccupation with ideas which the speaker's words bring to mind, (6) associative listening in which personal experiences are constantly recalled so that the listener does not actually react to the speaker's message, (7) occasional reaction to the speaker by making a comment or asking a question, (8) close and emphatic following of the speaker's train of thought, and (9) actively meeting the speaker's mind.

Althea Beery in *Language Arts for Today's Children* (8, p. 88) has made apparent the nature of the developmental stages through which the listening of maturing children passes. She quotes the goals set by an immature second-grade group and then lists the expectancies for pupils in the upper grades. Here is the second graders' list:

> We listen to people who have something to tell us.
> We think before we talk. We have something other people would like to hear.
> We look at the person who is talking. We stop what we are doing. We keep very quiet.
> We listen very carefully to the rules before we play a new game.
> We wait until the children are all ready to listen.
> We listen the first time; we listen to the *whole thing*.
> We stop and get in line when the fire bell rings.

The upper-grade abilities and activities went like this:

Hold the thread of a discussion in mind.

Watch for transitional phrases.

Listen to content even though it does not affect us directly.

Take notes during a speech or report.

Write a brief summary of an oral report.

Discount bias in a speaker.

Disagree with a speaker courteously.

Indicate by our remarks that we have turned over in our minds the ideas of others.

Reserve judgment in listening to different viewpoints in discussion.

How Listening Is Involved in the Curriculum

LISTENING is constantly demanded in the learning activities of the school day. By analyzing such situations, the teacher can identify the skills needed for listening and can take measures to build and improve the requisite skills.

SITUATIONS THAT INVOLVE LISTENING

In trying to build up children's ability to listen effectively, the teacher need not set up separate periods nor feel that he is having to add anything altogether new to the school program. The children do a great deal of listening anyway. His job is to see that they are helped to become increasingly effective in all their listening.

From the early school years, children have occasion to listen to *directions, explanations,* and *announcements.* In so doing they must acquire the habit of putting away any materials that might distract their attention, learn to lend an ear from the beginning, deliberately intend to hear the speaker to the end, and try to understand the speaker the first time he enunciates an idea. It is bad for a teacher to form the habit of repeating his directions and explanations since his pupils soon learn that he will explain two or three times; they consequently do not listen the first time he explains. He may actually be teaching them not to pay attention.

To ensure attentive listening, the teacher should be certain of what he will say and how he will say it. He must wait until he has close attention, speak simply with clear-cut phrasing, be brief, orderly, and clear in his directions, and use visual support through gestures, demonstrations, or drawings on the board of sketches that will clarify his meanings. Children should learn to pay close attention from start to finish to make sure they understand what the speaker is saying; and if they do not understand, they should feel responsible for asking questions that will elicit the desired information.

As pupils progress through the grades, directions and explanations become increasingly lengthy and intricate. Children who have learned to listen well in the lower grades can, with their added maturity, cope with the greater demands on their listening skills, but only if teachers continue to help them gain skills, such as noting the sequence of ideas and their relative importance, contradictory or unsupported statements, and bias. Upper-grade children, too, should assume more and more responsibility for making clear explanations and giving explicit directions to their classmates. Also, they should learn how to induce close and comprehensive attention on the part of their listeners.

Conversation is the commonest of the oral types of communication and, therefore, calls for much listening. However, groups are usually small, interests are directly personal, and listening usually comes easily. Even so, the school needs to provide guidance because most children need help in learning to wait their turn and to show courtesy as they listen and respond to the remarks of their companions. In speaking they need to be taught to help their own listeners by choosing a topic of interest to their companions, to feel responsible for taking part and drawing in a newcomer or too-shy child, to avoid or change a subject that is overly personal or embarrassing to a member of the group. Such learnings come in connection with a show-and-tell period of real significance, pupils' conversation during small-group and committee activities, and informal talk at intermissions. The teacher's guidance is usually incidental, and often individual, as he unobtrusively comments on matters of courtesy and effectiveness.

In school and out, children frequently participate in *discussion*. Unlike conversation that may ramble, discussion centers on a single topic and should proceed in an orderly way to a point of decision. When a pupil is part of a discussion group, he should feel responsible for knowing what topic is under consideration, following the thread of thought, being ready with a timely and worthwhile contribution, listening evaluatively to what his companions are saying.

In all curricular areas and in all the daily lessons, each child will alternately talk and listen as his group makes plans, states the problems it is meeting, suggests solutions, and reports on progress. He will join in his group's discussion of the pictures in the textbooks and other references, activities involved in a social studies or science unit, class picnic that must be planned, playground problem that involves the safety of younger children, and questions that have been raised about a geographic region of the United States or the life of some great citizen.

Reports become a major responsibility in the upper grades; but even the kindergarten child may report on his firsthand experiences, such as a weekend trip or the progress of the nestlings under his bedroom window. During the presentation of a report, listeners must follow the speaker's plan of organization—his selection and sequence of ideas—must attempt to select information that supplements the information already in mind, and

As their teacher reads or tells a story, children develop their listening skills and gain an appreciation of language and literature.

must evaluate the authenticity of what he is saying. Reports are called for as small groups engage in committee work connected with a class enterprise, as an individual observes or reads to learn the answer to a question raised in a learning activity, or as he experiments.

From kindergarten days through the upper-grade years many occasions arise when a child listens to *stories* whether they are told to him or whether he reads them orally. The teacher and classmates may read from books; they may tell stories or tell and relate tales based on personal experience; they may share creative writing. Here the listener should respond appreciatively, follow the buildup of the plot, envision the action that is portrayed, and interpret the feelings and motivations of the characters.

Appreciation is similarly called for as children listen to *poetry* and engage in choral speaking. Poetry is characterized by unusual structural forms, brevity, vivid word pictures, and deeply imaginative feeling; young listeners must visualize what the poem portrays and assimilate the ideas and feelings. Because poetry has melody and rhythm, it has great sensory appeal. Usually an adult reads or recites the poem while the children listen —a child reader can rarely do justice to the involved phraseology and economical, yet graphic use of words.

Modern living calls for a great deal of listening. Most homes have one or more of the following kinds of equipment: radio, television set, record player, and, of course, the telephone. All the types of listening are called for in the various listening situations: secondary listening when music plays softly in the background, conversational listening when called to the telephone, appreciational listening as good drama or fine music is presented, exploratory or interrogative listening as recipes or weather information is given, concentrative and critical listening whenever issues are discussed by politicians and experts in various fields.

While such devices call for much listening and may build up listening skills, they may on the contrary develop ability not to listen—to "tune out" instead. When radios and television sets are turned on hour after hour, the child listener almost surely learns to cut out either the conversation and discussion of the family group while he attends to the broadcast (or telecast) program, or he will ignore the program as he listens to his companions. At any rate the teacher has to deal with children who will tend to "tune out" any presentation that does not have much appeal. He has to be truly interesting and effective if he wants to attract and hold the attention of his pupil audience.

Typically, school situations frequently call for prolonged listening by large groups, as in school assemblies and programs. Often a large proportion of the children are too young or too old to be interested. Here the teaching staff should make sure that the presentations are suited to the maturity, background, and interests of the young audience. Otherwise bad listening habits and discourtesy are likely to result. Even when a program is well suited to the audience, each teacher should prepare his pupils for interested and effective listening by preliminary discussion, study of pictures, storytelling, and other means of building a background and eagerness to listen.

GENERAL POLICIES IN DEVELOPING LISTENING SKILLS

The psychological process of listening gives the teacher insight into his responsibilities for developing his pupils' listening skills. Let us first consider purpose, or motivation. Whenever the teacher or any of his pupils is to speak or read orally, he needs to consider what purpose is to be served. Are the children to listen for enjoyment? Then he should set the stage through a display of pictures or a discussion that will arouse curiosity and a feeling of anticipation as the girls and boys get set to listen. Should they listen with the intention of finding out the answers to certain questions that have been raised? As they tune in on the explanation to be read or told to them, they should be aware that "Now you will find out why leaves turn red and yellow in the fall. Listen as I read this page to you."

Do older pupils need to weigh the arguments for and against having a school carnival to raise money for a classroom radio? The issue is a live one. They will have a purpose in listening, but the teacher may have to help them to be ready to think objectively and critically. To think thus should be their objective.

Another psychological factor in listening is readiness. Are the children old enough to be interested in the topic? Have they had experiences and earlier learning activities that provide a meaningful background for interpreting what they are about to hear? Are there terms that need development before they listen? Having an adequate and pertinent listening vocabulary is an essential in listening readiness. Have any of the pupils prejudices and misconceptions that need to be cleared up before listening begins? Are classroom conditions conducive to good listening—proper temperature, comfortable seats and posture, no dazzling light in the eyes, quiet? Of such does readiness for listening consist.

The manner of children's thinking is another consideration in the psychology of listening. Children learn best when materials are concrete. The teacher should so plan what they are to hear that they can envision the actions, feel the emotion, or admire and dislike the characters portrayed in the graphic oral reading or storytelling to which they are audience. Young children sense best an organization based on time sequence. Upper-grade children can determine the main points in a discourse and make a mental outline of what they hear; or, at least, they should have acquired such ability if the teacher has provided proper guidance. Listeners profit if the speaker proceeds in orderly fashion and reiterates main points as he goes along. This reiteration is all the more important in view of the fact that almost any listener takes time out to reflect a bit or, perhaps, to recall a pertinent experience. In the process, he loses track of what the speaker has said in that brief interval of time.

The younger the child, the shorter is his span of attention. Here again the teacher considers the psychology of listening. He suits the length of the listening period to the maturity of the child; he brings in variety by showing pictures, discussing an interesting point, letting the children give a dramatic representation of an action in the story, and the like.

In utilizing opportunities for children to listen, the teacher does not need to add a period to his day in order to give listening experiences. He may test with an audiometer to make sure that a child's unrecognized partial loss of hearing is not handicapping him. The teacher merely is alert to the situations in which listening is appropriate, and he is especially sensitive to occasions that call for varied types of listening as, for instance, *exploratory, appreciational, conversational,* and *critical.*

In summary, the following suggestions for developing more effective listening on the part of pupils may prove helpful.

1. Provide a classroom atmosphere conducive to listening: relaxed, comfortable, quiet. Each speaker should feel secure and confident that his listeners will accept his contributions as worthwhile. Have young children sit close to the speaker in an informal arrangement. At all ages, a child with a hearing loss should be seated near the speaker and should be able to watch him easily. Encourage any child who cannot hear well to move quietly to a seat where he can hear better.

Whenever possible, reduce noises that cannot be prevented; for example, hall noises which can be softened by closing the door and outside noises muffled by closing windows. Modify room noises through teacher-pupil planning of changes that will substitute quieter activities for the noisy ones that distract the attention of a small group listening to a story or trying to follow the discussion of their companions.

2. Take advantage of the opportunities for listening that arise throughout the day.

3. Be sure that the children sense a purpose for listening and that the purpose is suitable to the occasion and the materials. Different kinds of thinking are called for in casual listening for enjoying a favorite poem or story, in thoughtful listening to locate answers to already verbalized questions about how to train a puppy to do tricks, and in critical listening to find flaws in an argument about public power projects.

4. Lead the pupils to expect meaning whenever they listen, and encour-

age them to ask questions in case they do not understand what they have heard. Encourage an attitude of mental curiosity.

5. Prepare pupils for what they are about to hear by recalling related familiar materials, by developing new vocabulary needed for their listening, and by stimulating questions and a feeling of anticipation.

6. Whenever possible, break up long listening periods by allowing the pupils to join in as a repetitive rhyme appears in a story, on an exciting step in the story, or to comment to make guesses about what the ending will be. Also the pupils should anticipate that they will make use of the materials soon after they have heard them. Help the pupils to realize that the speaker may not give complete answers to their questions, that they must select pertinent points, and that they must "piece together" and interrelate these points to achieve a final answer.

7. Suit the occasion and the materials to the maturity of the children: their span of attention, their interests, their capacity to understand, the relation to previous experiences.

8. Guide the older girls and boys in an evaluation of what they hear; sensitize them to the tricks of the demagogue's trade, in which gestures, facial expression, inflections of the voice, and other emotional appeals are used to disguise half-truths and false claims.

9. Set up occasions in which the pupils purposefully reproduce what they have heard: outline, summary, explanation to those who have not heard the original production, sketches, and the like.

10. Help the children to set up standards for effective listening so that they will know when to listen, what should engage their attention, and how they can listen well.

ACTIVITIES DESIGNED TO IMPROVE LISTENING

Teachers with ingenuity can easily think up many different kinds of activities that will promote keen, thoughtful listening by their pupils. A number of suggestions follow. Some of these situations may be used in the form presented here; others may need to be varied to suit the local situation.

Conversational listening. For improvement, the following procedures can be used: (1) alerting children to the need for improvement by discussing signs of listeners' inattentiveness which pupil speakers have noticed from time to time; (2) setting up standards for courteous listening and for becoming an interesting conversationalist on the basis of the discussion; (3) making a tape recording of a class conversation and applying the standards that have been set up; (4) making a gradually growing check list of standards for courteous listening; (5) evaluating class conversations according to the check list; (6) encouraging pupil self-evaluation by using the check list; and finally (7) letting class representatives evaluate. It will be noted that critical listening is involved as children work together to improve their listening habits.

Appreciational listening. Two different aspects must be considered in this type of activity: responsiveness and the cultivation of tastes. Again, creative listening is involved in many activities listed here. Oral reading will often be the background for responsive listening as the listeners (1) sketch an original cartoon of a character or situation portrayed in a story; (2) pantomime, activate puppets, or dramatize spontaneously in response to a story just listened to; (3) individually tell or write an original ending to a high-quality story; and (4) make sound effects with rhythm band instruments as the teacher reads a poem or story portraying different kinds of weather or rates of motion; for instance, as a character strolls, walks briskly, stumbles, lopes, pauses and walks softly, races, and leaps to safety.

Storytelling, too, gives opportunity for the children to learn to listen appreciatively and creatively; for instance, they (1) tell chain stories in which each participant carries on from where the preceding speaker stopped; (2) witness the first act of a play planned and presented by a committee, then spontaneously make up the next act; (3) listen for leads in prepared stories told by members of a special committee, these leads to suggest spontaneous stories on the part of the listeners; and, (4) for advanced pupils, keep notes of the ideas suggested by the poems and stories presented by the teacher or their classmates.

In trying to improve the pupils' taste in listening fare, the following activities may prove helpful: (1) making a tape recording of various pupils' favorite stories and poems and letting the listeners request a personal presentation of the ones that appealed the most, or else having the class discuss the qualities in poems and stories that have lasting appeal; (2) painting or drawing scenes suggested by favorite selections; (3) making a personal or a class "hit parade" of poems or stories heard over a period of two weeks when different children took turns reading; (4) making a similar class hit parade of local radio or television shows; (5) polling the class members' listening preferences for such programs, with a follow-up discussion of the qualities that cause the appeal; (6) making a cooperatively devised rating sheet for evaluating radio and television listening; and (7) appointing a committee to give advance notice of choice programs that are to be presented in a local theater or hall or on radio-television.

Exploratory listening. Improvement may result from activities like these: (1) In extending and deepening word meanings, the pupils may listen for certain words that have been listed on the board prior to hearing a selection read. They should get at meaning by noting the context in which each of the words is used. (2) After listening to a set of directions only once, the pupils will carry on a simple experiment or carry through some enterprise in crafts or construction. (3) After listening, the pupils will write out the directions, as, for instance, for lifesaving on the beach or for playing soccer. Or (4) they listen for new information on a topic already partially learned.

The prime way to help children listen for information is to see that they listen with a question in mind, that they have an explicit purpose for the listening they are about to do. The teacher may pose questions raised through class discussion or volunteered by an individual pupil who does not fully understand some stimulating experience. The teacher may devise special exercises: (1) He may build a file of news reports and published speeches that contain contradictory, obsolete, or absurd statements and have the pupils listen specifically for the contradictions and the out-of-date or ridiculous statements. (2) The teacher of gifted pupils may write contradictory or absurd statements for class listening, such as "Jimmy put on his warmest coat and cap and went out into the frozen garden to pick some pansies for his broken vase." (3) The pupils may listen to reports (personally presented or tape recorded by a previous class) or to an explanation to learn facts which correct former erroneous ideas. (4) The class may watch and listen to a sound movie with the intention of thinking up questions to guide group discussion.

A relatively advanced form of listening for information is the determination of the main idea in a selection that has just been heard. So as to have available materials for building exercises, the teacher should file clippings of suitable speeches, lectures, reports, and descriptions; or he can build up a file of tape recordings to use year after year. Before pupils attempt to find main ideas through listening, they should have had considerable experience in locating the main idea in numerous reading selections. The first listening activities should center about single paragraphs in exercises in which the pupils are asked (1) to select the truly central topic from a multiple-choice list of topics related to the paragraph, only one of which is the actual main idea of the paragraph or (2) similarly to select the topic sentence of the paragraph. The multiple-choice topics or statements will be written on the board or duplicated on paper so that the pupils can have time to consider them evaluatively. A still more advanced exercise in determining main ideas is based on three- or four-part selections. In this exercise the pupils are either (3) to write out, in proper sequence, a topic to represent the main point in the selection or (4) to write a statement for each. Seventh and eighth graders should be able to work out a still more difficult but valuable exercise as they determine the theme of an entire selection. Here again, multiple-choice items should be available for the pupils (5) to select the central topic-theme or (6) to select the sentence that best expresses the theme. The more proficient pupils should finally be able (7) to write out the theme independently. When instructing a college class, the writer had the following amusing experience. She was explaining how to teach pupils to find the theme of a selection and, to illustrate the point, she asked that each student try to tell the story of Red Ridinghood in a sentence of approximately eight words. She expected a sentence such as "A disobedient little girl runs into danger." A young bachelor in the class unintentionally convulsed the group as he bettered the instructor's direction by saying, "Girl outwits wolf." He had the idea, but implied more. After many lessons in locating main ideas the pupils should be able (8) to write summaries.

Another form of concentrative listening calls for the pupils' noting the sequence of ideas: (1) A simple game involves the children's repeating what has been said in the preceding pupils' cumulative statements: for instance, they may pretend to go Christmas shopping. Mary says, "I bought hose." Jane continues, "I bought hose and house slippers." Joe says, "I bought hose, house slippers, and a sport shirt." The game continues as long as the cumulative list is complete and in correct order. All kinds of situations may be substituted for Christmas shopping. (2) A second interesting assignment is the pantomiming of a three- or four-scene story which has been presented orally. (3) An alternative assignment is the retelling of the story in proper sequence. (4) Still another alternative is the drawing of a picture strip with the story parts portrayed in order.

Closely related to locating main ideas and determining their sequence is that of noting the speaker's plan of organization. Here again, the pupils should first read and analyze a number of printed lectures and speeches. They will note different ways of introducing a talk, such as a joke to attract close attention and relax the audience, a complimentary remark about the town or organization sponsoring the speech, or a personal experience which leads into the theme. The pupils will become familiar with transitional phrases ("next" or "in the second place") that highlight a change to the next main idea. They will also note the speaker's plan for closing his printed lecture.

Following considerable experience in analyzing printed lectures, the pupils should similarly analyze brief tape-recorded selections or printed speeches read orally by the teacher. (1) They will note the type of introduction. (2) They will watch for transitional words that lead into the next main point. (3) They will be alert to the speaker's plan for repeating the points he has already made before presenting the next one. (4) They will note the type of conclusion, such as the summary or the illustrative story that exemplifies the points the speaker has made. (5) In another interesting exercise, older pupils will listen to the introduction of a speech by a well-known speaker and try to predict the points he will make.

This boy is listening attentively for information that will guide him in making an illustration.

Somewhat related to experiences in noting main ideas and the speaker's plan of organization are activities in noting illustrative details. When pupils are to listen for details, they should first be apprised of the main points and ideas to be illustrated: (1) As the pupils listen, they should write down a topic or a sentence to represent each of the leading illustrative details. (2) The pupils may listen for details that will help them make an accurate sketch or detailed figure in a mural. The teacher will find it advisable to compile selections that feature clear-cut illustrative details by making clippings or tape recordings.

There come occasions when pupils need to take notes, as during interviews, lectures by a school visitor, and a trip to a museum or a complicated industrial establishment. The foregoing experiences in finding main ideas and following the speaker's plan will form a basis for making meaningful notes, which will be running notes for an informal talk and an outline for a well-organized presentation. Taking notes and making an outline while listening is quite difficult, and all but the most capable pupils should have very simple responsibilities.

Whenever children set up standards for good listening and put them to use, they are engaging in critical listening, a phase for which modern living makes heavy demands. It is important that children be guided in developing constantly improved taste in selecting the radio and television programs so common in their homes. It is important, too, that they learn to evaluate the conflicting statements in advertisements of competing products and also to consider objectively and judiciously the speeches and lectures which politicians and leaders in various organizations present in an effort to persuade and move their listeners to partisan action. Never in history has there been a time when citizens have had as much need for the ability to listen with a critical, yet open-minded attitude. The school should make much of the opportunities to improve the critical listening of its pupils.

One of the great lessons that the younger school child has to learn is the discrimination between fact and fancy. Every child has his Mulberry Street (as portrayed in Dr. Seuss's well-known book) where he walks and sees wonders that exist only in his imagination. It is normal for him to see the family cat as a stalking tiger, his daddy as the biggest and strongest man in the neighborhood, himself in an adult role as he sits "reading the paper" just as Daddy and Mother do each evening. Parents and teachers must help young children to distinguish between "what really happened" and "what is make-believe." Gradually more mature types of judgment are called for as children learn to distinguish between fact and opinion.

Pupils in the middle and upper grades may check on the authenticity of statements in situations such as the following: (1) Pupils may give off-the-cuff opinions and then get the facts to prove their oral statements in

Other students listen critically as a panel member states his position.

such matters as whose house has the most square feet of floor space or which of two almost equivalent routes to a nearby park or to a distant city is the shorter. (2) The teacher may clip or devise statements in which fact and plausible opinion are intermingled and ask the pupils to listen first for opinions and then for indisputable facts. (3) The teacher may tell or read orally short statements of opinion with the understanding that the listeners are to rewrite them into factual statements. (4) The pupils may listen to lectures and programs on radio or television and note instances when mere opinions have been stated as definite facts. They will report these to the class to determine whether the statement is actually opinionative. Children should learn to look for evidence as they listen. Did the speaker give enough facts to prove his point? Did he jump to a conclusion from insufficient evidence? Did he need more facts? Could he have given more and better reasons on the other side of the question he is discussing? Did he use examples that actually do help to prove his point? Were his sources of information up to date, reliable, unprejudiced? (5) The most discriminating and able upper-grade pupils may check on their own speech for instances in which they have stated mere opinions as facts. (6) These pupils may compile phrases which speakers utilize to conceal the debatability of their statements and make these seem factual; for example, "informed sources," "an authority who does not wish to be named," "leaders tell us," or "experts report." This kind of critical listening will appeal to bright minds because such phrases may sometimes preface proved facts, or they may reflect a speaker's effort to appear factual when he actually has no proof of authenticity. (7) A panel member or debater may quote some statement out of context and give a wrong impression to his listening audience unless the listeners make a thoughtful, objective appraisal of such quoted evidence.

Older pupils will find very enlightening and intriguing those activities in which they learn to listen for emotive language: (1) In the first place, they may list and compare the sound devices used by advertisers on radio and television to attract attention, such as screeching tires, gun shots, echo chambers, whistles, or unusual voice qualities. (2) Another interesting activity is the analysis of the sales psychology that underlies the advertisements. Is it sensory appeal, as in honey-sweet cereal or the smooth-as-silk feeling? Is it the so-called Scotch instinct of liking a good bargain? Is it vanity, as in the desire for a touchable skin or the glint on softly waving hair? Is it comfort, as in the instantaneous dissolution of a painkiller or the healing of "dishwater hands"? Is it the pinch of unpaid bills and the easy road to a kindly lender's door? Is it the neurotic's appetite for excitement and suspense? Is it the love of a rhythmic beat or harmony that is featured in the omnipresent singing commercial? These and many other psychological appeals may be analyzed. (3) The speeches of politicians and organization promoters may be similarly analyzed not only for the type of psychological appeal but also for language that features the spread-eagle and flag-waving techniques, the glittering and pompous generality, the catchword or slogan, or the folksy manner—any of which may be designed to appeal to the patriotism or high ideals of the superficial thinker and to prevent his grasping the true significance of the speaker's basic ideas. When speeches are emotion-tinged, listeners must give critical attention in order to determine whether the speaker is merely trying to be interesting and to hold attention or whether he is using emotion as a camouflage. (4) Another interesting comparison can be made between news reports and commentaries on radio and television. The teacher can use a home assignment or recordings of telecasts and broadcasts that have been made to help him in guiding the comparison.

SUGGESTIONS FOR STUDY AND DISCUSSION

1. In which types of listening have you engaged this past week?
2. List the skills needed in effective listening, especially those related to thinking along with the speakers.
3. Evaluate your own listening in terms of these skills.
4. Observe in a primary and an intermediate-grade classroom. Spend a half day in each. List the occasions for listening; classify as to types; evaluate the effectiveness with which listening was done.
5. What obstacles get in the way of listening? Which of these are also found in reading? Which are peculiar to listening?
6. What can be done to overcome these obstacles?

FOR FURTHER READING

1. BAKER, ZELMA W., *The Language Arts, the Child, and the Teacher*. San Francisco, Fearon, 1955.
2. BIRD, DONALD E., "Speech Education." *NEA Journal* (November 1960), 31–33.
3. BURNS, PAUL C., "Teaching Listening in Elementary Schools." *Elementary English* (January 1961), 11–14.
4. CANFIELD, G. ROBERT, "How Useful Are Lessons on Listening?" *Elementary School Journal* (December 1961), 147–51.
5. CYPREANSEN, LUCILE, "Listening as a Skill." *Childhood Education* (February 1961), 268–70.
6. DUKER, SAM, "Goals of Teaching Listening Skills in the Elementary School." *Elementary English* (March 1961), 170–74.
7. *The English Language Arts* (Chapter 14), Commission on the English Curriculum of the National Council of Teachers of English. New York, Appleton-Century-Crofts, 1952.
8. *Language Arts for Today's Children*, Commission on the English Curriculum of the National Council of Teachers of English. New York, Appleton-Century-Crofts, 1954.

9. LOBAN, WALTER, MARGARET RYAN, and JAMES R. SQUIRE, *Teaching Language and Literature* (Chapter 4). New York, Harcourt, Brace & World, 1961.
10. LOGAN, LILLIAN M., *Teaching the Young Child* (172–82). Boston, Houghton Mifflin, 1960.
11. NEVILLE, MARK A., "Listening Is an Art: Practice It." *Elementary English* (April 1959), 226–33.
12. NICHOLS, RALPH G., and LEONARD A. STEVENS, *Are You Listening?* New York, McGraw-Hill, 1957.
13. RUSSELL, DAVID H. and ELIZABETH F., *Listening Aids Through the Grades*. New York, Bureau of Publications, Teachers College, Columbia U., 1959.
14. SCHWARTZ, SHEILA, "What Is Listening?" *Elementary English* (April 1961), 221–24.
15. STRICKLAND, RUTH G., *The Language Arts in the Elementary School* (Chapter 6). Boston, Heath, 1957.
16. WEAVER, A. J., GLADYS BORCHERS, and D. K. SMITH, *Speaking and Listening*. Englewood Cliffs, N. J., Prentice-Hall, 1956.
17. WHYTE, WILLIAM H., JR., *Is Anybody Listening?* New York, Simon and Schuster, 1952.
18. WILT, MIRIAM, "A Study of Teacher Awareness of Listening as a Factor in Elementary Education." *Journal of Educational Research* (April 1950), 626–36.
19. WITTY, PAUL A., and ROBERT A. SIZEMORE, "Studies in Listening: A Postscript." *Elementary English* (May 1959), 297–301.

9

Developing Pupil Interest in English

Chapter 9 is based on the premise that English is more than a tool to sharpen language skills. The teacher who includes an occasional lesson on the subject matter of English—historical, dealing with the language of the past; comparative, showing relationships between different languages; current, dealing with structure today— will stimulate pupil interest in all language activities.

ONE of the purposes of the elementary school is to open the eyes of children to the wonders of their world. In language, as well as in many other subjects, young people can find much to stir their interest and curiosity. Under the guidance of a teacher who knows the language well and can translate that knowledge into terms appreciated by the pupils, children can begin from their first years in school to enjoy learning about language.

It has been said that English is a tool subject and that the function of English instruction is to sharpen the language skills. This statement is only partially true. English also has a subject matter of its own, with a body of knowledge fast increasing because of scholarly research in the field of linguistics. The subject matter is in part historical, dealing with the language of the past; in part comparative, showing the relationships between different languages; in part current, dealing with the structure of English as spoken today.

In catching and preserving pupil interest in English, teachers can make use of the subject matter of language to enhance their lessons and make them more meaningful. On occasion a lesson or a short series of lessons should be presented with the primary purpose of offering information about the language. Interest alone provides sufficient reason, just as it does in any of the humane studies, like history, music, or art.

At other times, in the course of developing skills in writing or speaking, practice and drill may grow tiresome despite courageous effort by the teacher. When the need comes for a change of pace, a different kind of lesson can serve the cause, one that is interesting enough to prick up the lagging attention and add zest to the study.

The Subject Matter of English

THE topics listed below are offered as suggestions for interesting lessons. For the most part, they bear directly upon the English language—its endless variety of sounds and tones, the stories of words, the range of choice in the vocabulary of English and the different purposes words can fulfill, the variety in sentence structure and how English sentence patterns are formed and transformed, what the basic structural features of the language are, and how the structure and the words have changed over the centuries.

THE SOUNDS OF THE LANGUAGE

Rhymed chants and sayings are a part of child folklore persistently repeated by succeeding generations of children. Long before they enter school, the sound of their language and its rhythm catch their fancies. In school their reading and writing lessons during the primary years present the first organized study of language sounds and symbols. To complement the work in reading and writing, the teacher can find frequent opportunities to create new awareness of language sounds and maintain the children's delight in them.

There are books with riddles in rhyme for small tots, rhymed couplets with final words left for completion, and jokes in jingles. And of course much can be done without books on the spur of the moment. The children may even be allowed a little time for creative fun during which they make up a language of their own. Alastair Reid in *Ounce Dice Trice*(18, p. 39) gives a numbering system made up of remarkably satisfying sounds to replace the numbers one to forty, beginning this way: "Ounce, dice, trice, quartz, quince, sago, serpent, oxygen, nitrogen, denim." They may enjoy playing with reduplicated forms, finding and listing words like *choo-choo, yo-yo,* and *tom-tom.* Pure foolishness in a sense, it is true, but a game that can spark interest in language and open a child's mind to the heritage he has always taken for granted. In language study during the early years the spirit of play should predominate.

As children mature, new reasons for the study of language sounds become obvious. In their informal speech and in oral reading, they can begin to note differences in stress and pitch of voice, and the effect of pause between words and sentences. The beginning reader often speaks in monotone, so engrossed is he in interpreting the symbols on the printed page. But when he can read with a little ease, the teacher finds it necessary to remind him that the story means more if he reads with changes in the tone of his voice. Some primary books print the words needing emphasis in capital letters: "What DO you suppose Teddy Bear did next? He ran ALL the way home in less than a MINUTE." Unless helped in their listening skills, some children do not hear the intonation of the voice—the rise and fall, the accent, and the pause.

The sounds of language may need attention in leading children to clear articulation, to correct pronunciation, and to the ability to distinguish syllables in learning to say words correctly. Spelling and punctuation depend in varying degree upon the ability of the individual to hear accurately the sounds of the language he uses every day. Without direct assistance, some children retain baby talk: *I fink he twied* for *I think he tried.* Some never make the effort to articulate or never hear their own errors in pronunciation as they use freely such puzzlers as *lashear* (for *last year*) or *Wyncha go?* (for *Why don't you go?*) or *Dijeejet?* (for *Did you eat yet?*). The teacher needs to help them to listen to the difference. Tape recordings of their own voices can provide much interest as well as much learning.

As a part of literature study, the sounds of language must inevitably be stressed. Children should be exposed to the rhythm of well-written prose, and their ears should be attuned to literary devices such as parallel structure and the balanced phrase, the long rambling sentence to establish one mood, and the series of short sharp sentences to develop another. Until children are mature, these learnings will be wholly indirect, a matter of experiencing much good literature read well in class. In reading poetry, children will experience sound as an integral part of its composition— rhythm and meter, rhyme, assonance, and alliteration. These devices should be enjoyed frequently in the elementary grades, with analysis usually left for later years. In the sounds of language, as in almost every aspect of linguistics, the range of interest can extend from early youth to a period of advanced scholarship.

STORIES OF WORDS

Even as early as the intermediate grades, when children have learned to use the dictionary, they can find there and elsewhere information about the origin and derivation of words. As part of the work in vocabulary development, the teacher can provide some interesting explanations about words or possibly stimulate the children to hunt for such explanations themselves. In their study of their own community, they will enjoy learning about place names. The street on which they live, their school, or their town may carry the name of a local or national figure. If so, the children may be able to gather interesting facts about the person.

In most parts of the country, Indian place names bear testimony to the former inhabitants of the land. Other names, originating in France, Spain, Holland, and elsewhere, suggest the early ancestry of American people. In many communities the surnames of citizens can lend strength to the teaching of democracy. As children compare their own last names, they prove the theory that America is a nation of many peoples from many lands.

Word study can also contribute to an appreciation of foreign lands. When a class studies our Latin American neighbors, an acquaintance with a few Spanish words will make them aware of another language. By noting similarities in some English and Spanish words, they can begin to realize the ties that link two different languages and people. In the early grades, when introduced purely as an interest element, the names of familiar objects or animals in a foreign language are of interest to children. What does a Frenchman call a cat? How do children in Mexico say *chickens*? If the teacher has a language background, such curiosity can be fostered. The educational objective of showing language to be conventional and a matter of choice with people of different lands, is worth the few minutes such incidental instruction takes.

As children study folk literature, they can be led to find many instances where words in daily use come directly from the stories handed down from Norse and Greek or Roman mythology. They can find such origins in the names of the days of the week (Thor, Saturn), or the planets in the sky (Venus), or the elements of earth (Uranus), air (Helios), and water (Hydra). They can find them in trade names of foods and tools. In this age of new scientific inventions and discoveries, new words are being added to the language. Children will find interest in discussing words of recent origin and may even be led to discover some on their own.

Some words have interesting histories of changing form or meaning. For example, the word *silly* once meant *blessed*, and *odd* meant the *point of a triangle*. The accounts of how such changes may have come about make interesting stories to tell young people. When children come to a riper age they will find, if their interest in words continues, that their own research is even more gratifying. As adults they may take pleasure in digging through pages of the *Oxford English Dictionary*, whose dated entries reveal new word meanings and when they appeared.

WIDE RANGE OF CHOICE IN VOCABULARY

The growth of a child's vocabulary from infancy to school age is remarkable. If he has any assistance from parents in providing him with

Here children learn that it is possible to communicate ideas in French as well as in their customary English.

many experiences and words to talk about them, he will come to school with a good start in vocabulary. It is an important part of an English teacher's work to see that this growth continues. Words have so much intrinsic interest for children that such work need never be dull. In addition to the increased vocabulary that naturally accrues from wide reading and class discussion of words in context, children will enjoy and learn from word games, puns, and verbal jokes. Little folks may like to think of as many words as possible beginning with the same letter. Older children may be stimulated by analogy games. For example, they can be given a phrase such as *a herd of cattle* and asked what to call a group of sheep, birds, geese, bees, chickens, cats, or people. Or in reference to the *beginning* of a trip, they may be asked to supply terms for the beginning of a day, a presidential term, a play in the theater, a journey by ship. Or they may be allowed to toy with analogies like this: *A page is to a book as a* (volume) *is to a set of books.*

Children can also stretch their minds and fix some new words in their vocabulary by building word chains. Starting and ending with a pair of opposites, they can see how many words they can fit between the two. For example, they might start with the word *love* and think of words suggesting a cooling ardor, arranging them in descending order until they arrive at *hate.* Or they could supply a similar series of words from *huge* to *tiny.* The good readers with large vocabularies might even be able to extend the boundaries of the chain by finding words that mean huger than huge or tinier than tiny.

The use of words often requires a knowledge of idioms. It is of interest to note how many idioms are based upon one word. Thus the word *play* changes meaning with the phrase *played out* or *play on words;* and the word *lie* varies in meaning with such idiomatic phrases as *lie back, lie down, lie of the land, lie over, lie to,* and *take something lying down.*

From exercises that develop the concept of a wide choice of words, the teacher may take the next step to show how a choice must be made to fit the occasion. Most children know that the language they use needs to be adapted to the persons they address, on the playground, in the schoolroom, or at home. If they have failed to make such transitions or to be aware of the need to do so, the teacher can help them to recognize the different demands upon language which different conditions impose. Children can learn how to change usage patterns to standard English for the classroom and for other semiformal situations, especially when their interest is stimulated by fun. Ruth Golden(7) tells how she made this point with pupils whose normal speech patterns were substandard. She used a tape recorder as one way of getting children to hear differences in usage and later found the children responding well to a "better speech campaign."

American slang deserves at least a small amount of attention when usage levels are studied, partly because of its prevalence among school-age individuals. Children need to understand what its advantages and its disadvantages are; when its use is sanctioned and when it is not. In the spirit of young linguists, pupils can enjoy keeping notes on various expressions that state the same idea in different words or phrases. Their examples may include parallel phrasing typical of substandard English, slang, informal standard and formal standard English.

VARIETY IN SENTENCE STRUCTURE

Even young children can appreciate the difference in sentence forms. The study does not have to be technical. What they need is experience and time to savor it. One way is through proverbs. The structure that permits so much to be said in so little space is worthy of observation:

> Haste makes waste.
> A stitch in time saves nine.
> Laugh before seven; cry before eleven.

The manipulation of sentence patterns is interesting and informative. An awareness develops, even in play, as children notice how statements are turned into questions, how agreements are changed to disagreements or contradictions, and how one arranges a sentence differently in saying yes or no.

STATEMENT, AFFIRMATIVE	He lives in France.
CONTRADICTION	No, he does NOT live in France.
STATEMENT, NEGATIVE	He doesn't live in France.
or	He does not live in France.
CONTRADICTION	Yes, he DOES live in France.
QUESTION	Does he live in France?

Children all know these patterns, of course, and use them easily, but by bringing them to the level of consciousness, the teacher is preparing for a later day when they can choose their phrases with the knowledge of different pattern effects.

Children can also begin to see that choices exist when they compare patterns that use active or passive verbs, or approach a statement directly or indirectly by use of expletives. Again, these patterns may be examined without much technical language even before children have studied grammar. For example, they can look at these pairs of sentence patterns:

> John carried her books.
> Her books were carried by John.

> Going on a picnic is great fun.
> It is great fun to go on a picnic.
>
> Seven children were at the table.
> There were seven children at the table.

Or, this trio of patterns:

> My father gave me a dog.
> A dog was given me by my father.
> I was given a dog by my father.

The first step in such manipulation of sentences is to develop a concept which some children never get, that sentences once stated are not frozen or incapable of being changed. After differences have been observed, children can begin to see rhetorical reasons for exerting choice.

Most of the discussion of the relationships of words and phrases in a sentence is included under the section on grammar in Chapter 20, "Teaching Usage and Grammar." By the start of the upper grades most pupils are experienced enough in their understanding and use of language to approach grammar in an organized way. But in the intermediate grades, grammar can be presented functionally, with explanations made to apply to improvement in expression. Often at that stage of development, children fall into habits of writing run-on sentences either without any punctuation at all or with overuse of *and*. These children need to hear and see the sentence as one unit among several that compose a paragraph. They can be shown by example until they begin to recognize the sentence *idea*. In this connection they will find comfort in learning that the patterns of the English sentence are relatively few and distinctive.

Sentence word order is important in the study of English. Children can discover some common arrangements for themselves if directed by questions posed by the teacher. They can observe, for example, such things as these: when *a, an,* or *the* appears in a sentence, it can usually be counted on as a clear signal that a noun will follow; when adjectives also modify the noun, they come between the signal word and noun (a pretty little girl, the monstrous tiger); though adjectives usually precede the noun (unlike those in some other languages) adverbs may move rather freely within the sentence to answer such questions as *where, when,* or *how.*

The presentation of compound parts of a sentence can be introduced simply with reference to *and* and *but.* Children can use these connectives in the patterns they have already discovered, making new patterns with compound subjects, or compound verbs, or compound modifiers. Knowledge of some of the elements of sentence patterns and a beginning acquaintance with the language of grammar can thus begin early as a matter of interest, preparing children for an organized study of the sentence structure later in their school years.

BASIC STRUCTURAL FEATURES OF ENGLISH

It is generally agreed that the study of grammar requires some maturity and that a technical approach to the subject should be left at least until the upper grades or junior high school. Whenever it is presented, however, this word of warning might be helpful to the teacher. Young people will find greater understanding and develop an interest when they look at the problem as a whole. Rather than confining grammar instruction to a series of isolated lessons and exercises, the teacher will gain the desired goals more effectively by making sure that the pupils are understanding the basic structural features of their language. Unless precautionary steps are taken, children could miss these in the clutter of details. Again the teacher is referred to Chapter 20, and to the five major concepts emphasized for classroom instruction in grammar: the inflective and derivative changes in word forms; the commonly used patterns by which words are arranged in a sentence; the idea of modification, or the effect of one word, phrase, or clause upon another part of the sentence; the relationship between subject and predicate, with the idea that these parts of a sentence must agree; and the idea of coordination and subordination, whether the relationship exists between words, phrases, or clauses.

The study of English is full of complexities, and there is no suggestion here that these can be handled fully in elementary and junior high school classes. But certainly what is taught should be done thoroughly with full understanding of the underlying principles. Only then will the teaching enlighten the learners. As for interest, it is an element that is usually absent when meaning is not clear but frequently appears as a companion to understanding.

VARIATIONS IN WORDS AND STRUCTURE

When children are old enough, they should learn the story of their language, how it stems from Indo-European, from the Germanic rather than the Romanic branch (named after the Latin language of the Romans and including French, Spanish, Portuguese, Italian, and Rumanian). In the North, the tongues most closely related to English include Dutch, Flemish, German, and Scandinavian. English changed more rapidly than others because of historical influences. Examples of how some changes occurred will illustrate the point for pupils. In the first chapter of *Ivanhoe*, Scott indicates the influence of the French upon the early English language. The Saxon swineherd, Gurth, grumblingly observes that the laborer in the field who must look after the animals calls them simply by the names used by his forebears, but the ladies and gentlemen in the castle, who do not even know that the laborers exist, use fine names for their meat, transforming *swine* to *pork*, *calf* to *veal*, and *ox* to *beef*. The Norman rule over Britain was lengthy enough to establish great numbers of words suitable for somewhat elevated life, while everyday alternates were used in communication among the common people.

The merging of two tongues provided the English with vastly increased vocabulary. Through the ages Scandinavian, French, Latin, and Greek influences, in addition to more esoteric foreign words, all contributed to English and are still doing so. To understand English, pupils must understand its changing nature and the impossibility of chaining the language permanently even by rules in a book. The story of English is a demonstration of how language develops and how it changes as the people who use it change.

Children should learn that sentence structure, like that of words, has undergone great change. The shift from a highly inflected tongue to one with few inflections left may persuade some that their task is not too great when they are asked to remember the apostrophe for possession and to distinguish between the possessive *its* and the contraction *it's*. Verb forms and their meanings might be a point of interest for children as they compare modern interpretations of the traditionally named tenses: past, present, and future. They know that *he leaves* uses the verb in the present tense; yet in *he leaves every day at ten,* modified by the rest of the sentence, the verb carries the idea of past, present, and future. The verb in *I am eating* is present tense, but the verb in *I am eating after the meeting* carries a meaning of futurity. Likewise, the comparison of auxiliaries and their meanings is interesting; for example, the difference in saying *I can go* or *I should,* or *must,* or *may,* or *could.*

It must be admitted that much may be found in the spelling of English which cannot easily be explained. Still, most words have at least some parts that are spelled exactly as they sound, and a clear analysis of the pronunciation of the word in some cases, at least, will be helpful to those who have difficulty in spelling. Aside from the help that auditory discrimination can give, the knowledge that the silent letters, which now seem so unnecessary, once represented a part of the pronounced word may tend to stimulate interest in learning. The *gh* in *fought* and the *k* in *know* are examples.

Special kinds of spelling errors can be avoided if spelling is taught together with linguistic study. In the changing forms of words, for example, special attention can be given to the spelling problem of when to double consonants: (a) when the prefix ends with the same letter with which the stem begins (as in *immediate*), and (b) when the addition of a suffix occurs after an accented short vowel sound (as in *getting* and *beginning*). The generalizations treated in Chapter 18, "Improving Children's Spelling," should be considered a part of the word study. So, too, when the class studies the inflected form of the noun showing possession, the apostrophe and *s* should be considered part of the spelling instruction. In some cases knowing the origin of word meanings will help in spelling, such as *heard* from *hear, mariner* from *marine,* or *description* from *describe.*

A misconception to avoid is the idea that word changes, especially in choice of words and in pronunciation, occurred wholly in the past, since our language is still in flux. The variations in word usage and in pronunciation that occur in different parts of the country are an interesting aspect of American speech. To help children enjoy such natural variations, and to overcome any provincial feeling that whatever is unfamiliar must be wrong, a teacher could present some facts about dialect in the United States. Possibly an exchange of tapes or records from children in another part of the country would help to increase interest and understanding of regional dialects.

A few related topics are suggested, such as stories about the alphabet, early steps in the making of books, and the influence of the printing press. While these latter topics are peripheral to the study of English, they are important in the development of man and his society. In the elementary grades, where teachers are usually responsible for teaching both English and social studies, these subjects can contribute to learning in both fields.

STORIES ABOUT THE ALPHABET

In any language sounds come before the need to record them for one's self or others. Such records have not always been made by means of an alphabet. Before any culture group had progressed to our present simple system of using separate letters to stand for separate sounds, other systems were in use. Teaching children something of the history of man's struggle to develop an effective way of writing will give them some background for an appreciation both of their own civilization and of the influence of other civilizations dating back thousands of years. Their education should include something of the kinds of writing that preceded the development of the alphabet. They should see examples of hieroglyphics as used in Egypt, of cuneiform writing from Babylonia.

The story of the alphabet need not be complete—it is far too complex for that. Nevertheless, children should know that their alphabet comes from the Romans, and that the Romans got it from the Greeks, and they in turn from the Phoenicians. With every shift from one language to another, letters no longer useful in describing the sounds of the new language were either dropped or used for representing sounds alien to the former language which the alphabet served. Some interesting stories could be built around specific examples, such as the story of the letter called *thorn;* the story of *aitch;* and *izzard,* now the last of the alphabet (from A to Izzard), called Z in the United States and *Zed* by the British. Some of these stories are briefly outlined in dictionaries; others are to be found in various books written both for adults and for children.

As a point of interest and an illustration that man can devise many ways of delivering a message, some examples of codes may be given. The Morse code may be briefly described and its purpose and use discussed. Flag signals as used in the Navy and in scouting will serve as examples, supplied by the pupils. For children of preadolescent age, building a system for sending their own secret messages has a real attraction. They can do this if they are shown how to formulate a code by simple transposition of letters. By an enthusiastic response, children, without realizing it, will be spontaneously sharpening their curiosity about language, exploring some of its wonders, and keeping alive that interest which the English teacher is eager to preserve.

Two stories of interest to upper-grade children or above make use of different kinds of codes. The solution of Poe's "The Gold Bug" depends upon a code based on strange symbols for letters and the relative frequency of their occurrence in common words. The plot of O. Henry's story, "Calloway's Code," rests upon the use of clichés so familiar to the reader that he can recognize which words are omitted. The omissions form the secret message.

BOOKS AND THE PRINTING PRESS

Education is based upon book learning more than any other kind of experience. In the total curriculum, where schooling of the young child begins with his immediate surroundings, firsthand experiences are usually arranged. But as the child is introduced to an expanding environment, much of his experience comes from the printed page with its accompanying pictures. Within the covers of a book he finds the world spread before him—past and present, fact and fancy, prose and poetry. All this is his possession because mankind through the ages has thought it worth while to record facts and ideas and has sought a way of keeping such records for future generations.

Even a child in the intermediate grades can learn with interest about the beginnings of the making of books: how papyrus was used on the banks of the Nile before there were forests of trees to supply wood for writing, and so the bulrushes in the swampy land around the river were pounded into a substance fit for writing; how a kind of fine leather was used for the beautiful books written with such care in the monasteries of the Middle Ages, but the scarcity of the product made books impossible for most people to obtain; how paper was finally imported from China, its source a mystery

Language becomes exciting to these boys who are communicating by means of the Morse code.

for many years until the secret was broken and Western people found with joy that they had at hand the materials for duplicating the process in their own land.

The advent of printing marks a great new era in the freeing of the human mind. When books could be made and duplicated easily, the possibility of spreading education broadly throughout the land became a reality. Persons of all social and economic levels could become readers when books became available. As with other great inventions, no single person can be given credit for constructing the printing press. But the name of Gutenberg, considered the first European to use movable type, is an example of one whose leadership and skill helped to make the dream a reality. School children today would find interest in his story and in comparing the early printing presses with those of today. They might discover to their surprise the influence of the printing press upon punctuation and spelling. For example, the justification of lines, to form a good straight margin, often required the expansion or contraction of a word. In such cases, the printers, in an age before spelling was standardized, freely added a few letters as needed (for example, *shoppe* for *shop*), or saved necessary room by squeezing letters together (as in y^e [*the*], with the *e* imposed upon the *thorn* to save space).

English in Today's World

As YOUNG people begin to make a serious study of the other countries of the world, they will find interest in learning where the English language is spoken. They may be surprised to realize that, with the single exception of Chinese, English is used by more people than any other language in the world. They can trace the spread of English to colonial America where it became the common tongue for people from many lands, and later to other continents of the world as it spread with the British Empire.

The turmoil of shifting political and social conditions is now undoubtedly having its effect upon the use of English, particularly in Asia and Africa. India is an interesting example. In the wave of nationalism that spread through India when it first became an independent state, the impulse was to reject English. Hindi was proclaimed the official language. But India is a nation of many languages, and many people in non-Hindi speaking communities feared that the imposition of Hindi would be as distasteful as that of English had been under British rule. One of the promises in the new constitution was free and compulsory education for all in this country which had been so predominantly illiterate. The non-Hindi people did not want their own languages neglected in school. The new Indian government wisely provided for an interim period during which English would remain in use for official communication while the new education in Hindi proceeded. With the passing of time, the leaders became less rebellious against the language of a former colonial power and began to recognize the convenience of English for common communication with the Western world as well as its importance for learning in scientific and technical fields.

Some of its leaders now urge retention of English in the schools. Plans have been suggested for using two languages in the primary schools: Hindi, the official language of the state, and the local language. In the secondary schools some seven or eight years of English instruction would be given, with continued instruction available in the colleges and universities. The place of English in India and other Asiatic countries is still being decided.

In the United Nations, English is one of five official languages: Chinese, English, French, Russian, and Spanish. English and French (along with Spanish in the General Assembly and the Economic and Social Council), are the working languages.

The progress of our native tongue in the world of today is a fascinating thing to observe. Pupils in school should be aware of the present place of English and its future trends.

SUGGESTIONS FOR STUDY AND DISCUSSION

1. Find a book on word origins. Read to your class some of the stories about words.

2. Make a tape recording of your own voice. List ways in which you think your voice could be improved.

3. Listen to the enunciation, pronunciation, and intonation of the voice of each of the members of your class. Make a chart showing the voice faults of each pupil. What listening skills will help pupils hear the imperfections of their own voices and, in addition, make them wish to improve?

4. Discuss with your class the origin of surnames. What might have been the occupations of the first persons to use the names Baker, Farmer, Clark? Call the attention of the pupils to names such as Johnson, Olson, Prichard. What do they have in common?

5. Read some recent articles about English today. What has caused the English language to spread all over the world?

FOR FURTHER READING

1. AZIMOV, ISAAC, *Words from the Myths*. Boston, Houghton Mifflin, 1961. Grade 6 and up.
2. BARNES, FRANKLIN, *Man and His Records*. Chicago, Rockwell, 1931. Grade 6 and up.

GUIDING LANGUAGE LEARNING

3. BOWMAN, WILLIAM DODGSON, *The Story of Surnames.* London, Routledge, 1931. Adult.

4. DIRINGER, DAVID, *The Alphabet.* New York, Philosophical Library, 1953. Adult.

5. EPSTEIN, SAM, and BERYL, *The First Book of Words.* New York, Watts, 1945. Grades 5–8.

6. FUNK, WILFRED, *Word Origins.* New York, Funk, 1950. Adult.

7. GOLDEN, RUTH, *Improving Patterns in Language Usage* (Chapters 7–9). Detroit, Wayne State U. Press, 1960.

8. HOFSINDE, ROBERT (GRAY-WOLF), *Indian Picture Writing.* New York, Morrow, 1959. Grades 3–5.

9. —— *Indian Sign Language.* New York, Morrow, 1956. Grades 3–5.

10. IRWIN, KEITH GORDON, *The Romance of Writing.* New York, Viking, 1957. Grades 7–12.

11. LAIRD, HELENE, and CHARLTON, *The Tree of Language.* New York, World, 1957. Grades 5–12.

12. LAMBERT, ELOISE, *Our Language.* New York, Lothrop, Lee & Shepard, 1955. Grades 7–12.

13. OGG, OSCAR, *The 26 Letters,* rev. ed. New York, Crowell, 1961. Grade 8 and up.

14. OPIE, IONA and PETER, *The Lore and Language of Schoolchildren.* New York, Oxford U. Press, 1959. Adult.

15. MATHEWS, MITFORD McLEOD, *American Words.* Cleveland, World, 1959. Grade 7 and up.

16. MOORHOUSE, A. C., *The Triumph of the Alphabet.* New York, Schumann, 1953. Adult.

17. PEI, MARIO, *The World's Chief Languages,* rev. ed. New York, Vanni, 1960. Adult.

18. REID, ALASTAIR, *Ounce, Dice, Trice.* Boston, Little, Brown, 1958. Grades 3–8.

19. ROGERS, FRANCES, *Painted Rock to Printed Page.* Philadelphia, Lippincott, 1960. Grade 6 and up.

20. RUSSELL, SOLVEIG PAULSON, *A Is for Apple, and Why.* New York, Abingdon, 1959. Grades 4–8.

21. SALOFF, ALICE, *Words Are Funny.* Garden City, N. Y., Doubleday, 1952. Grades 1–3.

22. SCHLAUCH, MARGARET, *The Gift of Language.* New York, Dover, 1955. Adult.

23. STEWART, GEORGE R., *Names on the Land.* New York, Random House, 1945. Adult.

24. WITHYCOMBE, E. G., *The Oxford Dictionary of Christian Names.* New York, Oxford U. Press, 1947. Adult.

10

Language in the Kindergarten

Chapter 10 deals with the kindergarten child and the phases of his all-round development that underlie adequate language development. It presents the objectives of kindergarten instruction and describes an environment conducive to the attainment of these aims. There are detailed descriptions of such activities as sharing experiences, conversation, planning together, storytelling, and dramatic play.

TYPICALLY the child enters kindergarten well equipped in oral language. Having talked with his family and friends and through access to radio and television and perhaps some movies, he has learned to understand many thousands of words and to use nearly two thousand of them in his own speech. He may speak in sentences which are complete and varied in structure. He may be reasonably sequential when he is relating a personal experience or retelling a story he has heard. However, many young children do not possess such skills; they have problems in speech, do not use complete thoughts in expressing themselves, and cannot relate incidents in sequential development. If possible, these skills should be taught during the first years in school. However, it is not possible to teach such skills if total perception has not yet developed in the child or, for that matter, if total development has not yet taken place. It must be remembered that total development cannot be forced or "taught."

There are, of course, wide individual differences among kindergarten children. Some homes afford a much greater abundance and variety of enriching experiences and planning, the children from such homes having access to picture and story books, having manipulative materials for putting together a crude doll bed or a miniature airport, using crayons and paints for graphic expression, making trips to the zoo or the farm, and the like.

Other homes provide meager opportunities. Some children may have learned a foreign language at home and may be unable to understand English; other children may have had only illiterate speech patterns to imitate; still others may have had limited contact with their parents who both work outside the home; the more fortunate children will probably have had adequate opportunities to hear and use acceptable English. Further variation in language development will be due to both physical differences and differences in children's native ability, the brighter child having the advantage because of his greater alertness and capacity to understand and remember what he has observed.

The Contribution of the Kindergarten

FOR children deficient in earlier language experiences, the kindergarten will fill in many gaps through enriching experiences and many social situations. At the same time, the more advanced pupils will find further enrichment and sufficiently varied experiences to encourage continued growth.

AIMS OF KINDERGARTEN INSTRUCTION

Certain broad educational purposes control the kindergarten curriculum. These deal with desirable personality adjustment and the child's all-round development: social, emotional, mental, and physical. All through the day learning situations arise that will encourage the children to develop constructive social attitudes as they learn to share, to take turns, to cooperate with a companion or with a group in some joint enterprise, to be resourceful and self-directive and self-reliant. The first year of school is for many youngsters their first experience in living and learning with their peer group. It is most important that they do this in a happy, friendly atmosphere.

In the course of such social experiences, the children have much occasion to speak and listen to one another. As they construct a garage for their trucks from hollow blocks, as they seek clean paper for the easel, as the playhouse mother straightens up her house and sends her child out to the corner store for butter, as a committee cares for the hamsters, as the children plan and carry out their various enterprises, there is a constant flow of language.

Then come the quieter times when the entire group observes and listens to a classmate's show-and-tell contribution, when the teacher reads tuneful verse or tells an intriguing story, when a record is played or a filmstrip shown. Here are intake experiences that encourage subsequent conversation, discussion, and dramatic play.

The varied environment in this kindergarten room promotes the children's intellectual and social development.

Good eating habits, cleanliness and neatness, outdoor play and the follow-up rest period contribute to the physical welfare of the pupils. There are jungle gyms to climb, a slightly raised plank to walk, seesaws and swings, simple tools on a workbench, clay, fingerpaint, large paintbrushes, puzzles, and other equipment that contributes to increased eye-hand coordination and muscular control. As the children handle their building blocks in making a boat or train big enough to sit in and as they saw and hammer at new playhouse furniture, they are developing mentally, socially, physically, and emotionally; at the same time, they are using language abundantly. Multiple learnings are characteristic of kindergarten experiences.

THE KINDERGARTEN ENVIRONMENT

The surroundings in which the kindergarten child finds himself are an important influence in promoting his development, or—if barren and unhygienic—in inhibiting proper growth. The kindergarten room should be spacious, colorful, cheerful, and rich in suggestions for varied activities. The big hollow blocks of many sizes and shapes, the housekeeping or store or doll corners will suggest dramatic play. The small slide, the jungle gym, and workbenches call for lively physical activity while, in a faraway part of the room, quieter activities are suggested by easels, a clay table, puzzles, scissors and paste, magnets, plants, rocks, and other objects for touching and exploring. There may also be a reading corner with picture books on table or shelves, or an alcove where the sleepy child can curl up for a nap.

There are a piano, rhythm instruments, chalkboards, and record players for large-group activities. About the room is abundant bulletin board space to display the children's art or the teacher's ever changing array of clipped pictures that reflect the season, the children's currently prevailing interest, or a curricular area where the teacher is trying to initiate a worthwhile experience. Neatly kept open lockers suggest that the children are learning to be responsible for their care.

THE DEVELOPMENT OF KINDERGARTEN CHILDREN

The five-year-old brings to school a considerable body of information and a host of concepts; a large meaning vocabulary and a considerable speaking vocabulary. However, his background of experiences needs filling in and rounding out. He has difficulty authenticating facts, as he still has difficulty in distinguishing fantasy from fiction. He has to develop concepts of time and space. He asks many questions in order to get desired information; he enjoys new experiences, new words, and new concepts. He is a sociable creature who talks much of the time to anyone in the vicinity.

Alert children who have books of their own, have listened to stories at home, and who live in a family of readers will be interested in books when they get to kindergarten or first grade. Some will want to watch the page as the teacher reads from a book; most children like to see the pictures that parallel the story. Some children are advanced in this respect and may sit with a companion and tell a simple story from the pictures he sees as he turns the pages.

The five-year-old has lived in a world of television before coming to school. He has gained much from this medium in vocabulary and understandings, and he brings these learnings to the classroom. This experience for the most part has been an intake process. When he has the opportunity to question, tell, and discuss things that he has watched on television, he learns more because the outgo aspect of the cycle of learning is very important at this age to clear up words, understandings, and ideas. Some children in this decade have traveled rather widely. Here again is an opportunity to capitalize on sources of information for the development of understanding as well as to give the pupil the speaking opportunities he needs for the development of these skills.

Kindergartners tend to like school and to enjoy the activities of the day. A certain amount of routine is welcomed because children feel secure when they know what to expect next; for instance, they know that the story hour comes after the cleanup period or that the planning period comes early in the morning. Five-year-olds adjust easily to school under capable guidance; they experience little difficulty in moving from one activity to another, though they can persist in a group activity as long as twenty minutes. They like to finish what they have started, except that the more immature may need encouragement and guidance from the teacher in this respect.

Both parents and teacher are important to children of this age, who like to take home their pictures and little booklets to share with Mother and Daddy, and who like to bring their new toys and other gifts from home to show their teacher. It is also fun to display these possessions to their classmates.

In the changing pattern of the modern American home, the teacher is a parent substitute to a greater degree than ever before. In many homes today, both parents are working. Sometimes the child is left with a relative or baby sitter for long periods. The child needs parental love and attention, and the teacher must provide these whenever the home fails.

Kindergarten Language Activities

WHILE activity in itself is valuable to the young child, each activity takes on meaning and significance as he talks it over with his mother or some other companion. Language helps the child to react suitably to the world about him, to interpret what he sees, hears, feels, and handles.

SHARING EXPERIENCES

The child of five is still egocentric and is most articulate and interested when allowed to talk of "me and mine." The boy likes to show off his model space ship and tell about it; the little girl preens in her new dress as she displays it or proudly explains the unusual features of her doll. Early in the school year, the child's explanation may be very brief and incomplete, as for example, Jerry's comment on his new gun and holster: "It snaps when I shoot with it. I got this for my birthday." As the year progresses, the pupils' accounts become more vivid, exact, and sequential.

Often the experience to be shared is one for which a child has nothing to display. He may have gone to Uncle Tom's farm for Sunday dinner and enjoyed thoroughly the baby animals there. So he may come to school bubbling over with his enthusiasm for the funny baby pigs, the cunning little kittens, and the roly-poly puppies. As he talks, his young listeners will be reminded of experiences of their own, and an extensive sharing period may be launched.

At first, the discussion and conversation will tend to be parallel; that is, each child will be obsessed with his own experiences that have been suggested by his talking companions. Consequently, he will tend not to respond directly to what his classmate is reporting. Later, the more mature children may respond with questions and comments on what the child speaker is telling so that the give-and-take type of discussion occurs. Many children do not learn to give and take in this manner until they are in first, or even second, grade.

CONVERSATION

Five-year-olds tend to be great talkers. At first, all may want to talk at the same time and about their own individual experiences. One of the important learnings in the kindergarten is being willing and satisfied to take turns, to listen to what is being said without too much concern with "my, mine, and me." During the group planning, the evaluation period, and discussion of pictures and stories, the children can get experience in waiting their turn. The teacher will say, "Let's hear what Jimmy has to say"; or "I can't hear more than one at a time. It's Mae's turn now." However, much of the conversation should be completely free, probably occurring in groups of two or three when children are engaged in dramatic play, a work period, or eating lunch. The shy child should be unobtrusively placed near an outgoing, friendly child who will share playthings and involve the quiet one in some joint activity.

Since much of language is learned through imitation, the "model"

The child who creates, as in crafts, has ideas to share later with his companions.

teacher will be a polite and interested listener, will speak clearly in simple but complete sentences, will use vividly descriptive words, and will deliberately and frequently use correct expressions which he hopes his young listeners will adopt into their own language to replace some of their customary crudities; for example, he will try to use *saw* often in the hearing of a child who uses *seen* incorrectly. Sometimes he will be quite pointed, without being conspicuous, as he says to the child, "Didn't Teddy have fun Saturday when he *saw* the elephant at the zoo?"

CLASS EXPERIENCES

Early in the kindergarten morning comes the planning period when the children are grouped more or less informally around the teacher to talk over plans for the day. The attention of beginning kindergartners can be expected to be short spanned and easily diverted; they will constantly get off the subject as planning proceeds; and the teacher will, in a patient and friendly way, keep bringing the discussion back to the points under consideration. The decisions to be made must be kept simple; each individual must be able to decide just what he will start doing and where he will go as soon as the subsequent work period starts. The discussion must be very concrete, simple, and brief so that the young minds can stay with the discussion and follow the thinking.

Later in the year the children will have learned to stick to the point much better and to plan in greater detail. Their attention span will have increased.

Other class experiences will be concerned with listening. There will be many stories and much verse presented directly by the teacher or indirectly through recordings. The outcome of literary experiences will be enjoyment, growth in concepts and vocabulary, some information, and much insight into the thoughts and feelings of children like themselves. New York State's bulletin, *The Language Arts* (10, pp. 51–52), lists many other types of listening activities that will help children become aware of the great variety of sounds all about them and will help to build auditory discrimination. Part of the list follows:

> Reproducing sounds made by animals and toys with which children are playing
> Listening to stories with engine sounds, automobile sounds, etc., and imitating them
> Listening to poems in which there are sounds of water, of wind, of rain, and repeating the words used by the poet to create the illusion of sound . . .
> Listening and noting difference in sound of trucks and of passenger cars without looking; . . . of freight and passenger trains . . .

Listening to sound of vehicles that are going up hill, on a level, down
hill . . .
Listening to and imitating the sound of wind
Listening for bird calls . . .
Listening to the falling of dry leaves . . . other seasonal sounds
Imitating such sounds when possible
Practice in listening to and reproducing word sounds accurately . . .

Taking a school trip is another valuable class experience. The trip may
be to the custodian's room to get acquainted with the man who tidies the
classroom each afternoon and who will help with placing and fastening
heavy timbers to support the playhouse the children hope to build. Perhaps the class may walk around a near-by block to find signs of fall in the
yards and along the street. Preliminary to the trip the teacher should use
a planning session that will bring out purposes to be achieved through
the trip (the children may go just to enjoy the warm sunshine). He will
make clear just how the trip will be managed.

After the trip may come discussion or, more probably, dramatic play or
painting that has been stimulated by the experience. One teacher of young
children arranges for a stroll through the schoolyard or along the street
every day when the weather permits; then, upon the group's return, he
encourages the children to respond in any way they please. Some go to
the long strip of newsprint that is attached to a long wall space and proceed to paint their impressions. Others go to the worktable and with
scissors and paste, devise colored leaves and flowers and birds for the
bulletin board. The picture books and the housekeeping corner attract
others.

CREATIVE STORIES

Young children's original stories tend to reflect the stories that some-
body has told them or read to them. Creativeness lies in the changes they
make and in their inner emotional responses to the tales they are telling.
This is the story that Craig told his group:

Easter is here. On Easter Day the bunny comes to my house. He hides eggs
for me to find. They are all colors. I will put the eggs under my old hen. She
will hatch out little red and blue and yellow rabbits. They will play with me.

Listening to simple stories and verse and enjoying the colorful action
pictures that the teacher or various classmates display is a good way to
stimulate children to improvise creative stories and even simple verse.
Filmstrips, movies, and recordings are stimulating influences. Real experiences with pets and interesting objects make a contribution. It is well to
remember that young children have difficulty in distinguishing between

the true-to-life and the make-believe. The teacher should impress upon them the fact that made-up stories are make-believe stories. For instance, after Craig's story above, the teacher might say, "That's such a good story that you made up, Craig! It is fun to make believe, isn't it? What do you really do with the eggs that you find on Easter morning?"

The cumulative and the repetitive kind of story appeals to five-year-olds. They particularly enjoy the refrain that appears periodically throughout a story, such as "I'll huff and I'll puff and I'll blow your house in!" After chiming in on a number of stories with refrains, many children will begin devising stories with similar repetitive parts.

Children enjoy dictating their stories, especially when they see the teacher writing down what they say. The stories—or poems—should be written down exactly as the children dictate them. Children's writing should not be edited at this early stage.

DRAMATIC PLAY

Dramatic play is an intrinsic part of the young child's growing up. As he observes life around him, he imitates and assumes the characteristic behavior of those he sees and thus gradually identifies himself as part of the ongoing world around him. Many a father and mother have been startled to see themselves reflected in the spontaneous play activities of their child. With hands outheld, Mary says to her doll in a pleading voice: "Do be a dear, sweet baby. Please eat your oatmeal for Mommy." Then a deeper voice carries on: "Pick up your spoon and eat that oatmeal. Daddy will put you back to bed if you don't eat that oatmeal right away. Do you hear me? Eat that oatmeal!" Mary has picked up the essential characteristics of both her parents.

The writer remembers a genuinely embarrassing situation in her own home. The farmers in her area often exchanged work and were given a bumper meal at midday. Her five-year-old sister was fascinated with the uproarious laughter of one of the neighbors. He would slap his thigh and let out a mighty roar whenever greatly amused. The little lassie watched and listened a number of times; then she stood at his side and imitated him to perfection. The neighbor's sense of humor did not include being imitated by even a young child and he precipitately left the table. He did not understand the role of imitation in a five-year-old's life and the child's complete lack of ridicule. There was no occasion for his feeling hurt.

It is not only human companions that a child imitates in dramatic play. The barking of a pet dog, the gamboling of baby lambs, the gun battle on television's Western show, the horn and motion of the passing Diesel engine, the buzzing and zigzag of a passing bumblebee—any moving object that appeals to the natural dramatic instinct of the preschool child is likely to stimulate imitative action.

To him dramatic play tends to be serious business. His whole personality is involved, and he becomes one with the character or the object that he is portraying. The classroom needs to have many properties that suggest dramatic play; for instance, large project blocks for constructing semipermanent buildings; large hollow building blocks that can become an airdrome for the play airplanes or a big bus to ride in; a housekeeping corner with dolls, varied furniture, cooking utensils and dishes; a wardrobe of grown-up clothing and accessories for dressing up; or a puppet stage with paper bag puppets.

Puppet properties are particularly valuable for the shy children who when out of sight, but vocal, become free and spontaneous. Oak tag, a paper bag, or double butcher paper may be fashioned into a head, which is in turn affixed to a tongue depressor or lollipop stick and moved along just above the floor of the puppet stage or the top of a table which has been so curtained as to conceal its under parts. The more mature children can handle fist puppets made of papier-mâché heads and full skirts that conceal the fists of the players whose thumbs and fingers extend into the sleeves and up into the head and move the puppets through their play.

Puppetry is one type of dramatization that involves a story. Dramatic play is unstructured; the children live the parts of the characters they are portraying and let the action and conversation evolve naturally. The big hollow blocks of many sizes and shapes, small building blocks, movable toys such as trucks, police cars, express wagons, the housekeeping, store, or doll corners may all suggest dramatic play. Dramatization, whether puppetry or actual play, is based on a story and conforms to its plot. One kindergarten group was fascinated with the story of the "Three Billy Goats Gruff." They placed a chair at either end of a long kindergarten table to form a bridge. Under it hid the terrible troll; over it each goat tripped in turn. The children's dialogue and behavior were as much like the story's characters as the fictitious troll and goats could have been.

The stories that kindergartners will dramatize should be very simple with uncomplicated plots. The cumulative tale like that of the old woman and her pig, or Johnny and his pancake, is appropriate. Some children may wish to dramatize their own original stories and songs. There should be brisk, vivid action, and fast movement of the plot. There should be relatively little planning, and no rehearsal. Dramatization in the kindergarten should be very spontaneous and natural.

SUGGESTIONS FOR STUDY AND DISCUSSION

1. Observe three five-year-olds in the home and three in a kindergarten situation as they engage in undirected play activities. What are the characteristics and interests that you find?

2. Make out a floor plan for a well-arranged and properly furnished kindergarten room or suite of rooms. *Language Arts for Today's Children*, pages 262–71, and Gertrude Hildreth's *Readiness for School Beginners*, page 121 (for Grade 1), will be helpful, as will books devoted exclusively to kindergarten teaching.

3. Make a list of stories and poems well suited to listening by five-year-olds. Which are best told; which best read orally?

4. Prepare a brief written report on one or more of the following topics:

    a. How to help a shy child to adjust

    b. Experiences valuable to the child with a barren background

    c. Helping the foreign-language-speaking child to learn English

    d. Experiences that will encourage creativeness

FOR FURTHER READING

1. BARNOUW, ELSA, and ARTHUR SWAN, *Adventures with Children in Nursery School and Kindergarten*. New York, Crowell, 1959.

2. FOSTER, JOSEPHINE C., and NEITH E. HEADLEY, *Education in the Kindergarten*. New York, American Book, 1959.

3. GANS, ROMA, CELIA STENDLER, and MILLIE ALMY, *Teaching Young Children*. New York, Harcourt, Brace & World, 1952.

4. HARRIS, CORNELIA, "Individual Reading Conferences in the Kindergarten." *Elementary English* (February 1958), 96–101.

5. HEADLEY, NEITH, "To Write or Not to Write." *Childhood Education* (February 1961), 260–63.

6. HEFFERMAN, HELEN, and V. E. TODD, *The Kindergarten Teacher*. Boston, Heath, 1960.

7. HERRICK, VIRGIL E., and LELAND B. JACOBS, eds., *Children and the Language Arts*. Englewood Cliffs, N. J., Prentice-Hall, 1955.

8. HILDRETH, GERTRUDE, *Readiness for School Beginners*. New York, Harcourt, Brace & World, 1950.

9. LAMBERT, HAZEL M., *Teaching the Kindergarten Child*. New York, Harcourt, Brace & World, 1958.

10. *The Language Arts*, Bulletin of the New York State Bureau of Elementary Curriculum Development. Albany, State Education Department, 1957.

11. *Language Arts for Today's Children*, Commission on the English Curriculum of the National Council of Teachers of English. New York, Appleton-Century-Crofts, 1954.

12. LOGAN, LILLIAN, *Teaching the Young Child*. Boston, Houghton Mifflin, 1960.

13. MOORE, ELENORA HAEGELE, *Fives at School*. New York, Putnam, 1959.

14. MOORE, SALLIE BETH, and PHYLLIS RICHARDS, *Teaching in the Nursery School*. New York, Harper, 1959.

15. READ, KATHERINE H., *The Nursery School*. Philadelphia, Saunders, 1960.

16. STRICKLAND, RUTH G., *The Language Arts in the Elementary School* (Chapters 4, 5). Boston, Heath, 1957.
17. WARD, MURIEL, *Young Minds Need Something to Grow On.* Evanston, Ill., Row, Peterson, 1957.

11

Oral Expression in the Primary Grades

Chapter 11 points to the desirability of stressing the fact that oral communication is basic in the language arts curriculum. On the basis of accepted principles of instruction, suggestions are given for a program in the primary grades. Included are specific and workable instructional methods.

ORAL language is important in the life of the young child. He listens to others in order to get information and directions, to secure explanations, and to be entertained. He himself talks abundantly as he questions, informs, explains to, and entertains his companions. He can make his needs quite clear and express his feelings, tell about his experiences and observations, and amuse others with his imaginative or reproduced stories. However, with his expanding environment and growing maturity, the child needs further language experiences that will involve a constantly enriched vocabulary and the arranging and distributing of words into more involved sentences in appropriate sequence.

Oral language is truly basic in the language arts curriculum. In the first place, the preschool child listens and speaks, but does not yet read or write—except for possibly his own name and a few scattered words that have particularly impressed him. Through conversation and discussion in his family circle his observations and experiences take on meaning and significance. Throughout the primary grades, oral language continues to be the dominant means of communication between the child and his associates.

In a second sense, oral communication is basic because, in the everyday affairs of life, it is used more frequently than written communication. Through speaking, human beings exchange most of their ideas, express their emotions, attain their social purposes, and transact the bulk of their business. It is therefore especially important that the school concentrate on helping children to speak with satisfying clarity and impressiveness.

Oral language, in the third place, is foundational because the fundamental aspects of spoken language are similar to those of written communication. Correctly constructed clear-cut sentences, a rich supply of words to express precise meanings, the ability to organize ideas, and situations that encourage the purposeful exchange of these ideas—these are the essentials of both oral and written communication.

Oral Language in the Curriculum

IT IS by speaking that children and adults alike exchange most of their ideas, express their feelings, and carry on their social activities. Language is a social activity and, as such, requires instruction based on certain principles. These principles are outlined in a subsequent section of the chapter.

SOCIAL NATURE OF LANGUAGE

Present-day lessons in oral English are aptly called oral communication or oral expression. The pupil speaks because he has something to say; his message is of first consideration. His listeners have good reason to listen because they expect some interesting information or anticipate amusement or suspense as he speaks; they are a real audience. This audience may consist of all, several, or only one of his classmates, or any number of outsiders; but there is a guarantee of absorbed listening if the situation really centers about the exchange of ideas through purposeful speaking and listening.

Throughout the day, the modern school provides a setting for a constant interchange of ideas as the pupils learn together. Language activities are therefore all-day-long social experiences which cannot be limited to a single period within the school day. In all lessons the teacher and the pupils recount their background experiences, question one another, give explanations and directions, report on their observations or reading, tell stories, and dramatize situations; during recreation periods they experience similar but less formalized oral exchanges.

Even so, the teacher will find occasion to have periods devoted to special English lessons; within the school's program, English as such is taught in order to improve the pupils' effectiveness in their social intercourse and expressional activities. How informal and functional the ordinary communicative situations are in real life is shown in *Language Arts for Today's Children*(11, pp. 106–07):

> Throughout his school days and throughout his life, the child will probably use oral communication much more than any other of the language arts except listening. For every word he reads or writes, he will speak and listen to a thousand. He will find in speech an outlet for his emotions, a means of presenting and defending his opinions, a way of making himself a part of his vocational or social group, and a basic tool for all his school work. His speaking will help him to co-operate with other people; at the same time it will help him to maintain his identity as an individual. What he says, and to a great extent how he says it, will be a part of his total personality and will help those who observe him—his parents, companions, and teachers—to understand his actions. . . .
>
> Speech is an all-pervasive element in daily living. The child talks while he is building, painting, modeling clay, cutting out pictures, playing in the playhouse, looking at pictures, or working simple puzzles. He talks in planning his contribution to the science exhibit or in describing the trip his group took to the post office. He uses speech as an aid in ordering his thinking. He talks to relieve his tensions, to give vent to his feelings, to control the actions and thinking of others. He needs to talk to gain increased control over his speech mechanism—to use effectively his teeth, tongue, lips, and breath in speech that is meaningful. He needs to talk if he is to develop socially. He is, in many present-day classrooms, as free to talk as he is to move about. He must talk if he is to be in touch with others, if he is to communicate with them in the most efficient manner. At the same time, he recognizes that he must not interfere with what others are doing.

From the preceding quotation several implications on basic teaching procedures may be drawn. In the first place, oral language should receive emphasis in the school program. Oral language is said to be *the* language; written language merely records part of the ideas that might be spoken. Secondly, considerable oral expression is an accompaniment of physical activities and is a phase of social living in which much of the talk reflects feelings of companionship and is not particularly intended to convey ideas of significance. Teachers should, therefore, provide opportunities for children to chat as they paint, draw, construct articles, and look through their library books.

A related third point is that a class should often be subdivided into small groups which, while carrying on a joint enterprise, discuss their plans and problems, prepare committee reports, and report progress to the class as a whole. Children are known to be more effective—natural, poised, direct, forceful, clear—when speaking to a single child or a very small group of companions, rather than an entire class. Only rarely should pupils stand before a class and give a planned story or a formal report, though this type of procedure may be advisable if the production is for an assembly or program.

In the phrase "providing every possible opportunity for his development" the teacher will also have to consider a fourth implication: there is more to the oral aspects of language teaching than giving children frequent opportunities to speak. It is implied that the teacher should specifically design lessons to improve the quality of children's speech and to develop still further their skills of speaking.

A properly balanced program of oral language teaching will then include at least three types of lessons: (1) the informal exchange of ideas as the pupils are working on cooperative enterprises; (2) less frequently, compositional types of prepared talks for the benefit of the class as a whole or in preparation for an assembly; and (3) whenever need arises, training lessons with the specific purpose of improving language skills and techniques. At the primary-grade level, the last two types of lessons have much less meaning than in the higher grades. Most of the speaking that young children do should be informal and spontaneous.

The criteria for effectiveness in language are determined by its social nature. A child's speaking is successful to the extent that he engages the interest and thoughtful consideration of his audience and that they continue to be attentive and appreciative of what he is saying. The following standards may help the teacher, as well as the pupils, to judge the effectiveness of children's language:

1. Do my listeners show interest when I tell an experience?
2. Can they follow the directions I give?
3. Do they understand and accept my explanations?
4. Do I report accurately and clearly what I hear and read?
5. Am I respectful and tolerant of my companions' viewpoints?
6. Can I discuss and disagree without becoming angry or making my companions angry?
7. Am I an attentive, interested listener?

BASIC PRINCIPLES OF INSTRUCTION

Preceding chapters have outlined the considerations that underlie language teaching. Certain principles, drawn from those chapters, apply specifically to teaching oral communication:

Growth in oral language abilities parallels other phases of language development. The child then grows most rapidly in his powers of oral expression during his earlier years. Oral language is therefore particularly important in the early school years. The enrichment of vocabulary through broadening experiences, frequent opportunities to speak in situations that encourage the use of sentences, and the acquisition of ease and fluency of expression, are goals of major importance in the primary grades.

Children talk most effectively about the things they know best. Relating personal experiences, then, is an especially important type of language activity at the primary level. As firsthand experience expands the children's horizon, they increase their fund of ideas, enrich their vocabulary, learn to organize their thinking, and acquire fluency and clarity of expression. Thus children, who necessarily begin with the here-and-now, are led into expanding situations in which they become acquainted with less familiar and further removed conditions. They are led to observe more closely, to ask more discriminating questions, to attempt reasonable explanations, and to report their findings with increasing accuracy. Not until they have become thoroughly at home in a new situation or have grasped fully the pertinent features of any new experience are they ready to speak with any great degree of effectiveness. Fluency of expression results from familiarity with facts and situations.

All too often children are asked to express themselves before they have had sufficient firsthand or vicarious experiences to enable fluent speaking. Before speaking on topics not known through earlier activities, they should have looked at, listened to, touched and manipulated any unfamiliar objects; or they should have studied pictures, watched films, listened to recordings or a talk by an informed and interesting speaker, or read abundantly.

In the beginning stages of learning, the teacher should present in a concrete manner any unfamiliar but necessary language skill. Merely talking about such a skill as using a dial telephone for the first time or beginning a report with an interesting sentence will make little impression on pupils and will induce only a vague understanding of its nature. The teacher should show the children what the skill is like by using a carefully planned demonstration. For instance, he may give three possible beginning sentences for a report on a specific topic and guide the pupils in a discussion of the relative merit of each sentence. As a result, the pupils will develop for themselves standards of excellence for beginning sentences. Sentences to be evaluated might be like these:

"I'm going to tell you about a bird."
"A bird is pretty and useful."
"I think the bluebird is the best bird of all. Do you know why?"

Language should be considered a daylong activity. Since primary teachers rarely have a separate language period, they must be alert to language-learning situations that arise during the school day. Whenever children tell stories, exchange news items, plan their various classroom activities, discuss material they plan to read or have already read, or report informally on their observations, the teacher should seize every apportunity to extend and clarify vocabulary, to give experience in speaking in complete sentences, and to help children organize their thinking. Language instruction can be effective only if, throughout the school day, children are so guided that they are growing in language—both in quality of ideas and skill in expressing the ideas.

There should be definite, but not necessarily separate, instruction in listening. Since oral language activities presuppose a listener or listeners, the art of listening as a corollary of the ability to speak well needs to have attention in oral language situations. The teacher and the child speakers need to be explicit, interesting, and direct in their communication if they expect to attract and maintain attentive listening.

INCIDENTAL INDIVIDUAL CORRECTION

Much of the improvement in primary children's language will come through the use of the audience situation and their imitation of the teacher. As the children talk over their many enriching experiences, they will gain in vocabulary and will utilize sentences whose clarity and organization reflect the reminiscences of their speech. The teacher will introduce appropriate new terms, use sentences that are simple enough and yet as complicated as the children can cope with, enunciate clearly, use a pleasantly modulated voice, and otherwise act as a model which the children may imitate unconsciously.

The teacher will use incidental individual correction and will handle correction in such a way as to avoid embarrassment. Spontaneity in the child will probably not be inhibited by the teacher's suggestions for improvement if he gives them kindly and unobtrusively. Great benefit can come from suggestions given on the side to various individual children; for example, "You *did* it, Jimmy. Say 'I *did* my work.'" Or the teacher may say, "I didn't hear very well. Can you make me hear?" Thus a child may receive individual suggestions that will help him in particular to improve. The teacher may also follow the practice of saying the correct form after a child has made an error in order that the correctly used word may begin to "sound right" to the child in question.

A PROGRAM OF MEANINGFUL EXPERIENCES

The foregoing principles call for a developmental program in language teaching—one that takes into account the known facts of child development, that is concrete in introducing new skills, that provides constant guidance in all oral language activities, that is geared to the emerging demands of everyday living, and that makes daylong applications. The following activity illustrates some phases of such a development program.

One riverside city was served by a ferryboat that connected the harbor with a mainline railroad across the river; but many of the children in the city school did not know that the ferry existed. During a third-grade unit on transportation, a discussion of boats and travel by water arose. One of the pupils mentioned having seen the local ferryboat while riding in his father's motorboat one week end. Many questions arose and eventually one child asked if a school trip to see the ferryboat might be possible. Eventually the group planned to cross the river on the ferry. What a thrilling experience for the children!

During their ferryboat experience, the pupils increased their knowledge by quizzing the family at home, reading simple library books and looking at pictures, actually observing the local ferryboat, riding on it, and asking questions of the pilot. Skills that were involved in this experience were learning to use a dial telephone, introducing one's self and making clear-cut arrangements for a trip over the telephone (there was much classroom planning and most of the pupils rehearsed on toy telephones), asking pertinent questions of the pilot, and planning a sequential type of record of the ferryboat experience. The oral expressional activities included discussions at home and at school, explaining to parents the nature and purpose of the trip, discussing matters of safety and courtesy, talking over personal observations while riding on the ferryboat and after returning to school, and planning to record the whole experience.

In a truly developmental program, a child will be constantly broadening his experiences and deepening his meanings. Through such experiences he will build up a mental bank account of ideas to share with his companions; he will have a real message back of his speaking. *Intake,* or acquisition of ideas, is therefore the first half of the language program; *outgo,* or communication of ideas, is the second half.

NEED FOR SOCIALIZATION

The enrichment and deepening of experiences, however, are not enough. The developmental program must also involve many socializing activities in which the children learn to adjust to group living.

An observer noted the following social situations in one primary room. Two children were quietly discussing a new picture book. Five girls and boys were preparing the play corner for the doll's first birthday. In the play store, two others were shopping for food to serve at the party. Half a dozen girls had formed a sociable sewing circle, chatting as they worked on a new wardrobe for the doll. Gathered about the workbench were several boys busily engaged in making a table and chair just right for the doll to use. The remainder of the class were rehearsing for a program of poems and a play to be presented as a surprise to the doll family.

A class party is a pleasant social activity from which children can learn the give-and-take of human relationships.

The teacher must plan numerous occasions that call for the sharing of experiences, for the assumption of leadership in group enterprises, and for the willingness to cooperate and follow when someone else is the leader. The shy child needs to lose himself in individual and group enterprises that he will enjoy sharing with others. The overly aggressive child needs kindly but firm guidance to help him realize that others must often come first and that they merit their due share of time and activity. Through shared experiences, such as dramatization and group planning, the children in primary grades become adjusted to living together cooperatively.

Objectives to Be Attained

IF INSTRUCTION is to result in improving the quality of children's oral language, it must be in conformity to accepted objectives. This is all the more important in a program that is informal and integrated, as is the case in the primary grades. Without a check list of definite aims, language instruction may lack direction.

EMPHASIS IN THE PRIMARY GRADES

An oral language program that is geared to the facts of child development will vary in its emphases at the respective school levels. Beginners in kindergarten or first grade have previously been associated with a family whose members differ in age from the beginners'; therefore, helping the entering child to feel at home among a large group of children his own age is a major consideration for the teacher.

Because the six-year-old is a child of action, the teacher must provide much motor activity in the learning experiences of first grade. He should mix quieter activities such as listening to stories, looking at pictures, planning group enterprises, and working up cooperative chart stories with dramatic play, trips, building with blocks or boxes, painting with large movements, and rhythmic interpretation of music. The more mature seven-year-old, who tends to take in more than he gives out and who may be less active, profits from a quieter type of instruction. The interest of the eight-year-old in matters distant in time and space encourages a much broader program, and also an active one because he is a doer.

The major objective in teaching language to young children is spontaneity—a desire and willingness to talk with and to their fellows. The first prerequisite for fluent and unrestrained expression is an abundance of experiences that will provide plenty to talk about. While some children come to school with a rich experiential background, most of them need further enrichment through varied school activities.

A second requirement is an abundance of socializing experiences in which children learn to work and play together in many joint enterprises.

Such enterprises bring about much give-and-take of ideas through conversation, discussion, explanations, and other informal speaking activities. Thus children acquire a sense of belonging, a feeling of security, and a growing attitude of "otherness" in the school situation. As children find numerous occasions to talk among themselves in promoting their cooperative enterprises, they gain greater facility in their use of language—a wider vocabulary, clear-cut sentences, and correct enunciation to enable their fellows to understand their meaning. Excessive shyness or aggressiveness tends to disappear in such highly social activities.

SUPPLEMENTARY POINTS OF EMPHASIS

Two mechanical phases of language need special attention in the early primary grades: enunciation and the voice. Baby talk, lisping, indistinct speech, and substitution of sounds are among the simpler difficulties with which the teacher must deal. Deficiencies in voice pitch, quality, and volume need corrective instruction—the sooner the better.

Another important consideration in the primary language program is initial instruction in the organization of thought: (1) In discussion, the pupils should learn to stick to the point. (2) When telling stories, giving simple explanations, and making informal reports, the child should think sequentially and express his ideas in good order.

Training for language skills will become increasingly definite through the primary years; and eventually pupils should make an effort to attain currently set up standards in regard to clear-cut sentences, enunciation, sticking to the point, and interesting content. They should gradually become somewhat self-critical so that spontaneity will be tempered by their effort to improve their weak points. In training lessons, the more mature third-grade children may deliberately hold themselves to *brief* talks, with conscious effort to utilize good sentences, to narrow the topic, or to present their ideas in orderly sequence.

One set of evaluative standards set up by a third-grade group follows:

1. Did I choose a story that everyone would like?
2. Did I know it so well that I could talk right along?
3. Did I tell the parts in order?
4. Did I make the characters talk as they really would have talked?
5. Did I say my words clearly?
6. Did I use good sentences?

Types of Oral Expression and Methods of Instruction

ONLY the more informal types of oral expression are appropriate in the primary years. For instance, the children will find numerous occasions for group discussion, directions, explanations, and simple reports as they carry on their learning activities associated with their science and social studies experiences.

In connection with reading, literature, and personal experiences, they will converse, tell stories, engage in dramatic play, and stage spontaneous dramatization of the stories they read or hear. From time to time, they will have announcements to make to their classmates or to other groups.

Specific activities that will involve such types of language experience are these: (1) relating out-of-school happenings; (2) using the telephone when the occasion warrants it; (3) planning, carrying out, reporting progress in, and evaluating various learning activities; (4) explaining and giving directions for games, simple science experiments, and constructional activities; (5) reproducing rhymes and stories unfamiliar to certain classmates, or sharing favorite ones with them; (6) joining in the simplest types of group speaking; (7) engaging in dramatic play as well as creative dramatics based on plot situations; (8) telling original stories, which may sometimes be suggested by pictures that the teacher displays; and (9) reading orally when a genuine audience situation has developed.

CONVERSATION

Undoubtedly conversation is the most frequent form of expression. To the extent that school situations are lifelike, conversation will naturally enter in. Much of it will take place as the children work in small groups at the easels, as they build a play store with their blocks or boxes, or in the science center while they arrange an exhibit. Such conversational activities reveal to the teacher the children's individual interests and emotional stresses, their needs for corrective speech lessons, and their social characteristics. It is during such small-group situations that children speak with the greatest naturalness and fluency.

There are, however, occasions when the entire class will engage in conversation lessons. An occasional show-and-tell period gives the child reason for speaking about something he genuinely wishes to share with the entire group. His doing so is likely to elicit questions and remarks as some of his listeners are reminded of their similar possessions and experiences connected with these possessions. The teacher may sometimes act as the leader and direct the conversation so as to spread the opportunities to speak and to draw in the more reticent pupils. He may function as an informal model in his display of interest and courtesy. He will be pleasant and informal in manner, correct but unstilted in language usage.

As the year goes on—particularly with the older primary pupils—the teacher will gradually abandon his role as leader and act as a participating member instead. Gradually the pupils will become aware of the qualities of a good conversationalist and thus be ready to become leaders. They will come to realize that all should have a turn, that no one should monopolize the conversation, that each participant should select topics of genuine interest to his companions. They learn what constitutes being a good listener and how they may draw quiet classmates into the conversation.

Through conversation may come the realization of these aims: enriching experiences, building up a wide vocabulary, developing poise and spontaneity, and socializing, that is, effecting a joint participation of teacher and pupils.

DISCUSSION

Children find occasion for discussion as they plan together, consider their problems, settle each particular issue, or attempt to clear their thinking. The modern school day is likely to begin with a planning period to set up the program of learning activities for the day. Then, as the day proceeds, subsidiary problems arise so that discussion is called for time and again. It is possible that, in school situations, discussion is more commonly used than is conversation and that it calls for more direction. While conversation tends to ramble, discussion should be orderly and sequential; the pupils must stick to the point. In discussing issues, they need to define their problem, analyze it into its various aspects, and clearly define the points on which they need more information and clarification of ideas. Frequently the pupils will work up a list of questions to be considered.

For younger pupils, the teacher will record the questions on the chalkboard, or sometimes on a chart in cases where much lengthy investigation will be required. For older primary children, a member of the group may be able to act as secretary and keep a record of the questions that have been raised.

Discussion, if properly directed, should accomplish the following aims: orderly thinking, clear-cut sentences, and the use of precise vocabulary.

STORYTELLING

It is impossible to conceive of a primary school day without storytelling by both teacher and pupils. The stories may be about personal experiences; they may be the telling of favorite literary stories; or they may be original. Although the tales are often told to provide entertainment and pleasure, they may be sources of valuable and concrete information, vicarious experiences, and greatly increased vocabulary.

If storytelling is to make its greatest potential contribution to language growth, two prerequisites must be observed: informality and the audience situation. Much of the storytelling will take place as the children are comfortably seated in a rather compact group so that the speakers can remain seated and still be heard. At any rate, the situation should be such that the storyteller will not feel embarrassed or conspicuous; he should be at ease, natural, animated, engrossed in his story, and informal in manner.

In a true audience situation, the speaker is certain of the interest of his listeners because he has something fresh or enjoyably familiar to tell them. While children may request the retelling of a favorite tale, usually the materials will be entirely new to the majority, if not all, of the audience. A pupil may tell of an unusual experience of his own, make up an imaginative story, or reproduce one that only he has read—thus holding interest because of the freshness of his presentation. Or the audience may listen just as intently as they rehear a story they particularly like, one they are planning to dramatize, or one that is being retold so that the group may choose one of several storytellers to present the story in an assembly.

Storytelling provides an excellent means of developing children's ability to listen attentively. Whether the teacher or a pupil is telling the story, the opportunities to build up habits of courteous and close attention when another is talking are superior. There are times, of course, when the storyteller rambles or when he has selected a story with little appeal. Then his listeners tend to become restless and inattentive. Although the teacher should afterward discuss with the pupils the reasons why an audience should listen courteously, he should also tactfully help the child speaker to feel a responsibility for selecting interesting stories to tell and avoiding a rambling discourse. That is, the storyteller is fully as responsible for telling things of interest as the audience is for listening attentively. Storytelling is a two-way process.

Storytelling, if effective, should realize these aims: good enunciation, clear-cut sentences arranged in orderly sequence, poise and ease of manner, and responsibility for selecting an interesting story to tell.

CREATIVE DRAMATICS

The various curricular areas provide almost daily opportunities for dramatic play and dramatization. Situations in the social studies, natural science, reading, literature, and even arithmetic take on meaning and impressiveness as the children act them out. Whether children enact the home life of desert peoples, impersonate a raindrop and follow in action its course from lake to flower, play the story of "The Three Billy Goats Gruff," or learn to make change in their play store, they are not only learning the concepts present in the curricular materials but they are also developing the ability to talk fluently and to express ideas clearly and forcefully.

Because children have an innate tendency to dramatize, their dramatic activities aid in attaining several of the most important language objectives. Situations that might otherwise be abstract and vague take on clarity through lifelike dramatic presentation. The young children tend to identify themselves with the characters they represent and are therefore spontane-

This mock radio program provides experience in oral expression and is an interesting enterprise for listeners as well as for active participants.

ous and natural; the bashful and the overbold alike fit themselves into the group enterprise and thereby progress in their social adjustment. There is opportunity for originality and imagination. Language growth is promoted through words that children add to their speaking vocabulary. Children also gain greater facility in phrasing and ordering their sentences.

REPORTING

In the primary grades, a report is usually informal and only partially structured. For example, a boy may have seen a baby bird and will describe it in detail so that his classmates or the teacher may help him to identify it. Another child, after watching carpenters put up the framework of a house, will explain what he has observed to his interested audience (who may possibly be stimulated enough to plan a trip to see these same carpenters at work).

Presenting such a report demands a certain degree of organization of ideas. However, the organization will grow out of the nature of the topic or the experience upon which the report is based. To develop in the children a sense of organization, the teacher will plan special observational experiences, sometimes by observing pets or inanimate objects brought into the classroom and sometimes through planned trips. In preparation, he will see that questions are raised so as to direct the children's observation. On a first trip to observe spring birds, for instance, the class may help in devising a list of questions like these:

1. What is the color of the bird?
2. How big is it? Is it like a robin, a sparrow, a wren, a crow?
3. Where does the bird usually perch?
4. What kind of song or call does it have?
5. Where is its nest? Of what is the nest built? What shape is it?

In the later primary years, the child may occasionally give a planned report. Perhaps he is to tell how far his committee has progressed in carrying out an enterprise assigned to them by the class. He will probably organize this committee report in terms of the sequence of the committee's activities and conclude with a statement of things still to be accomplished. Sometimes a child may report on an out-of-school experience, such as accompanying his father to a grass fire in a nearby empty lot. Even though he reports according to sequence, he probably will highlight a vivid description of the scene of the fire. For the most part, the primary child's planning of a report will be in terms of the sequence of events. If the planned report is to be based on reading, the primary child should always have two or three questions in mind which his report will answer. Such questions, listed on the chalkboard during class discussion or written on paper by the teacher, guide the child's reading and help him to give a helpful and interesting report.

Some standards that one third grade developed for planning and giving a report follow:

1. Choose a topic that the other girls and boys want to know more about.
2. Plan an interesting way to tell it—show a sample, draw a picture or bring one, or tell it like a story.
3. Tell the facts in good order; stick to the facts as they are.
4. Say each sentence by itself.
5. Speak each word clearly and loudly enough for everybody to hear.

The values to be gained from reporting are varied. In the first place, the child must observe or listen or read accurately. He must note details of significance and later select those facts that will interest his audience and bring to them the most important facts—facts with which they are not yet familiar. He must give in proper sequence the facts that he has selected, and he must present them in a way that will interest the listeners and give a clear and accurate impression. The child will increase his vocabulary through the processes of gathering the information; he will have purposeful experiences in phrasing sentences effectively; he will have occasion to use his tongue, lips, teeth, and breath skillfully. The act of sharing information and attempting to be interesting and clear-cut in presentation will cultivate in him constructive social attitudes.

INSTRUCTIONS, DIRECTIONS, AND EXPLANATIONS

In an experience curriculum pupils are helped to learn by doing. Thus, three forms of expression—instructions, directions, and explanations—are much in demand. The pupils' planning of various group enterprises involves much working out of instructions and directions for work and many explanations of procedures. These forms of expression are usually the outgrowths of discussion, and the forms serve as a summary of the policies the pupils have adopted. There is also strong motivation for attentive listening as the teacher gives instructions, directions, and explanations to children who will utilize them in carrying on some joint enterprise. Expression that takes the form of directions, instructions, or explanations helps to attain the following aims in language instruction: sentence sense, clarity and organization of ideas, attentive listening, and precision of vocabulary.

ORAL READING

Oral reading is an activity through which the teacher or child shares with others the information, thoughts, and feelings of an author. The teacher who reads well actually "tells" the story or "says" the poem in the exact words of the author. In poetry and in many stories the language of the author should be preserved so that the full value of the selection will fall upon the ears of the listeners.

The pupil who reads orally must first understand the meaning and the feeling of the passage he is reading. He must also have learned the skills of interpreting the printed symbols on the page so that the phrasing and emphasis resemble that of conversational speech.

Some teachers may hesitate to spend time on improving the oral reading of children, thinking that reading aloud may retard the progress in silent reading. However, there are other teachers who feel that the skills of well-taught reading are actually an asset to improving the silent-reading skills. Good oral reading demands that the reader have a long eye span since he must look off the printed page to maintain eye contact with his listeners. He must also group the words for his listeners. Thus, he must use the skills already learned in silent reading in addition to oral skills for communicating thought and feeling to others.

This oral activity for children is most worthwhile if the purposes of the oral reading are specific and meaningful to the children. Listening must not be omitted from this activity, and the purposes of listening must be as well understood as those of oral reading.

There is little purpose served by oral reading when all children have one basic book from which one child at a time reads out loud. The language arts period should be one of varied experiences with many stories, poems, and activities. Oral reading is one approach which satisfies a variety of purposes and develops many skills and interests as well.

To teach the skills of oral reading, the teacher must understand the two-way process of communication. The cycle of communication is incomplete until the listener responds in some way to the thoughts or feelings expressed by the reader. This response may be silent but appreciative. The reader must acquire the skills of grouping and emphasis, must be able to interpret with facial and bodily expression, must learn to vary pitch, pause, rate and volume—all for purposes of interpreting to the listeners the thoughts and feelings expressed by printed symbols.

GROUP SPEAKING

At the early primary stage children enjoy motor and rhythmic activity. They enjoy saying rhymes together which have marked rhythms and interesting sound sequences. The old familiar nursery rhymes and other jingles are said over and over with evident enjoyment. Here, then, is the basis of a very valuable oral learning activity called *group speaking* or in the upper grades, *choral speaking*.

Through informal group speaking children enjoy and appreciate the rhythm, music, meaning, and mood of rhymes, jingles, and poems. There are many values derived from group speaking of the informal type. One important contribution is the social aspect of the language arts program. Every child in the group becomes a part of the whole production. The silent one is drawn into participation. The loquacious one learns the need for blending voices together and working with others. Listening and repeating together sequences of speech sounds in poetry or prose encourages the child to correct or to improve his speech without calling attention to specific problems. Moreover, group speaking encourages understanding, memorization, and the appreciation of children's literature that is an integral part of any good reading and language arts program.

There is no one way to begin group speaking. Most teachers encourage informal speaking by developing free response, including speech and rhythmic and dramatic activity. Selections like "Hickory Dickory, Dock," "Jack Be Nimble," "Little Miss Muffet," and other nursery rhymes contain opportunities for rhythmic speech practice and informal dramatic response. Poems such as Christina Rossetti's "Mix a Pancake," "The Little Turtle" by Vachel Lindsay, and "The Nursery Clock" suggest sound and action for interpretation with small children. The poem itself often dictates what the group will do and how.

For primary children "Say it with me," or unison method, which is used with rhymes, poems for sound or description, and some action poems is a popular way to begin. The refrain method which is used when the verse has a repetitive phrase or sentence is very easy and encourages good listening. An example of the refrain poem is "The Nursery Clock."* The teacher may read the line of verse and the children in unison or in groups, may come in on the refrain.

TEACHER: The nursery clock hangs high on the wall,
GROUP: Tick-tock, tick-tock;

TEACHER: And every morning I hear its voice call—
GROUP: Tick, tick, tock!

TEACHER: High on the wall it is running all day,
GROUP: Tick-tock, tick-tock;

TEACHER: Ticking the seconds and minutes away—
GROUP: Tick, tick, tock!

TEACHER: Each morning it hustles me out of my bed,
GROUP: Tick-tock, tick-tock;

* Louise Abney, in Louise Abney and Grace Rowe, *Choral Speaking Arrangements for the Lower Grades*, rev. ed., Expression, Magnolia, Mass., 1953.

TEACHER: At evening it's ticking while prayers are said—
GROUP: Tick, tick, tock!

The part method in which the lines are divided among pupils or groups provides extra emphasis for meaning and moods. It calls for a poem that can be set up for small group reading or speaking. Generally in the early grades the boys become one group and the girls another group or the teacher may divide the class arbitrarily down the center of the room. The poem is divided according to *meaning. No thought units should be broken in the reading or speaking.* "Five Little Chickens" is a good poem for the part method since one group may ask the question and the other group may answer it.

FIVE LITTLE CHICKENS

Said the first little chicken,
With a queer little squirm,
"Oh, I wish I could find
A fat little worm!"

Said the next little chicken,
With an odd little shrug,
"Oh, I wish I could find
A fat little bug!"

Said the third little chicken,
With a sharp little squeal,
"Oh, I wish I could find
Some nice yellow meal!"

Said the fourth little chicken,
With a small sigh of grief,
"Oh, I wish I could find
A green little leaf!"

Said the fifth little chicken,
With a faint little moan,
"Oh, I wish I could find
A wee gravel-stone!"

"Now, see here," said the mother,
From the green garden patch,
"If you want any breakfast,
You must come and scratch."

UNKNOWN

Primary teachers find that keeping individual poetry folders containing the "successful" poems used for group speaking is well worthwhile. Through work and experimentation the primary teacher will find many values in group speaking which make the language program more complete and effective.

SUGGESTIONS FOR STUDY AND DISCUSSION

1. What types of policies in primary instruction and management are likely to inhibit children's growth in language?

2. Which policies promote such growth?

3. Are there occasions when the children should refrain from talking and moving around? Explain these occasions: what they are; what genuine reasons pupils can accept for keeping quiet; what part such occasions will play in promoting social adjustment.

4. Observe for a full day in a kindergarten or first grade. Keep a log of the oral language situations you notice.

5. Evaluate the social adjustment of the children you observed.

6. What are the major ways to improve the quality and correctness of oral language in the primary grades?

FOR FURTHER READING

1. BAKER, ZELMA W., *The Language Arts, the Child, and the Teacher* (Chapter 2). San Francisco, Fearon, 1955.

2. BROGAN, PEGGY, and LORENE FOX, *Helping Children Learn* (Chapter 2). New York, Harcourt, Brace & World, 1955.

3. BURTON, WILLIAM H., *Reading in Child Development* (Chapter 10). Indianapolis, Bobbs-Merrill, 1956.

4. DEBOER, JOHN J., and MARTHA DALLMANN, *The Teaching of Reading* 205–13). New York, Holt, Rinehart and Winston, 1960.

5. GANS, ROMA, CELIA BURNS STENDLER, and MILLIE ALMY, *Teaching Young Children*. New York, Harcourt, Brace & World, 1952.

6. GILMORE, JOHN V., *Gilmore Oral Reading Test: Grades 1–8*. New York, Harcourt, Brace & World, 1951.

7. GREENE, HARRY A., and WALTER T. PETTY, *Developing Language Skills in the Elementary School* (Chapters 5, 11). Boston, Allyn and Bacon, 1959.

8. HATCHETT, ETHEL, and DONALD HUGHES, *Teaching Language Arts in Elementary Schools* (Chapter 5). New York, Ronald, 1956.

9. HERRICK, VIRGIL E., and LELAND B. JACOBS, eds., *Children and the Language Arts* (Chapter 6). Englewood Cliffs, N. J., Prentice-Hall, 1955.

10. KLAUSMEIER, HERBERT J., and others, *Teaching in the Elementary School* (253–68). New York, Harper, 1956.

11. *Language Arts for Today's Children* (Chapter 5), Commission on the English Curriculum of the National Council of Teachers of English. New York, Appleton-Century-Crofts, 1954.

12. LOGAN, LILLIAN M., *Teaching the Young Child* (Chapter 10). Boston, Houghton Mifflin, 1960.
13. PRONOVOST, WILBERT, and LOUISE KINGMAN, *The Teaching of Speaking and Listening* (Chapter 6). New York, Longmans, Green, 1959.
14. STRICKLAND, RUTH G., *The Language Arts in the Elementary School* (Chapter 6). Boston, Heath, 1957.
15. TIDYMAN, WILLARD, and MARGUERITE BUTTERFIELD, *Teaching the Language Arts* (Chapter 7). New York, McGraw-Hill, 1959.
16. WOLFE, DON, *Language Arts and Life Patterns* (Chapters 2, 4, 24). New York, Odyssey, 1961.

12

Oral Expression in the Intermediate Grades

Chapter 12 discusses the fundamental types of oral language activities, objectives and procedures in using expressional lessons and training lessons, dominating aims in the intermediate grades, and techniques in oral communication skills. Since the objectives and procedures in the intermediate and upper grades are the same, it is possible that the intermediate-grade teacher may secure some additional help by reading Chapter 13, "Oral Expression in the Upper Grades."

AT THE intermediate level, the child should grow constantly in his ability to evaluate the effectiveness of his own language and should thus be inclined to make a conscious effort to improve. As his experiences become broader and more complex, he can learn to organize his thoughts in terms not only of time sequence but also of a few major ideas with their respective supporting details.

He becomes aware of the underlying spirit of true courtesy and tends to act in accordance. For instance, he learns not to interrupt unnecessarily and yet he knows how to interrupt courteously when the occasion warrants. He tries deliberately to involve a reticent companion in the general conversation; he finds that he can disagree and still be considerate; and he learns how to avoid hurting the feelings of his associates (though he can be blunt enough on occasion). Heavier demands are made on his listening abilities as he takes more detailed instructions, alerts himself to contradictory or unsupported statements by a speaker, and engages in extended conversation and discussion with his classmates.

Discrimination in Purposes of Language Instruction

THE instruction at intermediate-grade levels continues to work for spontaneity, a dominant aim at the primary level. In addition, intermediate-grade teachers stress training in specific language skills and techniques so that the oral communication can become increasingly effective.

There are, therefore, two distinct types of lessons: (1) *expressional lessons* in which the communication of ideas is stressed and (2) *training lessons* in which the improvement of language skills is the major consideration—language skills for which needs have arisen in expressional situations. The objectives and procedures in these two types of lessons are quite different, and unless the teacher recognizes them to be so and adapts methods of instruction to the purpose of the lesson, the results will lack effectiveness.

EXPRESSIONAL LESSONS

In lessons stressing communication, the pupil is mainly concerned with the message he is trying to convey to his audience. He concentrates on *what* he is saying rather than on *how* he is saying it. The *how* may well take care of itself whenever the speaker has much to say and knows that his listeners will enjoy hearing his contribution. Here fluency, clarity, and good organization are characteristic in his well-thought-out presentation of ideas. He speaks for the same reasons and in the same way as he does outside of school: he converses; he advances and discusses plans; he explains; he tells stories and relates experiences; or he makes reports. In trying to get his message across, the pupil tends to lose self-consciousness or self-importance. To the extent that the expressional situation is a genuine one in which there is underlying purpose, he will be effective because of his earnestness, inner amusement, or thorough mastery of the information he is sharing. For those pupils deficient in oral language skills, the teacher should intersperse training lessons with the expressional ones so as to build up the automatic control of these oral skills.

TRAINING LESSONS

In the training lesson, the pupil's motive is to improve in some specific ability. His planning is centered more on *how* he is talking than on what he is saying. Each training lesson will concentrate on a particular skill that currently needs improvement. The pupil consciously tries to enunciate more clearly, to pronounce words correctly, to make his voice distinct and pleasant, to talk directly to his audience, or to maintain good posture. In trying to improve structure, he will deliberately limit his story or report to three or four sentences, each of which he keeps distinct from the others. In such lessons belong the repeating of tongue twisters, the reproduction of a familiar story in order to practice the skill of building to a climax, or the deliberate effort to add some new words to his speaking vocabulary.

STYLES OF SPEECH

The chief objective in language instruction is not so much formal correctness as the ability of children to suit the style of their discourse to the situation. For instance, it is now conceded that colloquial speech should be featured in English lessons whenever natural and informal social situations are dominant. In the conversation, discussion, dramatization, and informal reporting called for in group activities, pupils may well respond to one another in word groups that are not sentences and may sometimes even use bits of expressive slang to give punch to their speech. *Colloquial speech* is the comfortable, clear, idiomatic, forceful type that is used by literate persons when they are speaking in the informal situations of real life, whether in school or out.

However, the pupils should be helped to discard any *illiterate style* of speech, when crudities, mispronunciation, faulty enunciation, and serious errors in usage are evident. They should weed out expressions that are unacceptably provincial, mainly by substituting others that are more appropriate. Incidental individual correction by the teacher and individualized practice by the pupils are helpful here.

Occasionally there come occasions when a more *formal style* is demanded. For example, someone is to introduce a speaker, review a book, or demonstrate a process at a club meeting or assembly. Then the speaker must express himself in complete, well-rounded, and effectively phrased sentences. In developing a formal style, the pupil will need to study simple, suitable models, such as an illustrative report given by the teacher, in order to get proper standards in mind; he will purposefully rework and rehearse the proposed talk. Because situations that require formal talks come only occasionally, teachers are not justified in giving too much time to instruction on this style of speech. Most language teaching in oral communication should be concerned with the colloquial type.

Dominant Aims in the Intermediate Grades

ANY aims at the primary level that have not been attained when the pupils reach the intermediate grades should still be stressed. Those pertaining to the mechanics of oral communication should be well on the way to attainment—such as posture, poise and ease of manner, a pleasing and well-modulated voice, and clear accurate pronunciation.

Those objectives that bear on the content of the pupils' communication will still need to be stressed, largely in the direction of refinement. Vocabulary, for instance, should not only be enriched, but the use of

How to Tell a Story
(October)

1. A story should have an opening, its developing steps in good order, and a closing.

2. The opening may tell the time, place, and characters.

3. The story should keep moving.

4. The closing should be short, and it should not be given away ahead of time.

5. The speaker should show real interest in his own story.

This chart and the charts on pages 225 and 226 show the succession in one seventh-grade class's development of goals in storytelling.

words should become more and more precise. The older children may gradually learn the varied meanings a single word may have; they should study synonyms and antonyms in an effort to use words exactly and aptly. Such vocabulary study, along with the pupils' definite planning of talks so as to achieve proper organization of ideas, should yield increasingly forceful, fluent, clear, and pointed expression.

Although primary children tend to have satisfactory sentence sense, their sentences are characteristically short and choppy and frequently strung together with *and's, so's,* or *then's.* In the intermediate grades, pupils grow in their ability to perceive the interrelationships of ideas; they sense the subordination of some ideas to others. For instance, something is true *if* or *when* or *where* or *because*; and a simple sentence will not suffice to show the interrelationships of ideas. The demands for complex sentences have increased and children have to be helped to think through their sentences so that when relationships are causal, conditional, or related through time or place, connectives like the four named above are used in place of just *and.*

Gradually the pupils learn to achieve variety and style in their sentences by transposing the order of sentence parts. They will use phrases and de-

Storytelling Standards
(January)

1. Plan an opening, developing steps, a climax, and a closing.
2. Have an interesting beginning which may tell the time, place, and characters.
3. Include vivid details that will make the opening and action in the story seem very real.
4. Keep the action moving steadily and rapidly toward the climax.
5. Make the ending short and brisk.
6. Speak in an interested and interesting manner.

pendent clauses at the beginning of sentences (although the children may do this primarily to avoid beginning successive sentences with the same word). Also, in their planned and more formal talks, the pupils will make a conscious effort to open with a suitable and interesting introductory sentence and to conclude with a summarizing statement. As stories and reports become quite lengthy and inclusive, the pupils will profit from lessons on outlining which will help them to plan their talks.

SETTING UP STANDARDS

At all levels, children should help in setting up the goals for their language activities. In the intermediate grades pupils should take considerable responsibility for identifying their own goals and holding themselves to these objectives. If the goals are not complete enough, the class should come to that conclusion by noting any inadequacy in their list of goals as they apply the points to a talk, in an effort to evaluate its effectiveness. For instance, the pupils may apply the first draft of an evaluative list of standards to the teacher's demonstration of a report. Thus they check their

Guides for Storytelling
(March)

1. Plan your story according to this pattern: opening, development, climax, and closing.

2. Plan an opening that will rouse immediate interest by giving a hint of events to follow.

3. Make the characters seem real through their actions and conversation.

4. Add vivid details to your description of the setting (time and place), characters, and action.

5. Keep the action moving toward the climax. Follow the climax with a quick closing.

6. Show your own interest in the story by speaking with life and enthusiasm.

statement of goals for ambiguity of terms, overlapping of items, and omissions; then they may proceed to revise their list.

A class-made chart of standards should never be considered "finished," and a teacher may find it necessary to concentrate on a few items in the chart during any specific training period. If so, both the teacher and the class should understand why these items currently need emphasis.

Fundamental Types of Language Activities

ORAL communication is much more used in the affairs of daily life than is written expression. In school and out, adults and children converse, discuss their plans and activities, give and follow directions, explain, relate experiences, tell of their dreams and imaginary adventures, and report orally their progress or findings in some personal enterprise. There are many out-of-school days when a large number of people write not a single word; but how few there are who go through a day without saying something! And, because oral expression is so common and so necessary, it is a major part of the basic language program.

Speaking and listening may be separated for purposes of identifying specific skills and of listing activities, methods, and materials for promoting the improvement of the identified skills. However, in actual practice, speaking and listening are inevitably linked in the communication cycle. The quality of listening will be affected by the proficiency of the speaker. Needless to say, the speaker will be affected by the courtesy, attentiveness and expressed interest of his listeners.

CONVERSATION

Of all the types of oral communication, conversation (including telephoning) is the most commonly used in out-of-school living. In school, therefore, at the intermediate level pupils should have many opportunities to engage in conversation in order to learn the techniques and skills that underlie interesting, courteous, and appropriate conversation. Periods devoted to conversation should be informal, spontaneous, and lively. These may come during dramatic play, an occasional show-and-tell period when there is really something significant to display, art and constructional activities, and a free period when each child chooses his own activity (for instance, when the pupils are assembling before school opens in the morning). Children can learn to be courteous enough to give others a turn, to draw their reserved associates into the conversation, and yet be eager to participate themselves. The values of conversational lessons for the pupil lie in their contribution to his social development, in training in courtesy, and in the enrichment of ideas and vocabulary. In addition, the teacher has a rich opportunity to observe the customary speech patterns and fundamental interests of individual children.

DISCUSSION

Any modern schoolroom has countless occasions for discussion as the pupils plan their work and evaluate what they have already accomplished. Discussion is certainly one of the most valuable language activities. Through it, children clarify their thinking, gain new ideas, learn to think for themselves and to form reasonable judgments. Standards to be stressed in discussion are these: sticking to the point at issue; making only those remarks that carry the thinking forward; correcting misinterpretations; expressing ideas in clear-cut sentences; listening for specific points; following continuity in thinking; speaking clearly and with good voice projection so that all can hear. Pupils who are given many chances to discuss matters that are vital to the group and who are helped to keep the above standards in mind are likely to develop clear thinking and effective speech.

EXPLANATIONS

Closely allied to discussion are expressional activities that feature instructions, directions, or explanations. The standards for these language activities are much the same as the standards for discussion. Indeed, these three types of language activities are often imbedded within a discussion as children plan an enterprise, demonstrate it, carry it through to its conclusion, and evaluate it. In giving directions, instructions, and explanations effectively, children must necessarily be concrete and precise, accurate, terse, and well-organized in their statements. Perhaps of all the types of language activities, these three best reflect the quality of thinking and afford opportunity to improve the thought processes of the individual pupils through carefully guided practice. On the receptive side, pupils get excellent experience in *listening* attentively as their classmates give instructions, directions, and explanations.

REPORTS

Although reports may be in written form, those in the intermediate grades are frequently oral. In developing a child's ability to give an effective report, instruction is centered around the ideas that he wishes to express. The reporter-to-be must learn the techniques of reading and research that will aid him in locating materials; and he must acquire the ability to appraise and select pertinent facts and to make accurate, orderly notes. Furthermore, he must realize the necessity for a thorough mastery of the facts, ideas, or events to be reported and for his proper organization of them. He must learn by experience how to plan and think through what he is to report to ensure adequate comprehension and clear-cut impressions on the part of his listeners. As a part of preparation for presenting a report, he should learn to make a brief outline of main points and hard-to-remember data.

Properly motivated and well-prepared reports are a truly functional form of expression. The speaker-audience relationship is a highly desirable one; the reporter has a real message to convey, and the listeners are gaining interesting supplementary information. A good report is characterized by proper sequence and structure of sentences, an enriched vocabulary, and a businesslike directness and forcefulness on the part of the speaker.

The pupils observing this candlestick maker at work with authentic colonial tools are getting reliable information to report.

Another form of carefully planned, precise expression consists of special occasion talks. Here some pupil may introduce an outside speaker to the class and thank him after the talk; some child may go to another classroom and invite the group there to see a play his group has worked up; or a pupil may announce the play to a visiting group. Special occasion talks call for planning to ensure a clear, appealing, complete presentation of ideas.

STORYTELLING

Storytelling should have an important place in the language program of the intermediate grades. Children delight in stories, whether the teacher tells them (and he should tell many) or whether they themselves read and reproduce them. The teacher should encourage the children to write original stories. Some girls and boys have a flair for making up purely imaginative stories that are highly interesting. Effective storytellers use colorful words, plan an attention-getting opening, keep the action brisk, tell the events in proper sequence, keep the outcome in doubt until the end, and speak distinctly. These characteristics suggest the standards that the pupils should keep in mind.

DRAMATIZATION

Closely allied to storytelling is dramatization, which holds the appeals of the story but adds to it the pleasure of dramatic activity. Children tend to lose themselves in the parts they are playing, so that the timid and repressed child usually overcomes his reserve and his fear of an audience. Besides developing socially, the child who plays a story acquires new words and ideas, learns to think in good sequence, and tends to develop a more flexible voice and improved enunciation. To the extent that he is able to contribute original interpretation and action to his part, he is creative.

ORAL READING

Since the intermediate-grade period is a time when pupils acquire lifetime reading skills that determine reading rate, there should be less oral reading in this level than in primary and upper-grade levels. However, during silent reading the teacher may sometimes find passages that are just right for oral reading. Mildred A. Dawson and Henry A. Bamman say that by planning carefully, the teacher can provide an audience situation in which a group will listen expectantly to the reading of a passage by another pupil, even though the group may know already what is in the passage.

More important are new materials. They will provide a genuine audi-

A wealth of visual materials adds substance and interest to this girl's oral report.

ence situation because the plot of each passage has not already been revealed. Dawson and Bamman(4, pp. 208–09) have made a list of audience situations in which each pupil reads material new to the other members of the group:

Materials New to the Audience

I. Sharing of some favorite literature
   A. The pupil reads an entire selection in a single-copy reader.
   B. He reads part of a well-liked book so as to persuade others to read it for themselves.
   C. He displays self-made illustrations or the illustrations in the book and reads the part that has been illustrated.
   D. He pantomimes action, letting the audience try to interpret it, and then reads the actual account from the book or story.
II. Sight reading of simple materials, using either a periodical or a book
III. Reading of cut up stories (These are clipped from a magazine, then cut into sections to distribute among a number of pupils who prepare to read the parts in sequence.)
   A. The parts are numbered to help each reader to know his turn.
   B. The parts are unnumbered so that each reader is "on his guard" to recognize his turn.
   C. The title is omitted so that the main part of the story will suggest an original title to the pupils; later there is comparison with the actual title.
   D. The last section is retained by the teacher so that the listeners have an opportunity to make up original endings before the ending is read.
IV. Sharing of individually volunteered materials
   A. Jokes are clipped from a paper. (Teacher-approved, just to make sure!)
   B. Anecdotes about famous people may be read.
   C. Supplementary information that will help a class project is used.
   D. Materials are screened and selected for an assembly.

In addition to providing audience situations, the teacher should provide all intermediate-grade pupils with training lessons on specific skills. Elements to be trained are enunciation, voice, fluency, and emphasis on key ideas.

CHORAL SPEAKING

Good oral reading of prose and poetry expresses the meaning, rhythm, and mood which the author intended in the selection. Group reading should aim to do the same. It is important that children understand the meaning of a selection as a whole and, of course, the meaning of words, phrases, and thoughts before attempting to read the selection aloud to others. When words are grouped well, the meaning is clear. When words are emphasized well, as in good conversational speech, the meaning becomes clear to the listeners. When meaning, rhythm, and mood are expressed by an individual or group, the selection becomes real, vital, alive, and the listeners give response to the reading.

The teacher of intermediate-grade children must be careful to present group speaking so that meaning of the selection cuts across meter and rhyme. If this is not done either by the teacher's own reading or by a study of meaning *before* the group reads together, the result will be a singsong pattern devoid of meaning or beauty. If the child knows what the lines mean in the poem and if he reads it the way he would say it, consciously or unconsciously he can be encouraged to group or phrase his words in a conversational, meaningful pattern for his listeners to hear.

Prose pieces such as "The Pledge to the Flag" may be studied for meaning and followed by learning the skills of grouping, emphasis, and use of pause. Remember that marks of punctuation are for the eye and may or may not tell us what to do with our voice. The *meaning* of the selection and the *ears* of the listeners are guides to good conversational speaking and reading.

Fundamental Techniques in Oral Expressional Skills

IN TEACHING the skills demanded in the ideational phase of oral expression, the teacher should use certain basic instructional techniques. Pupils' curricular experiences in oral language should parallel their activities in other lessons and their out-of-school real-life experiences at home and in the neighborhood. To be effective in influencing pupils' ways of speaking, the language class should in itself be a true social situation with the best of group dynamics in constant operation.

At all ages, children learn through doing. They should acquire the skills of oral expression in a context of genuine social situations where they learn to be effective in actual conversation, purposeful discussion and explanations, shared storytelling, entertaining creative drama, and informational reports. Committees of successful teachers have found the following procedures to be advisable:

1. Set up, or take advantage of, a genuine occasion for oral communication.

2. Direct the pupils in an effort to meet this situation through the use of group dynamics and increasingly effective techniques of oral expression.

3. Advise with the pupils as they plan and prepare their more formalized reports and stories; also raise stimulating, evaluative questions to help pupils to see how they may improve the quality of unrehearsed, spontaneous discussion.

4. Through constant self-evaluation, lead the pupils to realize that they

are successful in their oral presentations to the extent that they convince, inform, or entertain their audience; help them to see what the causes of their success or failure may have been.

5. Encourage pupils to rehearse their planned presentations; provide needed practice in effective oral reading techniques, use of the voice, proper posture, good enunciation, and other specific skills.

6. Help the pupils to realize their specific progress, especially by comparing success on various similar occasions, by using tape recordings, and by referring to records kept as the class had applied their lists of goals as standards for evaluation.

In the more formal type of expression, which unusually gifted children may enjoy when important and hard-to-find information is to be presented, a definite cycle of steps may characterize the language lessons. Here the pupils need to plan with care and in detail. The cycle is as follows:

1. *Purposing.* The pupils suggest, or are led to suggest, topics about which they may talk and the audience situations that they may utilize.

2. *Setting up standards.* This step is a recall of needs as revealed by criticism in previous lessons or by an inventory. The use of a teacher's model will help to clarify any standards that are relatively unfamiliar to the pupils. The teacher can write the standards on the chalkboard, post them on a boldly lettered bulletin-board chart, or have the pupils file them in their notebooks.

3. *Organizing.* The pupils think through what they have to say while keeping the standards in mind.

4. *Expressing.* The pupils talk.

5. *Criticizing.* The teacher and pupils cooperate in giving first, favorable criticism; second, helpful criticism and suggestions.

SUGGESTIONS FOR STUDY AND DISCUSSION

1. Analyze a chapter in each of several language textbooks and determine whether expressional or training lessons are more stressed. (It should be a chapter containing considerable oral language experiences.)

2. Similarly, analyze several hours of lessons that you observe.

3. Training lessons in oral expression have to do with *how* the pupil talks. List some skills, other than those mentioned in this chapter, that could be improved by the use of training lessons.

4. Read several references on oral-language instruction in the intermediate grades. Keep separate notes on the expressional and the training aspects. Then make an outline of chief points in each area, and write a summary.

FOR FURTHER READING

1. BANY, MARY, "A Discussion Technique for Settling Conflicts." *Elementary English* (April 1958), 223–26.
2. BROGAN, PEGGY, and LORENE FOX, *Helping Children Learn*. New York, Harcourt, Brace & World, 1955.
3. DAWSON, MILDRED A., "The Role of Oral Reading in School and Life Activities." *Elementary English* (January 1958), 30–37.
4. —— and HENRY A. BAMMAN, *Fundamentals of Basic Reading Instruction* (Chapter 12). New York, McKay, 1963.
5. DEBOER, JOHN J., and MARTHA DALLMANN, *The Teaching of Reading* (205–13). New York, Holt, Rinehart and Winston, 1960.
6. GABEL, MARY THERESA, "Helping Children to Express Themselves Orally." *Elementary English* (November 1957), 459–61.
7. GILMORE, JOHN V., *Gilmore Oral Reading Test: Grades 1–8*. New York, Harcourt, Brace & World, 1951.
8. GREENE, HARRY A., and WALTER T. PETTY, *Developing Language Skills in the Elementary School* (Chapters 5, 11). Boston, Allyn and Bacon, 1959.
9. HATCHETT, ETHEL, and DONALD HUGHES, *Teaching the Language Arts in Elementary Schools* (Chapter 5). New York, Ronald, 1956.
10. HERRICK, VIRGIL E., and LELAND B. JACOBS, eds., *Children and the Language Arts* (Chapter 6). Englewood Cliffs, N. J., Prentice-Hall, 1955.
11. JOHNSON, LOIS V., "The Process of Oral Reporting." *Elementary English* (May 1958), 309–13.
12. JONES, MORRIS VAL, "Choral Speaking in the Elementary School." *Elementary English* (December 1958), 535–37.
13. KLAUSMEIER, HERBERT J., and others, *Teaching in the Elementary School* (253–68). New York, Harper, 1956.
14. PRONOVOST, WILBERT, and LOUISE KINGMAN, *The Teaching of Speaking and Listening* (Chapter 6). New York, Longmans, Green, 1959.
15. STRICKLAND, RUTH G., *The Language Arts in the Elementary School* (Chapter 8). Boston, Heath, 1957.
16. TIDYMAN, WILLARD, and MARGUERITE BUTTERFIELD, *Teaching the Language Arts*. New York, McGraw-Hill, 1959.
17. WOLFE, DON, *Language Arts and Life Patterns*. New York, Odyssey, 1961.

13

Oral Expression in the Upper Grades

Chapter 13 continues the discussion of oral expression begun in Chapter 11 and continued in Chapter 12. Expressional lessons and training lessons for older children are described. Emphasis in the upper grades is on specific language skills and techniques. Both formal and informal types of expressional activities are delineated. It is suggested that the teacher of the upper grades read Chapter 12, "Oral Expression in the Intermediate Grades," as a preliminary to this chapter.

THE preadolescent of the upper grades responds to nearly adult types of language situations. In speaking, young children evince little meeting of the minds. Each one speaks of some self-centered experience that is somewhat related to the topic at hand; but older girls and boys are ready to challenge one another, to note omissions and discrepancies in reasoning, and to thresh out a controversy. There is a group consciousness among older children that must be guided into fruitful channels and not allowed to develop into a destructive, gang-type organization.

Informal Types of Expressional Activities

As AT the primary and intermediate levels, *conversation, discussion, directions, instructions,* and *explanation* are important phases of the language curriculum in the upper grades. These types of informal expression are called for throughout the school day as lessons in various subjects include activities that implement the treatment in the textbook, as artificial subject-matter lines are broken down through curricular correlation and integration, and as the teacher emphasizes language all day long.

For instance, the class may develop a historical mural that summarizes progress in transportation due to a series of inventions; they may be preparing for a Book Week assembly featuring modern children's literature; or they may be at work developing a nature trail in near-by woods. Abundant opportunities for informal speaking arise in the course of carrying out such enterprises.

An especially important aspect of oral language in the intermediate and upper grades is committee deliberations where the skills required in group dynamics are important. It is through committee activities that pupils have occasion to learn (1) the responsibilities of leadership, (2) the difference between leadership and dictatorship, (3) the importance of having participation by all, (4) a way to keep a record of the percentage of participation, (5) the responsibilities of a secretary or recorder, (6) the desirability of consensus on questions that arise, and the like. In the upper grades, children must have clear objectives for carrying on effective committee work, meeting specific deadlines, and preparing frequent progress reports if the committee is a long-term one. There should, of course, be constant teacher guidance in committee work.

Probably a teacher should know his class pretty well before going far into committee work; gradually he should move into the practice of dividing a class into committees. For instance, early in the school year a question may arise which is suitable for investigation by two or three pupils working together. Before the teacher selects this first committee, the class should discuss thoroughly the setting of the problem, its clear definition, sources of information that may best be consulted, the ways of working as a committee, and the possible time and methods of reporting to the class. Thus, the members of this first committee appointed by the teacher can go about their work with confidence and efficiency.

From time to time, the teacher should select different pupils to work on committees; for example, to hold an interview to secure needed materials from different places in the community, to write letters for various useful purposes, and so on. Training for committee work should be a gradual process; only after most of the pupils have had some such directed experience with committee work should the teacher divide the class into various committees to work simultaneously on related activities. Gradually there will have been introduced the various processes of group dynamics that train pupils in leadership, participation, recording, and evaluation.

Another type of informal discussion that is common in the upper grades is the talking over of literary selections. Here the questioning by the teacher is a critical factor. Poor questioning will result in an ineffectual pupil-to-teacher reciting of isolated facts and details. On the other hand, thought-provoking questions that induce an insightful consideration of the setting, plot, characterization, and theme of a literary selection will arouse pupil-pupil as well as pupil-teacher discussion.

Good questions make pupils think, not merely remember. Such questions rarely begin with *who, when,* or *where*; rather they begin with *how, why, compare, contrast,* or *show.* There may be such questions as these: What would you have done? Which character would you have liked best? Why? When did you first suspect how the story would end? How might the story have ended if Tom had not received the message in time?

Formal Types of Expressional Activities

REPORTS

Among the most useful and interesting forms of planned talks is the report. Even so, teachers and pupils alike often dread hearing reports because pupils may use materials from reference books almost *verbatim,* and speak in an expressionless, disinterested manner. Teachers should have a series of lessons that will show pupils how to locate materials, select only the pertinent information, take running notes, organize the materials in an interesting manner, and present the ideas concretely. How to give a good report is not learned by accident.

While reports should be carefully and thoroughly prepared, they should not be memorized *verbatim.* The reporter should be direct, should maintain eye contact with his audience, and be almost conversational in manner. Therefore, he should "talk off" his report in an unstilted manner. He may need notes for reference so that he can keep his ideas in proper sequence and will have detailed data for exact presentation. The first section of an outline which was prepared to guide an oral report is given **below.**

An Archaeological Discovery

1. Description of document
   A. Clay tablets
      1. Over 4000 years old
      2. From Tigris-Euphrates valley
      3. With inscriptions in cuneiform characters
   B. Work of archaeologists
      1. Story assembled from 22 fragments
      2. Translation made from Sumerian language

When a report contains considerable detailed information that is relatively unfamiliar to the class and is known to be of value and interest to

This well-informed boy is reporting and demonstrating in a spontaneous and direct manner to an intrigued audience.

its members, the reporter is responsible for being highly effective. He may be the one source for presenting these particular facts. It may be that he should rehearse after preparing his notes. For rehearsal, the following procedures are suitable: (1) The students may pair off and, two at a time, may practice on their talks by giving them to one another in a distant corner of the classroom or in the hallway. (2) Each student may tape record his report and evaluate his own prospective presentation. (3) The entire class may be divided into groups of four so that each reporter can practice first with an audience of three before taking the time of the class. As small-circle groups are in operation, the teacher may go from one group to another with constructive suggestions.

Perhaps the most common weakness in any oral presentation that has been planned ahead of time is the speaker's reliance on reading what should actually be spoken. Without constant effort by the teacher, oral reports are likely to be largely copied from printed sources, or written hastily and then read before the class. The practice of providing each prospective reporter with a set of questions to be answered in his report will usually prevent copying materials and giving them *verbatim*. The questions help him to select and eliminate ideas, to organize, and to give ideas in his own words. Any class that has heard a report that is largely a duplicate of a section of the encyclopedia can easily tell why such a report is boring and ineffective and can understand the basic—though unintentional—dishonesty of presenting as one's own report something that has been copied from a book.

If an unusually significant report is to be written out and read aloud, it deserves careful preparation both in the writing and in the delivery. Preliminary planning by teacher and pupils should establish appropriate and inappropriate occasions for reading a report. In general, if notes are used as reminders, practice in oral reporting can develop pupils' ability to speak directly to the audience, with considerable freedom of expression within the boundaries of a planned outline.

Special guidance can help pupils to prepare satisfactory reports on current events. Without such guidance, the pupil usually gives one or two introductory sentences, then carelessly reads the item or snatches of it, often with poor phrasing and mispronunciations that indicate lack of preparation and understanding on the part of the reporter. Pupil-teacher planning should specify when current-events reports may be read and when they are better given without direct reference to the printed words. Only when the printed material is presented in an unmatchably superior style or when it is very detailed and statistical should a current-events item be read. Usually the report is a better one if the pupil does not refer directly to the printed words.

The first prerequisite for a report is a purpose for giving it. For ex-

The audience is absorbed in this debater's arguments, which may later be refuted or supported.

ample, the pupils may need additional information for carrying out some group project, or they may wish to find entertaining episodes to add to a play about Abraham Lincoln. Another requisite is that the reading matter should be simple enough for the pupils to understand. In assigning reports based on reading materials, the teacher should give a list of questions to guide the reader in selecting the important ideas. Pupils in the upper grades should be able to select crucial information for themselves, but they will need guidance in the techniques of taking suitable notes— including the exact reference and page—and organizing information taken from more than one source. Only through step-by-step training in a series of carefully planned lessons will pupils gain the ability to combine data gleaned from several sources into well-organized reports.

DEBATES

Formal discussion, such as planned debates in the upper grades, closely resembles the report in its make-up. In formal discussion, the pupils prepare ahead of time the arguments and validating proof in respect to some well-defined issue. Precision of vocabulary, exactness of statement, variety in sentence structure, and effective arrangement of ideas are necessary features when pupils participate in debates, symposiums, and other formal types of expression. Unless the research is adequate, the logic good, and the proof sound, argument is weak. Because many problems suitable for debate demand greater experience and judgment in public affairs than elementary children have, debate merits little emphasis in the language program except for the more mature and able among the older pupils. It is a relatively adult form of expression.

ORAL READING

Oral reading is another form of communication important in the upper grades. Occasionally a pupil may write out a report and later read it to the class. This will be when statements must be very precise, detailed, and technically correct; for instance, he may have found a news item that he wishes to read to his group. Literature is much enjoyed when individual pupils choose portions of their personally selected books that they wish to share with their classmates, or when a puppet play or pantomime parallels the oral reading of a story or play. In case there is any disagreement or uncertainty about a bit of information, a pupil may read orally from an authoritative source.

These are but a few examples of the kinds of oral reading situations that may arise again and again in any curricular area. It will be necessary, of course, for the teacher to select reading materials having a wide range of difficulty so that individual differences in children's reading proficiency can be met.

Some pupils need teacher demonstrations to show that oral reading can be done smoothly. The demonstrations show the pupils that, as listeners, they find it easy to interpret meaning because the teacher's phrasing is clear and the voice inflection is suited to the mood and action of the literary selection. Out of courtesy and respect for his audience, any child should read orally *only after careful preparation.* The oral reader must understand the meaning of his selection and know the pronunciation and significance of all the words. In all ways, he must do his best to give his audience an interesting, meaningful, authentic impression.

DRAMATIZATION AND STORYTELLING

Social studies and literature are especially fertile grounds for dramatization and storytelling. These activities take on a creative flavor as the pupils work out original plays and stories based on information and plots derived from their books but modified by interpretation. At times, it is appropriate for these older pupils to reproduce stories. This is true when a pupil tells part or all of an individually selected story for the entertainment or enlightenment of his listeners, or when he is trying to induce them to read it for themselves.

Mainly, however, such reproduction is done as part of a training lesson for practice on enunciation, sentence structure, or organizational thinking. For such training lessons, it is preferable that the teacher draw stories from study-type materials rather than literature. Using literary materials for such lessons might reduce the pupils' appreciation of the literature.

CHORAL SPEAKING

Today there are few schools where some form of group or choral speaking is not used. There are two distinct uses: the verse choir for audience enjoyment and the choral group speaking for classroom participation. Sometimes a group will become so proficient that they take part in an assembly or program. In the classroom, however, practice is chiefly for enjoyment and improvement. When the choral group become performers, they have reached a high enough level of achievement so that the audience enjoys and appreciates the selections read.

The values for upper-grade pupils are many and include: (1) building and developing an appreciation of poetry, (2) cooperating with a group with one purpose in mind, (3) learning the skills of good oral reading, and (4) enjoying good literature.

Choice of selections and arrangement of the selection chosen are very important to success with group speaking. The upper-grade teacher might well approach group speaking by studying a prose selection such as "The Gettysburg Address" for meaning. Skills of grouping, emphasis, pausing and variety in volume, rate, pitch and pause can all be taught in prose. Good oral reading is basic to good group speaking of prose or poetry.

The wise teacher will choose simple arrangements for the first attempt with poetry. A lively rollicking ballad with a refrain line for the chorus or humorous selections like "The Grand Old Duke of York," "Jonathan Bing," and "Poor Old Woman" are excellent for interest and relatively easy to say together. Solo and group parts may come next with the arrangement and choice always dependent upon the meaning and feeling inherent in the selection.

Pupils in the sixth, seventh, and eighth grades are well aware of differences in voice pitch. Grouping by pitch may be done quickly by the teacher if he asks each pupil to count to five in a good strong tone. Classes usually may be grouped by picking light and dark (high and low) girls' voices and light and dark boys' voices. After the initial division into four groups the teacher can check on wrong placement of voices by having each group count from one to five together since the high or low will stand out in the group response. By using this kind of grouping, differences in pitch and volume can be utilized in many selections that appeal to the upper-grade pupils.

The development of social values in the group process may bring many desired results; in addition, the opportunity to teach the skills of oral reading, the skills of speaking, and the art of good listening is, of course, of definite advantage to the upper-grade teacher. But whatever the reading selection and approach chosen, the teacher will do well to remember that appreciation and enjoyment of prose and poetry should be the first aim of this oral activity.

Improving Pupils' Expression of Ideas

MUCH of the improvement of oral language skills and techniques comes through training lessons. However, just as we learn to skate by skating, so do we learn to talk by talking—talking freely and naturally. In expressional lessons, much can be done to improve the quality of the pupils speaking.

Charlotte Wells(14, p. 202) states very well the functional viewpoint as she discusses speech in the full-school program. She says:

> But specifically, what can the teacher do? In what general ways can she assure the best possible speech habits in her pupils? First, she can stop taking for granted that the speech of the student is the best he can achieve. Second, she can create an environment conducive to good oral work. Third, she can observe the speech of her students and call the attention of the group to the most prevalent need for improvement. Fourth, she can

suggest specific approaches to improved speech. Fifth, she can maintain an awareness, in the group, of the importance of speech in all classroom discussion. Sixth, she can encourage her students to better speech by her example as a speaker.

THE AUDIENCE SITUATION

In the modern school the pupils are sharing their actual and vicarious experiences with their classmates whenever they speak. Listening should be made as important to them as speaking, for each member of a group must speak according to what he is hearing and to the way he interprets what he hears. Each speaker and listener must help to carry the group's thinking forward. The speaker realizes that he must be effective if he is to instruct, inform, convince, persuade, or entertain his audience; his listeners are conscious that they may miss something interesting and worthwhile, something that they may not be able to get elsewhere, if they do not listen intently when someone is telling something or reading aloud what he has prepared.

The presence of an audience that is interested in hearing what a speaker has to say is powerful motivation for effective expression. Any communication of informal or formal type can create a good audience response whenever the speaker is sharing information unfamiliar to his listeners, reporting on his part in some group enterprise, or entertaining through stories and dramatization—provided he has been wise in selecting his materials and that he presents them well.

IMITATION OF A MODEL

All through a child's school years, imitation influences the quality of his language. The teacher may be a helpful model if his enunciation is clear, his voice pleasant and well modulated, and his manner direct. Imitation may also lead to inferior language, as is shown by the child's tendency to adopt slang and incorrect usage picked up from some of his classmates because he prefers the approval of these classmates to that of adults.

The teacher can make constructive use of imitative tendencies by setting up a model or demonstration for some new standard. In the upper grades, and sometimes in the intermediate grades, a capable pupil may present a talk that illustrates clearly the use of such a standard for a stimulating opening sentence in a planned discourse.

The teacher should rely heavily upon repeated demonstration as a supplement to the pupils' spontaneous observation and imitation of their associates' speech. Lest the pupils imitate a model discourse too closely and allow their productions to become stereotyped, the teacher should avoid using the exact topic they will be using; still, there should be enough similarity in the topics to stimulate the children to think up interesting presentations of their own that conform to the standard. Wisely used, the model helps to improve the quality of the children's oral communication.

INCIDENTAL INDIVIDUAL CORRECTION

The use of incidental individual correction is effective in helping each pupil to overcome his particular weaknesses and difficulties. All during the day the teacher should be on the alert to notice the serious errors and emerging language needs of the pupils, no matter which subject is being taught at that moment. The incidental individual correction *should not interrupt* the pupil's line of thought or embarrass him. In most instances, the teacher will wait until the end of the period in which the error has been made and then unobtrusively tell the child the right way to use the word in question. This is particularly true in the case of word forms or speech habits that have not yet been given much direct teaching.

Whenever a pupil continues to make an error or shows a weakness for which there have already been several corrective lessons, the teacher should remind him of the correct form as soon as he has concluded his remarks. If there is a chart hanging in the room as a reminder of the correct way to speak, a nod toward the chart may be enough of a hint for the pupil so that he will voluntarily correct himself.

THE RIGHT USE AND CHOICE OF WORDS

Oral expressional lessons furnish pupils with an opportunity and an incentive to broaden their vocabulary and to develop their ability to compare words so as to choose the one best suited to express an idea exactly. The teacher may either write an ordinary composition—probably one that he has worked up—on the chalkboard and let the pupils suggest more graphic synonyms for expressions therein; or he may leave blanks for expressive verbs, adjectives, and adverbs to be provided by the children.

To stimulate pupil interest in graphic words, the teacher should give attention to unusually apt expressions in a literary selection. When they are dramatizing, the children should make a definite effort to include such words in their dialogue. Thus they enrich their vocabulary and become more precise in their speech.

Some pupils enjoy keeping a list of interesting words they find in their reading and putting such words to use in their own speech later. Study of word derivations and the analysis of words into prefixes, suffixes, and roots may be useful experiences. Upper-grade pupils should make a definite effort to develop their powers of discrimination, and they should cultivate an interest in the study of words, thus adding to their own effectiveness in speaking and writing.

PLANNING

Americans are notorious for not having (or taking) time to think. Probably one reason children in school do not make due progress in improving their language is that they do not have time to plan what they will say; and if they have the time, they do not know how to use it in making plans. Especially in the more formal types of oral expression, pupils should think through what they plan to say so as to have their ideas effectively arranged and to have in mind the words that will best convey their meaning. In the beginning, the teacher will probably have to have several training lessons in which he and the class will plan together a report or an explanation to be given in an assembly. In this way, the children can perceive what is involved in making plans.

CRITICISM

Not every expressional lesson should include criticism. Whenever appreciation or creativity is the purpose of the lesson, the teacher should keep criticism to a minimum. However, a large share of the lessons devoted to oral communication should include some helpful evaluation so as to keep each pupil acquainted with his current needs and to hold him to standards previously set up.

In the early part of each year's work, the teacher should offer most of the criticism, since pupils tend to notice trivial points and often fail to see the more fundamental qualities that make speaking either effective or ineffective. The teacher is naturally more discriminating. He will take care not to overcriticize the backward child; he will give favorable comments and praise, but only where it is merited; he will *avoid all destructive criticism* and give helpful criticism instead. He will not say, "Tim, you talk too fast"; but, instead, he will say something like, "Tim, that was an interesting story. We liked it. If you will remember to speak more slowly, we can enjoy your good stories even more."

Pupils should be inducted into criticism gradually. The teacher should ask them to consider a single standard while he is checking the others. Usually pupils will give several talks before any criticism is offered. For the sake of variety, the boys may be responsible for one standard, and the girls for another; or the pupils may choose one of their number to be the critic that day. From time to time, the teacher should introduce new ways of criticism; for instance, the use of the tape recorder may give the children an objective and relatively impersonal basis for criticism.

Whatever the system of criticism, these criteria should be kept in mind:

1. In the early stages, pupils should restrict their criticism to the standards that have currently been set up; the teacher should supplement this with further evaluation.

2. The teacher should make sure that pupils are trained to detect the really commendable and the essentially weak features, and not to concentrate on trivialities.

3. Pupils should always give favorable criticism first.

4. Pupils should give *helpful* criticism—suggestions for improvement of weaknesses. Negative criticism is out of place.

At the upper-grade level, the pupils are advanced enough to give pertinent and judicious criticisms. The critic and the criticized both benefit from the discriminating evaluation of the strong and weak features of an oral discourse.

Training Lessons in Oral Communication

THE sole purpose of a training lesson is to introduce or practice a specific language skill or technique. In such a lesson, spontaneity may be partially inhibited in order to stress a currently needed skill. In the early primary years, when spontaneity is a major objective, training lessons have little or no place, except perhaps in the area of speech skills such as enunciation. As more and more technicalities are introduced in the intermediate and upper grades, the need for training lessons increases.

A series of training lessons, which will usually include a lengthy and detailed development lesson and brief follow-up practice periods, should immediately follow the discovery of the need for such training. (The development lesson is described in the chapter on correct usage.) The pupils' need for training in a specific language skill will be revealed in various ways. The teacher may make notes of such needs as children are observed in their spontaneous conversation and discussion during their free time and in different classes; or on the other hand, he may take a systematic inventory through the use of a check list. However, upper-grade pupils should carry as much of the responsibility as possible for applying their goals as standards and identifying their own needs for training. This they will do as they give supplementary reports, use reference books such as the dictionary, and otherwise engage in language activities that require specific skills. That is, pupils will discover language needs as they engage in activities in which unfamiliar skills are required. Another way they will identify their needs will be through the helpful criticisms they give one another during expressional lessons.

When a teacher has identified a language deficiency in certain pupils, he should demonstrate clearly to these pupils the corresponding skill and see that they practice it thoroughly. Soon, they will come to use this skill automatically in their spontaneous oral communication. It is only as training lessons carry over into expressional lessons that the former type can

Compare the unpleasantly vehement delivery of this boy with the poise and naturalness of the speaker pictured on page 239.

be justified. Drill for its own sake is not an acceptable part of the language program.

SKILLS AND TECHNIQUES TO BE TRAINED

In Chapter 3, "Language Program in the Total Curriculum," the objectives for language instruction are itemized; they are listed under several categories, including content and mechanics. The former list has to do with the *what* of expression: choosing appropriate subjects, using sentences rather than fragments, organizing ideas properly, and acquiring an enriched vocabulary. There are also such techniques as those required in preparing reports; for instance, locating materials, taking notes, organizing materials, and also finding ways of making the presentation concrete and interesting. Similarly, each phase of oral communication has its peculiar techniques. Thus, conversation and telephoning, discussion, explanations and directions, and storytelling have their own techniques, some of which may need separate attention in a series of training lessons.

The mechanical phases of communication have to do with the *how* of expression: how good the pupil's posture is, how he enunciates and pronounces words, how he modulates his voice, and how direct and poised he is in addressing his audience. Here the skills of speech need training. (Chapter 7 is devoted to the improvement of speech skills.)

MATERIALS TO BE USED

The teacher can derive much practice material from a language textbook. All language books contain exercises designed to demonstrate the nature of each requisite oral skill and to provide directed practice in using it. The teacher should make use of such materials at a time when they are specifically pertinent to the emerging needs of the pupils by selecting from the exercises those materials that are currently appropriate.

It is possible that a textbook will set up instructional units so appropriate and well organized that any teacher who maintains a separate daily language period may feel it wise to follow the textbook page by page. Most modern-minded teachers, however, will use their textbooks selectively so as to relate their instruction to language needs currently arising in the various curricular areas. They will also use their textbooks to adjust their language teaching to the individual differences among their pupils, who will frequently vary in their language needs at any particular time.

Readers and various other textbooks will also provide materials that are suitable for training lessons. They include glossaries and indexes which are useful in teaching the techniques for locating information; the use of topical sentences and the construction of a good paragraph can also be taught with such books. For instance, pupils can analyze various selections to determine how topical sentences or good beginning sentences are used in information books and to note the organization of paragraphs in a several-page excerpt. The teacher should avoid the use of literary selections for any such analytical purposes.

At times, the pupils may also talk of personal experiences, even in a training lesson. Whenever they do, their consciousness should be centered on improving their way of expressing themselves.

PROCEDURES FOR IMPROVING SENTENCE STRUCTURE

Skill in sentence construction depends on a knowledge of what a sentence is. The problem, then, is to develop sentence sense. As an aid in solving this problem, the teacher should adapt the following suggestions: (1) The word *sentence* should be used from the very beginning of the first year of reading instruction. (2) From this time on, the teacher should insist on the use of sentences in oral communication whenever it is natural to use them. (3) Within a training situation, the children should think through what they want to say, then say one thing at a time, in a sentence. (4) The children who have poor sentence sense must have practice exercises that will help them to distinguish between a sentence and a sentence fragment. (5) In learning to eliminate run-on sentences, the children may give three-sentence stories and descriptions, the topic being selected from a list provided in the textbook or on the chalkboard, e.g., *my pet, my favorite game, my hobby.* The children should take time to plan the three statements before they speak.

Language Arts for Today's Children (10, pp. 239–40) gives the following advice on the development of sentence sense:

> The search for synonyms for overworked words is important in the intermediate grades to stimulate concrete and effective expression.
>
> Development of sentence sense at the intermediate grade level can be related to this problem. Building sentences by adding descriptive modifiers to such a base as *horse ran* or *boys rode* is a game children enjoy and one which helps them understand both the base of a sentence and the effective use of words. Reading aloud the resulting sentences shows the interesting variety of pictures presented.
>
> Reading aloud what they have written and listening to their sentences helps children to sense completeness, to discover omissions, and to detect elements lacking in clarity.

Some teachers utilize the children's learning of the grammar of the sentence for helping pupils to develop a better sentence sense. Bright pupils who are able to understand the abstractions of grammar can so use their learnings; but many upper-grade pupils have not yet attained the maturity to make use of grammar. A "meaning approach" is more likely to be helpful for most children. Here the children get their ideas clearly in mind, then work to phrase their sentences so as to make their meaning as clear as possible. Oral reading helps the pupils evaluate such sentences.

PROCEDURES TO IMPROVE ORGANIZATION

Pupils' initial experiences in organizing ideas come as they relate an event or a story in proper time sequence. Further experience comes as they dramatize stories, especially those in which there is a succession of acts or scenes. Storytelling based on pictures is one of the better means of providing practice in sequential thinking. By questioning along the following lines, the teacher can help the pupil to have a definite beginning and ending for his story:

1. What has already happened; or, how did the story start?
2. What is happening right now in the picture?
3. What do you think is going to happen next; or, how will the story end?

The good beginning sentence and a summarizing ending sentence are often appropriate in informational types of communication. Children may work at this scheme for developing a single paragraph. Subsequently, pupils will deal with talks that develop more than one main point and will therefore require more than one paragraph for their talks. The teacher will stress the fact that each paragraph must have a central idea; thus outlining becomes an essential aid. Outlining in connection with selecting the main ideas in brief selections in readers and textbooks will be developed, probably more in connection with written communication than with oral.

Some of the following procedures may prove helpful in developing the ability to organize: (1) The pupils should limit talks, especially in training lessons, to a single phase of a topic. (2) The pupils should begin a story with the four W's: *who, when, what, where.* (3) The pupils should think through their communication before giving it. (4) The teacher may utilize dramatization, picture stories, and reproduction as incidental means of developing a sense of the proper sequence of ideas. (5) The pupils may analyze and outline selections in readers and other textbooks. (6) Occasionally the pupils should work over some of the rambling talks that have been presented and tape recorded.

Setting Up Standards

TEACHERS in all school systems need manuals and guides to help them decide on the goals that should be stressed at the various levels. Committees of teachers should work with their curriculum director (their supervisor, their principal, or a group-chosen chairman) to set up developmentally sequential lists of goals. The one that follows was developed for oral expression in the upper grades and high school in the Portland, Oregon, public schools. Such a list gives the teachers a helpful background for subsequent cooperative pupil-teacher planning of goals.

Improvement in content and organization

1. Having something worthwhile to say
2. Organizing ideas through effective plans, outlines, or notes
3. Presenting ideas rather than memorized words
4. Speaking fluently
5. Expressing ideas clearly and sincerely
6. Using an adequate vocabulary, chosen for exact meaning
7. Avoiding sentences strung together with "and's," unnecessary repetition, and vague expressions
8. Moving from one idea to another in smooth transition
9. Presenting ideas with courtesy and awareness of the feelings and response of the listeners
10. Showing enthusiasm and interest in the subject

Improvement in technical skills

1. Keeping eye contact with the audience
2. Exhibiting poise and good posture
3. Pronouncing words correctly and articulating well
4. Using good inflection
5. Speaking loudly enough for all to hear, in a well-modulated voice
6. Using notes, if necessary, without distracting the audience
7. Employing good usage in verb forms, pronoun forms, adjectives, and adverbs; avoidance of double negatives, etc.

Frequent experiences in common speech situations to improve content and organization

1. Speaking in social situations; e.g.,
   a. Conversing in an interesting way
   b. Making introductions easily
2. Explaining or persuading; e.g.,
   a. Participating effectively in discussion
   b. Giving short prepared talks
   c. Contributing constructively in committee deliberation as a member or a chairman
3. Reading orally; e.g.,
   a. Reading prose and poetry
   b. Dramatization

Standards should be set up by pupils, under teacher guidance, as soon as the pupils discover a need for improving their oral language in some way. In a lesson following the setting up of standards, they will work to learn how to put the resulting standard into effect. Often the teacher can make a standard understandable by a demonstration. In expressional lessons, the setting up of standards should consume little time, and the teacher should not emphasize them to the extent of inhibiting spontaneity.

However, pupils usually should have certain standards in mind when they talk; otherwise, their presentation may be ineffective. The teacher should see that training lessons are interspersed with expressional ones whenever standards need lengthy consideration and practice. Pupils can be spontaneous and yet consciously hold themselves to being clear, orderly, and interesting in their presentation.

In the upper grades, pupils need much help and direction in setting up and applying standards to their use of *logic* and *evidence* in their speaking, particularly in discussion. They should learn to ask questions like the following: Did you think straight, or did you "get off the beam"? Why do you think so? What facts do you have for proof? Are they enough to warrant your conclusions? Where did you get your idea? Who said so? Was he qualified to know? Was he biased? Are your reasons good? Are there better reasons? The teacher should alert the pupils to their own tendencies to make broad, unwarranted generalizations or to be gullible when they hear such statements. Critical thinking is important.

In the early part of the school year, the teacher and pupils should consider only one or two of the most needed standards. If there are two, one may be on a mechanical feature, such as voice or posture; the other should be on the ideational side of speaking, such as using graphic words or keeping sentences separate from one another. Gradually the pupils will add other standards, though they should not try to set up more than two (or possibly three) in any one lesson. If learning is to be permanent, the pupils must occasionally review the standards they have already set up.

One of the most productive ways in which pupils can set up standards is for them to make a cooperative list of the things they believe they should keep in mind as they talk. They can make a chart from this list, and each pupil can copy it in his own notebook. Beside the list the child can draw narrow perpendicular columns, a column for each remaining month in the school year. Then each pupil may check off each standard on the month when he believes he has mastered its use. After the pupil knows what is meant by a standard and how to use it, an effective method of individualizing instruction is to have the child choose his own individual standard to keep in mind before giving a talk.

SUGGESTIONS FOR STUDY AND DISCUSSION

1. Why is it important that a child prepare carefully before he reads orally?

2. Why should criticism be kept to a minimum during expressional lessons?

3. Why are training lessons more appropriate in the higher grades than in the lower ones?

4. Read several references on oral-language instruction in the higher grades. Keep separate notes on the expressional and the training aspects. Then make an outline of chief points in each area, and write a summary.

FOR FURTHER READING

1. DAWSON, MILDRED A., "The Role of Oral Reading in School and Life Activities." *Elementary English* (January 1958), 30–37.

2. ———— and HENRY A. BAMMAN, *Fundamentals of Basic Reading Instruction* (Chapter 9). New York, Holt, Rinehart and Winston, 1960.

3. DEBOER, JOHN J., and MARTHA DALLMANN, *The Teaching of Reading* (205–13). New York, Holt, Rinehart and Winston, 1960.

4. GERBER, PHILIP L., *Effective English* (Chapter 7). New York, Random House, 1959.

5. GILMORE, JOHN V., *Gilmore Oral Reading Test: Grades 1–8*. New York, Harcourt, Brace & World, 1951.

6. GREENE, HARRY A., and WALTER T. PETTY, *Developing Language Skills in the Elementary School* (Chapters 5, 11). Boston, Allyn and Bacon, 1959.

7. JOHNSON, LOIS V., "The Process of Oral Reporting." *Elementary English* (May 1958), 309–13.

8. JONES, DAISY M., "So You Have Something to Say!" *Elementary English* (April 1959), 248–52.

9. KLAUSMEIER, HERBERT J., and others, *Teaching in the Elementary School* (253–68). New York, Harper, 1956.

10. *Language Arts for Today's Children,* Commission on the English Curriculum of the National Council of Teachers of English. New York, Appleton-Century-Crofts, 1954.

11. LOBAN, WALTER, MARGARET RYAN, and JAMES R. SQUIRE, *Teaching Language and Literature* (Chapter 9). New York, Harcourt, Brace & World, 1961.

12. PORTER, ELEANOR, "The Problem: To Say What You Mean." *Elementary English* (October 1958), 388–90.

13. PRONOVOST, WILBERT, and LOUISE KINGMAN, *The Teaching of Speaking and Listening* (Chapter 6). New York, Longmans, Green, 1959.

14. WELLS, CHARLOTTE, "Speech in the Full School Program." *Elementary English* (April 1951), 201–04.

15. WOLFE, DON, *Language Arts and Life Patterns* (Chapters 2, 4, 24). New York, Odyssey, 1961.

14

Written Expression in the Primary Grades

Chapter 14 explains how written communication is related to the other language arts and to the total curriculum. It describes writing experiences of graduated difficulty which can be successfully completed by children in the primary grades, beginning with the first sentences composed and dictated to the teachers and leading up to a variety of writing tasks to be done independently as soon as the mechanics of handwriting are learned. Suggestions are offered for measuring progress in writing ability, and a suggested program for each of the primary grades provides a guide to goals suitable for most children.

THE responsibility for developing skill in the use of written language, unlike oral language, lies almost entirely with the school. Children have help at home in learning to talk, and they enter school with considerable skill already developed. In writing, however, the instructional program begins in school, literally from scratch. As it becomes necessary for children to label their papers or possessions, to keep a record of their plans, to write the story of their experiences, or to express their original ideas, the teacher must deal not only with the thoughts to be expressed but also with the elementary skills of writing, even including how to form the letters and how to spell the words.

From the first, children's writing experiences should be directed toward the level expected of them when they complete their schooling. Indeed, the strength of a primary teacher's instruction lies in the fact that his efforts to help children develop power in the use of written language have long-range value as well as immediate worth in the day-by-day activities of a busy primary room. Primary children learn the importance of thoughtful writing at their own levels of maturity; for example, making correct statements, using words that say what they mean, and giving clear explanations. Their early writing experiences should help them to organize their ideas and present them clearly; to learn the common forms and conventions of written English and the ways of applying them appropriately in their daily writing; to appreciate the need for courtesy and promptness in writing messages; and to take pride in doing their writing tasks well.

Writing—An Integral Part of the Curriculum

THE degree to which a child expresses himself spontaneously and interestingly will depend largely on the number of stimulating facts and ideas he has to express. An integral and inseparable part of the language program, therefore, is the *intake* that the curriculum provides—that is, the acquisition of information and ideas. A teacher must stimulate his group in various ways. For instance, a story hour featuring exciting adventure is an experience that will challenge thinking, open new avenues of learning, enrich ideas, expand vocabulary, and provide many occasions for communication of ideas. The richness of the *intake* will determine the quality and quantity of the *outgo*. As children gain ideas and feel a desire to express them, the teacher can help the children to master the skills that will enable them to express their ideas with optimum effectiveness.

What kind of school environment contributes most toward this intake upon which a good program in oral and written communication relies? Usually firsthand experiences are most vivid; for example, articles to show and tell about, exhibits to arrange and explain, experiments to perform and demonstrate, a pet to feed and care for, a party for room mothers, a visit with a postman, a walk around the schoolyard, or a trip to the airfield. Sometimes films, filmstrips, and slides supply experiences that children cannot have at first hand. All such experiences introduce new words or give new meanings to old words and thus expand the child's vocabulary. They provide ideas to express; stimulate questions to be asked and answered; supply a need for making plans, listing duties, keeping records, and writing stories. Where such vital experiences are going on, writing tasks become a natural and important part of the curriculum.

Before children write, their teacher should always encourage discussion of the topic wherein they develop qualities in oral communication that also are desirable in writing. Sometimes the girls and boys tell or dramatize a story, thus developing a plan of organizing details. They learn to stick to the point. Their practice in choosing words to convey their meaning and putting new vocabulary to use helps them to develop a command of language that will serve as usefully in writing as it does in speech.

Reading and listening also contribute to a child's preparation for writing. A picture file and simple illustrated books at hand for browsing and reading stimulate his thinking. The teacher who makes time in his daily schedule for reading to his pupils from storybooks and poetry often finds that children respond creatively with stories and poems of their own. If the children are not yet skilled enough to write for themselves, they compose orally and sometimes dictate to the teacher so that he can take the stories or poems down.

Opportunities for creative expression in many other forms may stimulate further written language experiences. Painting, clay modeling, hand puppets, and papier-mâché work are engrossing, and they often yield satisfaction that serves as a stimulus for writing. A story explaining a child's painting or finger painting, an explanation of the object he has modeled in clay or papier-mâché, a dialogue for his puppets—all such activities make writing an integral part of the complete primary program.

Developmental Steps in Learning to Write

COMPOSING AND DICTATING TO THE TEACHER

The first steps in learning how to express ideas in writing are taken long before children can write for themselves. In order that skill in the use of language may be developed to the greatest extent possible, the teacher plans many opportunities for expression in which he serves as scribe. At first the pupils compose *cooperative compositions* wherein all join in dictating a story to their teacher. They plan the story as they go along, the natural sequence of the action reported providing the basis of organization. Stories of the pupils' own experiences, their plans, their responsibilities, and their records of information make them realize the importance of written communication, both for themselves and for others, for immediate reading and for later reference.

Experience charts can be particularly useful in preparing children for writing. The following purposes should direct the teacher in using them:

1. Have the children express their ideas on a topic that is familiar and interesting to them.

2. Stimulate thinking about the topic by questions or discussion.

3. Encourage the children to try consciously to express themselves well for the written record. Comments and questions can direct their thinking: How shall we start our story? Can someone think of a better way? Do you like that way of saying it?

4. Develop a sense of organization by guiding questions, if necessary,

A chart prepared by the children reflects the rich information acquired by caring for a hamster in the classroom.

such as these: What did we do next? How does our story end? What shall we name the story?

5. Help children to evaluate their expression of ideas. Ask them whether they have said what they mean; whether there is more that should be said; whether they have told their story in the right order.

The form in which charts are written should serve as a model of neatness and attractiveness. For group reading, paper 24 by 36 or 24 by 30 inches permits room for the story and an illustration. Letters should be well formed, large, and black enough to be easily distinguished. Margins should be observed, and, when appropriate, a child's picture illustrating the story adds to the attractiveness of the paper and furnishes picture clues for the reader. By starting each sentence on a new line, the teacher helps children develop an understanding of the sentence as a unit of thought. Writing in paragraph form may well be postponed until the third grade, especially for the average or slow learner.

In general, the teacher may be guided by the form used in the basal reading book which the pupils are currently using. If the book is arranged sentence by sentence, then the chart should be similarly composed. If the reading book uses short paragraphs, the chart may also use short paragraphs. As the teacher writes the chart, he should call attention, incidentally but consistently, to such conventions as a capital letter at the beginning of the sentence and a period, question mark, or exclamation point at the end.

At the primary level, one of the most useful types of written communication is the letter, usually in the form of a note with only the greeting for a heading. The child may address this note to Mother or to an absent classmate. Or he may address it to a commercial firm to request free materials or the privilege of making a visit. Usually, pupils first discuss what should be said in the note, plan the proper sequence for treating the topics, and then dictate sentences to the teacher.

One danger for the teacher to avoid in teaching cooperative composition is permitting the writing to become a formal exercise. The lessons should not be isolated, unmotivated exercises; instead, they should be vital, worthwhile, pupil-directed enterprises. Cooperative composition should arise in connection with activities that the pupils have a genuine reason for wanting to record.

Another possible danger to be avoided is the tendency to permit a few leaders to dictate for the group all of the time. Cooperative composition should involve the active participation of all, if possible; at the very least, the less aggressive members of the group should be encouraged to contribute their ideas.

Even after children have begun to learn writing in manuscript, the

These children are making silk screen prints for their class newspaper.

teacher frequently performs the function of scribe. In this way, he relieves children of the full burden of writing at a period when handwriting and spelling skills are not yet automatic. He knows that pupils cannot give full attention to content if they are doing their own writing and must give laborious care to the mechanics of writing.

Dictation may be done singly by individual children as well as cooperatively by a group. *Individually dictated stories* may merit a chart for the class to read, particularly if the news is important and interesting to others (like the arrival of a baby brother or sister), or if the individual needs the encouragement of having a story of his or her own creation made important. Other ways of sharing stories dictated by individuals include using the stories in a classroom paper which is duplicated for the children to take home; making them into a *Big Book of Stories* for the reading table; having them written on a section of the chalkboard labeled *Our Own Stories.*

Sometimes a teacher invites individual pupils to make up their own stories and dictate privately to the teacher. As each child is telling his story, the teacher may write it in manuscript or on a typewriter with primary type. The large print and neat-looking page that carries his message is indeed impressive to the young child who dictates it.*

Mary Bundy Gr. 2.

I have a pony.
His name is Trot.
Every time I call him,
he runs away.

This individually dictated story was written in the early half of the second grade. Mary had drawn a picture of her pony and wanted to write a story about it. The story was dictated to her teacher, who wrote it on a piece of paper. Later Mary copied the story from the paper.

Such experiences, whether devised by individuals or small groups or the class, make writing seem to be worthy of one's best efforts. In this way, children build favorable attitudes and attain practical experience in such

---

* Mildred A. Dawson, *Language Teaching in Grades One and Two*, New York, Harcourt, Brace & World, Inc., 1949.

matters as unity of subject matter, organization of thought, choice of words and phrases, and fluency of expression. Although pupils do not actually practice the mechanics of writing, observation of the teacher's writing, whether he writes in manuscript or uses a typewriter, furnishes some preparation for a later period when independence in writing develops.

DEVELOPING WRITING SKILLS THROUGH TRAINING LESSONS

In dictating their ideas to the teacher, the children are able to concentrate on the ideas they wish to express. However, they need to develop skill on the technical side of writing, and the teacher must plan to develop this technical skill. The demands of spelling, handwriting, punctuation, and capitalization tend to engage most of the children's attention and effort as they begin to do their own writing.

It is for this reason that *copying* is a desirable first step toward learning to put ideas into written form. The materials to be copied are those that an individual pupil has dictated to his teacher or those that have been worked out in the cooperative compositions just described. Many teachers do not make copying mandatory every time, but offer the suggestion that some pupils might like to copy the story from the board or from the chart to take home or to use in an illustrated booklet. Such an invitation is usually accepted by most children who are ready to profit by the effort of copying. Unless the teacher supervises the copying and gives individual help as needed, its value as a learning device diminishes.

After the slower-learning pupils have done some copywork and become familiar with the mechanics of manuscript form, capitalization, punctuation, and sentence form, they are ready to take *studied dictation*. (Quick-learning children more easily acquire a mastery of mechanics through observing the teacher write, noting usage in their printed reading materials, and copying the stories they have dictated.) In studied dictation, a group of children develops a cooperative story which the teacher writes on the board. Then the teacher helps the children to notice the placement and capitalization of the title, the capitalization and punctuation for each of the sentences, the margin, the spelling of any difficult words, and the shape of the letters used in the words (by examples in manuscript form).

The teacher should list on the board in the order of their occurrence any unfamiliar or difficult words that might prove troublesome. The children may then consult the list during the process of taking dictation. When they have completed the study, the teacher covers the composition by a map or curtain, but he does not erase it. He then dictates the composition from a copy he has made for himself.

Dictation requires a specific technique when given to immature and slow-learning children: (1) The teacher reads the entire story while the pupils try to recall the number of sentences and the punctuation to be used. (2) The teacher reads the entire first sentence while the pupils think about the capitalization, spelling, and end punctuation for that sentence. (3) The teacher reads the first phrase of two to five words while the pupils listen, then repeat it aloud. (4) The pupils write what they have just repeated. (5) The teacher reads the next phrase while the pupils repeat it, and then write it—and so on, phrase by phrase (6) The teacher and pupils treat each successive sentence in the same way. This detailed procedure provides for the short attention span of immature pupils and it assures the near-perfection that is desirable in developing new skills.

When the pupils can write creditably from dictation after preliminary study of the composition, they are ready for another training task, a step higher in difficulty—taking *unstudied dictation*. Again, the story is one which has been dictated to the teacher. Without the help of seeing the selection first, the child must recognize the sentences by ear and apply the forms he knows regarding manuscript writing, capital letters, punctuation, and spelling. When the selection includes words that might be misspelled, the teacher should write them in order on the board for reference as the children write from dictation. The composition should be brief and simple in construction. The procedure in giving unstudied dictation is identical with that for the studied type.

During the process of copying or taking studied dictation, the pupil's attention is largely given over to the mechanics or skills of writing rather than the ideas to be expressed. Most children need at least a few lessons such as these in order to learn the basic skills demanded in effective writing. Some children pick up such skills quickly, almost incidentally, and should not be held to a long series of training lessons in which they copy and take dictation. On the other hand, slow-learning children should have a considerable amount of such training, and, of course, the materials should always be simple enough to ensure that the slow learners get creditable results.

PROGRESSING GRADUALLY TOWARD WRITING INDEPENDENTLY

There are many kinds of writing experience that seem valuable and interesting to children, yet do not impose very heavy writing tasks. The teacher is wise to plan many experiences that are simple enough to be completed successfully as children begin to try their hand at independent writing.

The examples that follow will suggest good writing assignments for the beginning writer:

The *unfinished story*, as the name suggests, is developed to a point somewhere short of the conclusion. While the main part is written by the teacher, from cooperative dictation, the last sentence or sentences remain for each child to develop as he pleases. In the same way, an *unfinished letter* may be composed by the class and written on the board by the teacher. The last part may be left incomplete for individual responses. Here is an example of an unfinished letter:

COOPERATIVE COMPOSITION: DEAR MRS. STONE,
    Thank you for the party.
    The cookies and juice were good.
    The circus was **fun**.

CONCLUSION
    BY CHILD 1   I liked the clown.
    CHILD 2   I liked the band music.
    CHILD 3   I liked the elephants.
        They did a funny dance.
            Love,
            Marty

Writing *captions,* either titles or sentence descriptions of pictures, is another first step in independent writing. Children may draw or paint pictures to illustrate what they have seen and studied. They may write the caption for the picture on a separate paper or on a space ruled off below the picture. Its brevity makes it suitable for beginners, yet it demands some degree of maturity since either title or sentence description requires stating the main idea of the picture.

A variation of this kind of assignment is made for a series of pictures that tell a story, with one or more sentences to describe each picture. Here the teacher takes a long strip of paper and folds it into three or four sections. When the paper is laid out flat, the creases show dividing lines where each new picture begins. The drawings are explained by the captions written at the bottom of the paper. By such a simple writing experience as this, children become aware of sequence in time, and they soon develop a sense of appropriateness for beginning and concluding a story. Differences in ability are readily revealed in such an assignment, but each child can find satisfaction in completing his story at his own level of achievement.

Even the best pupil will at times wish to use words he cannot spell. The teacher should encourage him to follow some of these suggestions: (1) leave a space for the unknown word; (2) write as much of the beginning of the word as he thinks he knows; (3) write the probable spelling on an extra slip of paper and, if it looks right, use it; (4) think through the story before beginning to write and ask the teacher to list difficult words on the board; (5) keep a piece of paper on his desk so that the teacher may quickly write down any word asked for; (6) look up the word in the spelling word box or picture dictionary or in a reader where he knows the word can be found; (7) keep a spelling notebook with a separate page devoted to words beginning with the respective letters of the alphabet, including all the useful words that he would like to study for himself. From the first, the teacher should encourage the children to spell correctly and to be independent as far as possible in ascertaining the spelling of hard or unfamiliar words.

VARIED KINDS OF WRITING EXPERIENCES

The school day brings many opportunities for different kinds of writing. In planning the types of writing experiences, the teacher bears in mind the goals he hopes to have the children approach. Room records, duty charts, and all writing that children do in relation to room activities will require his particular attention to accuracy in the statements of facts. Children should write on charts their lists of room responsibilities and the names of leaders or committees. The charts should have shallow pockets that can be used to insert children's names as the names are changed from time to time. Announcements, such as reminders to other children or descriptions of lost-and-found articles, may require a regular space on the board.

After the sharing time, when the children have exchanged interesting information orally, many teachers have them dictate cooperatively some statements for their daily news. The teacher should see that the date is correct and that the children have selected the facts on the basis of importance or special appeal. Pupils should also record plans for room activities other than those related to studies. Weather records and records of the growth of plants or animals require the pupils' careful observation and accuracy in writing. They may organize listings of radio and TV programs, recommended for in-school and out-of-school listening, under classifications such as music, stories, science, health, or social studies.

Study time suggests other kinds of writing. Having the children list questions that need to be answered is often a first step for the teacher in presenting a new subject for study. Since it is important that the children keep the list as a guide for working and a source of evaluation later, they or the teacher should write the questions on a chart. Sometimes the subject they are studying requires classification of objects or pictures, or gathering of data. They may need a list of the books read by members of the class or a list of the books in their room that have stories about the subject they are studying. They may write and mail letters requesting information. Vocabulary lists can serve them as reminders of new words they have learned or as an aid in the spelling of words they may use in written work.

Outlines, explanations of facts, accounts of what happened from day to day, summaries of what was learned, and pupil-made questions and answers in review can provide the pupils with frequent opportunities to summarize the most important learnings in their unit of work. At the end of the unit, the class or individual members may draw up statements of evaluation and possibly the application of learnings, such as a listing of health practices or safety measures.

In addition, there should be opportunity for a more personal expression in writing. Children enjoy writing stories, created out of their imagination, about other people or personified animals (but often related to their own experiences, too). With encouragement from an appreciative audience of classmates and wise but unobtrusive guidance by the teacher, this kind of writing can yield gratifying growth in vocabulary development, in selection of detail and adherence to the point of the story, and in sensitivity to the choice of phrasing and even to the building of suspense or surprise.

Friendly letters also serve as a good means of sharing thoughts and feelings with others. Recognition of the need to write about things the reader would find interesting is a concept that children can develop particularly well through letter writing if they are sure they will receive answers. Some teachers make sure of a response to children's letters by instituting correspondence between two rooms of the same grade level in different schools, either in the same school system or far apart.

Children who hear poetry frequently often express their thoughts rythmically. When pupils express sincerely what they observe, feel, and think, teachers may write their sentences as poetry, regardless of the lack of rhyme or measured meter. One teacher, finding that a sentence in the midst of a child's story brought an expression of appreciation from the class, said, "It sounds like a poem, doesn't it? We can write it that way." And with the addition of a title, it did make a lovely poem.

CLOUDS

The clouds float by.
They look like ladies in lacy dresses
Dancing in the sky.

In this way the teacher helped the children to understand that poetic expression is more than a rhymed jingle, that it sets forth in lines of pleasing rhythm a word picture or a thought that rings true.

Rhymes and jingles, too, have their place in the children's writing experiences. The wonder of words, their meanings and double meanings, the music and humor of rhyme can furnish genuine entertainment along with a growing knowledge of the English language. Greeting cards, rhymed or unrhymed, serve as a satisfying kind of writing even when children are just beginning to write independently. Riddles and jokes may be written and tacked on the bulletin board so that everyone can enjoy them.

A Curriculum for Written Work

ONE of the best ways to keep a check on children's progress in written expression is to watch the skill develop over a period of time. By keeping samples of written work in folders for each individual, the teacher gathers evidence of progress to help himself, the parents, and the child himself. A page of writing done by a first-grade child in the first few weeks of school may have no more than the child's name and date on it. A few months later, a page neatly copied from a cooperatively dictated story written on the board will offer proof of rapid growth. For such records a teacher should save something every week or two during the school year.

Papers that represent different kinds of writing experiences should be kept and filed by the children themselves. As the children file them, they can periodically watch their progress by comparing former work with their current papers. The old adage, "Nothing succeeds like success" applies here, for children derive real encouragement from their improvement and they are inspired to further achievement.

The teacher's appraisal of each individual's written products must be made in terms of the child's potential ability, his background of experience, and the growth he shows in the skills and abilities which the teacher has tried to help him develop. While every primary teacher is aware of the wide differences in ability among his pupils and the consequent need for modifying any program to fit the needs of the pupils, it is valuable to have in mind the sequence by which skills are usually developed by children as they progress through the grades.

PROGRAM FOR FIRST-GRADE WRITTEN COMMUNICATION

When children attempt to communicate in writing, the product of their efforts can exhibit no more skill than their training and ability will permit. The unusually proficient pupil will be able to go far beyond this program; the one who is quite slow to learn should be expected to advance only as far as he is able. The outline below indicates the general aspects and major details in a desirable first-grade program.

Growth in vocabulary

1. Understand new words gained through experience, and put them to use.

2. Know and use technical terms such as *sentence, capital letter, small letter,* and *period.*

Acquaintance with sentences

1. Recognize a sentence in print or manuscript writing, usually by having it read orally.

2. Express ideas in short, clear, and interesting sentences.

Organization of ideas

1. Stick to the point in dictating experience stories.
2. Tell experience and fanciful stories in proper time sequence.

Writing skills (beginning stages)

1. Use correct manuscript form.
   a. Head papers in accordance with locally prescribed form.
   b. Write (in manuscript lettering) clearly and neatly.
2. Use capital letters correctly.
   a. Form capital and small letters correctly.
   b. Capitalize the first word of a sentence.
   c. Capitalize special names: the pupil's own; teacher; school, town and street.
   d. Write the word *I* as a capital letter.
3. Use correct punctuation.
   a. Use a period correctly in ending sentences.
   b. Use a question mark correctly in ending sentences.

PROGRAM FOR SECOND-GRADE WRITTEN COMMUNICATION

In the second grade, as in other grades, pupils differ widely in capacity and achievement in the area of written expression. Each teacher has the responsibility of planning his language program so that every child will progress at his appropriate level. Since children are more nearly alike than they are different, they may work in a single group or in several smaller teams in most aspects of the language program, with the teacher's giving individual help as soon as the need for it emerges. A little help given at the right time is usually adequate. A suggested outline for the second grade is given below, with the understanding that each child will achieve to the extent that he is able to perform.

Growth in vocabulary

1. Use correctly and appropriately new words met during ongoing learning experiences.
2. Recognize increasingly different meanings for the same word. Use intelligently such technical terms as *sentence, capital letter, small letter, period, question mark, comma, greeting, closing, margin.*

Acquaintance with sentences

1. Realize that a sentence tells or asks something.
2. Recognize the signs of a sentence: complete "sound" when read orally, and beginning capital letter and end punctuation—*stop* and *go* signs.
3. Express ideas in short, clear, and correct sentences.

Organization of ideas

1. Stick to the point.
2. Express ideas or facts in order of time sequence.

Writing skills

1. Use correct manuscript form.
   a. Head all written papers correctly according to locally prescribed form.
   b. Leave margins as prescribed.
   c. Write (in manuscript lettering) neatly.
2. Use capital letters correctly.
   a. Master the items listed for first grade.
   b. Capitalize special names: a pet's; terms: *Mr., Mrs., Miss.*
3. Use correct punctuation.
   a. Use period and question mark after statement and question, respectively.
   b. Copy correctly comma in date, after greeting or closing of personal note; periods after numbers in a listing.
4. Spell correctly through use of helps suggested by the teacher.

Major activities

1. Copywork
   a. From chalkboard
      (1) Cooperative story or personal note
      (2) Announcement
      (3) List or memorandum
   b. From teacher's note pad
      (1) Label or picture legend
      (2) Individual story or personal note
2. Dictation
   a. Careful observation of mechanics in story while having preparatory supervised study
   b. Attentive listening during dictation
   c. Conscientious effort to write correctly
3. Independent writing (by each individual whenever he is ready)
   a. Experience stories; creative stories
   b. Simple note of thanks or an invitation to assembly
4. Self-evaluation and self-correction
   a. In respect to all major activities itemized above
   b. Use of the model in the child's locating his own errors or weaknesses

With proper guidance and stimulation in the preceding grades, children in third grade should have acquired considerable ability in writing independently and in checking on their own accuracy in writing. Whatever skills have been initiated in the preceding grades will need continued practice and application in order to ensure habitually correct use in all the pupils' writing activities. The following outline of learnings for the third grade illustrates the fact that only a few items are introduced year by year and that each successive grade should build on abilities and activities that have already been introduced, by both extension and refinement.

Growth in vocabulary

1. Use newly learned words to express new facts and ideas.
2. Choose vivid descriptive words and action words to convey sense impressions.
3. Recognize sound quality of words through rhyming.
4. Understand and use technical terms for first and second grade, plus *indent, paragraph, apostrophe, contraction, command.*

Acquaintance with and use of sentences

1. Develop the concept of the sentence as a complete thought, and habitually check on completeness by reading aloud.
2. Understand the need for three kinds of sentences: statement, question, and command.
3. Begin to eliminate the run-on sentence and the *and* fault.
4. Compose correct and interesting original sentences.

Organization of ideas

1. Learn that a paragraph is restricted to a single topic.
2. Relate the events of a story in sequence.

Reading skills (as related to writing)

1. Use books effectively in collecting information for written work.
    a. Understand parts of a book: title, title page, table of contents, glossary, index.
    b. Use table of contents to find a story.
    c. Locate books in the library's classified sections.
    d. Use a book list.
    e. Read books selectively in terms of what is sought.
2. Keep a reading record.
3. Transfer word-analysis skills to spelling.

Writing skills

1. Use correct manuscript form.
    a. Utilize skills itemized for second grade.
    b. Use correct form in writing a personal note.
    c. Develop the habit of checking manuscript form.
2. Use capital letters correctly.
    a. Master items listed for second grade.
    b. Capitalize the first word in a line of verse.
    c. Write the words *I* and *O* as capital letters.
    d. Capitalize proper names: person, month, day, street, town, common holidays.
    e. Capitalize titles: book, story, poem.
3. Use correct punctuation.
    a. Master items listed for second grade.
    b. Use a period following a command and after *Mr.* and *Mrs.*
    c. Begin to learn the use of an apostrophe: contraction, possessive singular.
4. Spell correctly through use of helps suggested by the teacher.
    a. Acquire the tendency and ability to find the correct spelling of any word (from the teacher, a notebook list, a spelling box, a simple dictionary, a textbook).
    b. Form the habit of spelling all words correctly.
    c. Make progress in mastering contractions and homonyms.

Major activities

1. Fill out simple forms, such as library cards.
2. Compose and write class rules or standards.
3. Raise and list questions as guides for reading or writing.
4. Write a notice or announcement for the bulletin board.
5. Write a brief news story for a class newspaper.

SUGGESTIONS FOR STUDY AND DISCUSSION

1. Keep a log of the situations that call for written expression in a primary grade over the period of two weeks. Differentiate between occasions when the teacher acts as secretary and when pupils write independently (for student teachers and teachers).

2. In your college class, do the following kinds of peer teaching:
    a. Write an experience story on the chalkboard as your "pupils" dictate it to you.
    b. Supervise pupils as they copy a letter they have dictated.
    c. Teach a studied dictation lesson on the fable of the dog and the meat he dropped in the stream.
    d. Teach an unfinished story lesson.

3. Collect a set of primary written stories. What evidence do you find of individual differences? What kinds of help would be good for each type of difficulty you find?

4. Possibly someone in your family or circle of friends has samples of the same child's written productions for each of the three primary grades. If so, analyze for evidences of growth from year to year.

FOR FURTHER READING

1. BAKER, ZELMA W., *The Language Arts, the Child, and the Teacher*. San Francisco, Fearon, 1955.
2. BROGAN, PEGGY, and LORENE FOX, *Helping Children Learn* (Chapter 2). Indianapolis, Bobbs-Merrill, 1956.
3. BROWN, DOROTHY, and MARGUERITE BUTTERFIELD, *The Teaching of Language in the Primary Grades* (Chapter 8). New York, Macmillan, 1941.
4. BURROWS, ALVINA, and others. *They All Want to Write*. Englewood Cliffs, N. J., Prentice-Hall, 1952.
5. DAWSON, MILDRED A., *Outline for Teaching the Language Arts*. New York, Harcourt, Brace & World, 1959. Pamphlet.
6. GANS, ROMA, CELIA BURNS STENDLER, and MILLIE ALMY, *Teaching Young Children*. New York, Harcourt, Brace & World, 1952.
7. GREENE, HARRY G., and WALTER T. PETTY, *Developing Language Skills in the Elementary School* (Chapters 6, 12). Boston, Allyn and Bacon, 1959.
8. GUNDERSON, AGNES G., "When Seven-Year-Olds Write as They Please." *Elementary English* (April 1943), 144–50.
9. KLAUSMEIER, HERBERT J., and others, *Teaching in the Elementary School* (268–82). New York, Harper, 1956.
10. LOGAN, LILLIAN, *Teaching the Young Child* (Chapter 10). Boston, Houghton Mifflin, 1960.
11. PARKE, MARGARET B., "Composition in Primary Grades." *Elementary English* (February 1959), 107–21.
12. STRICKLAND, RUTH G., *The Language Arts in the Elementary School* (Chapter 12). Boston, Heath, 1957.
13. *When Children Write*, Association for Childhood Education International. Washington, D. C., The Association, 1955.
14. WOLFE, DON, *Language Arts and Life Patterns* (Chapters 21, 31). New York, Odyssey, 1961.

15

Written Expression in the Intermediate Grades

Chapter 15 discusses the basic purposes for written communication, from the strictly utilitarian, such as keeping exact records, to the highly personal, such as writing imaginative stories. The chapter describes a large variety of assignments to fit these purposes. Special attention is given to training lessons designed to raise the quality of written expression. As a guide to normal expectation, a chart is included which lists progressively advancing goals of instruction in written communication suitable to pupils at the intermediate level.

BECAUSE children vary widely in their rate of maturation and capacity to learn, their interests, the quality and diversity of their experiences, and their inclination to verbalize their ideas and emotions, teachers in the intermediate grades should expect a wide range in children's ability to express their ideas in writing. Some pupils will approach high-grade adult proficiency before they reach the upper grades and will, by the fourth grade, have become quite independent in the planning and execution of their writing activities. Others will need careful guidance and detailed instruction in the writing of sentences and paragraphs, in spelling and other mechanical aspects of written communication, and in deciding what to write about and how to say it.

The pupils in a typical group will probably range all the way between these two limits of proficiency. Average pupils of the upper intermediate grades should be able to write one to three well-organized paragraphs of four or five sentences, each with correct end punctuation and relatively correct capitalization and spelling.

It is important that the teacher accept all children as he finds them and be ready to provide differentiated instruction to benefit them according to their needs. He should allow the more able children to work up to their capacity, giving them the stimulation and guidance they need to promote optimal growth. He should guide the less proficient pupils in building up habits of independent work. Those pupils who have made the least progress in their ability to write independently will find it necessary to continue some cooperative writing, to copy written work under the close supervision of the teacher and also to write from dictation both studied and unstudied compositions, like the exercises described in the preceding chapter. By careful observation and systematic inventory, the teacher can gauge the degree of independence that the various pupils can assume and should then provide as many opportunities as possible for each pupil to write as independently and maturely as he can. Of course, children who are motivated with a deep interest in their topics and who know that their readers will welcome their ideas will tend to learn and use skills with relatively little effort.

Background Experiences to Promote Good Writing

THERE are good ways and poor ways to plan assignments requiring written work. If an assignment requires a child to state facts which he does not know thoroughly, to explain ideas which he does not understand thoroughly, or to compose paragraphs for which he sees no purpose, we can expect the results to be less than satisfactory. If his writing is to be a constructive experience, related in a meaningful way to all that he is learning in school, it must be planned as a natural and important part of the curriculum.

The less experienced the child, the more dependent he is upon ongoing firsthand experiences to provide him with knowledge and understanding. As he matures, he becomes more able to profit by vicarious learning through reading, listening, and viewing, since his maturity increases perceptiveness and his widening contacts with reality provide him with background upon which to base his interpretation of the words he hears or reads. Children at the intermediate-grade level are not yet ready to do much writing on subjects with which they are not familiar either through firsthand experience or through abundant reading that is supplemented by visual aids and discussion. Their writing tasks should be related to the things they know about or are learning something about.

The best preparation for good writing is based upon the extension of meaningful experiences. Observation, experimentation, field trips, the viewing of pictures and films, as well as reading and discussion, provide a background of understanding that will make a writing assignment a matter of clarifying, organizing, and expressing ideas that have already become a part of the child's own thinking.

Reading by itself, especially when the subject matter is unrelated to a child's immediate experience, is often not enough to prepare a child of intermediate-grade level for understanding and expressing ideas clearly in writing. Assignments that call upon him to write what he is unable to digest from his reading often lead to plagiarism. Fearful of straying far from the language of a textbook or encyclopedia because he does not fully understand it, he solves his problem by copying the words from the book.

The teacher must prevent this tendency by both direct and indirect means. He should teach the pupils how to take notes in reading, if their assignment depends upon reference to an encyclopedia; how to close the book and write from notes only; and how to use quotation marks where a quotation will have greater impact and clarity than anything they can say. But indirectly, the teacher can help children avoid the inclination to plagiarize by providing enough enlightening experiences to develop understanding of materials found in books before children are required to write on any given topic. This he can do through actual experiences such as trips or demonstrations by pupils or through the use of audio-visual aids like recordings, filmstrips, or movies. He can also teach the pupils to use a list of questions to guide their selection and organization of ideas.

Good writing demands a purpose in the child's mind. Too often the purpose is clear only in the mind of the teacher. If the writing is to elicit the child's best efforts, however, it must seem important to him. Certainly it may be important for any of several reasons. Many of the writing tasks he encounters will be primarily connected with his school studies or activities. Here the purpose will be utilitarian. A record to be kept, a summary of a discussion to be made, a business letter to be composed—these exemplify some of the types of writing that will frequently occur as a part of his learning in all subject fields.

On the other hand, there will also be opportunities for a more personal kind of writing, such as writing a friendly letter, a story, a poem, or a play —types of writing which for some children are as compelling as any writing done for the work-a-day world. Whether the writing is utilitarian or a more personal type of expression, it will serve as a developmental experience for the pupil only if he knows what he is trying to do and if he puts an effort into doing it well.

Probably the surest way of ensuring a pupil's best effort is to provide him with the knowledge that someone will read what he has written. Basically there is little urge to write except for the purpose of communication. Any

On a field trip these children collect information that will help them to write fluently later on.

writer wants to be assured that there will be a reader. In the case of the school child, it is not satisfying if the teacher is consistently the sole reader of all he writes. For the lessons that he recognizes as training lessons, the teacher's reading and correction may be enough; but for other writing there should be a real reason for the transfer of thought from person to person across an interval of space or time. In the case of utilitarian writing, pupils should file their records for actual use later, they should be sure that the reports of their experiences will be read by fellow pupils or others, and they should mail their letters with hopes for answers in reply. In the case of personal writing, the best stimulus for writing personal letters seems to lie in the pleasure of sharing it with classmates through oral reading. Alvina Burrows(1, p. 248) brings out this point:

> The sharing of original stories with the group is a valuable part of children's social orientation. A few may not wish to read theirs and such wishes should be respected. Their reservations usually melt away as the stories of others are enjoyed without fear of criticism. To read a story of one's own making to a rapt audience of one's peers is a keen satisfaction. It gives power. A child who does this once wants to share his productions again. And in so doing, again and again, lies the secret of improvement.
>
> The audience, too, gains from such intimate exposure to a creative act. Hearing a story fresh from its source, with the author still glowing over his invention, is like having a vicarious share in creation. There is a unique intensity of communication in the atmosphere. There is no substitute for this face-to-face situation in effectiveness. To be frequently one of an eager audience, and occasionally its center of attention, makes listening an active process and story-making a compelling desire.

Purposes That Lead Toward Goals

IN PLANNING the writing experiences for children, a teacher may well stop to ask: What are the qualities that are characteristic of good writing? Toward what goals should these pupils progress? Leaving technical aspects of written English aside for the moment, what should be considered as desirable substance in writing?

Certainly the answer would begin with some of the following points: (1) Written statements of fact should be accurate. (2) Explanations should be adequate, clear, and well organized. (3) Reasons and conclusions should be logical. (4) Words and phrases should be precise in their meaning; where feeling is to be conveyed, they should also be expressive. (5) Both sentences and paragraphs should be well developed and to the point. (6) Ideas should be based upon honest and (when possible) original thinking. (7) In addition, certain kinds of writing call for other specifics, such as a well-planned plot in a story. If such goals seem far from achievement in the middle grades, they still supply a challenge for the teacher.

With these goals in mind, the teacher can plan writing experiences to develop such characteristics—experiences that will have real purposes in the minds of the children. Some of the purposes and the ends they can serve are listed here.

KEEPING EXACT RECORDS

A number of different kinds of writing tasks might fall under the general classification of keeping exact records. Any one of them might be used by the teacher to stress the importance of stating the facts accurately, giving a true picture, and choosing words that say exactly what is meant.

In the early intermediate grades, some teachers like to follow the practice of keeping a daily news record. The writing may be done as a group project with a pupil writing on the board or a chart as his classmates dictate to him. Items of most importance in the class, the school, the community, and the country may be selected by the group. Though the statements may be brief, they must be correct and must be worded so that any reader now or later will understand the facts.

A class log accomplishes somewhat the same kind of practice. In this case, each pupil or a class secretary may keep a day-by-day account of the development of the class unit of work. Upon the exactness and completeness of the record will depend the evaluation of individual and committee work as measured against the plans made at the beginning of the project.

As the school work progresses, the teacher may have the children write announcements and relay messages or, occasionally, write and post some information about class and school activities. He should always check such writing for exactness of information and clarity of expression. The writer should always test his work with these questions in mind: Will the reader understand exactly what I want him to know? Is the statement clear and complete?

In relation to any kind of study, pupils may find it necessary to gather data. It is sometimes a difficult task for children to keep a record of facts in such a way that anyone who reads it can see the complete picture. Writing the steps of an experiment and all the items noted during experimentation, for instance, calls for keen observation and meticulous care in recording the facts. Writing a description of a plant or animal at different stages of growth necessitates a quick eye for minute details and the exact word or phrase to make the small differences plain to the reader of the account. Sometimes pupils need to make a narrative of events, as when they make out a chart of their own health habits—showing how many minutes for work, for exercise, for eating, for leisure activities, for sleeping, and the like.

All these types of writing can have a meaning for children if they constitute an important part of their ongoing activities. When they see a real purpose in writing they will, with guidance, consistently and gradually take steps forward toward the goals the teacher has in mind.

MAKING CLEAR EXPLANATIONS

A good deal of the writing that most people do in a lifetime might fall under the classification of explanations. At intermediate-grade level, children need to explain how to do things (for example, how to build a campfire without matches) or how something works (the Cartesian diver). They need to write letters for information, explaining what they want to know and enough about themselves and their purpose so that the recipient can send them information suitable to their age and to their need. They must learn to see relationships between facts, to recognize causes and results in almost everything they study.

Teachers can help them learn to find these relationships in writing and to explain them with sound reasoning and adequate proof. All types of expository writing—business letters, rules, instructions, answers to questions and general explanations—may be an outgrowth of regular school studies, thus serving a purpose in the minds of the children. At the same time, these types of expression afford the teacher opportunity to teach toward the achievement of writing goals which may well prove crucial in daily living. It will be the teacher's responsibility to help pupils think and organize their ideas *before* they write, make clear and accurate statements of fact, express opinions based upon adequate reasons, and present their conclusions, if such are called for, in effective words and phrases.

RECORDING EXPERIENCES IN IMAGINATION

Frequently, at intermediate level, teachers catch pupils' interest by getting them to inject themselves into the new situations they are studying. Children like to study other parts of our own country or other countries by taking imaginary trips there, meeting imaginary people, thus seeing what they are like and how they live. They may follow somewhat the same procedure when they study about the historical past. They can imagine themselves as colonial children and write about life in colonial days, or they can tell about the Boston Tea Party as if they were there.

Such writing is imaginative only in the sense that a personal narrative runs through the account. The children can describe the places, the kind of people, and the life of the times with as much accuracy as can be gained from books and pictures. Letters, diaries, illustrated travel book-

A boy who has built replicas of satellites is able to explain them lucidly.

lets, explanatory "chapters" for a book of travels, and dramatic sketches provide a variety of forms for this type of writing. In this kind of writing, children can develop a close adherence to accuracy of facts and a sensitivity to other ways of living and to the feelings of people of the long ago or far away.

The teacher can make such writing interesting and vivid by the inclusion of specific details and the choice of exact words and phrases. If the imaginative experiences are written as a play or radio or television skit, the teacher has an especially good opportunity to develop skill in the organization of material as the children plan the presentation by acts or scenes.

SHARING THOUGHTS AND FEELINGS

Writing does not need to be all work and no play. Though many writing experiences may be essential to school work, the teacher should also give encouragement to the expression of personal feelings and ideas written exclusively for the individual satisfaction derived. In such writing there may be little or no need for discussion to precede the writing.

Since personal writing should be truly the child's own, and not an assigned task to be criticized and graded, the teacher must plan other ways in which to raise the level of writing. He may do this in part by separate training lessons, using samples of writing such as those that may be found in textbooks to point out commendable features. Samples of friendly letters, for example, appear in most language textbooks and serve to point out appropriate content in terms of the reader's interest, effective ways to make the message interesting, and proper form to meet conventional standards for letters.

To teach the writing of courtesy notes, such as letters of invitation, thanks, or appreciation, the teacher can have the children study samples and then try sample writing of their own. They should discuss the importance of promptness in courtesy notes and the basic requirements for all personal letters, such as sincerity, thoughtfulness, and individual ways of expressing a thought. But children must be able to recognize sample letters, like sample diaries, for what they are. The real experience comes only as the writing is self-motivated, rather than assigned, and as the child himself wishes to share his thoughts and feelings with a classmate or to record them so that he can later read what he has written.

Occasionally a child writes to relieve himself of strong feelings, a kind of therapeutic act which helps him to get something "off his chest" by the mere act of putting it in words. Though this writing may be highly personal, children who have complete confidence in their teachers often seem willing and sometimes even anxious to have their writing perused by the teacher. Careful guidance by the teacher can raise the child's writing above the level of his ordinary proficiency; but to do this, the teacher must restrict his comments to the positive side, building upon the strength observed in the writing. Mention of a particularly apt phrase or a word that conveys deep feeling may help the child to become aware himself of a goal in writing.

SHARING ORIGINAL STORIES AND POEMS

Another type of personal writing which many children enjoy is story writing. It should be encouraged *but not required.* Such writing should be free from some of the burdens associated with regular written work related to school tasks. The teacher should not impose deadlines but, instead, should develop a feeling of gentle urgency. When a child has completed a story to his own satisfaction, he will be sure to find an interested audience waiting to hear it.

Emphasis upon the mechanics of good writing, which the teacher must always stress in work related to school assignments, can be relaxed somewhat when the children are sharing a story by oral reading. Of course, the children must observe the conventional standards of good composition if the writing is to be read by others; but a listening group can enjoy a story, with no thought of such matters as spelling, punctuation, and capitalization. However, the writer will have a much easier time if he has sufficient mastery of these technicalities so that he does not have to stop and puzzle out when a sentence ends or what word this conglomeration of letters was intended to represent. When a child has completed a story and is permitted to read it to the class or hear it read by the teacher, the natural expressions of praise from an appreciative audience are likely to stimulate him to continue to write, and to do so with more and more discrimination.

Sometimes it is a child with unusual imaginative power who sparks the interest of others in this kind of writing. But it is certainly not the gifted alone who find pleasure in creating characters, animal or human, and putting them through imaginary adventures in an imaginary world. And all children who enter into such experiences, from the most gifted to the least, can profit from the realization that writing can be entertaining to others when they use care in selecting the right word, the apt expression, and the original comparison, or in developing mounting suspense and a well-planned plot.

Poetry writing, like storytelling, should not be a required assignment; yet if poetry is frequently read in the classroom, there will be those who are pleased to try their hand at writing it. The poet's observation of details, his choice of expressive words, his understanding and feeling for a situation are characteristics which the teacher may promote through a group experience in writing.

The poem below was a class enterprise. A teacher and her fifth-grade class walked around a city block with the purpose of noting as many signs of autumn as they could find. When they returned, each pupil expressed in writing the things he had seen, or heard, or felt, that spoke to him of fall. With all the papers at hand, the teacher selected phrases from each and put them together to make a poem.*

This is the poem that the teacher and children wrote:

MR. ROBIN REPORTS

October! Getting colder!
White mists in the morning,
Blue skies at noon.
The wind sings in the evergreens while
A crisp brown fir-cone falls to the ground.
The green hard cover of a walnut shines in the grass.
In the fall so much falls to the ground.
Children walk in the red-brown leaves
Hunting for dark brown chestnuts.
The juniper berries are blue-green
And dogwood petals are falling gracefully.
There are more roses on the bushes than stars on our flag.
The atmosphere is clear and cold,
But the gardens are warm with marigolds.
Other birds are going south.
I think I'll stay!

R. REDBREAST

Limericks and nonsense rhymes are fun for children who like to play with words. While posing the challenge of fitting words to a pattern of meter and rhyme, they permit the nonsense that seems to appeal particularly to children of the intermediate grades. Such writing, though without serious purpose, yields personal pleasure and gives a sense of added power in the use of language.

Training Lessons for Improving Writing Skills

THOUGH the teacher may plan the work of the class so that the children feel that there is real purpose in writing, and though the background of their experience has been adequate to provide them with sufficient facts and ideas to write about, the skills of written expression are likely to be only partially learned. Children need actual training in how to write effectively. Training lessons may precede assignments that call for inde-

* Isabel McLelland and class, Ockley Green School, Portland, Oregon.

pendent writing, with the purpose of establishing good writing habits for the work that follows. Or they may come after the teacher has appraised some written work, with the intent of discovering typical weaknesses.

TEACHING THE TECHNICAL SKILLS

In utilitarian writing, handwriting and spelling need constant attention to provide the required instruction and to keep children interested in putting forth their best efforts. Whenever they write, they should have dictionaries within easy reach, and the teacher should encourage the children to use them as needed. There should be vocabulary lists posted as units of subject-matter progress. The teacher should promote interest in legible and neat handwriting by encouraging the children to evaluate their own work. A study of models in the textbook and a display of children's papers exemplifying good form will remind pupils of basic manuscript form, including the headings for papers (which should be uniform within a school), placement of title, width of margins, and indentation of paragraphs. More regarding instruction in these areas may be found in Chapter 17, "Developing Handwriting Skills," and in Chapter 18, "Improving Children's Spelling."

Capitalization and punctuation likewise are technical matters that the children must practice in writing situations. In the intermediate grades, the teacher must present to the pupils new uses of capital letters and punctuation with adequate explanations. In simple cases the explanation should be brief, but in complex cases (like the use of quotation marks) the explanation may be presented in a series of lessons.

The teacher must explain the use of words and sentences as needs arise and as children's levels of ability permit. The fourth grader, for instance, who previously had no trouble writing the short sentences encouraged in the primary grades, may find himself in difficulty as he tries to express his more mature ideas in complex sentences beyond his training in punctuation. In the process, he is likely to write adverb clauses as sentence fragments and will need definite instructions in writing these adverb clauses as an integral part of the sentence. More about usage and grammar will be found in Chapter 20.

The training phase of instruction is intended to improve the quality of composition as well as the mechanics, and it is somewhat in the nature of an exercise. Its effectiveness will rest upon whether the pupils recognize its purpose and its relation to their own need for improving their skills in written communication. There are several kinds of training lessons that have proved effective with children of intermediate grades. The use of a variety of methods is desirable. Several possibilities are described on the following pages.

DICTATION

As in the primary grades, children in the intermediate grades can profit from dictation exercises. First, the pupils should study a model composition written on the board, and the teacher should draw their attention to specific points on which they need help. They should note the content, the organization, the sentence structure, spelling, capitalization, and punctuation. After the teacher has erased or concealed the model, the children write it from his dictation. For pupils who are immature, the teacher should use the dictation procedures described in the preceding chapter. In unstudied dictation, the same experience, except that the preliminary study is omitted, challenges the pupils to catch the sentences by hearing them, to apply the rules of capitalization and punctuation as they already know them, and to spell correctly from memory (with the help of the teacher for unusual words). Though the instruction in dictation exercises is usually aimed toward improvement of mechanics, such as capitalization, punctuation, or matters of form like margins and indentation, the models should exemplify good paragraph development, simple enough for intermediate-grade children.

SOCIALIZED CORRECTION

Training in self-appraisal can get its start in teacher-directed group criticism. As pupils work with one another in improving compositions, they are learning the techniques for appraising their own individual compositions.

Socialized correction should be initiated in the following way: Two or three pupil compositions should be copied on the board (or better still, projected on a screen) exactly as they have been written. One should represent some highly creditable writing and will serve as a pupil-written model for other pupils to study in setting up standards for self-appraisal. The other one or two should have difficulties representative of those most common in the writing of the class; these will help the children to find difficulties like those in their own papers and to know how to remove such weaknesses.

Each writer (whose material has been copied on the board or projected) in turn should go through his own composition and make all the suggestions for improvement that occur to him, the teacher meanwhile making suggested changes on the original or the chalkboard copy of his paper. Usually he will read aloud the entire composition, then make suggestions concerning sentence structure and the general organization. Next he will proceed, sentence by sentence, to suggest detailed improvements, especially in mechanical features such as capitalization and punctuation. At the conclusion of this self-appraisal, which is usually fruitful because the writer is more likely to notice the major weak spots after his composition has become cold, his classmates give supplementary suggestions, always from a constructive standpoint.

To make it easy for each pupil to suggest improvements in his own composition, the teacher may suggest that the pupils list in detail the points to look for when correcting a composition. A general list which the pupils could make more detailed would include such main points as interesting words, sentence structure, paragraph structure, usage, spelling, capitalization, punctuation and (if the composition is projected) appearance of manuscript.

The one or two other compositions that have been written on the chalkboard are similarly treated. On concluding this part of the lesson, the teacher and class identify cooperatively the spots where the compositions have needed improvement; they then compile a broad list of the ways in which improvements have been made. All the compositions are returned to their respective writers so that the writers may appraise these in regard to the points that have been listed. All make revisions on the original papers, which may be filed for future reference or use in the school newspaper or a booklet. Such papers should be copied only if they are to appear in some publication or to be sent through the mail. The teacher should keep in mind that children learn more by writing a fresh composition in which they try to improve on the preceding ones than they do from copying revised papers.

The following transcribed account describes what took place in a fifth-grade class involved in socialized correction of stories the children were writing. They were retelling their favorite incident from *The Adventures of Pinocchio*. The teacher* had copied on the chalkboard a few sentences from a child's paper. "Here is a paragraph from one of your stories," she said. "I have copied it here because I wanted us all to look at it together to see how we could improve it."

> Then blue fairy waved her wand and said Pinocchio would be a person.
> There was a light and then he moved his arm. He said,
>   "I'm alive.

TEACHER: Could you suggest a way to make the story better? What do you think of it as it is?

PUPIL 1: Well, it isn't very interesting. That was an exciting part of the story. I think we could change it and make it sound a little more exciting.

PUPIL 2: Yes. It sounds dull. I think we could change *would* to *shall*, and say "Pinocchio shall be a person."

PUPIL 3: Couldn't we change it and have Blue Fairy wave her wand and say, "Pinocchio, you shall be a real little boy."

* Alvina Flatt, Hosford School, Portland, Oregon.

TEACHER: With all these suggestions, I can see we're going to need a secretary. Ruth, could you listen carefully and make the changes that the class agrees upon? How many think Patsy's idea is a good one? (They all agreed.)

PUPIL 1: Ruth should write Blue Fairy with capital letters.

TEACHER: Why?

PUPIL 4: Because that was her name.

TEACHER: That's right. I'm glad you noticed. I see you noticed it too, Ruth. Now, how shall we go on?

PUPIL 5: You could say, "Right away there was a light," or a "flash," or something. (Many suggestions for vitalizing this part followed in quick succession, culminating in this: "Suddenly there was a brilliant flash. Pinocchio moved his arm.")

PUPIL 3: I don't think "said" shows how he felt when he came alive.

TEACHER: What word do you think would show exactly how he felt as he said those words?

CLASS: "Said with surprise." "Shouted." "Cried." "Exclaimed." (They reach an agreement on "shouted.")

PUPIL 6: Ruth should put a different mark after "I'm alive" to show how he shouted. I mean instead of a period.

TEACHER: What do we call that mark? (Two said, "Exclamation point.") And I see another mistake in punctuation.

PUPIL 3: It's those little marks after "alive." (Another pupil said, "Quotation marks.")

TEACHER: Now let's see how it looks. (She reads the revision from the board.)

> Then Blue Fairy waved her wand and said, "Pinocchio, you shall be a real little boy." Suddenly there was a brilliant flash. Pinocchio moved his arm.
> "I'm alive!" he shouted.

In this lesson, it is interesting to note that the children gave their attention first to the need for exact, appropriate, and vivid words, subsequently to the mechanics of capitalization and punctuation.

If certain particular kinds of weaknesses in written work are evident in a class, or a group within a class, the teacher may prepare a paragraph including such errors. Duplicated copies distributed to the children provide them with an exercise that requires analysis and correction. Group discussion follows, similar to that involved in socialized correction.

CHECKING WRITTEN WORK

As soon as children are able to express themselves independently in writing, they should learn that the writing task has not been completed until they have (1) written a rough draft, (2) polished up the rough draft, and (3) made a final copy of their composition. In the rough draft they will get their ideas down fluently, without being restrained by trying to be perfect on detailed mechanics; then, in going over the draft, they will polish up vocabulary choice, sentence structure, usage, capitalization, and punctuation. After that, the final copy should be written as well as they know how. Pupils will accept these three points if the teacher will impress upon them that all good writers tend to use a rough draft.

When the children become more proficient, they may appraise their compositions on the basis of a list of guiding questions that have been worked out in a chalkboard list or filed in the language notebook. These questions will guide the pupil as he checks his own paper. Some will relate to mechanics, others to the content; for instance:

1. Is your story told in good order?
2. Does it move right along?
3. Is the end kept a surprise?
4. Is each paragraph about one central topic?
5. Can you think of words that will be more clear and interesting?
6. Did you keep your margins?
7. Is the title correctly placed?
8. Is it correctly capitalized?

A most effective procedure is to have the pupils compile cooperatively a list of such questions on the basis of emerging standards over a period of weeks. Gradually they can add standards as the school year proceeds and can file the list in a notebook so that it may be used each time they check a paper written in connection with any curricular area. Doing this will promote independence and a feeling of responsibility for holding to consistently high standards of work.

Such lists of questions may also serve as guides for pupils whenever they exchange papers or work in teams to help one another improve the quality and correctness of written work. Cooperative work in improving papers should take place in connection with utilitarian writing, as a rule, though individual pupils may voluntarily request friends to work with them in improving their creative compositions. In case of a general exchange of papers—and it is not wise for the teacher to suggest this too often, since the children should learn to rely on themselves—the exchange should be between a capable and a weak pupil. Then the weak pupil can gain more knowledge of how to write effectively, and the capable pupil will use his ability to note ways to improve the paper he is appraising.

The socialized correction described above may serve as a good training ground for teaching the slower-learning children to correct their own errors; but able writers should not be held to socialized correction unless the weaknesses to be considered are present in their writing. It can be repeated frequently to the slower children's advantage. But children must learn to consider their own individual responsibility to check their work every time they write. True, the task is not exciting in itself and it comes at a time when the pupil wants to be done with his job of writing. The child who is unwilling or untrained to exert care in the details of writing is likely to omit it, unless he is writing something of real moment to him— and it is the teacher's responsibility to see that the child's writing does seem worthwhile. Even so, teachers will remind children regularly when they are completing their writing, to check it; to provide time for the checking as an important and integral part of writing; and occasionally to use variations in methods of checking that will renew interest and increase effort.

In some classes the pupils establish, for a limited period, a committee with duties to serve as consultants for other pupils before they hand in their papers. Pupils may not ask assistance from the committee members unless they can say that they have carefully checked their own work first. Then with help from a member of the committee, the pupils can make suggested corrections on their papers before handing them to the teacher. The teacher can then appoint pupils as members of the committee on the basis of technical accuracy in their own writing.

If committee membership rotates from time to time, some disadvantages are avoided, such as using too much of an able pupil's time in helping others; but some advantages are gained, such as giving more children the responsibility for examining written work carefully for its technical form and for explaining clearly to another why corrections are needed. Members of such committees never take the place of the teacher, but they may act as assistants occasionally to their own advantage as well as that of the other pupils.

The main emphasis in teaching the checking of written work should be (1) to instill the attitude that a final careful survey of one's own writing is important and (2) to develop skill in seeing and removing the careless errors that are inevitable in a first draft.

FIVE-MINUTE DAILY WRITING PRACTICE

Another type of training lesson involves regular writing practice every day for a short period of time. One fifth-grade teacher found the five minutes after lunch to be a good time for training children to have tools at hand and to get to work promptly. For such writing, the teacher should encourage the free choice of subject matter. However, he can also suggest topics of general interest, especially those which do not require study but are a part of the children's close experience. Here are some topics that he might use:

WHAT OUR CLASS DID THIS MORNING

A PROJECT I AM WORKING ON AT HOME

AN INCIDENT IN A BOOK I AM READING

AN INTERESTING TRICK I LEARNED ABOUT

WHAT I SAW ON THE WAY TO SCHOOL

The first object in daily practice writing is to get children to overcome a mental block toward writing and to develop some fluency by writing on familiar topics. The second object is to use the child's own composition as the basis for correction *he* needs. It is a way of discovering his common errors as he expresses his ideas in writing. As every teacher knows, the best way to determine errors in composition is to examine the individual's composition. Children who fill in blanks or write out sentence exercises from a textbook correctly, following standard forms, easily overlook errors as they turn their attention to the idea they wish to express. By establishing a brief practice period for free composition (with checking), the teacher can see what specific help each child needs individually.

The third object, to administer instruction as needed, can be rather easily handled in the following way. Pupils need to provide themselves with a spiral-bound notebook, so that their practice writing can be kept together for analysis and measurement of progress. At a given time each day, they start their entry with the date, followed by as much of a paragraph as they can write in the time allowed. If time is called promptly, some children will have no more than the date, at first; yet the persistence of the daily assignment is likely to make them bring pressure upon themselves as needed—to have their pencils ready and to come to the writing task with something to say.

In this kind of training lesson, the teacher must come to an agreement with the class that the grading will be done for only three booklets each day, rotating through the class as fast as possible. He will mark one page of each notebook, suggesting improvement on that page. In the two weeks or so that may elapse between grades, the pupil practices applying the teacher's suggestions on the page that he marked. A conference with the child may be possible, so that the teacher can explain mistakes to the child as he marks them. Otherwise, written comments in the notebook should help the pupil to recognize his special needs. Here is the chance, also, for the teacher to express appreciation for the vivid word or phrase, the good topic sentence, the interesting detail, the well-expressed idea. The teacher's dated note is the guide to the child's progress.

On a back page of his notebook, each pupil should tally the kinds of mistakes he has made and the words he has misspelled. The notebook writing and the tally give a good record of the progress he is making through applying writing skills. When it becomes obvious to the teacher that many individuals are showing the same kind of weaknesses, he should use class or group instruction as extensively as needed. Daily practice writing does not take the place of well-organized reports, summaries, stories, letters, or other purposeful writing described in previous pages. The pupil needs both purposeful writing and training lessons.

USE OF THE TEXTBOOK

A well-selected language textbook will provide help in organization and expression of ideas in all commonly needed types of written communication. It will present constructive suggestions for building skill in using the conventional forms of written English, including grammar and usage, spelling, punctuation, and capitalization. It will indicate sources of difficulty frequently met by children and will provide practice material to help establish correct forms to replace incorrect ones.

But a textbook without a good teacher can never be adequate to help the individuals in the class to develop their full capabilities in writing. The following suggestions for the use of the language textbook may serve as a guide in planning instruction to improve written communication:

1. Use textbook ideas regarding assignments but alter the topics to make them apply to current work being done in any subject in the curriculum.

2. When special types of writing are to be used for the first time (business letters, book reports, and the like), turn to the book to find a model. Use this in discussing content, organization, and effectiveness, as well as the conventions of form.

3. When mistakes or weaknesses in writing are generally evident in classwork, explain the correction orally to the class, using the chalkboard to illustrate the error and the correction. Difficulties in the use of the language need to be explained in the most simple and direct fashion. Such face-to-face presentation gives you an opportunity to see from the pupils' discussion and expression which ones need further explanation. No textbook can take the place of this direct assistance.

4. Following this explanation, refer pupils to the textbook for supporting emphasis. Use it also to establish familiarity with the book as a source of reference when it is needed again for assistance on the same matter.

5. Use drill sentences in the textbook *after* you are reasonably sure most pupils understand the point the sentences exemplify. They are useful as

a check on your explanation and the child's understanding. Children who do not measure up to expectation may need further explanation or help in interpreting the explanation in the book. Too much emphasis on grading drill sentences may build a feeling that the drill is more important than the written communication it is supposed to strengthen. You may prefer to keep a record of achievement on drill sentences but not enter a grade in your books; that is, use the drills as a diagnostic check to determine further need for language instruction.

6. Use the textbook as a general guide in planning the instruction in the specific skills in written English and in the terminology and understandings about the language appropriate to the grade level. Plan modifications as needed, according to the variations in ability within the class. However, a well-chosen textbook series will have a developmental plan from grade to grade and can serve as a guide to progress that is generally expected from children of average or better ability. As you use the language textbook as a source of help during the year whenever specific needs arise, you can devise and keep a check list of items presented. If, as the year progresses, certain check-listed items of importance have not come to the attention of the class, take special pains to see that all items appropriate to the maturity of the pupils are included in the class's consideration. Avoid undue gaps.

7. Consult the textbook to find interesting and suitable expressional situations, such as real broadcasts or telecasts to serve as the culmination of an ongoing social studies unit. A language textbook suggests many stimulating situations to encourage purposeful writing.

A Curriculum for Written Work

ASIDE from the day-by-day evaluation of written work, in which both pupils and teachers participate, there needs to be some kind of a check list that will help the teacher to note the pupils' progress.

CHECK LIST FOR INSTRUCTION

Day by day the teacher must be on the alert to note the needs of the class, to stimulate their interest and enliven their purpose in writing, to offer instruction as needed both to the entire class and to the individuals. The following outline may serve as a check list indicating the major matters for instruction at each grade level. He cannot expect children of low ability to perform at these levels, and he certainly should not hold back children of high ability. However, teachers need to see the developmental progress expected of the large number of children who can make normal progress.

Growth in vocabulary

1. Maintain and extend at each grade level a discussion of word meanings, a choice of exact words for accurate and clear expression of ideas, and the use of vivid words to convey sense impressions.

2. Maintain the use of technical vocabulary learned in primary grades: sentence, capital and small letters, period, question mark; apostrophe, contraction; paragraph, margin, indention; greeting and closing of letters.

3. Introduce at Grade 4: use of the junior dictionary (beyond picture dictionary) for increasing word meaning. At Grade 5: with simple illustrations, indicate derivatives through root words, prefixes, and suffixes; introduce examples of words having regular and specialized meaning, indicating importance of reading in context. At Grade 6: extend use of dictionary and introduce other specialized word sources to able students, such as a thesaurus or book of synonyms and antonyms; choose words for variety and precision.

Acquaintance with and use of sentences

1. Maintain and extend the practice of composing clearly stated and interesting sentences to express thoughts, the concept of what a sentence is, the understanding of the need for three kinds of sentences (statement, question, and command), the correction of run-on sentences and the *and* fault.

2. Using grammatical terms functionally, without stress on definition, introduce in Grade 4: subject, predicate, and word order, showing the difference in word order in sentences expressing statements, questions, or exclamations. At Grade 5: the use of common and proper nouns as subject or object, with their singular, plural, and possessive forms; sentences that use *and* or *but* to join two parts, each with a subject and predicate; use of adjectives and adverbs with nouns and verbs. At Grade 6: the use and form of pronouns as subject or object, the use of prepositions and conjunctions to introduce subordinate parts of a sentence.

Organization of ideas

1. Maintain the understanding introduced in primary grades that a paragraph is restricted to a single topic. Provide practice in relating events in sequence.

2. Extend instruction in all intermediate grades regarding clear organization of ideas as expressed in sentences and paragraphs; the development of a paragraph; organization by simple outline.

Reading skills (as related to writing)

1. Maintain skills in the use of a book: title, table of contents, classified section; the ability to use a book list; the ability to read selectively in

terms of reading purpose. Teach the use of a dictionary for definitions. Continue to relate skills in word recognition to the spelling of unfamiliar words.

2. Introduce at Grade 4: the use of a book index; the use of a dictionary for learning pronunciation and syllabication; the use of an encyclopedia. Extend these skills throughout the intermediate grades.

Writing skills

1. *Manuscript form.* Maintain and extend (as more detail is needed) the use of the approved form for heading papers; the use of manuscript lettering for charts, maps, and so on; the use of margins, indentation of paragraphs, legible handwriting; careful checking.

2. *Capital letters.* Maintain primary skills in the use of capitals: the first word of a sentence; the word *I*; the names of persons, school, street, town, month, day; titles; the common holidays; the first word in a line of poetry. Introduce at Grade 4: the names of countries and people of the country; titles before names (like *Uncle* and *Aunt*); the first word in each topic and subtopic in an outline. Introduce at Grade 5: the first word in a quotation; all geographical names; the names of organizations. Introduce at Grade 6: the name of the Deity and sacred writings (such as the *Bible*); the departments of government; historical events.

3. *Punctuation.* Maintain primary skills in the use of end punctuation: comma in date, after greeting and closing of letter; period after abbreviations and after numbers in a listing; apostrophe for contraction and possession. Introduce at Grade 4: quotation marks, exclamation point. Introduce at Grade 5: extension of use of apostrophe for possession; comma in direct address; colon after greeting in business letters; hyphen in separating word at end of line. Introduce at Grade 6: comma in a series; comma between two sentences joined by *but* or *and*.

4. *Spelling.* Maintain the habit of checking spelling in writing and skill in finding how to spell a needed word. Extend throughout the intermediate grades: study of homonyms; use of apostrophe in contractions and possessives; spelling of plurals ending in *s* and *es*, words changing final *y* to *i* before *es*, words dropping final *e* in adding *ing, er, est, ed,* or *y*. Introduce at Grade 4: plurals changing *f* to *v*; doubling the final consonant in adding suffixes like *ing, ed, est* (to keep short vowel sound). Introduce at Grade 5: plurals of words ending in *o*; words keeping the final *e* in adding suffixes like *ness, ment*; plural possessives; words with *ie* and *ei*. Introduce at Grade 6: adding prefixes like *un, im, dis*; capitalizing proper nouns and adjectives formed from proper nouns.

Usage

1. Maintain and extend instruction in usage only as needed, attacking

gross errors first if they are noticed in the speech or writing of the class members.

2. Use technical terms only at appropriate grade levels.

3. *Verb forms.* Maintain primary instruction to eliminate such errors as the following: *he come, he seen, he done, he run, he brung, he et, he busted, he learned me, leave him go.* Extend to instruction in other verb forms as needed.

4. *Subject-verb agreement.* Maintain an effort to eliminate errors such as the following: *there is two of them, here's three pencils,* and *it don't.*

5. *Pronouns.* Introduce instruction to eliminate errors such as the following: *them books, him and me went, haven't no pencil, hisself, theirselves, the boy he, hisn, hern, it's, this here.*

6. *Adjectives and adverbs.* Introduce the distinction between *good* and *well, a* and *an, easy* and *easily.*

SUGGESTIONS FOR STUDY AND DISCUSSION

1. Make an extensive list of experiences that will build a background of ideas and beliefs that should be the basis for writing; for example, a speaker brought into the school or the use of a radio broadcast.

2. Research has shown that children write more correctly when they write fluently. From your own experience, did you find this true? If so, what are the probable reasons?

3. What are the different ways in which a pupil may "publish" his writings—at school, and outside? (Consider bulletin board, dittoed products, posting, and so on.)

4. How does instruction in utilitarian writing vary from that for make-believe writing?

5. Which of the grade goals are likely to be unattainable by very slow learners? How can you provide for their getting satisfaction out of putting ideas on paper?

FOR FURTHER READING

1. BURROWS, ALVINA TREUT, *Teaching Children in the Middle Grades* (Chap ters 9, 12). Boston, Heath, 1952.

2. —— and others, *They All Want to Write.* Englewood Cliffs, N. J., Prentice-Hall, 1952.

3. DANFORTH, HELEN, "First Aid in Children's Writing." *Elementary English* (April 1960), 246–47.

4. DAWSON, MILDRED A., *Outline for Teaching the Language Arts.* New York, Harcourt, Brace & World, 1959. Pamphlet.

5. —— and FRIEDA HAYES DINGEE, *Children Learn the Language Arts.* Minneapolis, Burgess, 1959.

6. EDMUND, NEAL R., "Writing in the Intermediate Grades." *Elementary English* (November 1959), 491–501.

7. GREENE, HARRY A., and WALTER T. PETTY, *Developing Language Skills in the Elementary School* (Chapters 6, 12). Boston, Allyn and Bacon, 1959.

8. KLAUSMEIER, HERBERT J., and others, *Teaching in the Elementary School* (168–82). New York, Harper, 1956.

9. *Language Arts for Today's Children*, Commission on the English Curriculum of the National Council of Teachers of English. New York, Appleton-Century-Crofts, 1954.

10. LEWIS, GERTRUDE M., chairman, *Educating Children in Grades Four, Five, and Six* (Chapter 4). Washington, D. C., U. S. Department of Health, Education, and Welfare, 1958.

11. STEGALL, CARRIE, "Take a Number from One to Ten." *Elementary English* (January 1962), 33–40, 49.

12. STRICKLAND, RUTH G., *The Language Arts in the Elementary School* (Chapter 13). Boston, Heath, 1957.

13. WARE, INEZ MARIE, "Business Letters That Should Be Written." *Elementary English* (May 1958), 305–06.

14. WATTS, A. F., *The Language and Mental Development of Children*. London, Harrap; Boston, Heath, 1947.

15. WOLFE, DON, *Language Arts and Life Patterns* (Chapters 21, 31). New York, Odyssey, 1961.

16

Written Expression in the Upper Grades

Chapter 16 discusses means of approaching major goals for written communication: logical thinking, good organization, effective expression, technical writing skills, and suitable format. Ideas for both class and individual instruction are explained in the light of certain basic principles important in planning and evaluating instruction. The problem of relating instruction to all written expression in the school day is considered, especially as it applies in schools with different types of organization in the upper grades.

IN MANY respects the problems related to writing in the higher grades are similar to those discussed in the preceding chapter. It is just as important that pupils feel an important purpose in their writing at upper-grade level as in intermediate grades. Their purposes will not differ greatly; however, their methods of achieving their purposes and their degree of success should be more advanced.

A warning is in order, however; for teachers should recognize that language ability does not always advance uniformly even when able pupils direct their attention and effort toward improvement. The increasing complexity of the subjects with which pupils deal, the greater dependence upon knowledge and understanding gained through their reading rather than firsthand experience, the increased demands for use of abstract thought, and their need for language forms with which they have not yet become familiar make it possible for them to suffer what appears to be a set-back in their writing skills. The skillful teacher exercises control over some of these natural hurdles to prevent discouragement and the development of unfavorable attitudes toward writing.

As with younger pupils, those in the upper grades should have experience both with personal writing calling for originality and imagination and with utilitarian writing, with its emphasis upon accuracy and completeness of information. It should be remembered, however, that it is utilitarian writing that is crucial in the lives of many individuals. In later life, family and business security may rest upon ability to assemble facts accurately, explain terms completely, present opinions convincingly, and think through to sound conclusions. Questions that call for answers that explain the how or why of a situation are a challenge to young writers. Problem situations that need to be thought through to conclusions and justifiable action make writing a thoughtful task as it should always be. Practice and instruction in this type of writing should be frequent and thorough, making use of the many different kinds of writing experiences.

Personal or creative writing has value not only for those who are particularly gifted but for all pupils. It gives them opportunity to write what they know firsthand, to express their feelings, to give special consideration to words that will create sympathetic response in the reader. Values in both utilitarian and personal writing contribute to a child's growing power in the use of language.

Suggestions given in the preceding chapters regarding the use of dictation and the socialized correction lesson, in addition to brief daily periods of practice writing, can be as useful to a teacher at upper-grade level as at intermediate-grade level. Many upper-grade pupils still need much help in their writing activities. Dictation exercises are particularly good for teaching punctuation and capitalization to those pupils who are backward in learning these mechanics.

Goals for Written English

BY THE time most pupils have reached seventh grade, they are mature enough to direct their efforts in writing toward ultimate goals which they wish to achieve; that is, they are ready to write with real purpose. They and their teachers should keep such goals in mind, evaluate written work in terms of the goals, and plan instruction where the needs may be, in order to progress toward the ends desired. The teacher and class might construct a check list of goals, listing the major items that are treated in the following pages and filling in specific points that arise in discussion of pupils' papers.

GOOD THINKING

It is little wonder that writing is considered by most people a difficult task. Its first requirement is that it be based upon good thinking. The upper-grade level is not too early to begin to teach the first steps in logic. Indeed, English teachers can ill afford to let pupils get beyond this stage before impressing them with their responsibility for having accurate information and reasoned opinions in all utilitarian types of communication. If teachers sometimes leave the impression with pupils that their main concern is in the placing of commas and capital letters, it may be that their zeal for improving technical writing skills has led them to neglect an emphasis on good thinking and reasoning.

The items that follow are fundamental in the logical communication of thought; they deserve the teacher's continuous effort every time he marks a pupil's writing and gives instruction to a pupil or to the class.

In any subject that departs from the familiar, there will be occasion to use new words or old words with new meanings. The *definition of terms* is a first step in communicating ideas in order to place the reader and writer on a common ground of understanding. The teacher should check each pupil's writing to see that the pupil defines new words or new uses of old words and that his definitions are accurate and complete enough to give the right idea.

The teacher should work with pupils to check statements for *unwarranted assumptions.* Careless thinking based upon assumptions that are not valid will lead the writer to unjustified conclusions. The pupil who writes, "The janitor should have picked up our lunch papers," assumes that the responsibility was the janitor's. If the responsibility was the pupils', the teacher should challenge the writer's conclusion. Boys and girls must learn that good writing depends upon good thinking; they must be able to justify their written words.

When a writer states his own opinions, he should be ready with accurate and sufficient *evidence.* The facts or information he uses should come from firsthand knowledge or reliable authority. It is easy to fall into the habit of making *unsupported assertions.* Pupils must be taught that merely saying something is so does not make it so. If they have incorrect facts or only part of the facts, if their source of information has provided them with facts that are unreliable or out of date, then the conclusions they draw cannot be sound. In examining their own writing or that of their classmates critically, they should be taught to say: Where did you get the facts? How do you know? Who said so? And particularly, they should learn to avoid placing confidence in the dubious authority of "they say" or "everybody knows."

One of the common weaknesses in writing, which pupils must be taught to guard against, is *jumping to conclusions.* To reason that what is true in one case or a few cases must be true in all is seldom justified. Pupils should learn to recognize that qualified statements are more trustworthy than broad generalizations if the latter have no solid basis in fact. For example, pupils can be taught to change this kind of statement: "Dogs never bite a friendly person," to this: "I've never known a dog to bite a friendly person." There should be many a class discussion related to instances when an individual or group has jumped to an unwarranted conclusion.

Other mistakes to watch for include errors in reasoning, where cause and effect relationships are not justified. When pupils learn to check their own thought processes carefully as they write, their writing becomes a mental exercise that gives them practice in good thinking. It establishes, also, the habit of a scientific approach to problems they face.

Long ago the great philosopher and essayist, Sir Francis Bacon, wrote: "Reading maketh a full man; conference a ready man; and writing an exact man." All that has been said about the need for being precise in the use of facts, exact in expressing ideas, and logical in drawing conclusions might apply to speech as it does to writing. Yet writing is often the better medium of instruction in critical thinking; the writer's words are there on paper for reference as teacher and pupil look back at them to check meaning and expression. Upper-grade pupils will learn these lessons of exactness in thinking if the teacher directs them wisely. As they learn to restrict their statements to correct information, to opinions supported by good evidence, and to conclusions drawn from thoughtful reasoning, they are establishing habits of good thinking, the first essential of good communication.

GOOD ORGANIZATION

Upper-grade pupils may need considerable help in establishing skill in organizing their thoughts. In the primary grades the first step in organizing is to follow the sequence of time in telling events. In the intermediate grades, experiences in simple outlining are customary. By the seventh grade and higher, the outline should be a natural step in organizing ideas. Because of the differences in ability and training found in most classes, and the increased difficulty of the subject matter studied in upper grades, it may be necessary for the teacher to plan specific demonstrations and to show the children how to organize before writing. A class problem can be used as a sample, and the class can prepare on the chalkboard an outline showing how to organize material for a written report. Once the class has prepared such an outline, even though all the pupils follow it, the individual differences will be interesting to note. In the over-all presentation of a report, the teacher should explain to the pupils that a report should have a brief *introduction,* a development of *main points,* and a *conclusion.*

The parts of an outline are useful in illustrating the terms *coordinate* and *subordinate.* The outline need not go far beyond the simple steps used in middle grades. However, the pupils should understand thoroughly the concept of coordinate ideas, each written in parallel steps of the outline, and subordinate ideas, listed as supporting subtopics. By dealing with compound and complex sentences, and making sure that the ideas are presented in proper relationship to each other, pupils can see an analogy between sentence parts and the parts of the whole composition. Organization should be evident not only in the total report but in paragraphs and sentences as well.

Transition words and phrases should be explained as a means of passing smoothly from one idea to another. The time to teach transitions, of course, is when needed. Use of the chalkboard or an opaque projector to display a written report that lacks transitions will permit analysis by the class, discussion of the need for transitions, and suggestions about words or phrases effectively chosen for such purposes.

In teaching the development of a paragraph, it is well for the teacher of the higher grades to see that pupils get frequent practice in writing a single, well-developed paragraph. By emphasizing the *topic sentence* as the key to the paragraph, the teacher can develop the concept of unity (keeping to the point) and coherence (logical sequence of ideas). Pupils should understand that the paragraphs they *read* may have topic sentences at the beginning, middle, or end of the paragraph, or may have topics implied rather than expressed by a sentence at all; however, as beginning writers, they will do well to write the topic sentence at the beginning of the paragraph. Often the teacher might wish to place on the chalkboard two or three topic sentences from which pupils might choose; the class would first discuss ways to develop the paragraph, and then be asked to write the paragraph. The topic sentences thus developed might relate closely to any topic recently studied or a topic of current concern to the pupils.

When boys and girls have been untrained in the organization of their writing, their tendency is to paragraph on intuition. With many, intuition moves them to indent for a new paragraph every sentence or two. The teacher can redirect this tendency by teaching them how to develop a topic sentence adequately. In the discussion preceding writing, pupils should explore different ways of *developing the paragraph*; for example, (1) by defining a term, (2) by giving reasons, (3) by listing examples, and (4) by using a comparison or contrast to bring out the point. The need for adequate development of the topic sentence is an important learning which pupils should apply in all expository writing.

EFFECTIVE EXPRESSION

Effectiveness in writing may depend upon such characteristics as exactness in choice of words, the inclusion of vivid details, the selection of appropriate language, or the conciseness of the statement. Each writing situation is unique and requires its own best methods of development to be selected from among many. The following illustrative paragraphs suggest characteristics which many pupils at upper-grade level can begin to develop as they try to increase their effectiveness in writing.

Exactness in the choice of words may seem to be a standard which sometimes gives even professional writers trouble despite a lifetime of practice. The teacher's responsibility seems to lie mainly in maintaining pupils' natural interest in words, in helping them to become aware that the selection of the right word makes writing more effective, and in stimulating their efforts to find precise words to convey thoughts and feelings. A few sample exercises will indicate some methods which the teachers may use in working toward vocabulary development. Here are the exercises:

1. Writing a definition can be a brief but challenging form of composition because it demands precision in the choice of words. It necessarily brings up the question of which word or phrase to use. Have a pupil write a sentence on the chalkboard to show the word in context first. Then let the class work out a definition that satisfies the meaning of the word in the given sentence.

2. Keep a section of the chalkboard for listing words newly mastered through discussion in class. Every day one or more should be added. Review their meanings as needed while the study continues and encourage their use in oral and written expression.

3. See how far around the class you can go as pupils substitute verbs that produce a specific word picture for the verb in a sentence like this: "The man walked to the station."

4. Have the pupils substitute an adjective with specific meaning for the adjective in such a sentence as this: "Maggie had a bad time."

5. For nouns suggesting complex concepts such as democracy, freedom, or responsibility, have the pupils define the word in one or more paragraphs by showing in specific cases how it works. This procedure, which produces a definition in operational terms, is often a more meaningful process than defining by synonym or brief phrase.

6. Keep alive the attitude of intellectual curiosity about words by using words that may be new to many and that are appropriate to the subject being discussed. Then pause for a parenthetical explanation of the words or a brief discussion of their meaning. Your attitude of interest in words can go far toward stimulating the intellectual curiosity of the pupils.

Another way to gain effectiveness in writing is to use *specific details to support a general statement.* Pupils can readily grasp this concept as it applies in description, narration, or exposition. The details are the convincing part of a description, as pupils can see if they develop a paragraph from sentences like this: "The day was very humid." The liveliness of a narrative depends upon specific items. A pupil may write: "We did a very delicate experiment." But unless he tells what was interesting about it, he fails to transfer his feeling of interest to the reader.

In explanations, the facts that lead to the generalization, the reasons that draw forth the conclusion, the examples that prove the case—these are the specifics that children need to learn to use so that they can develop paragraphs adequately to carry their ideas vividly to their readers.

Another characteristic of effectiveness is *courtesy* or *tact*. In the expression of an idea the writer must keep in mind the feelings of the reader, recognize how he might react to the idea and, in some way, through choice of phrase or an added explanation, provide for a feeling of good will. Probably one of the most difficult lessons of life is to learn how to disagree with one another and not engender ill will. A teacher can emphasize the importance of sincere respect for others and a courteous manner in expressing any kind of opposition. Letter writing may be a good medium for such a lesson. The factor of human relationships may be as vital as the idea itself.

Related to tact, and implying the same desirability of keeping in mind the reader's likely response, is the characteristic of *appropriateness*. Choice of words and phrases and the general tone of the writing may be dependent upon the age of the persons for whom the communication is written, the degree of familiarity between the reader and writer, and the subject of the communication. The point may well be discussed with pupils, especially in contrasting the tone of friendly letters with business letters, that language is capable of conveying endless shades of meanings. In written communication, since one sends the thought across time or space, the reader cannot see the writer's frown or smile, or draw interpretation of the words in part from gestures or a friendly handclasp. The tone of the occasion must be established by the writer's careful choice of appropriate language.

Some pupils need special help in developing *conciseness* as a help toward effective expression. A. F. Watts(18) suggests the value of the three-sentence exercise in which all that the writer considers important about a certain topic should be expressed in exactly three sentences. It is a procedure that can be used for correcting the tendency to ramble and for developing skill in expressing thought compactly. Such an exercise illustrates the advantage of substituting an exact word for a general word with modifiers ("at the intersection" instead of "at the place where the streets cross"), the proper use of subordination ("The eastbound car was probably going over sixty," instead of "The car was going east and it was probably making over sixty"), and the avoidance of unnecessary repetition ("I had a huge, big serving").

TECHNICAL WRITING SKILL

The old saying that practice makes perfect is as true for the skills of writing as for other skills—and as misleading. The repetition of the act of writing produces improvement only when the effort is directed intelligently toward eliminating weakness and building strength. The teacher's responsibility, therefore, is to provide many writing experiences that seem purposeful to the pupils, to use their writing as the basis for identifying their needs for instruction, and to give them help in overcoming the mistakes they make. Psychologically, the best time to provide the help is before the pupil makes the copy of his first draft; that is, in time to make corrections for the "reader." Expository writing done for utilitarian purposes lends itself to this analysis better than creative writing.

The following plan has been used successfully by teachers and can be administered fairly easily. The teachers can work with the entire class in matters of concern to many pupils and work with the individual pupil in cases where errors are not common to others in the class. Each pupil is provided with a mimeographed tally sheet like the one below.

Name_____   Room_____ Date_____
Mistakes I make in writing   *Words I misspelled*
       (Tally errors.)   (List words; tally repetitions.)
Sentences
    Fragments_____   _____
    Comma faults_____   _____
    Run-on sentences_____   _____
Verbs_____   _____
Pronouns_____   _____
Spelling_____   _____
Word division_____   _____
Capital letters_____   _____
Punctuation   _____
    Commas_____   _____
    Semicolons_____   _____
    Colons_____   _____
    Apostrophes_____   _____
    Quotation marks_____   _____
Other mistakes   _____

_____   _____
_____   _____
_____   _____

Tally sheets of this kind may be issued for each grading period. Pupils will file the tally sheets with their written compositions in their individual folders. They tally their errors from all written work that has been checked by the teacher during that period. At the end of the tally period, the teacher asks for a show of hands to see how many made each kind of error. For those errors made by many of the pupils, the teacher plans time for class instruction. For errors made by only a few, he may gather the small group around a table for instruction. After the errors have been identified and the way to correct them understood, the teacher can help pupils clinch their learning by assigning corrective lessons from the textbook.

Since most language textbooks provide for some practice exercises on the kinds of correction listed on the tally sheet, these assignments may be prepared in advance by page numbers referring to the texts available. The teacher then assigns the corrective lessons individually according to the capacity of the pupil and the greatest needs indicated by his tally sheet.

A plan such as this can be modified as necessary to fit a teacher's own classroom situation. If he follows the basic principles, pupils will respond with interest in improving their writing. They understand that the instruction is directed to their own needs. In the end, instruction *must* be individualized, for writing is an individual skill. Each child must face his own weaknesses and overcome them.

From one tally period to another during the year pupils can watch to see their own progress. As in other skills, learning is stimulated in children when they can observe their own improvement.

Many times pupils make mistakes in writing through carelessness rather than ignorance. Particularly in writing their first draft, when they are more concerned with the thoughts to be expressed than the conventions of usage, spelling, punctuation or capitalization, they are likely to leave a trail of avoidable mistakes. These should and can be corrected in checking. The difficulty lies in making the job of checking important in the eyes of the pupils and in providing time for its accomplishment.

Some teachers announce time for checking a short while before collecting papers, thus calling this procedure to the attention of the pupils. (Often it is wise to have pupils file their papers until the next day before checking them. Pupils are more likely to note errors and weaknesses when their writing is cold.) Some ask their pupils to check carefully, make corrections, and then sign a statement at the end of the paper signifying that they have completed a careful checking. For variety's sake, teachers sometimes allow the pupils to receive help in checking from their classmates.

If two or three specific technical skills have recently been the object of study, the teacher may ask the pupils to draw columns in the left margin headed by the skills, such as punctuation, capitalization, or sentence structure. Then in groups of four, the pupils circulate their papers, each reader checking in the indicated marginal column any errors discovered in a line-by-line analysis. The pupils must have a few minutes to verify the need of corrections marked by their classmates and to make the corrections. This they will do before handing their papers to the teacher.

Though exchanging papers for checking sometimes stimulates interest, it does not take the place of the pupil's own checking based upon careful analysis of his writing. Nor does it replace the teacher's reading and scoring with marginal notations followed by an occasional pupil conference. When assignments can be made in a classroom so that most pupils will be occupied by reading references in order to meet a deadline, the teacher can call a few of the pupils to his desk and have a brief period for discussing their writing individually. Nothing will prove more useful than the face-to-face conference in which pupil and teacher read the paper together and try to see how they may avoid difficulties and develop good writing.

NEAT MANUSCRIPT

The appearance of the paper in written communication is as important as the dress and manner of the person in oral communication. Upper-grade pupils need to have certain standards in mind; further, they need to be encouraged to measure up to these standards. They should come to feel that an untidy, illegible manuscript constitutes a discourtesy to anyone who is to read it. Specific suggestions regarding the development of attitudes and skills in producing a good-looking paper are made in Chapter 17, "Developing Handwriting Skills."

One teacher surprised his pupils early in the school year by glancing over the papers they had just handed in and marking with a red pencil a high grade on a few papers. These he held up before the class, who were shocked to see that he had graded the papers without reading the content. Then the teacher explained that occasionally during the year, when he found papers that were superior in neatness and penmanship or that showed great improvement, he would give them a separate grade for appearance in addition to the grade for content, organization, and technical skills. Though grading is obviously an extrinsic motivation for learning, it undoubtedly stimulates some pupils. A more valid motivation, educationally speaking, would be for the teacher to plan, as often as possible, to have the pupils' written work displayed or read by others besides himself—since motivation increases when people write in order to communicate with specific people separated from them by time and space.

Basic Principles to Guide Instruction

IN PLANNING instruction to lift the performance level in written communication, every teacher is influenced either consciously or unconsciously by certain basic principles. These principles may vary in educational value. An example of an unsound principle, which might never be put into words but might still determine a teacher's procedure, is to believe that pupils should not write until they know grammar. If such an assumption served as the guide to instruction in writing, the efforts of both teacher and pupils in elementary school would be primarily concerned with learning *about* language rather than practicing to *use* it effectively. Such an emphasis is neither suitable for the age level (because it does not take into account the complexities of grammatical concepts) nor agreeable to the psychology of learning (because it neglects practice and guidance in writing).

In order to evaluate the principles that shape the teacher's plans, it is necessary to put them in words. Then they can be given the thoughtful consideration they deserve. The following statements (in italic print) seem worthy of being considered guiding principles in helping pupils to write well.

Writing is for the purpose of communicating ideas. Pupils need help to see that writing serves a purpose only when it conveys a meaning to a reader. When children write, they must use words that convey clearly their ideas to their readers. They must use these words correctly and must follow the precepts of good grammar and correct usage. When the teacher makes communication the heart of instruction, the teaching of usage and grammar becomes rightfully a means to an end rather than the end in itself. Then he can spend the major amount of time on the real experiences in writing—experiences designed to meet the need for conveying ideas. Pupils should have guidance from the teacher when they try to express their thoughts on paper. As he watches them write, he can suggest corrections and improvements according to their recognized needs and their ability to understand.

Emphasis upon communication places the responsibility for critical thinking upon the writer. If the main aim is to keep a record, convey a message, or share thoughts and feelings, the writer must be as concerned with the correctness of his facts and the soundness of his reasoning as he is about the use of conventional forms or technical writing skills. In short, instruction in written expression should aim primarily at communication as demonstrated by actual performance of this complex human activity, and evaluation of writing skill should be based primarily on the degree to which the communication is or can be successful.

Not all the specific goals in teaching writing are equally important.

A teacher must bear in mind the relative importance of instructional goals. It is not as important for the margin to be a certain width as it is for the thought to be clearly expressed. It is not even as important for the spelling to be correct as it is for the reasoning to be sound, though spelling is admittedly important and an easier target for both teachers and the public. These suggestions are not meant to persuade teachers to lessen their efforts to improve the mechanics of writing. Almost all teachers of English are already keenly aware of this need and, if not, they will soon become aware of it through public pressures.

The warning indicates, however, that other goals are important too; they should be seen in proper perspective and sought by devoting proportionate time for instruction. It would be unfortunate if a teacher should bear so heavily on one major goal that he could give little or no attention to others. Neatness, technical skills, effective expression, organization of ideas, and critical thinking each require direct instruction applied to the pupil's writing.

Perhaps the technical skills have tended to usurp attention because they are so much easier to measure or so much more easily supported by a "rule." Some of the goals essential in good communication cannot be found in a rule book. They may, however, be as vital as those that are. From among the many specific aims directed toward good writing, English teachers are responsible for putting first things first as they guide pupils toward more effective written communication.

Language is a changing manifestation of human behavior. When a person studies language development over a long period of time, it is easy for him to see how it changes. Chaucer's way of expressing thought looks very different from our own when he writes

> Whan that Aprille with his shoures sote
> The droghte of Marche hath perced to the rote,
> And bathed every veyne in swich licour,
> Of which vertu engendred is the flour.

The language of Shakespeare, or even that of characters in books written in the nineteenth century, reveals how language has changed from the past to the present. What shall be the authority for good language today? Not even a textbook on language usage of twenty-five years ago can be the reliable authority for the language of the present time. The criterion must be based upon the practices of educated people today.

Since language is a living thing and changes as people change, its standards of acceptability vary not only from one generation to another but also from one situation to another. Appropriateness of language is measured in different usage levels. One teacher used an interesting analogy when he spoke of the use of the white-collar word *go* for everyday business occasions, the more dignified word *depart* as a white-tie-and-tails term, *scram* for no tie and slacks, and *git* for run down at the heels. Only the last is at all times taboo by social standards; the other words are right when used at the right time.

If English teachers do not accept change, they open themselves to just criticism from people who establish their standards upon the language of the educated. When there is so much that is essential to teach, they cannot afford to expend their efforts in holding to standards that are out of date or inappropriate to the occasion.

People learn by doing, in writing as well as other skills. This principle implies that the best way to have children learn to write is by practice in the whole competency involved. Neither diagraming sentences nor filling in blanks will accomplish improvement in expressing ideas in writing. Only practice in writing develops such skills as organizing ideas, checking the validity of one's ideas, developing a paragraph adequately, choosing words well, observing the conventions in one's own sentences, and producing a neat and attractive paper.

Some teachers, who agree to the principle of learning by doing, restrict somewhat regretfully writing activities because they lack time for extensive correction of papers. They do not wish to have pupils write anything that cannot be carefully corrected. Their argument should be seriously questioned. A teacher can correct writing at regular intervals but he does not have to correct it every time the children write. When he does give instruction during a writing lesson, his suggestions should be quite specific. The pupils can benefit from these suggestions during later practice writing periods in which there is no help from the teacher and before another conference points up other things to work on.

Some things the pupil writes can be carefully analyzed; some will have to be merely "checked in." But unless children find real purposes for writing and apply serious effort, their progress in writing will be too slow for them to measure and therefore not satisfying to them. When pupils write often with earnest purpose and save their written work in individual folders, the year's work will speak for itself. They will be able to note progress in their ability to express themselves in writing.

Good writing depends upon a mind furnished with ideas. Someone has said that no good writing ever comes from a vacuum. What the pupil has done and seen, what he has read and heard about, serve as a source upon which he must draw when he writes. If little is there, he cannot write effectively. The demand for writing must be preceded by experiences that have furnished his mind with knowledge and understanding. Schools that give pupils many experiences of value and vividness serve best in preparing them for instruction in writing. Beyond that point, each pupil

The curator's explanations make these pupils' observations in a natural history museum meaningful and enhance their written reports.

must labor for himself with the teacher showing him the way when he tends to lose sight of the goals.

Walter de la Mare, in *Memoirs of a Midget*,* had Miss M. address a great author, asking him how to write. "Lord have mercy upon me," he said, "*to write*, my dear young lady. Well there is only one recipe I have ever heard of. Take a quart or more of life-blood; mix it with a bottle of ink, and a teaspoonful of tears; and ask God to forgive the blots."

Upper-Grade Writing and School Organization

THE problem of instruction in written communication will vary at the upper-grade level according to the type of school organization in which the teacher works. If the upper grades are organized somewhat like the self-contained homerooms prevalent in the lower grades, the opportunities for relating instruction in daily writing to any of the school experiences, regardless of subject matter, are unlimited. A class log of a unit on health and safety, or a report on a science experiment, for example, may provide the natural motive for learning to give accurate information in complete sentences. The need to request information in a study of state government may be the basis for learning about the form and content of a business letter.

In school systems organized under the junior high school plan, large blocks of time may be arranged, with English and social studies, and possibly other subject areas, grouped under the instruction of one teacher. Here too the writing may be related to the diverse needs found in many kinds of learning activities.

Where English is taught in a program similar to the typical high school plan, as a separate subject under an English teacher, the teacher may find it necessary to use more ingenuity to relate instruction in writing to the pupils' general needs. The importance of doing so is worth the effort, however; pupils who can see the direct influence of their instruction in writing, and who can observe increased effectiveness in written communication, will be ready to receive direction in improving their skill.

By serious planning within those school faculties where each teacher instructs in only one subject, schools can develop methods of cooperating to help boys and girls recognize certain needs: in improving pupils' written expression in all subjects; in seeing that pupils receive needed instruction and that they apply the instruction in all their writing. Such cooperation in the faculty must be an honest, two-way effort. English teachers can plan with others some methods of arranging their instruction so that it applies to writing done in other classes; other teachers can plan with English teachers some basic criteria for good writing which students

* *Modern Writers at Work*, J. K. Piercy, ed., New York, Macmillan, 1930.

will be expected to follow in all classes. Such interplanning offers strong support to the efforts of any English teacher. And it is right to expect all members of a faculty to recognize some responsibilities in common regarding instruction in English. Improved communication of ideas is a basic aim of education and essential in a democracy. It cuts across all subject boundaries as much as moral and spiritual values.

For instance, every teacher wants pupils to use the vocabulary of his subject with precision in meaning and spelling, to see that their facts are accurate and their opinions supported, to express their ideas so that others will understand them, to write legibly enough to be read easily. These are some matters upon which teachers of different subjects can put forth a united front. What are other ways in which English teachers can make their influence felt beyond a single hour in the day? The best way to find out is to get faculty members together to work out a plan that offers mutual satisfaction.

SUGGESTIONS FOR STUDY AND DISCUSSION

1. Collect two or three sets of informative or expository papers. Analyze each paper for each of the characteristics discussed under "Good Thinking" early in this chapter.

2. Analyze a textbook in language to find lessons that will help pupils learn how to organize a written report or story.

3. Keep a week's diary of situations when you need to use words precisely.

4. Try to develop a paragraph from the following topic sentence by each of the procedures mentioned for paragraph development, page 302. "Power brakes are a great asset in an automobile."

5. Make a list of words that have many interesting synonyms which are too rarely used. List the synonyms with each word.

6. How do motivation, guidance, and evaluation of utilitarian writing differ from the treatment of creative writing?

FOR FURTHER READING

1. BATEMAN, DONALD R., "More Mature Writing Through a Better Understanding of Language Structure." *English Journal* (October 1961), 457–60, 468.

2. BURROWS, ALVINA TREUT, and others, *They All Want to Write*. Englewood Cliffs, N. J., Prentice-Hall, 1952.

3. CARLSEN, G. ROBERT, "English for the Ungifted." *English Journal* (May 1961), 329–33, 337.

4. COOK, LUELLA B., "Writing as Self-Revelation," *English Journal* (May 1959), 247–53.

5. DUSEL, WILLIAM J., "How Should Student Writing Be Judged?" *English Journal* (May 1957), 263–68, 299.
6. GORDON, EDWARD J., and EDWARD S. NOYER, *Essays on the Teaching of English* (Part II). New York, Appleton-Century-Crofts, 1960.
7. GREENE, HARRY A., and WALTER T. PETTY, *Developing Language Skills in the Elementary School* (Chapters 6, 12). Boston, Allyn and Bacon, 1959.
8. GROSE, LOIS, "Essential Conditions for Teaching Written Composition." *English Journal* (April 1961), 246–51.
9. JOHNSON, ERIC W., "Stimulating and Improving Writing in the Junior High School." *English Journal* (February 1958), 68–76, 91.
10. KLAUSMEIER, HERBERT J., and others, *Teaching in the Elementary School* (268–82). New York, Harper, 1956.
11. LABRANT, LOU, "Inducing Children to Write." *English Journal* (February 1955), 70–74, 116.
12. *Language Arts for Today's Children*, Commission on the English Curriculum of the National Council of Teachers of English. New York, Appleton-Century-Crofts, 1954.
13. LOBAN, WALTER, MARGARET RYAN, and JAMES R. SQUIRE, *Teaching Language and Literature* (Chapter 10). New York, Harcourt, Brace & World, 1961.
14. MERSAND, JOSEPH, "What Has Happened to Written Composition?" *English Journal* (April 1961), 231–37.
15. OLSEN, HELEN F., "What Is Good Teaching of Written Composition?" *English Journal* (April 1961), 238–45.
16. POOLEY, ROBERT, *Teaching English Usage*. New York, Appleton-Century-Crofts, 1946.
17. SMILEY, MARJORIE B., "Do Your Classroom Procedures Really Teach Communication?" *English Journal* (February 1958), 81–85.
18. WATTS, A. F., *The Language and Mental Development of Children*. London, Harrap; Boston, Heath, 1947.
19. WOLFE, DON, *Language Arts and Life Patterns* (Chapters 21, 31). New York, Odyssey, 1961.

17

Developing Handwriting Skills

Chapter 17 discusses handwriting in terms of skills and attitudes which need to be developed through the elementary grades. Problems concern readiness for instruction, manuscript and cursive writing, and the transition from one to the other. Legibility, ease, speed, and attractiveness are presented as major goals. Suggestions are given for approaching such goals with due consideration to individual problems like left-handedness, with an emphasis on application of handwriting skill in all written communication.

HANDWRITING is sometimes called a tool subject. Its importance lies in the fact that it is the medium through which most people can record their ideas for their own use or for the use of others. If the tool is to serve its purpose, instruction in the elementary school must lead to the major objective, that of writing legibly, and two other important objectives, those of performing the writing task with ease and speed while producing a neat, attractive paper. Fundamental to the acquisition of these skills is the favorable attitude that is built up about handwriting.

Since writing by hand tends to be individualistic in expression, it is likely to be affected by at least two things: the more stable characteristics of the person, such as his temperament; and the stresses of the moment, such as his mood, his need for haste, or his feeling about whether what he is writing is important enough to merit his best efforts. Handwriting instruction must therefore include attention not only to the development of the specific skills involved but also to the attitudes that foster a desire for improvement and a willingness to put forth effort.

To achieve these ends, most school systems plan a developmental program in handwriting which begins with a period for measuring and building readiness, proceeds with instruction in manuscript writing, and moves into cursive writing in second or third grade. The initial instruction and the period of transition from manuscript to cursive are both periods that require special care in establishing habits.

From the earliest presentation of writing, on through the elementary school, handwriting must be an integral part of instruction in the language arts. The need for the written word will arise in the classroom whenever children's ongoing experiences are important and interesting to them. Out of their need comes a natural interest in learning how to write legibly.

The teacher should see that instruction periods are followed by ample opportunity for the child to put the instruction to use in practical situations that seem important to him. Thus a handwriting program evolves which includes careful instruction, drill or practice needed to promote facility, and application of the skill to children's daily work. When the teacher makes sure that motivation is stimulated by the need to write, that standards for handwriting are kept high, and that instruction is based upon frequent individual diagnosis of handwriting, the improvement in children's handwriting should be continuous.

The Primary Program

EVEN the first step in handwriting should not be taught by and for itself. From the start, a child should have something to write and a genuine purpose in writing it. For instance, the teacher can show the first grader how to put his name on a picture he has drawn or how to label an object he has placed on the science table. Further demands for writing arise as he learns to add a caption to his picture, copy a notice or announcement to take home, or write a simple story to accompany the picture strips he is making into a booklet. Not single letters, but words and even simple phrases and sentences are the units that the young child will find essential for his written communication. Gertrude Hildreth(12, p. 4) pointed out that as early as the 1900's Dr. Ovid Decroly, the Belgian educator,

> advocated teaching children to write by beginning with whole, meaningful words such as they used in speaking and were learning to read. He concluded [that] learning to write is not achieved best by motor imitation but by expression of ideas graphically. The visual images of whole, meaningful words are most easily retained because they express ideas.

Practice on selected letter forms should follow as the child exhibits the need for added proficiency. In the early stages of writing during the primary grades, the teacher will be at hand to show the child how to make letters that offer him some difficulty—where to start the pencil, the direction in which to move it, the shape of full-bodied letter forms. When a pupil needs help, the teacher will provide a good model of the letter forms by writing them on the child's paper or on the chalkboard. The immediacy of this kind of help, offered repeatedly as the child is occupied with practical writing tasks, seems to be more useful in fixing the writing habits of the beginning pupil than a formal handwriting period.

This is not to say that there is no value in practice. Practice by beginners, however, should consist of the application of improved skills in a functional writing experience rather than the use of unrelated drill exercises.

READINESS FOR WRITING

Maturation in the area of visual perception is an important factor in readiness for writing. The intricacy of the psychomotor processes involved in writing is brought out by Gertrude Hildreth(11, pp. 583–84):

> Learning to write is not a mechanical, lower-level reflex response, but a thinking process, entailing activity of the cortical nerve areas. Smooth motor coordination of eye and hand, control of arm, hand, and finger muscles are acquired in the process of learning to write and are needed for legible results. Learning to write also requires maturity adequate for accurate perception of the symbol patterns. Writing from memory demands the retention of visual and kinesthetic images of forms, not present to the senses, for future recall. . . . From earliest infancy, the eyes guide the hand, and the hand may be considered the instrument which carries out impulses received from the visual organs. The capacity for graphic representation, such as writing requires, depends on the motor function of the eye and is coordinated with the eye movements.

Teaching practices are changing according to the increasing knowledge about child development. Teachers now postpone instruction in writing until children are sufficiently mature and have a genuine need for writing; children use simplified letter forms for easier learning; teachers allow beginners to write on the chalkboard or on sheets of unruled or widely spaced paper.

Inasmuch as children develop at different rates, the up-to-date teacher takes continuous inventory of the children's prewriting experiences that promote or help to indicate readiness for writing, such as drawing on paper or chalkboard, cutting paper, modeling with clay, or using tools in construction activities. He notes the relative proficiency of eye and hand coordination attained by the children, their keenness of visual perception, and their general stage of development. He gives small-group instruction only to group members with common levels of achievement and similar need to express themselves in writing. He sees that children begin their learning in such a way and at such a time as to permit optimal progress.

MANUSCRIPT WRITING

When children are ready for their first writing experiences, the teacher plans instruction at a time when they are not fatigued or shaky after vigorous exercise. Usually the first writing a child wishes to accomplish is the writing of his own name. The purpose is immediate and important. He repeats the writing often, whenever he needs to sign a drawing or a painting, label a personal possession, or sign a letter. When the chalkboard is used, the teacher should see that the words to be copied are written level with the child's eyes. Later, when the teacher wants the child to copy from the board, he allows the child to move close enough to see clearly.

Manuscript writing is comparatively easy to learn: letters are discrete, movements are short, the letter forms resemble the print in books. Moreover, wide research shows that the beginner who is taught the manuscript letter forms, rather than the cursive, writes more legibly, makes fewer random movements, and gets better results with a minimum expenditure of effort. The reason is that the straight line and circle, or half circle, and the spacing used in manuscript writing follow the natural arm movements of young children. In other words, in manuscript writing children simply do what comes naturally. The child's use of manuscript writing also facilitates his learning to read since the letter forms closely resemble print. So well known are the advantages of this writing for children in the early primary grades that most schools are now using it in the first two or three grades.

Although some schools permit pupils to continue the use of manuscript writing in the higher grades, it is common practice to make a transition to cursive writing in the third grade or, less often, in the second. Since manuscript writing is so legible and almost as rapid—perhaps fully as rapid for some children—as cursive writing, one may well ask why make the transition at all. However, most parents want their children to "learn to write"; the pupils, who often consider manuscript form "baby" writing, prefer to use the kind of writing that the older members of the family use; teachers in the higher grades frequently prefer the tradition-sanctioned cursive writing; and most children have acquired the requisite muscular coordination by the time they are in the upper primary grades.

There is a diversity of opinions regarding the use of the two styles of writing. Virgil E. Herrick(9, p. 252) states that "less than one in twenty-five schools teaches either one exclusively." It follows, then, that more than ninety-six per cent of schools teach both manuscript and cursive.

TRANSITION TO CURSIVE WRITING

The proper time for introducing cursive writing is still a moot question. Research has established that many pupils can make the transition in the latter half of second grade. Children have not yet so fixed the manuscript forms that there will be much interference as they take on the somewhat different forms of the cursive alphabet and learn to connect letters within a word. Even so, current practice seems to be tending toward a delay in making the transition.

Postponement of the transition is justified on several counts. In the first place, many children are eight, or even older, before they have the necessary coordination for cursive writing. Then, there is the problem of reading. If manuscript writing facilitates learning to read, it is possible that changing to cursive writing before reading skills are far enough developed may slow up the reading process. An even more important consideration is that the continuation of manuscript writing seems to facilitate the child's learning to write out his ideas independently. When the manuscript forms have become automatic, the child can concentrate on what he is trying to express. It seems unwise to shift from the use of manuscript writing just at the time the child is beginning to write independently. Good writing habits and attitudes can take root if the teacher does not rush the child from an acquired skill in manuscript writing to the new requirements of cursive forms. By postponing the transition, he gives the child time to develop his power of independent expression relatively undisturbed by the mechanics of handwriting. Then, when the child is older, his added maturity gives him power to change to cursive writing with less difficulty.

In general, teachers find that children accomplish the transition from manuscript to cursive quite easily if they are not rushed. Manuals for the various handwriting series give explicit directions. More and more teachers are settling on the following policy: Offer instruction in cursive writing when the children appear to be ready to make the change successfully; but if individuals do cling to the familiar and easy manuscript form while thinking and organizing their ideas, let them use the form they prefer.

Certain types of evidence in the child's manuscript writing usually guides a teacher in determining his readiness for instruction in cursive writing. Frank N. Freeman(6, p. 371) gives this advice:

> First, he should have a fairly good mastery of manuscript before changing to the more complex form of writing, as indicated by a good recognition of the forms of the letters and a satisfactory control of the movements of writing them. This will warrant us in expecting that he will be able to form a clear idea of the form of the letters and the words in the cursive form, and

Mark Schlossberg September 30, 1960.   100
                        Language   A

1. Mr. and Mrs. Brown live in Albany, New York.
2. Mary owns a cat named Fluffy.
3. Tomorrow the month of October begins.
4. Nancy and Peggy may may go to the movies on Sunday.
5. He and I go to Hoover School.
6. Does he live in Bergenfield, New Jersey.?
7. Soon she and I will go to school.
8. I think Jim will have a birthday party in November.
9. Do Mr. and Mrs. Smith own a dog called Spot?
10. Miss Jones will visit us Wednesday night.

Mark Schlossberg   A   February 24, 1961
                Spelling

                The Lame Crow

        One day Mr. Howe found a baby
crow with a broken leg. It was by the
side of the gate near the road. Mr.
Howe held the crow in his hand. It
blinked its round eyes and flapped its
wings.
        Mr. Howe did not want the baby
crow to die. He tied its leg with a
splint and some string. Soon the crow
could stand on one leg and watch Mr.

Samples of a third grader's written work show his transition from manuscript to cursive forms in five months' time.

will be able to acquire the continuous and more complex movements involved in forming the letters and connected strokes of cursive. These, along with the child's desire to change and ability to apply himself, will indicate that he is ready.

An evidence of readiness for cursive writing, familiar to most primary teachers, is the tendency for a child to slant his letters and form some loops and connecting lines, rather than to adhere strictly to the vertical lines and separate letter forms. His own requests about when he can begin what he sometimes calls "real writing" indicate his interest. The ability to write a simple story a few sentences in length without undue fatigue or overdependence on the teacher's help and a span of attention long enough to accept instruction are other characteristics that the child must have if he is to be successful in the transition to cursive writing.

The teacher should face the fact that cursive writing will not necessarily come easily to children because they already know manuscript writing. Throughout the change-over period he should provide systematic instruction and careful guidance.

Teachers may find helpful Gertrude Hildreth's(12, p. 10) suggestions about the mechanics of changing over:

> Converting from print style writing to cursive longhand after three or even two years of systematic training in manuscript represents an abrupt change in a motor skill. This is not a simple matter of joining the letters but of learning new letter strokes and proportions, and slant. Some letters differ considerably from print style; the pen is not lifted from the paper in writing each letter of a word; and there are connecting strokes linking the letters within the words. In making the change-over teachers are asking the pupils to change their handwriting movements. Letters that begin at the base line in cursive begin at the top in manuscript style. The strokes required in cursive style and manuscript writing are diametrically opposite for a number of the letters; compare "b" and "d," "f" and "h," "l," "k," "r," "s."

Cursive longhand is not a natural development from unjoined writing. Most children will not join the letters spontaneously; joining must always be taught and drilled. Unless instruction in the shifting process is persistent and thorough, children may show confusion in styles and never become fully proficient writers.

The Intermediate and Upper-Grade Program

SOME school systems teach only manuscript writing throughout the elementary grades. In such systems teachers should give some direct attention to teaching the reading of cursive writing. By doing this, they can obviate criticisms that might arise when manuscript writers of third-grade level or above have difficulty reading cursive writing. In most systems, however, children enter the intermediate grades with a beginning knowledge of cursive writing.

If such is the plan, intermediate and upper-grade teachers should take definite steps to help children maintain their skill in manuscript writing while developing cursive writing skills. There are certain kinds of writing activities that teachers and pupils can carry out most successfully if manuscript writing is used. Labels, proper names on maps, and items listed on a chart are examples. The need for writing such things recurs frequently, and teachers should encourage the use of manuscript for these occasions. It is a waste of effort to allow a child's skill in manuscript writing, developed in the first years of school, to die for lack of use; and this waste is needless since the child really should use manuscript writing rather than cursive in the specific writing activities mentioned above.

A check against the basic objectives of handwriting instruction may serve as a help in surveying common needs at intermediate- and upper-grade level. The goals, it may be recalled, are legibility, ease and speed, and neatness and attractiveness of the written paper. Development of these qualities, together with a favorable attitude toward improvement efforts, is the concern of the teacher.

LEGIBILITY

The most important goal of instruction is legibility. Teachers who take time to observe how children make their letter forms often discover awkward methods in making certain letters; for instance, the child will start at the wrong end and guide his pencil backward to the first stroke of the letter. The teacher can give direct and immediate help in such instances, with enough practice at the board or on paper to give the child a feeling for the new method.

In addition to letter formation, there are problems of keeping the slant uniform and not exaggerated, avoiding extremes in the size of letters and keeping rounded parts "fat," using enough but not too much space between letters and between words, and keeping letters straight on the line and spaced so that upper and lower loops do not intersect each other.

Each of these problems, related to legibility, can be solved by direct attention through group and individual instruction. Even in large classes, the teacher's ability to discover individual needs and administer appropriate instruction becomes the crucial point on which the program rests.

As in other skills involved in the language arts, such as spelling, punctuation, capitalization, and usage, the teacher will obtain the best results if he will offer to the group a well-planned developmental program, supplemented daily by incidental instruction given to individual pupils while the pupils are putting the specific skill to use in the normal course of their schoolroom experiences. In the case of handwriting, he should probably devote more time to group instruction and practice in the intermediate grades, while the skill is still being developed, than in the upper grades. The exception would be for those upper-grade children who have special need for improvement.

Group instruction in handwriting need not be unrelated to the writing required in other school assignments. If the teacher will give instruction in some aspect of handwriting before a written assignment is to be checked, corrected, and copied, the pupils can apply the instruction as they proceed with the copying. Whether he uses lessons from commercially prepared materials or from those developed by the school, he can find a practice word or sentence that leads directly into the written assignment. It is often effective to combine the lesson in spelling with instruction in handwriting. Habits of carefulness developed in writing are likely to affect spelling favorably, and *vice versa.*

The length of time that the teacher devotes to direct instruction should differ according to the need, but he should see that no period extends beyond that point of saturation when fatigue or loss of interest cancels the values that the children receive. Some research has indicated that children gain as much from fifty minutes a week devoted to group instruction as from a hundred.

As for incidental instruction, the teacher must observe the writing process, as well as the product that each child hands in on his completed paper. In many cases, a change in the position of the child's paper on the desk, a correction in the manner of forming small or capital letters, a suggestion about moving the paper while writing across the page, and other such constructive guidance, will mean most to the pupil if the teacher offers the suggestion at the right time; that is, when it will make a difference in the paper the child is producing. To give such help at the teachable moment, the teacher must watch for opportunities while the children are writing.

EASE AND SPEED IN WRITING

Since freedom from physical tensions is likely to permit increased speed without loss of legibility, the problems of securing ease and speed in writing are related to each other. Ease in writing is promoted by good posture and correct handling of the pencil or pen. Though children usually conform to good standards in posture during a handwriting lesson, they are likely to need a reminder from the teacher as they work on other writing assignments. Pupils sometimes get the bad habit of sitting on one foot or dropping one shoulder by placing the unused hand on the seat.

If the pupil's head is bent too low over the paper, the teacher may suspect a weakness in his vision. His grasp on the pen or pencil, though firm, should not be so tense as to produce cramped writing or fatigue. The teacher should check frequently to see that his thumb is not stiff. Most handwriting experts advise that the child hold the pencil an inch or an inch and a half from the point. They recommend that the child use a combination of arm and finger movement in cursive writing, and current practices prove this recommendation to be sound.

Wrong habits once developed are hard to uproot. For that reason it is particularly important for the teacher to supervise posture and the position of the pen or pencil in the hand during the initial experiences of the child. A crucial time for habit formation in writing occurs when the child begins manuscript writing, and again when he begins cursive writing. At these times the teacher needs to make frequent corrections of faults that must never be allowed to become habitual.

The teacher should not emphasize speed until the children's basic letter forms are so well established that the act of writing has become automatic. By the time pupils have reached this stage, however, some individuals have fallen into a pattern of such slow movements that they need prodding to be able to finish their assignments. All children need to consider the problem of good writing in relation to their rate of writing.

Researchers have found that quality of handwriting tends to deteriorate with age. Because of the increased time pressures on most individuals as they grow older, schools should develop handwriting skills that can be maintained with a reasonable degree of speed. Occasionally, the teacher can give three-minute check tests on speed when the children are writing something so familiar that they do not have to pause to think of the words.

NEATNESS OF THE WRITTEN PAGE

One of the aims of handwriting instruction should be to teach what form is acceptable on the written page. For example, the teacher can explain that margins are a means of giving the page the appearance of a frame. Just as a picture needs a frame to be shown off to advantage, a page of written work needs a margin of clean paper on all four sides of the page. Keeping the left-hand margin straight should be well established; but some may need to be reminded to leave the right-hand margin wide enough to avoid the appearance of crowding words at the end of the line. If pupils forget about leaving margins or have a very crooked left-hand margin at first, the teacher might suggest that they draw a margin line wherever needed.

After the pupils learn to write legibly with a fair degree of ease and speed with pencil, they should use ink for formal writing, including the final draft of assigned compositions in any subject and letters to be sent

This boy writes with ease because of his proper position at his desk.

to persons outside the school. If the written paragraphs require planning, organization, and final checking (as most do), the children have had training enough by now to expect to copy the final draft, and to copy it in ink.

DEVELOPING INTEREST IN HANDWRITING

The ability to create and maintain interest in producing good handwriting is one of the problems confronting every teacher. He can solve it satisfactorily by providing frequent experiences in writing which are so important in the eyes of the child that a natural sense of pride inspires his best efforts. The advantage of developing interest in handwriting in contrast with some of the other skills lies in the observable progress which the child can measure. In planning to keep alive his interest, the teacher will want to make use of the child's handwriting evaluation and self-diagnosis that he does in the course of his regular work.

The best way to promote evaluation is to have pupils file written compositions weekly in their individual folders. Paragraphs relating to social studies, health, science, literature, or other topics of current interest serve best as a basis for measuring improvement in handwriting. Periodically during the year, the teacher may ask the students to select from their folders the paper representing their best handwriting. Some teachers like to give an occasional separate grade on the appearance of the paper, particularly if the pupil's improvement merits some recognition. This is extrinsic motivation, to be sure; but as a supplementary way of increasing interest, it may have its value. At least it assures the pupils that handwriting and the general appearance of the paper are important in the estimation of their teacher.

A handwriting scale against which to measure progress may be used occasionally to stimulate interest in improvement. One of the well-known handwriting scales (1), conveniently posted on the bulletin board, can give pupils a basis for judging their own writing and possibly raising the level of their standards for themselves. Frank N. Freeman(5) quotes a study which placed the average quality rating of fifth-grade writing at slightly above 50 on the Ayres Scale and of eighth-grade writing at almost 63.

The class group or individuals may make handwriting scales from specimens of their own writing. Five or more of a pupil's papers, saved over a period of three or four months, furnish the basis. He will take random cuttings of a few lines from each paper, arrange them in order of the quality of handwriting, and paste them with the best at the top. He should date each sample to indicate whether his improvement has been erratic or steady. If a pupil files this writing scale in the fall and follows a similar procedure in the spring, he has a good indication of his progress in handwriting during the year.

Dear Marion and Ed,

I thank you for those jackets you sent us. Did you see the Eagles play the Cardinals?

I'm sure you didn't. But anyway thankyou for those jackets.

Walter bought us a football suit. And we almost play football every afternoon.

Monday March 23, 1959
2705 Ave. R.

Dear Aunt Marion,

We now live in Snyder, Texas. Of course you know where your mother and Father live.

I thank you for what you gave us for Christmas. I've forgotten what it was but any way thank you.

Our Spelling words this week are fireman, beautiful, Friday, fire, morning, fine, say, handy, hour, bad, called, look, bell, none, rain, pull, hit, brown, field, pulled, dead, once, threw, and throw.

Two letters written four months apart illustrate the improvement in a third grader's cursive handwriting technique. These samples also demonstrate the value of courtesy letters as exercises in writing.

Many teachers find the use of the opaque projector to be effective in improving handwriting. For this purpose, a teacher plans one lesson with the projector so that handwriting is the principal subject of study. By looking at papers of many individuals and discussing ways of improving the handwriting and appearance of the papers, pupils acquire new understanding of their needs and a sense of the importance of good handwriting. While they are observing strong and weak points in the samples, the teacher may lead them to list the characteristics which they consider desirable themselves. Standards that they construct through their own participation are likely to be more impressive than those they read in a book.

Individual Problems in All Grades

DEFECTS in handwriting cannot be treated intelligently without identifying their nature and understanding their probable causes. Difficulties in letter form, slant, spacing and alignment, lack of readiness or lack of interest and purpose, and left-handedness are common defects. Individualizing instruction involves recurrent diagnosis of needs by the teacher with evaluation by pupils and teacher following the necessary instruction.

A check list prepared by upper-grade pupils is printed below as an

MY HANDWRITING CHART

Date	*Sept.*	*Nov.*	*Jan.*	*Mar.*	*May*
1. Capitals should be at least twice as large as small letters.					
2. The difference between *o*'s, *c*'s, and *a*'s should be clear.					
3. Round parts of *m*'s, *n*'s, and *u*'s should be clear.					
4. Loops on *f*'s, *j*'s, *g*'s, and *y*'s should be clearly drawn below the line.					
5. Loops should not intercept writing on lines above and below.					
6. *T*'s should be crossed and *i*'s dotted (not with a circle).					
7. Letters should not be crowded together.					
8. Letters should all slant in the same direction.					
9. Words should be separated by clearly defined spaces.					
10. A page of manuscript should have pleasing margins.					

A left-handed child places his arm correctly in relation to the paper and uses a wire pen holder to improve his penmanship.

illustration of an individualized approach to improvement in handwriting. The teacher encouraged the class members to examine their handwriting and to state in their own words standards for which they might aim. The pupils marked the check sheet once every two months on the basis of a critical analysis of their own handwriting on a page of some regularly assigned paper. They marked + for improvement, — for retrogression, and × if the quality of their handwriting remained the same.

LEFT-HANDEDNESS

Since between five and ten per cent of the population are left-handed, the teacher is apt to have two or three left-handed pupils in class each year. If the dominance of the left hand is strong, the teacher should accept the fact without reluctance. He should make the child feel that being left-handed is a rather common characteristic that need not be a handicap in his writing. The child must recognize that left-handedness does mean that he must be careful in the way he holds his pencil and places his paper on the desk.

He should place the paper on the desk so that the bottom edge is at right angles to the left arm. He should grasp the pen or pencil an inch or an inch and a half from the point, thus allowing him a chance to see what he is writing. The pencil should point over the left shoulder. In this position, he will be able to write without smearing pencil marks or ink (as he would if his grasp on the writing implement were lower), and without slowing his performance and increasing strain (as he would if allowed to rest his hand in a hooked position above the line on which he is writing). The correct position for left-handed children is likely to produce vertical writing or a slight backhand. For beginners, especially in cursive writing, the teacher may need to supply the left-handed child with a model written in the slant which the child can copy comfortably.

Since the child has usually fairly well established his writing habits (like pencil grasp and paper placement) in the first years of school, the primary teachers are particularly responsible for giving the left-handed child a good start. At all grade levels, teachers who observe their pupils' writing habits will undoubtedly discover a left-handed writer who needs correction and instruction.

THE TEACHER'S HANDWRITING

Though the teacher's handwriting may lack the perfection of the copybook or wall chart, it should conform as closely as possible to the high standards set up as goals for instruction. When the teacher writes on charts or on the board, he should write large enough for all to see; he should leave enough space between lines so that letters do not overlap; and he should make sure that his letter forms are clear and legible. The teacher should keep unused portions of the board neatly erased. When he makes notations on the child's paper, he should write with care. Teaching by example, and not by word only, places upon him the responsibility of providing a model worthy of being copied.

SUGGESTIONS FOR STUDY AND DISCUSSION

1. Use a handwriting scale to evaluate your own handwriting; then practice on the elements that need improvement.

2. Observe in a classroom to note these things: typical pupil posture when writing, evidences of poor motor coordination on part of some pupils, adjustments to care for left-handedness, teacher's use of chalkboard and bulletin board, provision for individual differences, use of cumulative files of pupils' writing.

3. List policies likely to develop a real interest in writing all papers legibly and neatly in good form.

FOR FURTHER READING

1. AYRES, LEONARD P., *Ayres Measuring Scale for Handwriting*. Princeton, N. J., Cooperative Test Division of Educational Testing Service, 1912–40.
2. ENSTROM, E. A., "After Manuscript Writing—When Shall We Begin Cursive?" *Elementary School Journal* (October 1960), 24–27.
3. ERLEBACHER, ADRIENNE, and VIRGIL E. HERRICK, "Quality of Handwriting Today and Yesterday." *Elementary School Journal* (November 1961), 89–93.
4. FREEMAN, FRANK N., *Evaluation Scales for Guiding Growth in Handwriting*. Columbus, Ohio, Zaner-Bloser, 1958.
5. ——— *Teaching Handwriting*. Washington, D. C., Department of Classroom Teachers, American Education Research Association of the National Education Association, 1954.
6. ——— "The Transition from Manuscript to Cursive Writing." *Elementary English* (October 1958), 366–72.
7. GROFF, PATRICK J., "From Manuscript to Cursive—Why?" *Elementary School Journal* (November 1960), 97–101.
8. ——— "New Speeds of Handwriting." *Elementary English* (December 1961), 564–65.
9. HERRICK, VIRGIL E., "Handwriting and Children's Writing." *Elementary English* (April 1960), 248–58.
10. ——— "Manuscript and Cursive Writing." *Childhood Education* (February 1961), 264–67.
11. HILDRETH, GERTRUDE, *Learning the Three R's* (Chapters 19–21). Minneapolis, Educational Test Bureau, Educational Publishers, 1947.
12. ——— "Manuscript Writing After Sixty Years." *Elementary English* (January 1960), 3–13.

13. HORN, ERNEST, "Questions for Research on Handwriting." *Elementary School Journal* (March 1962), 304–12.

14. HUNNICUTT, C. W., and W. J. IVERSON, eds., *Research in the Three R's* (Chapter 9). New York, Harper, 1958.

15. LOGAN, LILLIAN M., and VIRGIL G., *Teaching the Elementary School Child* (301–14). Boston, Houghton Mifflin, 1961.

16. MAGARY, JAMES F., "The Psychologist Views School Language Activities." *Elementary School Journal* (February 1959), 282–85.

17. NULTON, LUCY, "From Manuscript to Cursive—How." *Elementary English* (December 1957), 553–56.

18. ——— "Readiness to Change from Manuscript to Cursive." *Elementary English* (October 1955), 382–83.

19. TEMPLIN, ELAINE, "Handwriting—the Neglected 'R,'" in "Research and Comment," *Elementary English* (October 1960), 386–89.

20. ——— "How Important Is Handwriting Today?" *Elementary School Journal* (December 1960), 158–64.

21. TIDYMAN, WILLARD F., and MARGUERITE BUTTERFIELD, *Teaching the Language Arts* (Chapter 15). New York, McGraw-Hill, 1959.

22. WEST, PAUL V., *American Handwriting Scale*. New York, A. N. Palmer, 1929–49.

18

Improving Children's Spelling

Chapter 18 describes a program for continuous improvement in spelling through the grades. The chapter discusses spelling readiness and informal instruction for early primary years, then formal spelling instruction and supplementary materials for succeeding grades. Ways of individualizing the word list are suggested and instructional activities for increasing spelling skill are listed. Examples of experimentation, in individual classrooms and throughout a city, suggest methods for pupils and teachers to diagnose spelling needs and evaluate spelling skill.

CARL SANDBURG* speaks of the occasional opportunities for schooling that Abraham Lincoln had when he was eight years old.

He learned to spell words he didn't know the meaning of, spelling the words before he used them in sentences. In a list of "words of eight syllables accented upon the sixth," was the word "incomprehensibility." He learned that first, and then such sentences as "Is he to go in?" and "Ann can spin flax."

Those who have an opportunity to look at one of the old blueback spellers by Noah Webster, long a best seller in American schools, can find the very pages and lines to which Sandburg referred. It is an interesting mark from which to measure changes in aims of instruction, materials, and methods used down through the years in the teaching of spelling.

In those earlier days spelling could occupy a larger portion of the curriculum than is possible in the modern school with its broader educational goals and its more complex problems. Spelling bees no longer serve as a frequent reason for community get-togethers, but good spelling is still

* Carl Sandburg, *Abe Lincoln Grows Up*, New York, Harcourt, Brace & World, 1928.

considered one of the social graces. In the culture of the American people, skill in correct spelling is a requirement among educated people; and though everyone knows some highly intelligent individuals who are respected despite their lack of spelling skill, anything short of perfection at the adult level is generally unacceptable.

The aim of spelling instruction today is to prepare boys and girls to spell correctly the words that they need in the course of their daily writing and the words they will need to write when they are adults. Those pupils from whom normal progress can be expected should learn to spell automatically the words most commonly used and to apply to other words the common rules that usually hold true in spelling. Pupils should be able to use the dictionary for its pertinent information regarding spelling—homonyms, syllabication, roots, prefixes, and suffixes. They should develop a pattern for learning words difficult for them to spell.

They should likewise develop a sense of responsibility that will lead them to use the dictionary whenever they are not sure about the spelling of a word and to check their papers with care whenever they have completed any writing. It is only as pupils develop this sense of responsibility that they will concern themselves about correcting the careless errors that appear in the first drafts of their written work, even the drafts of those pupils who are the best of spellers.

Fortunately for teachers and pupils, research in recent years has brought to light some important information about the writing vocabulary of young people and their accuracy in spelling the words they use most frequently, as measured at each grade level. Leaders in the field of spelling instruction have made it possible to identify more clearly the vocabulary that children need to know and (at least to some extent) the methods that are likely to prove effective in teaching the vocabulary.

Spelling in the Total Program

A SPELLING improvement program is basically dependent upon a good experience curriculum. When children are constructively occupied in learning through firsthand experiences and through purposeful reading and listening, they develop a natural desire to communicate their ideas in speech and writing. Spelling becomes important to them if they feel that what they are writing is important.

Many of the language skills that pupils develop in their day's activities are applicable in more than one way. Reading and spelling, for example, usually advance together with fairly high correlation, even though striking exceptions may be found. The help in phonics and structural analysis (syllabication, prefixes, suffixes) presented in modern reading programs seems to assist children in spelling; for, though a large percentage of

English words are not wholly phonetic, many have at least parts which are. Moreover, a broad reading program introduces children to a large vocabulary and extends word meanings for them; and spelling accuracy increases with the understanding of the meaning of words. The use of the dictionary and the direct attention given to spelling a word when locating it in the dictionary seem to account for some improvement in spelling.

Spelling also receives an incidental boost in classes where oral communication stimulates care in pronunciation, discriminative listening to sounds, and precision in articulation. Likewise, improvement in handwriting can benefit spelling, and such technical writing skills as the syllabication of words or the use of the apostrophe have direct effect upon spelling. But more important than the specific items of instruction that tend to "kill two birds with one stone" and to improve spelling along with other written English skills, is the attitude of the children. If they come to feel that what they write is important, that others (besides the teacher) will read what they write, and that in writing they are expressing an important aspect of themselves, they will be ready to make an effort to spell correctly. The teacher who works to improve the spelling of a pupil without recognizing that the first and most important step is to see that he has something worth writing, with correctly spelled words, overlooks the fundamental purpose the child may have in learning to spell.

While spelling does benefit from instruction in other areas such as reading, writing, speaking, and listening, certainly such instruction cannot replace direct spelling instruction as soon as children have enough experience to benefit from such a direct approach. In the child's earliest years of school, however, preparation for success in spelling calls for a readiness program.

Spelling Readiness

As in reading, readiness for spelling will depend on several factors, such as emotional control, physical condition (hearing and general health), maturity sufficient for the child to discriminate among words both seen and heard, muscular coordination, the background of general experience and language experience, and the individual's meaning vocabulary, as well as his interest and attention span.

Spelling becomes of value to children only when they first feel the urge to write. When the first writing activities begin in the first grade, spelling experiences begin; but all through the first grade (and in some school systems through the second grade), the teacher keeps the spelling instruction on an incidental and informal basis, largely in connection with immediate writing needs. This may be true even when the books of a spelling series are used in the first and second grades. A first-grade speller is necessarily a readiness book as is the first part (or perhaps all) of a second-grade speller. The teacher must also see that the instruction is highly individualized to meet the spelling needs the child faces in completing his regular writing tasks.

Gertrude Hildreth(9, p. 50) feels that formal, or systematic, teaching of spelling should not begin until pupils have achieved:

A mental age of 7½ years or more
A speaking vocabulary of some 5,000 words
The ability to enunciate words distinctly
Ability to recognize and pronounce 300–400 of the commonest words met in reading
A beginning in phonics—the commonest letter-sound combinations
The ability to write the letters of the alphabet correctly
The ability to copy simple words correctly
The ability to write a few simple words from memory

FIRST- AND SECOND-GRADE SPELLING

Spelling readiness, like reading readiness, involves the building of a vocabulary that has meaning for the child. In relation to the experiences he has, whether firsthand or verbal with the aid of pictures, the teacher must introduce new words and new word meanings, and he must discuss them sufficiently to make them a part of the child's vocabulary. Pronouncing new words correctly and using them naturally in conversation is an important step that pupils will make toward relying on them in writing. Experiences planned to help children in word building will help toward later work in spelling. Thus work planned to develop visual and auditory discrimination will contribute to spelling ability.

During the readiness period the teacher's program for developing awareness about words should include such activities as these: observing words with phonetic similarities—words that begin the same way, rhyming words, and word families (demonstrating the interrelationship of words, thus making children observe that they can spell new words by changing the beginning letter or letters in their basic spelling words); associating pictures of people or animals with names (Mother, Billy, Skippy); seeing basic words in derivatives, such as go in going; making new words by combining smaller words, such as outside; noting how to make a word plural by adding s or es. Such experiences will lead children to greater care and accuracy in spelling while advancing them in beginning reading.

Each child should learn to observe and spell correctly the words that he needs for his daily writing. The first step will be handwriting exercises in which children learn the relationship of straight lines and the circle

By carefully studying a word on the board, this boy learns to spell it and other words with similar sounds.

by tracing or copying letters. The next step will be the straight copying of words. Even the beginner should be taught to notice and use capital letters or lower case when needed. Bobby, for example, needs to use the two cases of the letter *B*, so that from the first he becomes used to *Bobby*, not *BoBBy*.

The teacher should see that writing experiences that are more than straight copying, such as completion stories or letters that include some parts which each pupil can select for himself, are introduced with plenty of preparation for children's spelling needs. The teacher may prepare a vocabulary chart containing currently needed words, or he may ask what words are likely to be needed. On the chalkboard close at hand, he writes in response to pupil suggestions such words as *Dear* and *Mother*, *come* and *party*, *please* and *love*. As children grow more practiced in writing, the words they ask for before and during their writing should be freely given by the teacher either at their seats or on the board. Writing need not be a fearful experience. No child should be afraid of making mistakes; but the teacher should encourage his desire to spell correctly and should meet cheerfully his requests for aid.

In late first grade or early second grade, a child may also profit from occasional experiences in alphabetizing. This skill is one closely related to auditory and visual discrimination, so it is to be expected that children will be ready to accomplish such a task at different stages. Keeping the roll of the class or of the children at one table, and marking the absentees, is a kind of experience even very young children can do successfully. Learning to file papers in individual folders can sometimes be a successful experience for a young child.

Six-year-old Margaret, for example, was busy looking for her folder in the bottom drawer of a filing cabinet when a visitor entered. In response to the visitor's question, Margaret explained that she found and identified her own folder first by knowing that *M* was in the middle of the alphabet, and next by recognizing the picture she had pasted on the cover, since there were two Margarets in the class.

Keeping individual dictionaries also gives practice in noting initial letter sounds and alphabetizing words. The pupils can make these diction-aries by stapling half pages (cut the length of the paper) and marking pages conspicuously in one corner to show the letter of the alphabet. When the child asks for help in spelling a word or when the teacher sees he needs to correct the spelling of a word, the teacher should enter that word in the child's own dictionary in the page designating the initial letter of the word. Usually the teacher should enter the word for the child because the spelling must be an accurate model. If such booklets are at hand, it is not difficult to help children establish their individual word

Word bingo, good for remedial reading, also contributes to spelling readiness.

list of commonly used words—words that they will later need continually in their writing.

Much the same kind of experience, but planned as a community project, is the use of a word box. The teacher may wish to use a box for each large table if the room furniture is arranged for such seating, or he may use a single box for the entire class in a place convenient to all. A small cracker box is useful because it has room for cardboard dividers lettered alphabetically. When a child requests a word for spelling, the teacher can write it in large letters on a slip of paper that has been cut to fit the box. Practice in filing words or afterward locating them in the file box is a good spelling readiness exercise.

Picture dictionaries should be available for children when they write. These books are interesting to some children as browsing material, but as pupils mature, they can use the picture dictionary to find words they need for their writing. Searching for words in alphabetical order is helpful preparation for several needed study skills. In the primary grades, however, it is not necessary for children to alphabetize words beyond the first letter.

The teacher should encourage even primary-grade children to check their writing. Comparing what they have written after copying a word from the dictionary or the word box should become a habit with children at as early an age as possible.

Not all children will be ready for direct instruction in spelling at the same age. Besides having a real desire to write his own thoughts, the child who is ready for direct instruction should have had considerable opportunity to write and a familiarity with some words often repeated in the natural course of his writing. Then the first steps in instruction are not likely to lead to failure. The beginning speller should have good enough muscular control to ensure handwriting that is legible and easily performed. Because of this, he can give thought to his spelling and not focus it upon the effort of making letters. Hearing, seeing, and remembering the likenesses and differences in letter forms and words (learned through reading and speech instruction at the first- and second-reader level) must be within the child's ability before he is ready to study spelling. If the teacher does not observe these common indications in a child's performance, probably he should not trouble the child with spelling lessons. Instead, the teacher should let him spend his time in doing things that will develop spelling readiness.

Many experienced primary teachers feel that readiness for spelling can best be developed through the natural learning activities of the classroom. Seeing and doing interesting things and having the opportunity to talk about them and share them with others provide the background for writing about them in stories or letters.

The Formal Spelling Program

THE content of formal spelling instruction is most commonly guided by materials that are prepared and published in graded sets, either in consumable workbook form or in book form. Most series begin with Grade 1 or Grade 2 and go through Grade 8.

Graded spelling series usually provide for continuous development through a weekly instructional program, which includes work on word meanings and provides such related instruction as phonetic clues, capitalization, use of apostrophes, homonyms, syllabication, and formation of plurals and possessives. Many series suggest a remedial plan to help children whose spelling skills are weak by showing sound study methods. In some series a pretest plan is used to help the pupils to identify the words they need to study before the final weekly test. In schools where teachers are not provided with spelling books, they must organize their programs from the language experiences of the pupils.

PLANS OF INSTRUCTION

Two plans for teaching spelling are used in most schools—the *test-study* plan and the *study-test* plan. In the former the teacher gives a weekly pretest to find out the words that each pupil cannot spell. Then the pupil studies only the words that he has missed. In the latter the teacher gives the pupils a list of words to study and then tests them on all the words. Research has shown that the test-study individual plan is more effective in grades 4–8 and with bright pupils; the study-test group plan is more effective in grades 2–3 and with slow-learning pupils.

To determine which plan to use, the teacher can give a preliminary test at the beginning of the year. If the pupils misspell almost all the words, the study-test plan should be used. If the pupils misspell only half the words, the test-study plan will prove more efficient and more economical of time. To take care of individual differences, the teacher can use the test-study plan for the brighter members of the class and the study-test plan for the slower-learning members.

SELECTING WORDS FOR STUDY

In most schools the books in a graded series provide weekly word lists. In other schools teachers are encouraged to build their own weekly word lists to meet individual and class needs. To prevent lists from straying too far from the basic words and tending toward the obscure words seldom used in writing, teachers need lists of words that have been established by research as words most frequently used.

The Rinsland list(18) presents an extensive survey indicating which words were used most frequently at each grade level in a word count from children's writing. This and other research, including that of McKee-Fitzgerald, Horn, Breed, Dolch, Durrell, Fitzgerald, and Brittain, is compiled in briefer form in James Fitzgerald's *A Basic Life Vocabulary*(4). This study points out the most commonly used words: nearly five hundred which compose about seventy-six per cent of the words used in children's writing; about five hundred more which, together with the first group, make up about eighty-five per cent of children's writing; and other words commonly used but not quite so frequently.

Gertrude Hildreth(9) points out that while most of the words in the first two groups named above are very well understood by third graders, many children in higher grades are still troubled by their spelling; thus, these words should be their first concern. Another publication, Harry Greene's *The New Iowa Spelling Scale*(6), gives added information to show what the spelling accuracy is for each word as used by children at each grade level. School systems that do not use a commercial spelling series should have these publications at hand.

INDIVIDUALIZING THE WORD LIST

While prepared lists include the words that research indicates are likely to be needed in children's writing, they cannot be expected to include just the right words to cover the immediate spelling needs of any given class week by week. Probably the greatest waste in spelling instruction comes from having the able spellers in the class study and practice words they already know, or permitting poor spellers to spend a large portion of their spelling study time on words they seldom use, meanwhile continuing to misspell words commonly used in everyday writing. Consequently the better spelling series make provision for individualized reviews. If the teacher uses a prepared list, such as that of Rinsland or Fitzgerald, or a commercially published spelling book, he should augment the weekly word lists from two sources—words misspelled in the previous week's written work and words likely to be used soon because they pertain to matters that are being studied currently. For slow learners, these supplementary words may make up most of their spelling lessons. A teacher who guides his pupils in making up their own spelling lists should check words listed for study against a basic list. It is possible for any teacher to plan a spelling instruction program with a rather highly individualized method.

The following plan for weekly organization of spelling study permits individualization while remaining easy to administer. The words in a standard speller's weekly list are supplemented with misspelled words, jotted down by the teacher at the time of grading papers, and words that pupils or the teacher suggest as related to current study topics. They can be arranged roughly in order of their importance in writing and numbered accordingly (for example, words included on Fitzgerald's list of the five hundred most frequently used words coming first).

A pretest is used at the start of the week for children beyond primary grades. The words are dictated and written by number. With his mistakes discovered by the pretest, each child knows which words he needs to study. If desirable, the teacher may require that all the pupils include certain words in their study list whether they were misspelled or not in the pretest. Each child lists the numbers of the words to be studied, including as many as the teacher assigns, or fewer if the pretest indicates he does not need to study that many. Those who have special difficulty in spelling may be given fewer words for study, but learning the assignment should then be as firmly required of the poor spellers as of others. Spelling study during the week includes time for individual and class activities. Individual study is devoted to the words in the individual lists; classwork is applied to general needs, such as work on homonyms, or use of capital letters, or recognition of unphonetic elements in certain words, or similar spellings that can be generalized by a rule.

When the final weekly test is given, each pupil writes on a paper which he has prepared by listing only the numbers of the words on his own list. As the teacher dictates the words by number, he writes those which he has studied. The plan provides for a direct relationship between spelling study and the needs of an individual's daily writing; it provides a lesson for each individual which is suited to his own needs and abilities; and it permits flexibility in assignments to take care of handicapped spellers.

SUGGESTIONS FOR DIRECT INSTRUCTION

In the interests of regularity, it is advisable that the teacher have a weekly schedule for direct instruction, beginning sometime during the second or third grade and continuing through the eighth. By the third or fourth grade, most children profit from a pretest (such as that suggested in many standard spelling books) given early to help them to discover which words need study. The teacher should help the pupils to establish special methods of learning to spell, and he should use them continuously. Most spellers instruct pupils in such methods. Commonly, the pattern is similar to this:

1. Look at the word carefully.
2. Listen as someone says it aloud.
3. Say it aloud, checking the pronunciation with someone who knows.
4. Write it without looking at the copy.
5. Check it against the correct spelling.

344] GUIDING LANGUAGE LEARNING

For those children who might profit from kinesthetic sensation, the teacher might suggest tracing. Tracing seems most helpful to some pupils if the word is written in large letters and the fingers (one or two) are used to trace the letters on the paper. When a degree of certainty is attained, the child should turn his correct copy over, write the word from memory, and then check the spelling with the perfect copy.

The teacher should use certain terms in speaking with pupils about their spelling problems. Those listed below should be familiar to the pupils from the time the terms are needed in reading or in language. If the spelling series does not include a planned program for the development of such understandings and a review for those who need reminders, the teacher should check to see that the pupils have understood the terms.

A Terminology for Spelling

Vowels	A prefix
Consonants	A suffix
A silent letter	Compound words
A schwa	Roots or root words
A syllable	Derivatives
An accent mark	An antonym
Diacritical marks	A synonym
A contraction	A homonym

During the spelling period the teacher plans instruction to meet the needs of the class, of individuals, or of small groups as the situation demands. Some of the following activities prove useful in helping pupils overcome certain types of difficulties in the words they are to study: (1) analyzing difficult words: dividing them into syllables; noting prefixes or suffixes; identifying the phonetic parts; noting silent letters; observing exceptions to rules; (2) using word-building activities: finding the root or forming other words from the same root; listing words with similar prefixes to note meaning of prefix; (3) observing certain rules: listing singular and plural forms in columns; using words ending in *ch, sh,* and *x* or words ending in *y* preceded by a vowel; comparing words ending in *y* preceded by a consonant; noting words ending in *f* or *fe;* listing words combining *i* and *e* in three columns under headings *i before e, following c,* and *sounded as a;* listing words that retain silent *e* before a suffix; listing words that drop silent *e* before a suffix; (4) developing their auditory discrimination: listening to words dictated by the teacher and writing initial sounds or ending sounds, telling the number of syllables, or showing vowel sounds in the word by using correct diacritical marks; (5) using short dictionary drills: locating words in the dictionary; using guide words; using pronunciation guide; using diacritical marks; checking syllables; learning definitions; learning synonyms; (6) checking written work: checking paragraphs each time before giving them to the teacher; checking with a committee set up for that purpose; checking paragraphs by use of the opaque projector; listing in individual books the words misspelled in written work; (7) studying capitalization and punctuation: making statements of rules for capital letters; making statements of rules for periods after abbreviations; (8) studying synonyms, antonyms, and homonyms: making lists of word pairs; showing differences in meaning by graphic representation; using words in sentences to show similarities or differences in meaning.

ACTION RESEARCH IN SPELLING

With careful planning of problems and methods for checking rules, it is possible for the teacher to set up some fact-finding projects of direct benefit to a school system or to a classroom. Without the strictly controlled situations possible in true research, some careful, practical experimentation making use of objective data together with the judgment of a trained teacher may yield helpful results. Such procedure is sometimes called "action research." Here are three examples:

A city school system wished to determine which words were most frequently misspelled by school children in their everyday writing. It was hoped that the children's awareness of such words might reduce the amount of misspelling. Pupils from fourth through eighth grade were asked to keep a list of all words marked as misspelled in their daily writing. Teachers sent the lists to a central office at the end of each month for a period of three months. The teachers felt increasingly the importance of indicating to the children which words were misspelled. The pupils began to see how many times the same words were misspelled and how it was possible to reduce the number of misspelled words by taking care. Many teachers commented that nothing had ever before impressed their pupils so much as this continuing record taken from daily work.

Research people obtained data from the survey by making a spot survey of results in one month in about fifteen per cent of all the schools engaged in the research. Because the survey was limited, the results were combined with those of a nationwide survey to develop a basic word list for spelling at each grade level. Teacher-pupil participation in the work increased the understanding of the problem, and an interested teaching staff accepted the results more readily because of their share in the project.

In a classroom, a teacher explained to the pupils about research that indicated which words were used most frequently in children's writing and which words caused more errors in spelling at each grade level. The pupils determined to find out where their own errors lay. They kept the record of their misspellings, taken from their regular written work as marked by their teacher or a checking committee. At the end of each month they compared their spelling errors with the words in *A Basic Life Vocabulary*(4), listed according to frequency of use. From their own misspelled words they planned a part of their weekly spelling list for several weeks to come. They tackled first the words misspelled in the first five hundred in frequency. They could see that it was most important for them to eradicate mistakes in the most frequently used words first.

An upper-grade class became interested in the types of spelling errors they were making. They listed common reasons for making errors and checked against this list each time they had a word marked for misspelling on their written work. The list looked like this:

Reasons for Spelling Errors

1. Not hearing or pronouncing the word correctly, as *probly* for *probably; wich* for *which*

2. Being careless or uninformed about homonyms, as *its* for *it's*

3. Not using the apostrophe correctly, as *the Brown's dog* for *the Browns' dog*

4. Not forming plurals correctly, as *citys* for *cities*

5. Not using a prefix correctly, as *disatisfy* for *dissatisfy*

6. Not knowing whether to double the consonant before adding the suffix to retain the long or short vowel sound, as *shinning* for *shining*

7. Not checking for careless errors, as *the* for *then*

8. Not using *i* and *e* in the right combination, as *recieve* for *receive*

9. Not remembering the spelling of words with especially difficult letter combinations, as *nabors* for *neighbors*

Day by day they listed their own misspellings under the heading of the type of error that seemed to apply best. They themselves began to be aware of their own kinds of errors and, with special instruction offered to groups with the same kinds of problems, the teacher helped them overcome their spelling weaknesses.

While standardized spelling tests give an indication of skill in spelling, they never seem wholly adequate to measure the degree in which pupils improve in their daily written work; this is where correct spelling really matters most. One standard spelling test is planned as a diagnostic test to accomplish better understanding of pupils regarding their own types of errors. Whatever teachers can do to help pupils feel that spelling is important whenever they are writing something for others to read, is good. Yet one word of warning seems appropriate. Here, as in every area, too much emphasis could lead to fear and dislike, even to the extent that pupils may purposely avoid the choice of the best word in order to be sure of a word they can spell. On the other hand, the teacher should encourage a natural interest in spelling accurately, and he should give children special help toward their individual needs.

SUGGESTIONS FOR STUDY AND DISCUSSION

1. Examine several lists of commonly used words that have been determined by research. Which of these words are your personal "spelling demons"?

2. Look over sets of pupils' papers. Compare their misspelled words with a graded list established by research. Which words would be stressed for slow learners and which for proficient spellers at the grade level of your choice?

3. How would you present these troublesome words?

4. Observe the same spelling class for a week. Write an evaluation on the basis of policies advocated in this chapter.

5. Write a two-week plan for spelling instruction.

6. How is instruction in reading, listening, and speaking related to spelling readiness?

FOR FURTHER READING

1. BREMER, NEVILLE H., "Ways to Improve Spelling in the Elementary Grades." *Elementary English* (May 1961), 301–07.

2. CAMPANALE, EUGENE, "Survey of Methods in the Teaching of Spelling." *Elementary English* (May 1962), 446–55.

3. EISMAN, EDWARD, "Individualized Spelling." *Elementary English* (May 1962), 478–80.

4. FITZGERALD, JAMES, *A Basic Life Vocabulary*. St. Paul, Minn., Bruce, 1951.

5. GILSTRAP, ROBERT, "The Development of Independent Spelling Skills in the Intermediate Grades." *Elementary English* (May 1962), 481–83, 485.

6. GREENE, HARRY A., *The New Iowa Spelling Scale*. Iowa City, Bureau of Educational Research and Service, State U. of Iowa, 1955.

7. ——— and WALTER T. PETTY, *Developing Language Skills in the Elementary School* (Chapter 12). Boston, Allyn and Bacon, 1959.

8. HALL, NORMAN, "Individualize Your Spelling Instruction." *Elementary English* (May 1962), 476–77.

9. HILDRETH, GERTRUDE, *Teaching Spelling* (Chapter 3). New York, Holt, 1955.

10. HUNNICUTT, C. W., and W. J. IVERSON, eds., *Research in the Three R's* (Chapter 10). New York, Harper, 1958.

11. IBELING, FREDERICK W., "Supplementary Phonics Instruction and Reading and Spelling Ability." *Elementary School Journal* (December 1961), 152–56.

12. IKENBERRY, NELDA B., "Teaching Machines." *Elementary English* (October 1961), 395–97, 407.
13. *Learning to Spell: A Research Report,* Bureau of Elementary Curriculum Development. New York, State Education Department, 1960.
14. MALONE, JOHN R., "The Larger Aspects of Spelling Reform." *Elementary English* (May 1962), 435–45.
15. PETTY, WALTER T., *Improving Your Spelling Program.* San Francisco, Chandler, 1959.
16. PLESSAS, GUS P., and WALTER T. PETTY, "The Spelling Plight of the Poor Reader." *Elementary English* (May 1962), 463–65.
17. POPOFSKY, RUTH, "Can We Drive the Demons Out of Spelling?" *Elementary English* (May 1962), 456–59, 473.
18. RINSLAND, HENRY, *A Basic Vocabulary of Elementary School Children.* New York, Macmillan, 1945.
19. SCHOEPHOERSTER, HUGH, "Research into Variations of the Test-Study Plan of Teaching Spelling." *Elementary English* (May 1962), 460–62.
20. TIDYMAN, WILLARD F., and MARGUERITE BUTTERFIELD, *Teaching the Language Arts* (Chapter 14). New York, McGraw-Hill, 1959.
21. WOLFE, DON, *Language Arts and Life Patterns* (Chapter 12). New York, Odyssey, 1961.

19

Stimulating Creative Expression

Chapter 19 develops further ideas for stimulating creative expression which have been touched upon earlier.
Creative language is defined in broad terms, with a de-
lineation of its purposes and values. It is also related to
utilitarian writing. Attention is given to dramatic play,
creative dramatics, dramatization, creative stories and
original verse in turn.

PEOPLE vary in the avenues through which their creative
expression emerges. Some are born storytellers; others are dramatic, either
in planning original plays or in portraying parts in plays written by others;
some break forth in verse whenever vivid, emotion-arousing experiences
move them to expression. Small children naturally tend to engage in
dramatic play as they play house, school, or cowboys-and-Indians. Dramatic play is creative.

Presumably all individuals have potential creativity, but not necessarily
in a verbal sense. Nonverbal "creators" may express their inner selves
through the rhythm of the dance, the line and color of art, the melody
and swing of music, or the design of a hat or dress.

Creativeness has many different avenues, and teachers must open the
way for each child to express himself according to his special aptitudes.
While some talk and write, others should be encouraged to draw and
paint, to arrange bouquets, to sing and dance, or to build. Remember that
all children are creative, but they must have opportunity to express themselves in their own way. Most of them will not create adequately unless
they receive encouragement and stimulation through enriching, vivid experiences and frequent opportunities to "let themselves go" through creative expression.

Requisites for Encouraging Creative Expression

ONE requisite for encouraging creative expression is *rich living at school and at home*. Only as the child builds up an abundant store of ideas and vivid impressions can he express himself creatively. In the first place, he must have wide and varied real experiences in which he observes and participates in many activities and which he discusses meaningfully. He must be helped to observe and interpret phenomena and processes about him so that the obvious becomes meaningful; for instance, noting the formation of buds in the summer preceding their opening, learning to recognize common trees through the arrangement of buds on the twigs, gazing on the rainbow formed as the sun shines on fountain sprays, watching machines chew into the earth as excavations are being made, or observing the pull of the magnet.

It is important to realize that seeing, hearing, tasting, and feeling may result in only vague impressions if parents and teachers fail to talk over the experiences with the children. That is to say, observation and learning activities are not complete until the children have been helped to understand and appreciate them through thought-provoking discussions and explanations.

In the second place, the child must have many vicarious experiences as he listens to what others have experienced, watches television and movies, looks at pictures, listens to descriptions and explanations, and reads or hears scores of stories and poems. Increasingly, pictures and the printed page will enrich his background. Constantly he should widen his acquaintance with literature; often he should hear the creative stories, plays, and verse of his classmates and of the pupils who have preceded him. Both real and vicarious experiences are necessary in a program designed to stimulate creative expression.

A second requisite for encouraging creative expression is a *friendly, nurturing classroom atmosphere*. In the first place, the classroom teacher is the most important factor for he makes all other factors possible. Jeraldine Hill(10, p. 25) describes aptly the teacher's role in the creative classroom:

> The role of the teacher is not like that of the conductor of an orchestra who gives the signal for each instrument to play. Nor is it the role of sentry standing guard lest someone disturb the king. Each of these is the enemy of creativity. The role of the teacher is that of being aware of each child's ability, interest, activity. For in a classroom with creative permissiveness, the teacher has confidence and trust in each child's capability of creating. When and if the child needs a bit of help, he will turn to the teacher because this teacher has earned his trust and respect. Whenever we have earned a child's confidence by our actions and attitudes toward him and

towards his classmates, then he respects our judgment and trusts us to help him. If we encourage the faltering flights to inventiveness; if we praise the primitive beauty of the young artist's work; if we give an honest appraisal when the child is wanting our criticism, then we are making a pilgrimage to the mecca of all true teachers, the loving trust of a child. If we always feel in our hearts that the child can do better, while, at the same time, accepting what he does now, we are fulfilling the role of the teacher who fosters creativity.

The teacher must be an appreciative, understanding person who not only savors the original expression of his pupils but who may occasionally be spontaneously creative himself. Such was the second-grade teacher who wrote the following bit of verse to share with his pupils:

> Some poems tell stories
> With words that sing.
> Some poems paint pictures
> Of a beautiful thing.
> Some show a poet's feelings:
> Is he sad? Is he gay?
> Come, be a poet
> And write a roundelay.

An approving smile, a friendly word of praise or an exclamation of surprised appreciation encourages the child to feel secure and successful, free to give vent to his moods and original ideas. The teacher who can enter informally into the children's dramatic play, who can quip with kindly humor, who easily makes up rhymes or illustrative stories, who can sketch an imaginative cartoon at a moment's notice, is a teacher who can release children's creative tendencies.

Such a teacher will also constantly develop and utilize opportunities for encouraging his pupils' creativity. A second favorable factor in the creative classroom is the rich environment provided by the teacher—pictures, books, movies, trips, and varied materials with which to be creative such as a play corner, a collection of funny masks, easels and paint, rhythm band instruments, a bulletin board for posting the pupils' pictures or original verse and stories, or a tacked-up tagboard portfolio where children may unobtrusively drop their creative productions and later feature them in a sharing period. Activities will include reading and telling stories, sharing experiences, and dramatizing stories. For older pupils, there may be some class publication that will feature original stories, plays, and verse that pupils wish to submit.

One highly successful second-grade teacher begins early in the year to read orally his former pupils' stories and poems and to display their pic-

Karen Corbo

We went to the the zoo. We went on a bus. We saw reptiles, an elephant and a hippopotamus. I ate ice cream. We bought souvenirs.

A first-grade child records and illustrates her experiences and impressions after a trip to the zoo.

tures. These he has kept in a special file. As his new pupils view and listen to the productions of their older brothers, sisters, and neighbors, they begin to use their own free time at school and at home to try their hands at drawing, painting, and writing. Quietly they place the resulting productions on the teacher's desk with the knowledge that these will later receive friendly recognition.

When the flow of materials becomes quite free and general, this teacher helps the children to plan a special bulletin board for their creative efforts. For this, each child prepares a self-designed, colorful folder to hold his original pictures and writings. From this time on, the children enter the classroom agog with interest in what the bulletin board will hold. They make a beeline for the display space—some to add a contribution, all to take a peek under the covers to see what their classmates have done. It is amazing to see how abundant, how free, how unusual and high-quality the creative productions come to be.

This teacher's classroom typifies a third favorable factor: the so-called permissive atmosphere—relaxed, friendly, cooperative, tolerant. The children are helpful, both to the teacher and among themselves. They become genuinely interested in what their companions produce. Each child knows that his rights as an individual will be respected and that whatever he originates will be warmly received and treated as something valuable. He feels completely secure and willing to "let himself go" as he paints or devises rhymes and tunes. Since children feel most comfortable in small groups, the teacher of the younger children will often join clusters of two or three pupils and work with them on their creative efforts.

There should also be a measure of flexibility in the day's program. While a certain amount of regularly scheduled routine gives security, children still welcome occasional deviations so that they may enjoy the first snow of the season, welcome the songs of returning robins, or react to a stirring current event. One upper-grade group was quite indignant because they had heard a news report critical of the United States as quoted from the statements of a foreign visitor who had spent a few days in a very limited area. The English teacher saw in their feelings an opportunity to get some earnest expression from his pupils and suggested that the pupils write any responses that would express their feelings. Among the editorials, slogans, and letters he found the following paragraph:

> How can a visitor in America know our country if he has stayed for less than a week in the vicinity of a single city? I have lived here all my life and, with my family, have traveled from coast to coast for the past two summers. Even so, I feel I still know too little about my native land.
> A recent visitor to the United States has expressed his dislike for our country after a five-day visit limited to one metropolitan area. He has con-

demned the nation as a whole on this narrow basis. That is not fair. If he knew even as much as I do about the United States and its people, he would know that there is much to admire and love as well as certain features to condemn. I love my country and think that visitors to our shore should be well informed before they publicly condemn it.

One of the most inhibiting factors in the field of creative expression is the rush and pressure of the daily schedule; it is essential that the child have time for quiet thinking and individual writing whenever the teacher realizes that he has been stimulated by some interesting and emotion-stirring experience.

A third requisite for developing creative tendencies in the children is *productive guidance that gives praise only to the really good results of the children's expression.* In an entire story, there may be only one phrase or sentence of real merit. This portion should receive praise. As children listen to one another's productions and learn to recognize the meritorious parts, they gradually absorb standards and spontaneously bring forth expression of an improved quality. In the beginning, the teacher should call attention to the parts that deserve commendation. Later the children are likely to acquire the desire and ability to exchange suggestions for improvement, but only after they have gained self-confidence and an awareness of what is really good.

There may be occasions when children's creative efforts should not be shared as, for instance, when a child is giving expression to disturbing, pent-up emotions or when he is extremely shy. As a rule, however, children enjoy sharing their original stories and verse with their classmates. An essential in a program for stimulating creative expression in children is an opportunity to share productions whenever the young authors wish to do so.

USEFUL OUTCOMES

There are some useful outcomes of creative expression. Many children have pent up inside them hidden emotions of resentment, jealousy, fear, or inadequacy. Often their pictures, stories, and original plays reveal these corrosive inner feelings, and therapeutic treatment can be begun. Mauree Applegate(1, p. 260) believes that "children who can learn to explode on paper often are able to keep from screaming at home or at school." Without conscious purpose, therefore, children can find relief and release through creative expression. In doing so, they improve their mental health and strengthen or develop more desirable personality traits.

Another important outcome is the cumulative effect of creative expression upon the person who is creating. Ruth Kearney Carlson(4, p. 166) says, "Creativity, then, is not the sudden emergence of a poem, or a dance;

it is a process which is ever renewing. As one creates a poem or a picture, he is also changing. Man is continually becoming more creative. Being creative is an active process."

PROCEDURES TO BE AVOIDED

A teacher should never praise a child's production beyond its merits; but, on the other hand, he should make sure that standards are not on a level beyond the child's capacity. What might be crude for a ten-year-old may be commendable for a seven-year-old. A production of modest merit by a mediocre pupil may be praiseworthy because it reflects improvement, but the production of a gifted child in the same class should be commensurate with his ability. The teacher should praise only when praise is deserved.

Never should a child's creative efforts be subjected to ridicule; never should he be laughed at. One such experience may kill forever a child's tendency to paint or speak and write in an original manner, even though he has great capacity for creativeness.

Some teachers approach the writing of verse through the listing of rhyming words and the scanning of lines. Here the skeleton of poetry may get in the way of really creative writing, which is based on ideas, not on matters of form. When children think of rhyme and patterned rhythm in the early stages of writing, they are likely to write trash and to attain a forced style. Instead of thinking of patterns, children should express simply and vividly their emotional reactions to an experience.

In a ninth-grade class the pupils were enjoying Carl Sandburg's *Abe Lincoln Grows Up*. They selected favorite sentences* and wrote them as if they were poetry. One example follows:

> So the woman, Nancy Hanks, died,
> Thirty-six years old, a pioneer sacrifice,
> With memories of monotonous, endless everyday chores,
> Of mystic Bible verses read over and over for their promises,
> And with memories of blue wistful hills and a summer
> When the crab-apple blossoms flamed white
> And she carried a boy-child into the world.

Note how freedom from stereotyped rhyme and rhythm patterns resulted in naturalness and genuineness in a vivid, yet simple expression of sensory responses. These children are unlikely to make forced and meaningless rhymes in their future writings. They will not strive for artificial emotional effects. If the teacher helps the children to observe closely

---

* Carl Sandburg, *Abe Lincoln Grows Up*, New York, Harcourt, Brace & World, 1928.

and thoughtfully, if he allows them to discuss their experiences in order to amplify meanings and to build appropriate vocabulary, if he encourages them *to express their ideas* (not to play with words) in vividly descriptive phrases, they are likely to be genuine in their creative efforts.

Promoting Creative Language

CHILDREN get genuine pleasure out of sharing their original stories and verse with their classmates. The social nature of human beings guarantees the pleasantness of such sharing. Too, the child's natural desire for status in his group can be met as he shares his creations with his classmates. After a child has once received the appreciative responses of his classmates, his pleasure in sharing his original expression and his prospective attainment of status may partly motivate his creative language.

WHAT IS CREATIVE LANGUAGE?

To some extent, authorities disagree as to what constitutes creative language. Some insist that the ideas expressed must be unique, that the way of expressing them must be completely original, and that presumably the purposes of the person expressing them are not utilitarian.

Other authorities are less insistent on uniqueness; they maintain that whatever a person says in his own individual way, even for utilitarian purposes at times, is creative. They would agree that imaginative stories, plays, and verse are truly creative; but they believe that conversation, discussion, letters, or reports may contain creative elements when expression is colored by the personality and feelings of the speaker or writer. It is even possible, in their opinion, for creativity to be present in the reproduction of ideas as, for instance, in a personally conceived interpretation of the lines of a play or in a telling reorganization of materials so as to cast a new light on them and reveal possible implications not previously apparent.

PURPOSES IN CREATIVE LANGUAGE

Creative language occurs when the stimulation of a stirring experience and a resulting urge of ideas demand expression. In the words of Hughes Mearns, the child feels an itch to write. A rich environment, abundant living, opportunities to see and hear and feel and do many things, and encouragement to express their reactions to such experiences are likely to lead to much creative expression. Just as measles is contagious, so is the inclination to give vent to ideas and feelings through original stories, plays, verse, pictures, and melodies. As a result come feelings of release and achievement. A little experience in creative expression is likely to lead to more experiences in that area.

A junior high school pupil living in the ski-jump areas of the Sierras responded to the first deep snow of the season with the following poem. It was the first he had ever written, or considered writing. He said, "It just came to me. I was thrilled to see the snow and to know I could go skiing."

BACKGROUND TO SKI

And the snow has come with the dawn of winter,
The first sharp blasts from "Old North Wind."
There is peace in the forest now,
As if a Lordly voice had said, "Let there be peace."
And all at once the familiar sounds of the world were still.

For now the thirsty earth is covered, it would seem,
With a cool moist blanket of softly glowing diamonds which when woven
With the green of the forest and blue of a clear sky trimmed with fluffy clouds
Blend to display nature's masterpiece, commonly known as Background To Ski!
First, mix well the trees of the hillsides with crisp, fresh air,
Add a sprinkle of snowy flakes caught in a sudden swirl of wind,
Conclude the recipe with the mellow rays of the sun
Floating lazily down through the treetops, finally to reach the ground
And reflect from the dazzling crystals the warmth and friendliness found
When experiencing the Background To Ski.
Add all these together with the joys and happiness of being alive and free
On this beautiful and changing earth, and you are
On the road to the experiencing of the sport called skiing.

It is really very simple to have the breath-taking feeling of conquering
Time, speed, and all natural laws of nature.
All you need is a pair of skis and the Background To Ski!

BOB WILLIAMS

FORM AND CORRECTNESS

Although it is highly desirable for children to use good form and correct language when writing creatively, these are not the matters of first concern. Rather, it is essential that the child center his complete attention on the original ideas and feelings surging within him and seeking an outlet in word, line, or melody. Gertrude Hildreth(9) says that there should be a momentary disregard for matters of form and correctness whenever a child is expressing his own thoughts and impressions.

There is another kind of writing requiring learning skills and language usage: the utilitarian. It is when the child is learning to write a good letter, to organize and present a clear-cut report, to make an outline, or to be effective in any other type of utilitarian writing that he should learn the mechanics of written expression. Whenever a need for a specific skill or for correcting a definite error arises, it is time to present a development lesson (see Chapter 20) and to have follow-up practice and drill to fix the skill. As children gain an automatic mastery of such skills and of correct usage in connection with their utilitarian writing, the teacher can expect their creative writing to incorporate these desirable items without the child's giving conscious attention to them.

Stimulating teachers who have been highly successful in developing children's creative powers, have found consistently that the quality and correctness of pupils' creative language have improved in the process of sharing it with their classmates. They have pride in their personal achievement; they have a growing sense of courtesy and a feeling of responsibility for making their products easy for their friends to read by writing legibly and correctly. In their social exchange of suggestions for improvement, the pupils show a desire to use creative language free from flaws.

Creative Stories

SOME children have a flair for storytelling and they spin fanciful yarns with intriguing original qualities. Creativity is the essence of such stories. Other children look at the world around them and interpret their impressions in unusual phrases as did the child who saw taxis in the street far below as "little yellow ants crawling on wheel feet." The ability to interpret real-life experiences in unique terms is also creative.

Since creative language is the verbal expression of inner personal reactions to a vivid experience, it is possible to be creative and yet not use unusual expressions. Ordinary words can convey emotion to the listener or reader and build clear-cut concepts. Note the two stories told by a small child, the first to his teacher as she wrote it down to use later as a reading chart, the second to his mother. The first is a utilitarian story stripped of all feeling; the second expresses how he felt as he listened to the rain.

> It rained this morning.
> It rained very hard.
> We had to stay inside.
> Mrs. Litt read us a story.
>
> . . . . .
>
> The rain came pat, pat, pat;
> Then peck, peck, peck,
> Splash, dash, and pour.
> It sounded like my dog
> Sneaking into the house,

Trotting to find me
And rushing away when
Mother gets the broom after him.

Even a life-hardened adult is touched by the latter story in which the child's emotions shine through every word. Although there is no picturesque phrase in it, creativity pervades the whole story. Creative language need not be ornate or fanciful or unusual; but it must reflect the inner self and express the storyteller's own ideas.

DEVELOPMENT OF ABILITY TO CREATE STORIES

As with any other aspect of creative language, *abundant living* based on wide and varied experiences and keen observation, a *permissive atmosphere* in which individual thinking and spontaneous verbal expression are nurtured through friendly interest and helpful suggestions, and *time set aside* for telling or writing personal reactions, are factors that develop fluent storytellers. Children should do things, go places, see and hear the world in action, read stories and verse, watch television and films, and in all possible ways extend and enrich their experiences. From their rich store of ideas and feelings will come creative expression; often this will be in the form of stories.

Some children will need little encouragement in storytelling. They are born storytellers. Others will need stimulation and guidance. Hearing the stories of classmates, listening to stories read by the teacher, and reading lively stories for themselves help children to develop the ability to relate graphically their own personal experiences. Praise from the teacher for well-chosen phrases will often open the portals of the less responsive pupils who have natural, but as yet unreleased, aptitude for storytelling.

Still others may have little imagination and slight confidence in their own ability to speak or write their thoughts interestingly. For them, there should be no pressure. However, the teacher should consistently but unobtrusively praise even the smallest effort of pupils to relate their experiences. In helping them to gain confidence in their writing ability, he will help them attain importance and respect. Since children, as well as adults, like to do what they do well, their teacher's expressed appreciation of their efforts should encourage reluctant writers to continue to write and, perhaps, even *want* to write. He should also be quick to praise every instance of a well-chosen word.

Children enjoy telling chain stories in which the teacher or one of the pupils starts an imaginary—possibly fantastic—story, reaches a crisis, stops and asks a classmate to continue until another crisis arises, and so on, until several pupils have contributed to the development of the tale. At first, the more imaginative pupils may volunteer most of the chain of

Morning Work

Betsy   May 16, 1961

Which Is That One?

"On my ninth birthday, my father said "Betsy, you may go to the pound and pick out a dog for a birthday present."

Then Betsy said "Oh father do you really mean that? I can have a puppy all my own? "Yes, Betsy thats exactly what I mean."

So right after breakfast Betsy went to the Scarsdale Pound and looked around. Finally she saw a nice dog, so she told the poundman she would take the dog.

In a few days the dog had a puppy and now she can't tell which is which because they are twins.

By,
Betsy

Betsy is able to write interestingly about an important event in her life, and in the process she gains familiarity with new elements of punctuation.

incidents that make up their original story; but gradually the less spontaneous among the pupils will come to take a voluntary part in building up the story.

The beginning sections of a chain story that a second-grade class improvised on St. Patrick's Day follow:

> TEACHER: Mike was sound asleep in his trundle bed. At the stroke of midnight, a rattling of his window woke him. He lay still a whole minute listening. Then he decided that someone wanted to come in. So—
>
> BILLY: Mike ran to the window and opened it. He waited for Shep, his dog, to jump in because Shep often begged to be let in during the night. But nothing happened. Mike tried to see who had rattled the window, but there was no moon.
>
> SUSAN: The stars were shining brightly. So Mike looked very hard. There was nothing on the ground under his window. Then he heard a little squeak right at his elbow.
>
> JERRY: On the window sill, he saw the funniest little leprechaun who was holding out a gold piece to Mike. "Hi, Mike," squeaked the leprechaun. "I need your help. I have work to do but I need a moon to see by. I want you to take this gold piece and—

A simpler variation of the chain story is the unfinished story for which a single pupil makes up an original ending.

A less spectacular way of stimulating imagination in storytelling is to encourage children to change the endings of the stories they meet in their readers, library books, and teacher-read books. It is fun for them to devise a different ending, then to share it with other members of the class. Children get much pleasure in comparing the various endings that the members of a class can think up.

Writing Original Verse

VERSE-MAKING potential lies within every child, because it consists of his emotional reactions and thoughtful interpretations of personal experiences. In a social atmosphere that nurtures the child's spontaneous expression of his impressions and his feelings, whether at home or at school, rhythmic, cadenced phrases that serve to express his inner self are likely to bubble forth from his lips. Who has not heard a small child chanting rhythmic phrases to himself as he propels his "bike" back and forth before his home, or sits dangling his legs from the edge of the porch? Children create naturally, often in poetic words. One second-grade girl responded to the sight of a windmill as follows:

> The windmill
> The windmill

Is on a daisy hill. He pumps,
And pumps, and never stands still.

LINDA HARLEY*

A second-grade boy wrote about the sun:

The sun sparkles on tree branches.
It warms robins.

NICKY KLIRONOMAS†

Linda's words came out as rhymes; Nicky's verse is poetic in many ways because of its imaginativeness and imagery even though there is no rhyme and the lines are uneven in length. In fact, many children write only doggerel if they strive for rhyme and metered rhythm. It is preferable that they be completely spontaneous and uninhibited as they release their ideas and feelings in words.

Nature and its wonders stimulate much creative expression, as in the case of the third grader who told about a flower:

I saw a little daffodil
Who lived up on a little hill.
She wore a pretty yellow dress
And all the rest was green, I guess.
She wore a little crown to match
Her little silken dress.

MAUREEN HEASLIP‡

Almost all children like to use words that are formed in imitation of natural sounds. This second grader made use of onomatopoeia in a poem he wrote:

OUR HELPERS
With a tap, tap, tap,
And a tap, tap, tap,
The cobbler makes our shoes.

With a rap, rap, rap,
And a rap, rap, rap,
The carpenter makes our houses.

With a swish, swish, swish,
And a swish, swish, swish,
The washing machine washes our clothes.

WESLEY TUSSING§

* Laura Wasson's pupil, Meadville, Pennsylvania, Elementary Schools.
† Lucie Dean Patton's pupil, Marvin Marshall School, Carmichael, California.
‡ Dorothea Schaffner's pupil, Meadville, Pennsylvania, Elementary Schools.
§ Lucie Dean Patton's pupil, Marvin Marshall School, Carmichael, California.

Older children still turn to the supernatural to explain the phenomena before them. Mark, after returning from a visit to the mountains, wrote:

> The roaring falls are never stilled.
> They're like a giant's cup
> That's just been spilled.
>
> MARK HERNDON*

Though children have within themselves the ability and the tendency to express their individual reactions, teachers can do much to increase sensitivity and to encourage a greater abundance of living and thus to stimulate expression. Children who hear much poetry, who learn to savor favorite bits that amuse them or have a strong sensory appeal, are inclined to express themselves poetically. This sixth-grade girl put down her reactions to butterflies:

> I see them fluttering through the skies,
> The airy, lovely butterflies
> Soon sitting on a dewy rose,
> As through my flower plot they flit,
> They display their hues so exquisite—
> Then up into the clear blue skies
> With rainbow wings they gaily rise.
>
> THERESA FAETH†

A relatively easy way to create a poem (either as a group or individually) is to enumerate a series of impressions. Melissa, in the sixth grade, wrote:

> NIGHT
> Through the night the crickets are
>   calling,
> Katydids cry,
> The mist is falling.
>
> In the pool the peepers peep,
> Bats fly around,
> And people sleep.
>
> MELISSA CLARK‡

A stirring experience can stimulate a well-read, sensitive child to vivid and beautifully poetic expression. A drifting dandelion seed viewed

---

* Annual poetry collection, San Diego, California, Schools, Vol. 15, p. 81.
† Clayton B. Wire School, Sacramento, California.
‡ Margaret Barr's pupil, Meadville, Pennsylvania, Elementary Schools.

against a background of water and the sunset's glow led a sixth-grade girl
to write as follows:

DANDELION IN AUTUMN

Drift away, a silken star.
Shiver in the autumn breeze,
Shimmer in the dappled light,
Land in a pond; and I see before me
A floating garden of Xochimilco.
Like a blossom, leaves outspread,
You float by the shore.
A scarlet maple leaf, a gold poplar leaflet,
Both join to make your base.
Down you drift, a snowy blossom,
To join the leaves and rock gently on a pond,
A mirror-like lake reflecting the forest.
It's sunset. I leave you
Floating on a lake of fire,
The trees aflame around you.

MARY ANN STROUD*

APPROACHES TO CREATIVE VERSE

A teacher who sincerely enjoys literature, art, and music, who is always
seeing something new in nature, who quietly and genuinely expresses his
enjoyment or wonder, is fully as important to the child as are the enriching experiences that form the essential background for creative expression. Such a teacher will offer pupils every opportunity to give their
personal reactions to stimulating sensory experiences. He will provide
time for discussion, for thinking out imaginatively what their impressions
mean, and for dictating (if young children) or writing their impressions.
A vivid emotional response or a sharply defined impression of natural
beauty may stimulate some apt phrase, a verse, a couplet, or a stanza.
There is likely to be no rhyme; the rhythm may be broken. So, while
keeping his inner eye on the ideal expression, the child should polish his
product until it represents as true and graphic an expression as lies within
his capability—probably no rhyme, but smoother rhythm and more vivid
words.

It is essential that children become familiar with the simpler patterns
for lyrically expressing their ideas. With much hearing and much oral
reading of rhythmic poems and graphic prose, the children may unconsciously adopt some pattern and adapt it to their own uses. Probably the
teacher should casually call the pupils' attention to verse forms that are

* Annual poetry collection, San Diego, California, Schools, Vol. 17, p. 99.

simple and appropriate; yet he must never let form overshadow the message. Children like to make their words bump along regularly, and even to achieve rhymes in some instances. On the whole, publicity and praise should be sparing, confined to the truly revealing and expressive phrases; otherwise the genuine spirit of creativeness may be lost, and superficial, insincere effusions may result. (Remember, too, that some children will express themselves through stories, plays, or pictures rather than through verse.) And richness of inner experience, inward growth, is after all the goal.

Oral Reading

ORAL reading of literature may not of itself be creative; but it does serve to convey creative expression to an audience. The reader must have complete understanding of the meaning of the selection, be master of the specific voice skills that are requisite to proper interpretation, realize the importance of correct pronunciation, and know how necessary it is to practice his oral reading of key passages prior to his appearing before his audience.

Dramatic oral reading involves such situations as (1) pantomiming as a classmate reads, (2) pantomiming or dramatizing orally a part that has been read aloud, (3) assuming the part of a character in a story and reading the corresponding dialogue, and (4) similarly reading the parts in a play. Any upper-grade pupil who is to read verse aloud must prepare for it carefully. The reader must be sensitive to the mood and intrinsic meaning of the poem, must rehearse many times so that he can read smoothly and meaningfully the intricate word patterns of the poem, and must convey the spirit and beauty of the verse. In a way, an oral reader is creative, since he must identify himself with the mood and significance of what he is reading.

Dramatic Activity

ONE of childhood's natural impulses is acting out life situations which the girls and boys have observed. With them, such dramatic play is serious business, and they tend to identify themselves completely with the characters their actions reflect. The play mother really feels irked when her child comes into the living room with dirty feet, and the juvenile father tries hard to balance the load that he is placing on his truck. It is through dramatic play that children take on grown-up characteristics and identify with the world around them. Dramatic play is a part of growing up.

As children become familiar with literature and come to know their favorite stories well, they tend to replace dramatic play and creative dramatics with dramatization. Again the children identify themselves with the characters they portray; but they are acting out scenes in a play, not a situation observed in real life.

Dramatic activity is an important phase of a child's language development. The child observes and listens—the *intake* aspect of language growth; as a result, he experiences feelings and develops concepts that he reflects through dramatic action—the *outgo* or expression. Consequently, he builds up his vocabulary, his sentence structure, his organization of ideas, his social understandings, his emotional reactions and control.

DRAMATIC PLAY

In dramatic play, a young child spontaneously acts out situations which he has actually experienced or observed. There is neither beginning nor ending—the child is someone else and acts as that person would act in the same situation. Occasionally children select an impressive character from literature and act out situations without story plot. The sixth-grade boys in the incident described below are examples.

For several days, a group of television-stimulated sixth-grade boys had been reading the merry adventures of Robin Hood. One afternoon they remained in the classroom after dismissal and, with no apparent premeditation or external stimulation, began to enact scenes that might have occurred in Sherwood Forest. With sword or dagger in hand (yardstick or ruler) or with invisible bows and arrows, they sallied forth from their hide-out in the forest (deep lockers behind folding doors) onto the highways (wide aisles) to rob the rich and help the poor.

Never was there a stronger and bolder Little John, a braver Robin Hood, or more wily Friar Tuck than was found among this group of boys. Each child had lost all consciousness of the twentieth-century world and was living in the romantic past. Each had shed his own personality and had become one of the old-time characters.

These boys were engaging in real dramatic play because they were living someone else's experience so fervently and wholeheartedly that they had temporarily lost their actual identity. Dramatic play is spontaneous, free of immediate adult suggestion and control, almost as real as life itself to the performers. As a rule, dramatic play is associated with younger children as they play with their dolls, play doctor, play school, play house, and otherwise assume the identity of another person and behave as this other person would behave. But older boys also engage in dramatic play in their cops-and-robbers and cowboy games.

Dramatic development in children. The younger the child, the greater is his identification with the part he is playing. The girl or boy in kindergarten is lost in whatever character he is portraying—a mouse, a dog, an engine, or a bossy adult—but such impersonation is likely to be brief in duration. The first-grade child, however, will be Mother, mischievous Molly, or Mother's visitor as she plays house for much longer periods. So engrossing is the play of these younger children that they are rarely conscious of an onlooker.

On the other hand, older primary-grade children may be conscious of the fact that they are playing a part. They tend to become self-conscious and to lose spontaneity when they notice older persons observing them; they engage in more and more complex activities that reflect their growing maturity and their increasingly complicated living; they exhibit a continuity of action from day to day as the life situations (imaginary, of course) that they are portraying unfold. Older children are less likely to engage in dramatic play during school hours, except at recess periods when they may play Indian, Robin Hood, or cops-and-robbers, in surroundings removed from adult stimulation and supervision.

Stimulation of dramatic play. If younger children are to engage in dramatic play, there must be a nurturing atmosphere. Kindergartens, for instance, should have a supply of cast-off adult clothing so that the girls and boys will have an opportunity to dress up for playing house. There should be a play corner with child-sized furniture and housekeeping equipment. An essential is building blocks or light-weight small wooden boxes (with smooth finish)—which children may develop into a big train or boat or airplane on which the young passengers will take an imaginary ride.

The primary rooms, too, need to have play corners and make-believe stores where the children are stimulated to spontaneous dramatic play. They should also have many opportunities to listen to stories and poems with appealing characters and lively action. The teacher, in the meantime, will remain in the background so that whatever dramatic action does evolve is spontaneous and child-initiated.

Values of dramatic play. Important among the values of dramatic play is the opportunity it affords for emotional outlet. Pent-up feelings may be released; drab existence may take on color as the child identifies himself with a character who is lively, resourceful, happy. Over the days, the child will take on the personality and behavior of a variety of characters and thereby gain familiarity with widely varied feelings and reactions. As he projects himself into dramatic situations, he thinks intelligently and sensitively, gaining an appreciation and sympathetic understanding of other people's problems.

Integration of personality and organization of experience are parallel values to be found in dramatic play. As a child interprets personalities in different situations, he tends to unify everything he knows about each of them.

It is through the child's own personal living that he gains the attitudes and standards that will govern his life. However, it is sometimes difficult to have firsthand experiences that relate to certain attitudes about manners and morals, safety and health. Then, the teacher may read stories to introduce dramatic situations that represent desirable attitudes and appropriate reactions by fictional characters. Children will often play-act such fictitious situations and thereby may absorb into their own lives some of the desirable standards and attitudes portrayed in the stories that they have heard and liked.

Obviously an important outgrowth of dramatic play is the development of the creative abilities of children. As they identify themselves with other persons and imaginary situations, they must do creative thinking and react in the way that those other persons would.

CREATIVE DRAMATICS

Creative dramatics is an informal type of dramatization in which pupils, under guidance of the teacher, make up and perform plays, improvising the action and dialogue as they go along. Here is a rich opportunity for natural growth in expressional abilities and for socializing experiences. Free play of the imagination, complete submergence of the self in the part to be played, spontaneous expression of ideas and emotions afford pupils a chance to think creatively and to create as they perform. Jean De Sales Bertram(34, p. 518) describes what happens to the child when he takes part in creative dramatics:

> We must not forget that when the child is enjoying an aesthetic experience, seeing relationships for himself, and approaching life with a sense of wonder and mystery he is moving toward the achievement of the ultimate. The teacher has, withal, the privilege and responsibility of bringing out hidden and unusual power, skimming away the fear.

How often children exclaim, "Let's play the story!" as they enjoy such tales as "The Golden Goose" and "Three Billy Goats Gruff." And so they play it, with fervor and due regard to the developmental events. Their characterization is excellent and their emotional responses are in line with those of the personnel in the tale being portrayed.

Children may play simple stories with no preparatory planning; but as they meet more complex situations and settings, they may need to make a few simple plans. For instance, the pupils may wish to settle on the characters and number of scenes to be portrayed, on placement of the action in parts of the classroom (the teacher's desk for the fox's den and the reading center at the left corner of the room for the forest), and two or three castings of pupils to play the various roles. The simpler the story, the less preplanning there should be; but older children, enacting a longer and more complicated story, may find it advisable to make preparatory plans. However, the teacher should allow the players to make up the developmental action and the accompanying dialogue as they go along. Only in this way can the creative values of dramatics be retained.

Young children, particularly, should have frequent opportunities to play their stories. When given many such opportunities in the lower grades, they usually retain the tendency to want to dramatize in the intermediate grades. It is lamentable when older children have lost their natural dramatic tendencies simply because they seldom were given the privilege of playing their stories in their early school years.

Creative dramatics is for fun and should have little criticism. In order to encourage originality and to distribute the opportunities to participate, there may be more than one set of children to represent the characters in the story. The different groups may do their necessary planning and rehearsals in different rooms or, if need be, in widely separated parts of the same room. Thus each group can present its own interpretation without being inhibited by the plans and performance of the others. Pupils who do not appear as actors may constitute the audience and sometimes may act as judges to select a cast to present the play later in an assembly.

One type of creative dramatics that is likely to appeal to upper-grade children is the dramatic portrayal of historical events. The writer recalls going into an eighth-grade classroom where the pupils had requested that the scheduled recess period be given over to continuing their acting out a session of the Virginia House of Burgesses on the day of Patrick Henry's speech. They had divided themselves into Whigs and Tories and were heatedly and realistically debating the issues of prerevolutionary days. Another valuable experience in creative dramatics is role playing in which the participants come to understand other persons' feelings and responses through acting out situations that have caused concern.

In planning a play, the teacher should allow the pupils to do as much of the planning as possible. The teacher and pupils should follow these steps:

1. Divide the story into parts, scenes, or acts.
2. Name each scene or act.
3. List the characters in each such part (orally, unless the play is quite involved).
4. Discuss the setting: time, place, surroundings.
5. Review the action and principal conversation of the first part; discuss the necessary equipment; decide the places for the action.

6. Choose a cast for the first tryout of the first part.

7. After the tryout, give constructive suggestions—never unkindly—and choose another cast for playing this part.

8. Repeat steps 5, 6, and 7 for each part of the play.

9. Choose the final cast.

10. Write out the conversation and action sometimes, but do not make a rule of this.

There are various degrees of formality, and teachers may omit almost any of the steps named above. Experienced teachers know that pupils tire of dramatization that is too formal and, gradually, these teachers learn to manage activities with fewer and fewer of the formal steps.

FORMAL DRAMATIZATION

Formal dramatization is thoroughly planned ahead of time and may even be put into written form by a committee or by the entire group working cooperatively. Here creativeness may be at a minimum. However, there may be creative possibilities as the children devise variations in the action and dialogue, make additions, work out stage settings and possible trappings to add atmosphere, and make up simple costumes. Principally, the creative opportunities lie in each character's personal interpretation of his role by identifying himself with the personality he is portraying. Unless a child is able to put himself into the part, there is little creative value in his formal dramatization.

Some teachers like to take already prepared plays from magazines or books and assign the parts to selected pupils for memorization.

If the play has real literary merit, the memorizing of lines may be a valuable experience. With mediocre plays, however, such procedure can scarcely be justified. The creativity and spontaneity of creative dramatics are to be preferred to a cut-and-dried demonstration of memorized speech and action. Writing out a play for subsequent dramatization may offer good practice in creative writing, but unless a perfectly finished product is desired for a program or an assembly, children can benefit most by acquainting themselves with the plot and characters and then extemporizing their lines.

VARIATIONS IN DRAMATIZATION

In our daily living, gestures and facial expression are important means of communicating our impressions and attitudes. These same avenues of communication are employed in *pantomime* where bodily action carries the message and plot. Pantomime is an enjoyable variation of dramatization and particularly valuable for inducting a timid child into dramatic activities. He may, for instance, be a tree swaying in the wind or a little

Junior high school pupils discuss the interpretation of their roles in a play.

First graders pretend to be ocean waves.

rabbit hopping through the forest as Hansel and Gretel pick strawberries. The teacher can motivate oral reading by having a cast of characters pantomime the action as one or more pupils read a dramatic story; or pupils may act out in pantomime a part of the story so that the watchers may later find the proper part and read it aloud—a thought-provoking activity.

A popular variation of dramatization is the puppet show. Interest in this activity is likely to develop in the upper primary grades. Young children do best if they use cutout figures fastened to one end of a ruler or long stick. The teacher may convert a large box into a simple stage by removing the front and back and using a drawstring to pull curtains across the front; or she may string curtains on the front side of a table so that the children may crouch behind the table and move their puppets just above its back edge.

Next in simplicity are paper-bag and fist puppets. Here the puppet consists of a loose gown with sleeves; the gown is attached to a head. A child then uses his thumb and two fingers to move the head and arms of the puppet. It is possible to make the head from a paper bag or a coarse white stocking partially stuffed with cotton.

Only older children are able to operate puppets attached to strings. Carrie Rasmussen(46) gives excellent suggestions for this type of puppetry.

SUGGESTIONS FOR STUDY AND DISCUSSION

1. Try to get examples of children's creative writing from an elementary school. List phrases and sentences that are unusual.

2. Interview several experienced teachers. Get their ideas on what constitutes creativity, how to stimulate it in children, and what to do for children who are reserved or phlegmatic.

3. In your own words, define creative expression.

4. Try out your own powers of creative language. The following topics may present helpful suggestions. Notice emphasis on the sensory.

    a. Sights that please your eye
    b. Pleasant smells (or tastes)
    c. Drifting in a canoe: feasting of eye, ear, nose
    d. Early morning
    e. Baking day

5. What are the values in creative language to the speaker or the writer?

6. What are the values to the listeners or the readers?

7. Summarize teaching procedures for developing creativeness in children.

FOR FURTHER READING

1. APPLEGATE, MAUREE, "Hoppity . . . Skippity . . . Serendipity." *Childhood Education* (February 1960), 259–62.

2. ARNOLD, FREIDA, "A Creative Writing Activity." *Elementary English* (May 1961), 298–300.

3. BRACK, KENNETH H., "Creativity in Writing Is Where You Find It." *Elementary English* (February 1961), 89–90, 98.

4. CARLSON, RUTH KEARNEY, "Emergence of Creative Personality." *Childhood Education* (May 1960), 402–04.

5. —— "Seventeen Qualities of Original Writing." *Elementary English* (December 1961), 576–79.

6. —— "Stimulating Creativity in Children and Youth." *Elementary English* (March 1961), 165–69, 174.

7. CARPENTER, REGAN, "Creativity: Its Nature and Nurture." *Education* (March 1962), 391–95.

8. HARDY, HILDA, "The Child, a Creator." *Elementary English* (November 1961), 491–93.

9. HILDRETH, GERTRUDE, *Learning the Three R's*, 2nd ed. (Chapter 3). Minneapolis, Educational Test Bureau, Educational Publishers, 1947.

10. HILL, JERALDINE, "Fostering Creativity." *Elementary English* (January 1960), 23–26.

11. HOOK, EDWARD N., "A Dozen Methods for Stimulating Creative Writing." *Elementary English* (February 1961), 87–88.

12. MEARNS, HUGHES, *Creative Power*, 2nd rev. ed. New York, Dover, 1959.

13. PORTER, ELEANOR, "The Problem: To Say What You Mean." *Elementary English* (October 1958), 388–90.

14. PRYOR, FRANCES, "We Can't Afford Not to Write." *Elementary English* (November 1961), 509–12, 520.

15. SCHWINGER, FLORENCE W., "First Comes the Word." *Elementary English* (May 1962), 486–89.

16. STENDLER, CELIA B., *Teaching in the Elementary School* (Chapter 12). New York, Harcourt, Brace & World, 1958.

17. SVOBODA, LAURA SIEL, "Creative Writing and the Classics." *Elementary English* (January 1961), 29–32.

18. TORRANCE, E. PAUL, "Priming Creative Thinking in the Primary Grades." *Elementary School Journal* (October 1961), 34–41.

STORY WRITING

19. BERRY, ELOISE, "Films and Creative Expression." *Elementary English* (October 1958), 383–86.

20. EDMUND, NEAL R., "Story Writing in the Seventh Grade." *Elementary English* (May 1957), 305–06.

21. —— "Writing in the Intermediate Grades." *Elementary English* (November 1959), 491–501.

22. HEMINGWAY, HELEN FITTS, "A Cooperative Effort in Creativeness." *Elementary English* (March 1958), 164–67.

23. HILL, MARY EVELYN, "Creative Writing: First Steps." *Elementary School Journal* (May 1960), 433–36.
24. LARON, HENRY V., "Sixth Graders Write Good Short Stories." *Elementary English* (January 1960), 20–23.
25. WOODWARD, ISABEL A., "We Write and Illustrate." *Elementary English* (February 1959), 102–04.

VERSE WRITING

26. ABERNATHY, HELEN B., and EARLENE BURGETT, "Let's Write a Poem." *Elementary English* (February 1962), 119–28.
27. DE BASE, LUCY, "Fun with Poetry." Elementary English (May 1958), 299–301.
28. FRIEND, MIMI, "Developing a Unit in Writing Poetry." *Elementary English* (February 1960), 102–04.
29. HENDERSON, HAROLD G., *An Introduction to Haiku.* Garden City, N. Y., Doubleday, 1958.
30. LACHMAN, FLORENCE, "Writing a Group Poem." *Elementary English* (May 1957), 319.
31. McENROE, KATHLEEN, "The Process of Creative Writing." *Elementary English* (March 1958), 159–62.
32. SCOFIELD, ELIZABETH, "Haiku, a New Poetry Experience for Children." *Elementary English* (January 1961), 24–26.
33. VALLETUTTI, P., "Developing Creativity Through a Unit on Poetry." *Elementary English* (October 1959), 385–89.

DRAMATIZATION

34. BERTRAM, JEAN DE SALES, "Creative Dramatics in the School." *Elementary English* (December 1958), 515–18.
35. BRACK, KENNETH H., "Creative Dramatics: Why? How? When?" *Elementary English* (December 1959), 565–67.
36. BUSBEE, VIVIAN, "Dramatic Interpretation in the Elementary School." *Elementary English* (October 1957), 394–96, 424.
37. DURLAND, FRANCES C., *Creative Dramatics for Children.* Yellow Springs, Ohio, Antioch, 1952.
38. GRAUBARD, PAUL S., "Adapting Literature to Drama." *Childhood Education* (March 1962), 322–25.
39. ——— "Pantomime: Another Language." *Elementary English* (May 1960), 302–06.
40. HERRICK, VIRGIL E., and LELAND B. JACOBS, eds., *Children and the Language Arts.* Englewood Cliffs, N. J., Prentice-Hall, 1955.
41. KAMERMAN, SYLVIA E., *Children's Plays from Favorite Stories.* Boston, Plays, 1959.
42. LEASE, RUTH, and GERALDINE SIKS, *Creative Dramatics in Home, School, and Community.* New York, Harper, 1952.
43. LEWIS, GEORGE L., and ANN KAMMERLING BURKART, "Creative Dramatics: A Selective Bibliography." *Elementary English* (February 1962), 91–100.

44. LLOYD, BRUCE A., "Make Your Play." *Elementary English* (March 1959), 176–77.
45. POPOVICH, JAMES E., "Creative Dramatics." *NEA Journal* (November 1960), 29–30.
46. RASMUSSEN, CARRIE, *Speech Methods in the Elementary School* (Chapters 9, 10, 15). New York, Ronald, 1949.
47. SCHWARTZ, SHEILA, "New Methods in Creative Dramatics." *Elementary English* (November 1959), 484–87.
48. STARKS, ESTHER B., "Dramatic Play." *Childhood Education* (December 1960), 163–67.
49. WARD, WINIFRED, *Playmaking with Children*. New York, Appleton-Century-Crofts, 1957.
50. WOLFE, DON, *Language Arts and Life Patterns* (Chapter 26). New York, Odyssey, 1961.

20

Teaching Usage and Grammar

Chapter 20 establishes the major aim of instruction in correct usage and grammar to be the building of good language habits. The importance of motivation in the learning process is stressed. Emphasis is placed upon (1) the value of a language inventory to determine needs and (2) a definite cycle of procedures to develop or strengthen the use of approved language forms, including both class and individual work as needed. The chapter concludes with suggestions for classroom instruction in grammar according to the linguists' point of view.

OF ALL the phases of language instruction, the phase devoted to correct usage is possibly the least successful in terms of the effort expended. Errors that were in the children's speech when they entered school tend to persist in spite of the fact that most of these errors have repeatedly been the subject of correct usage lessons year after year. Why are errors so hard to eradicate? Several reasons have been identified.

A child establishes the language habits of a lifetime in his preschool years. He has learned speech through hearing others speak, then imitating the speech patterns he has heard. If he lives in a cultured atmosphere, he will have few problems in correct usage; but if he has been born into a home and community where illiterate and crude usage is prevalent, only a strong motivation and highly efficient type of instruction can improve his speech habits. His errors have become pretty well fixed by the time he comes to school because he has again and again repeated incorrect and illiterate speech patterns.

Typically the child continues through his years in school to live in the same type of environment as that into which he was born. If his family is illiterate, he has continuing experience in speaking incorrectly and in hearing poor speech as he associates with his family and his neighborhood companions. His hours in school are comparatively few, and he has relatively little opportunity for talking during school hours as compared with his chances for talking outside of school.

Many children who are most in need of lessons in correct usage are not particularly interested in improving their speech. They fit well into their social environment when they are speaking, just as their families and friends do; they are comfortable in doing this, whereas they are likely to be embarrassed if they use the unnatural (to them) language that the teacher has stipulated. Besides, a child is more concerned with *what* he is trying to say than with *how* he is saying it. If he can make himself understood by speaking effortlessly in his customary speech patterns, why should he make the effort to express himself in the unaccustomed correct forms?

The school itself may be negligent in providing enough experiences in which pupils feel the need of lifting the level of their normal speaking and writing. Whenever teachers have a separate period for language, it becomes easy to teach English as a subject unrelated to the rest of the curriculum. The few minutes that the teacher devotes to developing in children an understanding of correct word forms and to seeing that they practice them during the language period can make little impression if he makes no further effort throughout the school day to impress the forms and to see that children continue to practice them.

The separate language period should be a time when the pupils' language needs that have been revealed in other lessons and learning activities are met. In such a period the teacher will concentrate on the treatment of the skill or usage for which need has arisen. Subsequently he will see that the pupils use correctly this usage or skill in all learning activities where its use is pertinent. When the teaching of language is divorced from other curricular areas, there can scarcely be effective teaching of correct usage.

Lessons to impress correct usage may be, and often are, taught ineffectively. They may be poorly motivated. Too often, the teacher concentrates on certain items of usage because they are included in the course of study or the textbook rather than because these are the pupils' actual usage errors. He may not make the instruction fit the individual; and as a result, all of the pupils must drill on usages that only a few need. He should not force pupils to take part in usage lessons that involve errors they *do not make*. Sometimes the teacher presents all the usage drill in written form even though the errors are in the speech of the pupils. Instead, he should see that oral practice predominates. Sometimes he tries to teach too many items each year, each one superficially. In these and other ways, correct usage lessons may prove to be ineffective in eradicating errors.

Aims of Lessons in Correct Usage

A RATHER commonly stated objective of lessons in correct usage is the elimination of errors in the pupils' speech. By taking an inventory, or even by consulting a list in the course of study or a textbook, the teacher determines certain items of word usage that are to be taught. Then through a series of repetitive lessons, the pupils attack each error in its turn. But all too often speech patterns remain the same even though the children may actually *know* more acceptable forms.

Modern language teaching does not emphasize primarily the elimination of gross errors—such an attack would be negative—or even merely the knowledge of better forms, because knowledge alone avails little in the area of habits. Rather, the predominant aim is the building of good language habits. Instead of relying entirely on identifying errors, the teacher should see that lessons emphasize the *use of correct expressions* appropriate to the occasion, setting them up as objects of approval and as models for imitation.

The positive approach is preferred in modern teaching: *Do*, not *Don't*, is the slogan for the teacher of correct usage. In situation after situation, the pupils find a constructive opportunity to put the more acceptable form to use in their discussions, reports, and other language activities throughout the school day. The habit of using the more acceptable form can be built up only when it becomes familiar to the ear and the tongue. The positive approach is designed to build habits that gradually displace those of inappropriate or incorrect usage.

The ultimate goal is adequacy and effectiveness in the colloquial, comfortable language of everyday. Niceties, formalities, errors of slight moment, should not be emphasized. Instead the teacher, in cooperation with the pupils, notes which gross errors are prevalent in the speech of the whole group and which ones plague only a few of the pupils, possibly only an individual child. Then he sets up a program that stresses the adequate and effective ways of speaking that he wishes to substitute for the undesirable speech patterns.

Happily, few items merit attention in the elementary school. Instruction can therefore be thorough and not too time consuming. The teacher will be able to stress communication, not correctness, most of the time. Thus pupils can achieve an easy, vivid, clear-cut, reasonably acceptable way of speaking and writing everyday language.

First Steps in Forming Habits of Correct Usage

MOTIVATION

A familiar formula for habit formation includes four steps: motivating; making a clear impression; repeating again and again with no intervening use of incorrect forms; consistently putting the correct form into practical use. The problem of motivation is a serious one and must be met first: how to develop pupils' interest in usage lessons and arouse in them a genuine desire to replace inappropriate or incorrect forms with forms that are acceptable.

Any attempt to change language habits from those that are acceptable within a child's circle of family and friends is likely to elicit no interest. Such an attempt may even create a feeling of resentment. Language is considered by many to be a very personal expression of themselves as individuals, a thing to be defended against criticism. A suggestion by the teacher that another language form would be an improvement must be approached with tact and real understanding. He should see that the child's pride in himself, his family, and his friends is left intact.

Even small children understand the concept that some expressions are more appropriate for one occasion than for another. A teacher who wishes to develop a language habit like "I did" to replace "I done" may find the instruction more acceptable to the child if the recommended form is presented as the one expected in school, or in making introductions, if that is the current need, or in writing letters if the correction applies there. The teacher must be sensitive to the implications of any remark that might be interpreted as a personal criticism. When a rapport exists between teacher and pupils, they may come to a common agreement that certain forms are inappropriate among certain groups of people, and that reminders and corrections are often necessary.

Since gross errors in usage usually form very real barriers to people who wish to lift themselves to a higher socio-economic level than the one to which they were born, it is the responsibility of the school to help children overcome flagrant mistakes and develop habits of speech that are acceptable as standard English. For such a basic change in language patterns, the child must feel that real effort is worth while.

School experiences in speaking and writing must be impressive indeed to create the urge to change. The real stimulus comes when important occasions arise—important in the eyes of the pupils—and they *want* to discard an old language pattern for a new one. Such occasions are most likely to arise when the speaking or writing is done for a visible audience, either of classmates or of persons from outside the classroom. A report to a mothers' group, an assembly for other classes in the school, a report for the class, a record of school events, a personal experience to be shared with his classmates—these may be looked upon by the pupil as real reasons to use the language forms expected in his school.

Work prepared for the teacher alone, no matter how beloved the teacher, does not have the stimulus that a larger audience provides. One child said to his teacher, "Let me give you my report after school. I don't mind if *you* hear it. *You* already know how dumb I am." But the teacher had the good sense to respond, "We couldn't do it that way, John. The class really wants to hear your report. If you practice it once with me after school today, perhaps you'll feel ready when your turn comes in class."

Another teacher, working with a shy child, helped him prepare by recording his practice on tape. Too ill at ease to fa the his group, he consented to have the tape played for the group. Their approval gave him confidence in himself. In both cases, the group exerted a powerful effect in motivating learning.

When the teacher uses real or lifelike situations for stimulating effort to improve usage, he should be careful that the pupil prepares for the situation in a normal way. For instance, the pupil should not memorize his introduction of a speaker in an assembly, and certainly the teacher should not write the introduction for the pupil to memorize. Preparation might include the pupil's writing his talk first, to establish what is to be said and a good way to say it, with correct language forms; but oral practice should follow, and the oral practice should not be repetition by rote.

Or, for example, in writing a letter for information, the child's rough draft may serve as the basis for suggested change in usage. The motivation that lies in the importance of this letter-writing situation is not fully exploited unless the child does his own revision, with needed help from his language textbook or his teacher.

Aside from the unusual and highly motivating experiences that can be arranged from time to time, the teacher will seek to develop in the children a continuing sense of pride in their language, some understanding of its changing qualities and the levels of usage expected under different situations, and a desire to develop better language patterns wherever the need may be. A clear understanding on the part of the children of desirable forms and the reward of an appreciative nod when they do use the forms correctly, will keep some children striving toward the established goals.

RESTRICTING LESSONS TO NECESSARY PHASES

At the beginning of each school year, each teacher needs to take inventory to determine what aspects of language instruction are needed by the children in his classroom. A check list can be useful as a guide. The list should include items that are still likely to be unmastered (even though they have previously been taught), along with those currently needed and as yet untaught. Such a list, made out at the beginning of the school year, will no doubt require revision during the year as needs emerge.

Suggested Outline of Language Phases

I. Types of communication (used for currently appropriate topics)
   A. Oral communication
      1. Conversation
      2. Informal discussion
      3. Brief talks and reports
      4. Oral and choral reading
      5. Storytelling
      6. Dramatization
   B. Written Communication
      1. Letters (business and friendly)
      2. Records, news items
      3. Reports, explanations
      4. Outlines
      5. Stories, plays, poems
II. What to observe
   A. Content
      1. Originality or fresh approach
      2. Correct facts
      3. Adequate information
      4. Opinions supported with reasons
      5. Word choice; vocabulary
      6. Courtesy, tact
   B. Organization
      1. Sticking to the point
      2. Sequence of sentences, or main ideas
      3. Appropriate beginning and conclusion
      4. Effective sentences (avoiding choppiness, overuse of *and* and *so*, run-on sentences)
   C. Technical speech skills
      1. Voice (loud enough; distinct, pleasing)
      2. Articulation; enunciation; pronunciation
      3. Poise and posture
      4. Directness; enthusiasm
   D. Technical writing skills
      1. Capitalization
         a. List new items to be taught
         b. List old items not yet mastered
      2. Punctuation
         a. List new items to be taught
         b. List old items not yet mastered
      3. Spelling

    4. Appearance of manuscript
      a. Heading, title, margins, indentation
      b. Handwriting
      c. Use of ink (at appropriate ability level)
  E. Usage and grammar
    1. List sentence errors to be considered
      (fragment, comma fault, run-on)
    2. List verb forms to be considered
      (ain't, he done, have did, I seen, he run)
    3. List subject-verb errors to be considered
      (There's ten going. They was happy. He don't.)
    4. List pronoun errors to be considered
      (us kids saw, my brother he, them papers, tell me and Jim [impolite])
    5. List other common errors to be considered
      (a apple, haven't no, that there)

Teachers will recognize that no arbitrary list of items will fit the needs of all classrooms. Some suggestions on usage are made in this book at the end of the chapters in written expression in the primary and intermediate grades (Chapters 14 and 15). These suggested learnings are intended to show a plan for a continuous, developmental program consistent with the maturity of children and their needs. They cannot be assigned to grade levels without having adjustments made for individuals.

> Growth in language is not like building a wall by adding one stone here and another there. It is far more like growing a tree by letting it live in the rain, the sunshine, and the wind. No one would presume to divide up the growth period of a tree and demand that in the first period three branches must develop, in the next period five, and in the third period seven. The number of branches that develop on a tree in a given period depends on the type of tree it is, the kind of soil from which it grows, and the amount of rain and sunshine it receives.*

Since children vary from class to class and within the class, the items in which they need instruction must be checked by teacher observation. In schools where care has been given to the selection of a good language series, items given in the textbook may serve the teacher as a check list while he observes language needs.

An influential guide for teachers as they plan instruction in language is

* From: *The English Language Arts*, p. 36. Prepared by the Commission on the English Curriculum of The National Council of Teachers of English. Copyright, 1952, The National Council of Teachers of English. Reprinted by permission of Appleton-Century-Crofts.

Robert Pooley's *Teaching English Usage* (18, pp. 180–81). Pooley emphasizes selectivity in teaching usage and the necessity for attacking with the class only those errors that the majority make, beginning with the least complicated and most objectionable mistakes.

His list of errors for elementary school (Grades 3 through 6) is rather short. It is accompanied by another list recommended to receive no class instruction before junior high school level, but appropriate for individual correction during earlier elementary years if the child makes none of the gross errors listed for class study. Similar lists of errors for direct class instruction and for individual correction at junior high level are given.

Pooley offers the following errors to be attacked in the elementary school:

ain't, or *hain't*	he *give*	he *run*
hair *are*	I *got* for I've *got*	have *saw*
a orange	*my brother, he* (and other	I *says*
have *ate*	double subjects)	he *seen*
he *begun*	*her, him,* and *me* went	*them* books
was *broke*	*hisself*	*theirselves*
he *brung*	*there is, was* four	*this here*
climb (short *i*)	*knowed, growed,* etc.	*that there*
clumb	*learn* me a song	*us* boys went
he *come*	*leave* me go	we, you, they *was*
have *did*	*me* and Mary went	with *we* girls
he, she, it *don't*	*haven't no,* haven't *nothing*	have *went*
I *drunk*		have *wrote*
didn't, hadn't ought		it is *yourn, hern, ourn, theirn*
was *froze*		

Among the uses that Pooley recommends should receive *no* class instruction in the elementary school are the following:

None of us *are, were* there.
Can I go?
Do the work *good.*
I haven't *got* a pencil.
I couldn't *hardly* do the work. I haven't *hardly* any.
She gave it to John and *I.*
He *lays* down every day, is *laying* down, *laid* down, has *laid* down, etc.
Do it *like* I do.

He acts *like* he is cold.
It is *me, him, her, them.*
Everybody, everyone said that *they....*
Who did you choose?
If I *was* you, I'd play ball. I wish I *was* you.
Who are you waiting for?
I *will* probably be late.
One of my brothers *were* here.

It is assumed that no teacher would find his pupils making all of the errors that Pooley lists for attention in the elementary school. It is recommended that the staff of each elementary school make a survey of usage patterns in the local school in order to determine which of them are incorrect. Then the errors that are actually found may be divided among the grades above the second for direct teaching. In the instructional program, only errors common to most of the members of a class would receive whole-class teaching; most of the errors would be treated in small-group or individual instruction so that only the children who make the errors would engage in lessons on correct usage.

A LANGUAGE INVENTORY

A systematic inventory of class needs can be made by checking a list like the one on pages 382–83. With respect to oral language, the teacher will listen whenever the pupils are speaking—particularly informally—and check the errors he hears. In regard to written language, analysis of the writing pupils do will serve to indicate how well each pupil uses language; at the higher-grade levels this method may well be supplemented by a short diagnostic (teacher-made) test to see how well the pupils know how to distinguish between correct and incorrect forms.

From time to time certain parts of the check list may be highlighted. The inventory chart below shows how a teacher may keep a record of the

INVENTORY CHART

Substandard Usage Items	Mary	June	Jack	Dick	Ruth	Fred
ain't						
done *for* did	S	S			SD +	
don't *for* doesn't		SN+			SD	OD+
busted, broke *for* broken		S				O
learn *for* teach				O	D	
I and you			S			
for we girls						
there was several					SN	
this here book					SD +	

pupils' individual needs and their improvement in some of the usage items which have been the subject of instruction. The chart indicates the progress of the pupil (+ means improvement) and the time the check is made (S means September).

As suggested in an earlier chapter, children may compile a list of standards to be met in their communication lessons. As they use such a list in self-checking, they will be taking their own inventory to determine the progress they have made and their continuing needs.

A Definite Cycle of Procedures

INCIDENTAL INDIVIDUAL CORRECTION

Incidental individual correction should be used from first grade through eighth. Together with the children's natural imitation of the teacher's speech, incidental individual correction is the principal means of teaching correctness in the first grade, and possibly the second. Drill lessons should not be used much in any of the primary grades, where enrichment of ideas, spontaneity, and socialization are the chief aims.

In incidental correction, the teacher makes a kindly and unobtrusive comment after an individual pupil has made an error that a child of his maturity should not make. He will say, "You said, 'I seen it,' Sue. You should say, 'I saw it'; Say, 'I saw it.'" This, or some similar remark, will help Sue become conscious of the usage she should watch; but she will not be embarrassed because presumably she alone has heard the teacher's comments. There are times, of course, when an entire class needs to be helped with pronunciation or use of a specific word. Then the teacher may make his comments to the group, but will not identify any particular pupil as the one who has made the error. If a teacher consistently corrects the really flagrant errors of individual pupils in such a manner, he is likely to get favorable results.

IMITATION

The teacher should serve as a model for the children, especially with technicalities. Because children at the elementary school level tend to be too immature to comprehend the grammatical structure of sentences and the bases for the various syntactical forms of words, their imitation of correct forms is the major technique for helping them to improve their usage. In attempting to teach usage to children in the elementary school, a teacher should not depend too much on making explanations; rather he should show at least the younger pupils what is correct, and he should let them imitate him in learning the correct usage.

Haverly Moyer(16) tells of an effective experiment in improving usage and oral expression by ear training. Tapes were used to accustom intermediate- and upper-grade pupils to the desired form and to help them to listen to their own expression critically. No written drills or formal exercises were used, but the speech habits of the pupils improved perceptibly.

Language teaching can never be restricted to a period devoted specifically to English instruction. If correct usage is to become a habit, the children must practice the correct use of each newly learned item in all their classes and also on the playground. This assumes that the items are limited to flagrant errors and that colloquial terms are acceptable in everyday speech. After a series of language lessons on some item of correct usage has been completed, each pupil in the classroom *should hold himself responsible* thereafter for using that item correctly. A teacher who builds up a language morale by insistence on correct usage—kindly but firm insistence—is going to get the kind of results that he wants.

Placards or charts featuring correct usage forms (as in the following examples) are likely to help the pupils to form clear impressions and correct habits. These teaching aids should be displayed as soon as the pupils begin to realize their need for a particular form. If necessary, the teacher can use the bulletin board or chalkboard instead of these placards:

am not	*isn't*
I *am not* ready.	Joe *isn't* here.
I *am not* late.	*Isn't* that a robin?
I *am not* hungry.	Anne *isn't* coming.
I *am not* tired.	*Isn't* it cold today?

aren't	*haven't*
The books *aren't* here.	*Haven't* you a pencil?
Aren't you going?	We *haven't* voted yet.
You *aren't* my partner.	*Haven't* you seen Sue?
Aren't we invited?	I *haven't* any crayons.

NOTEBOOKS

In the middle and upper grades, each pupil should have a correct-usage section in his notebook. There he should record the right way to use each word he finds troublesome. He may also file drills and exercises in which he has practiced the use of such items. In addition, he may keep any papers in which he has used troublesome words correctly.

THE DEVELOPMENT LESSON

After a pupil has realized his need for help in mastering some item of correct usage, he is ready for a series of lessons designed (1) to give him an understanding of the way this particular word should be used and (2) to afford repetitive practice that will help to fix the habit of using the word correctly.

In a development lesson, the first step is to understand what the correct usage is. Usually there are several sentences that show in a simple, explicit way how to use the word in question. By comparing these sentences, the pupils discover a formula for deciding when and how to use this word. Then they may state their self-made rule.

The following sentences are typical of the kind appropriate for use in a development lesson. They are short and similar except in the one phase where discrimination is to be built up. In these sentences, the critical feature is the difference between the use of *was* and *were*. Thus the pupils will be encouraged to concentrate on the point at issue.

1. The boy was here.
2. John was here.
3. The boys were here.
4. John and Tim were here.
5. Their books were lost.
6. Their book was lost.

In reading the sentences preceding, the children will notice how much alike they are, and then note the critical usage of *was* and *were*. After analyzing these sentences, they can easily derive a rule for using the words properly.

The next step in a development lesson is an exercise in which the teacher helps pupils to recognize the right word (*was* or *were*, in this instance) by using it in a set of completion or multiple choice sentences. Probably the first set of sentences should be worked out orally so that the teacher can be sure the pupils understand the rule they have just made. Then he may follow the oral exercise with a written exercise; the pupils should read this aloud afterward for oral practice.

The teacher must realize that the development lesson is merely a starting point in breaking up a wrong habit and replacing it with a correct one. He should be careful to tie up the exercises in the development lesson and any subsequent drill with the daylong language activities of the children.

CLASS AND GROUP DRILL

On the days immediately following a development lesson for the class, the teacher should arrange brief and lively drills on the correct usage. Children learn habits through repetition of the desired learning, and through elimination of the incorrect form. Best results will follow if the teacher can make sure the practice situation is as lifelike as possible; since errors in using word forms first appear in speech and are most common in speaking, most drill on correct usage should be oral. If the teacher uses any written drills on word usage, the pupils should read the sentences orally after they have written them. Research(21, 23) has shown two techniques to be most effective in teaching correct usage: oral repetition of the correct form, and the choice between right and wrong forms *after* the pupils have learned the principle that guides or determines correct usage.

All too often teachers fail to see drill as only one part of the process of habit formation. They concentrate on drill, hoping for mastery through repetition. But drill is of no effect unless pupils have purpose and understanding. Otherwise filling blanks in sentences or selecting the preferable form from two or more possibilities is an activity performed either at random or with reliance on another person. Rather than submit any pupils to such poor experience, a teacher must be careful to assign drill exercises only to those who understand the processes which the drill intends to fix.

Drill exercises serve their purpose better when they are not lengthy. A short period with high interest gets better results. When the children's hearts and minds are in their work, short drills may serve to double check their learning and clinch their newly acquired skill.

INDIVIDUALIZED DRILL

Although individual incidental correction may take care of much of the pupils' need for improving their patterns of speech, the more deeply ingrained habits will need rather intensive follow-up drill. How to find time and opportunity to give individual practice on skills and usages is a problem for any teacher. Increasingly, as children grow older, they will be able to identify and record their own errors. They can also take considerable responsibility for getting practice on the various items of correct usage if they find drill materials available.

Language textbooks often contain exercises pertinent to an individual pupil's needs, and the teacher can hold him responsible for using them. Some workbooks have oral exercises, but they are more likely to have written exercises. In the latter case, the pupils may read the exercises aloud after they have finished writing them, thus providing oral practice on word usage. Pupils should write the drills on capitalization, punctuation, and spelling, of course. The teacher should provide oral practice on the skills and usages that appear in speech; he should provide written practice for skills and technicalities applied in writing.

A workable and extremely simple procedure that will provide some measure of individualization in practicing correct usage is as follows: from old, discarded language textbooks and workbooks, clippings from teachers' magazines, and files of teacher-made exercises, the teacher can develop a set of practice materials that the pupils may use during their free time. He should place each exercise in an envelope and label it. He can then file the various envelopes in a substantial box as wide as the envelopes are long.

Any pupil who needs practice on a certain phase of correct usage or a specific language skill may then go to the file and select from it a practice exercise related to his known needs. The teacher or a competent pupil may check the accuracy of his work. When the pupil has completed an exercise satisfactorily, he signs his name on the enclosing envelope. Although this procedure can be considered no more than supplementary, it can be helpful because practice is suited to individual needs and the pupils enjoy selecting exercises and doing them on their own initiative.

One procedure in individualizing written drills involves the collection of numerous exercises by cutting up various workbooks. The teacher arranges the lessons according to kind; for example, all lessons on the same type of capitalization together. He mounts each sheet on stiff paper. He can also mount a table of contents, showing the arrangement (probably alphabetical order by type) and the sheet numbers of the exercises. On another sheet he will have a widely spaced alphabetized list of the pupils' names. In this way he can list the items each pupil needs and can make a cumulative record of the exercises the pupil has completed satisfactorily. For a file the teacher can use a strong box of suitable size and shape.

To prepare for a lesson using such materials, the teacher (or a competent pupil) consults the list of pupils' names and their language needs to determine which exercises are needed by each of the pupils. Out of the file he pulls an exercise for each pupil and arranges the sheets in the order of the pupils' seating. In this way, the teacher will consume little time in passing the materials out. It is possible for each pupil to pull out his own exercise on occasions when only a few pupils are to use these materials. After the teacher has corrected the exercises, a pupil can easily replace them in the file since they are numbered and an index is available.

PRACTICE BY APPLICATION

Drill, as the word is used in preceding paragraphs, designates exercises of a somewhat formal nature; the word *practice* is reserved for the application of the learning in natural situations. Drill usually takes a specific item out of context, to highlight its form for the moment. Practice puts it back into context, emphasizing the use of the correct or appropriate form under all the varied situations in which it may be needed.

This is the hardest part of the formula for establishing new habits: putting into practice what has been learned. To remember *how* to express the thought when the mind is concentrating on *what* to say is a very real challenge. But the only way to produce approved forms automatically is through continued employment of them even when the setting is new each time and when the need for the phrase comes unannounced in the normal course of speaking or writing. The adoption of new language patterns is bound to be a slow process.

A SUMMARY OF CLASSROOM PROCEDURES

It is easy to fail to give proper emphasis to one or another of the steps involved in the complete program for habituating correct or appropriate usage in the speech and writing of pupils. The following check list may serve to determine which of the steps, if any, have been neglected:

Inventory

1. Observe the needs made manifest in the pupils' customary spontaneous speech and writing.
2. Administer the inventory tests as they are needed.
3. Help the pupils to check on themselves constantly.

Highlighting the correct forms

1. Provide for the pupils' inductive discovery of the correct way to use words, as contrasted with the incorrect way.
2. Give instruction in such a way as to focus the pupils' attention on the preferred usage.
3. Minimize explanations and stress the pupils' imitation of correct forms.

Variety in drill

1. Have the pupils begin by frequent oral reading of sentences that illustrate everyday cases of the correct use of troublesome words.
2. Use recognition exercises immediately after the pupils' inductive discovery of the rule governing usage.
3. After giving the pupils frequent and diverse exercises, lead them into conscious practice of the correct form in language activities during the day. Give individual help as well as classwork.

Practical application

1. Notice, and help the pupils to notice, the opportunities for using the correct forms that have already been taught.
2. Devise supplementary opportunities that will call for natural use of the correct forms.
3. Recognize and comment upon the pupils' improvement in putting into practice the preferred language forms.

Maintenance

1. Have a maintenance program that will give well-distributed drill and practice on each item that has been introduced.

2. Give mastery tests whenever they are needed, or take continuous inventory through observation.

3. Have a good follow-up program to strengthen correct usage that has not yet been mastered.

Grammar in the Elementary School

THE term *grammar* is sometimes loosely used to include many of the technical skills involved in writing, such as spelling, capitalization, and punctuation. Here it is used in the more specific sense commonly employed by linguists. In this sense it refers to the study of language, including words (and their inflectional forms), phrases, and clauses, and their relationship to each other within the sentence.

For more than fifty years, educators have tried to discover whether the teaching of grammar tends to improve children's ability to express their ideas clearly and correctly. Percival M. Symonds(23) reported an investigation comparing methods of teaching correct forms of usage directly. He found that a knowledge of the right and wrong forms, together with much oral repetition of the right form, was twice as effective in improving the pupils' usage as was the method of teaching the grammatical point involved.

In an assessment of the significance of the various studies and investigations, John J. DeBoer(5, p. 417) observes:

> studies of the relation between the teaching of formal grammar and the improvement of pupils' speaking and writing, extending over a period of fifty-five years . . . and covering both the elementary and high school levels, exhibit a degree of unanimity that is rare in the field of educational research. The findings dramatically confirm the views of modern psychologists as to the way in which language is learned. Language learning is a complex task, and it requires abundant and constant practice in meaningful, supervised communication.
>
> It must be admitted that the total number of studies published or cited in publications over this long period is small compared to the number reported for other problems perhaps no more important, such as the teaching of reading. Moreover, a close examination of some of the reports of investigations of the effectiveness of grammar instruction might reveal flaws in research design or conclusions not fully warranted by the evidence. The impressive fact is, however, that in all these studies, carried out in places and at times far removed from each other, often by highly experienced and disinterested investigators, the results have been consistently negative so far as the value of grammar in the improvement of language expression is concerned. Surely there is no justification in the available evidence for the great expenditure of time and effort still being devoted to formal grammar in American schools.

Many leaders in the area of elementary language teaching, on the basis of such investigations and their own practical experience, came to advocate major emphasis upon direct practice of correct forms and minimum attention to grammar as a means of achieving correct usage. Perhaps the situation is not very different today. Usage is based upon language habits which need attention long before the complexities of language structure should be introduced. But the contribution to human knowledge which has been made by the linguists has been felt, as in this sound stand taken in *The Language Arts* (14, p. 144).

> Technicalities of grammar lie outside the minimum essentials expected of children in the lower grades; but the teacher in these years nevertheless establishes the child's first impressions of the science of language. In fact, she can contribute something that is more valuable and enduring to the child than a memorization of grammatical definitions—she can help him understand what language fundamentally is, and why its various elements exist. Every day the class comes upon situations in which an alert teacher can lead elementary school pupils to understand the functional basis upon which the many elements in our speech and writing exist. . . . The several classes of words, for instance, are necessary because each class meets a definite need in daily life: one class to designate or label the objects to which we refer; another, to tell what the objects are doing; and still another to give an idea of the appearance of those objects. Correspondingly there are reasons for all of the other parts of speech. In similar nontechnical fashion the pupils can look upon written punctuation as a system necessary to help the eye see the relationships of written words, phrases, and sentences.

Classroom Instruction in Grammar

With a truer description of the language, such as the linguists have supplied in recent years, some of the tasks of the teacher are clarified. In the past, many repetitive lessons on definitions and sentence analysis left little more than an abiding dislike for the subject in the minds of some pupils. Some of the definitions of parts of speech were inadequate and misleading, some of the diagrams more instructive in architectural drawing than sentence relationships. The description of English too often assumed a false resemblance to Latin.

With these differences in mind, some grammatical *ideas* seem appropriate for instruction even as early as primary grades if the teacher limits selection of such elements to those which the children can understand. Functional grammar has a place in the intermediate years, and an organized approach to the subject can begin with most pupils at junior high school level.

At least five concepts having to do with morphology and syntax should be developing in the minds of the pupils during their elementary years. They are identified and briefly discussed below.

INFLECTIVE AND DERIVATIVE WORD FORMS

Most children learn the plural effect of *s* or *es* in primary reading so that they can distinguish between *boy* and *boys, box* and *boxes, city* and *cities*. In the intermediate grades they may be introduced to the name for such words. The concept is already there, but the word *noun* will be new to them. The structural characteristics will help to make recognition of nouns easy: (1) their plurals are usually formed by adding *s* or *es*, (2) they can show possession with an apostrophe and *s*, and (3) they are often introduced by *a, an,* or *the*. These clues will help more than the use of the traditional definition alone, that a noun is a name word or the name of a person, place, or thing.

Verbs too have their characteristic features, some of which are recognized in primary reading, like *ed* for the past. In the intermediate grades, when the children can understand, other structural clues, like the *ing* and the various auxiliaries, can be explained. Confusion of personal pronouns should be treated by lessons in usage in the elementary grades. The grammatical approach can be made when understanding and interest will justify the explanation of the different inflective forms to fit changes in person, number, gender, and case.

The study of vocabulary leads naturally to a recognition of many words derived from the same stem. It begins at an early age with words needed in reading, such as the words *happy* and *unhappy,* and continues through the years with examples taken to suit the maturing needs of the pupil. The meanings of common affixes and stems should be noted in the instructional program wherever they fit naturally—in spelling, writing, reading, speech, listening, or language study.

ARRANGEMENTS OF WORDS IN SENTENCES

Even before the child has completely learned to read or write, the teacher calls his attention to sentences by noting the capital letter at the beginning and the period at the end. English is a language that is dependent upon word order to express meaning. A study of sentence structure by older pupils reveals the common patterns of word arrangement. Four patterns are repeated most frequently. If they are presented in fairly simple sentences, those of average ability or above can come to recognize them as basic structures:

1. NOUN, VERB: *The candle burns.* The subject comes first; the verb that follows completes the sentence. Modifiers can enlarge upon the idea, as

in this variation: *There on the desk the flickering candle burns brightly.* The basic pattern is still noun, verb: *The candle burns.*

2. NOUN, LINKING VERB, ADJECTIVE: *The candle is tall.* The subject comes first, then the verb, completed by an adjective that describes the subject. Here the verb *is* links the subject to the predicate adjective.

3. NOUN, LINKING VERB, NOUN: *The candle is a column of pure white.* The subject comes first, then the linking verb, completed by a predicate noun, *column,* that represents the subject. In this case the predicate noun is modified by a phrase.

4. NOUN, VERB, NOUN: *The candle throws its light across the room.* Here the subject comes first, the verb next, followed by an object, *light.*

THE IDEA OF MODIFICATION

As the sample sentences above demonstrate, even very short sentences are likely to contain modifiers. Young children may become familiar with modifiers, as with the different sentence patterns, by seeing them in sentences and learning to imitate the structure in building their own sentences. Starting with a simple subject and predicate, children can add modifiers that supply details and limit the interpretation to a specific meaning. For example, the word *plate* is so general that the reader receives only a hazy mental image. By adding *blue* the writer draws a clearer picture; but further additions may serve to clarify it still more, like this: *the blue willow plate in my grandmother's room.* The adjectives represent the simplest form of modification in this sentence, but once the idea is clear, the principle of modification will be understood as it applies to phrases and clauses too.

PREDICATION AND THE SUBJECT-VERB-COMPLEMENT IDEA

The sentence patterns explained above illustrate the idea of subject-verb and subject-verb-complement relationships. They should be presented one at a time, discussed and illustrated amply, and then used as a basis for building sentences on the same pattern. There is no need for hurry either in presenting the idea or in moving from one pattern to another. Pupils need time to understand a pattern. To make sure of it, they can make sentences of their own to illustrate a pattern and find examples in their own speech and in that of their classmates or in newspapers and books. They will discover patterns most easily if they look for the verb first, then the subject, and at last for a complement. When predication is studied at a more advanced level as a part of language study, pupils will learn how to test subject and verb to see that they agree, or to test the subject and a complement following a linking verb to see that they refer to each other.

THE IDEA OF COORDINATION AND SUBORDINATION

The child will use coordination and subordination long before he is ready to analyze his use of them or determine their effectiveness. His first introduction to the problem of coordination may occur when he is criticized for overuse of *and*. Here the teacher explains that *and* introduces another part of the sentence that is of equal importance. The use of sentence patterns will clarify the point. The problem is not one that suggests an easy solution. Perhaps all his life the individual will face similar situations because each new idea poses new problems of expression. Subordination, likewise, involves the relationships of ideas and a weighing of their comparative importance. Clear thinking as well as effective writing is involved. But recognition of certain subordinate parts of sentences, like those introduced by such words as *when, after, which, who,* and the like, may help a child to avoid the common error of writing fragments as if they were sentences.

NEW DIRECTIONS IN GRAMMAR INSTRUCTION

The foregoing paragraphs may seem to imply that an understanding of grammar is related to effectiveness in writing. This relationship is not inevitable. Examples from history might be used to prove that some of the world's outstanding writers were unschooled in grammar and that some grammarians did not write well. But the assumption is reasonable that speakers and writers can use the tools of their expression more skillfully if they understand them.

The grammar that may be taught in the intermediate grades in a functional way, or introduced as language study in the upper grades, should be considered humbly as only a beginning in a vast field of scholarship. No textbook at the primary-grade level can "cover" grammar. The teacher can use the textbook as a guide in introducing some of the basic facts about words and sentences. Beyond that starting point, children can pursue the study, as their curiosity and natural interest prompt them, to learn more from their own observation and analysis of the language as they hear and see it.

SUGGESTIONS FOR STUDY AND DISCUSSION

1. How would you go about a positive attack on correct usage problems in the early primary grades? middle grades? upper grades?
2. Explain any difference in your approach at the three levels.
3. In your reading, find as many suggestions as possible about ways to individualize the teaching of correct usage items.
4. Why should drill be kept separate from expressional lessons?

5. Write a development lesson teaching the use of *don't* and *doesn't*.

6. Why do teachers have trouble giving enough oral drill on usage items? Give practical suggestions for emphasizing oral practice.

7. Read several articles on teaching grammar. Write your conclusions as to the wisdom of teaching grammar in the elementary school.

8. After reading from Fries and Jesperson, discuss the bearing of their viewpoints on the teaching of language.

FOR FURTHER READING

1. ALLEN, HAROLD B., ed., *Reading in Applied English Linguistics*. New York, Appleton-Century-Crofts, 1958.

2. BALLENGER, H. L., *Iowa Language Abilities Test: Grades 4–7, 7–10*. New York, Harcourt, Brace & World, 1946.

3. BATEMAN, DONALD R., "More Mature Writing Through a Better Understanding of Language Structure." *English Journal* (October 1961), 457–60, 468.

4. CONLIN, DAVID A., "Form and Function: A Quandary." *English Journal* (October 1960), 457–63.

5. DeBOER, JOHN J., "Grammar in Language Teaching." *Elementary English* (October 1959), 413–21.

6. *The English Language Arts,* Commission on the English Curriculum of the National Council of Teachers of English. New York, Appleton-Century-Crofts, 1952.

7. FRIES, CHARLES C., *The Structure of English*. New York, Harcourt, Brace & World, 1952.

8. FURNESS, EDNA LUE, "Pupils, Pedagogues, and Punctuation." *Elementary English* (March 1960), 184–89.

9. GEIST, ROBERT J., "Structural Grammar and the Sixth Grade." *American Speech* (February 1956), 5–12.

10. GERBER, PHILIP L., *Effective English* (Part VI). New York, Random House, 1959.

11. GOLDEN, RUTH I., *Improving Patterns of Language Usage*. Detroit, Wayne State U. Press, 1960.

12. GREENE, HARRY A., and WALTER T. PETTY, *Developing Language Skills in the Elementary School* (Chapter 14). Boston, Allyn and Bacon, 1959.

13. JESPERSON, OTTO, *Language: Its Nature, Development and Origin*. New York, Macmillan, 1947.

14. *The Language Arts,* New York State Bureau of Elementary Curriculum Development. Albany, N. Y., State Education Department, 1957.

15. LOBAN, WALTER, MARGARET RYAN, and JAMES R. SQUIRE, *Teaching Language and Literature*. New York, Harcourt, Brace & World, 1961.

16. MOYER, HAVERLY O., "Does Ear Training Help?" in C. W. Hunnicutt and W. J. Iverson, eds., *Research in the Three R's*. New York, Harper, 1958.

17. POOLEY, ROBERT C., "Grammar in the Grades." *NEA Journal* (September 1958), 422.

18. POOLEY, ROBERT C., *Teaching English Usage*. New York, Appleton-Century-Crofts, 1946.
19. POSTMAN, NEIL, "Grammar and the Education Controversy." *English Journal* (October 1960), 487–89.
20. SHANE, HAROLD G., *Research Helps in Teaching the Language Arts*. Washington, D. C., Association for Supervision and Curriculum Development, National Education Association, 1955. Bibliography.
21. SMITH, DORA V., Forty-Third Yearbook (Part II), National Society for the Study of Education. Chicago, U. of Chicago Press, 1944.
22. STEGALL, CARRIE, "Linguistics and I." *Elementary English* (April 1961), 229–31, 263.
23. SYMONDS, PERCIVAL M., "Practice Versus Grammar in the Learning of Correct English Usage." *Journal of Educational Psychology* (February 1931), 81–96.
24. TIDYMAN, WILLARD F., and MARGUERITE BUTTERFIELD, *Teaching the Language Arts* (Chapter 11). New York, McGraw-Hill, 1959.
25. WOLFE, DON, *Language Arts and Life Patterns* (Part II). New York, Odyssey, 1961.

21

Evaluating Language Instruction

Chapter 21 deals with policies and procedures involved in evaluating children's learning in the areas of listening, speaking, and writing. It shows how the objectives of instruction serve as basic criteria for evaluating the materials and methods of instruction and, most of all, for determining the relative success of the pupils in learning to use their language effectively.

EVERY teacher of the language arts is constantly asking himself such questions as these: How well did this lesson achieve the goals which my pupils and I set for ourselves? How should I select materials and procedures so as to get better results? What progress have my pupils made in the past month or in the year to date? What are they ready to go into next? That is, the teacher and his pupils are constantly evaluating as they plan for, work at, and gauge the results of the various language activities. By observing pupils, analyzing their language usage and testing results, every conscientious teacher constantly seeks evidence that learning activities are actually bringing about desirable changes in the behavior of his pupils. In so doing, he makes every effort to have the pupils themselves participate in the evaluative processes.

Purposes of Evaluation

WELL-CONSIDERED evaluation of the language arts program can serve many purposes and enlighten many people. While the pupils and their teacher are most immediately concerned, the administrative and supervisory personnel of the school, the parents, and the community in general are interested in knowing how successful the instructional program is. Testing can show them *how much* the children have learned; further evaluation through observation and analysis of the language products will further reveal *how good* the program is—if it suits the maturity, interests, abilities, and needs of the pupils involved in the learning activities.

Evaluation measures the individual's progress toward the objectives of the language arts program. As the children listen, speak, and write, the teacher observes their behavior—evidences of interest, the ease or difficulty of performance, versatility, accuracy, clarity, organization of thinking, and the like. He likewise examines their written products and analyzes their speech to find evidence that the goals of instruction are being realized or at least approached. Tape recordings and files of the pupils' papers may be studied to determine long-time progress and evidence of needs still existing or just emerging. To be effective, evaluation must be continuous—whether day by day, month by month, or year by year. Only thus can each child be guided in the light of his peculiar interests, abilities, and needs.

Evaluation motivates and guides further efforts of the teacher and the learner toward the objectives of the program. To the degree that pupils help to define objectives and to evaluate their progress in achieving their goals, they feel real concern and will work to attain success. They are constantly being motivated to further efforts. Knowing exactly what their individual weaknesses are and finding proof that they are making progress promote interest. The teacher, too, is motivated as he evaluates his pupils' learning, finds evidence of improvement and success, and gains a knowledge of exactly what weaknesses to attack next with both individual pupils and the group as a whole.

Evaluation measures the progress of a class, school, or system toward the objectives of the program. Measurement is an essential part of the evaluation process. To measure the many objectives in the usual language arts program, teachers, principals, counselors, and supervisory personnel use a variety of evaluation techniques: tests (both teacher-made and standardized), rating scales, check lists, questionnaires, interviews, records and reports, case studies, and the like. The kind of technique or device that should be used depends upon the kind of objective that is to be measured. A variety of the best measurements that can be secured, applied continuously to clearly defined objectives, will indicate how much progress has been made toward those objectives.

Evaluation obtains evidence needed in building or revising the curriculum in language arts. The school curriculum, which sets up general goals and suggests basic materials and procedures, is itself the product of evaluation as its makers consider and decide upon "the knowledge of the most worth." The teacher of any particular group of pupils then selects from this curriculum the specific objectives to be stressed at any one time on the basis of an evaluation of his pupils' readiness, interest, and need for instruction. He studies records of previous performance, the results of tests, and samples of children's recent work, then carefully observes their current language behavior in order to determine the direction in which to move next. Part of his observation takes place while the children are helping to make plans and, in the process, are revealing their concerns and their needs.

An effective language arts program is never static, but always flexible and adaptable—in a state of flux or else capable of being changed as soon as revision is advisable. Having determined what the objectives of the program should be, the teacher and his pupils plan a program designed to achieve these goals; then they evaluate it. A need for revision will probably be indicated and the means of improvement will be considered. The change having been made, further evaluation of results ensues. Here too, evaluation needs to be a continuous process.

Evaluation of the Materials of Instruction

MUCH of a teacher's success in language instruction lies in the wise choice of his instruction materials. He will constantly examine whatever language textbook the children are using and select from it the lessons that the pupils currently need. Used in this manner, a textbook serves its purpose as an aid to learning best. Likewise, the teacher considers what topics are especially fitting at any particular time so that the children may speak, listen, and write with interest and profit.

The topics for language lessons are legion, and the teacher must constantly consider which are most appropriate and fruitful. The children's expressed interests and known needs are always bases for selection. For instance, if abilities underlying effective storytelling should be dealt with next, the topics may well be drawn from literature or from personal experiences; if the skills of discussion and explanation need attention, current lessons in science, history, or arithmetic may furnish topics. Thus in evaluating the materials of language instruction, the teacher will start with the current interests and needs of the children and will select topics which will best bring the desired skills into play. The topics may be drawn from everyday experiences, lessons in other subjects, the children's personal reading, suggestions in the language textbook, or any source that provides topics that are timely and suitable to the maturity and ability of the pupils. Quite often, the language textbook will provide excellent suggestions for teaching skills, but the topics included in the lessons may not be as appropriate as some that the teacher can draw from other sources. In that case, it is wise to follow the textbook's suggestions for teaching the skills but to substitute topics freely.

Several questions follow as suggested guides to a teacher who wishes to evaluate the materials of instruction. Thoughtful consideration of such questions can help a teacher to decide on the best materials to utilize.

Are the materials timely? Do the topics conform to the known interests of children of the pupils' age, as shown by recent investigations? Is interest in some topic or activity running high right now? Does some holiday or the season of the year suggest appropriate topics? Which lessons in the other subjects could be greatly enriched and extended through reporting, storytelling, dramatization, and discussion based on further reading, trips, and the like? What topics will best lead to practice on the skills currently needed? If materials are truly timely, the teacher can actually "strike while the iron is hot."

Are the materials of suitable difficulty? The textbook itself may be one of the considerations here. Since almost any class has pupils whose reading is retarded, the instructions and illustrative materials may be too difficult for them to read. For such pupils, simpler materials may be available; or the teacher may present the textbook suggestions orally to these children while the remaining children work independently after a brief but pointed presentation of the assignment to be worked out. In one way or another, the teacher has to see that the materials of instruction are of varying difficulty so that the bright pupils are challenged at the same time that the slower learners are not overwhelmed. All should succeed—each at his own potential-level.

Does the subject matter have value? Do the instructional materials have cultural value? The language lessons should at times parallel activities in children's literature, music, art, and biography so that the pupils extend their knowledge and appreciation of great myths, legends, children's opera, paintings, true adventure, and famous deeds. It is as children share their personally appreciative reactions to cultural materials that language serves to enrich life.

Or current events and activities may provide the content. Are the topics appealing to this particular group of children? Are they close to the pupil's personal experiences? Has work in other lessons shown the topics to have unusual appeal? Or are the current language lessons directly useful in learning the language skills which the pupils now need for effective expression of ideas?

Are the materials well organized for teaching? In evaluating the organization of the skills in the language arts curriculum, teachers must consider the psychological principles that underlie effective learning. These are some of the questions he will ask himself:

1. Is the motivation for lessons for learning skills genuine and strong?

    a. Are the lessons based on established, known needs?

    b. Can and will the skills be put to immediate use?

    c. Will systematic check-ups show each pupil how he is progressing, what he has mastered, and what he still needs to work on?

2. Is there a thorough introductory lesson that inductively leads the pupils to an understanding of the skill and its uses?

    a. Do the pupils analyze simple, specific examples in order to derive the rule for themselves?

    b. Do they immediately apply the rule in carefully supervised practice?

3. Is the follow-up practice properly spaced?

    a. Is there provision for short and frequent practice soon after the development lesson?

    b. Are there review exercises at increasing intervals?

4. Are there many opportunities to put each newly taught skill to use in expressional lessons?

5. Are there periodic check-ups so that the pupil and his teacher can determine any further need for practice or reteaching?

Are the materials adaptable to the school organization? In evaluating the organization of the "content" of the language arts instructional material, the teacher will be guided by the policies that have dominated the organization of the curriculum. If correlation of subjects is to be the rule, then the teacher will consider how well the materials in the language lessons parallel his instruction in other lessons, since many of the topics for oral and written language lessons will be drawn from current lessons in science, social studies, and literature. Or if integration is the established policy, he will consider how well such language activities as discussion, storytelling, reporting, note taking, and letter writing are carrying forward units like "How All the Citizens of Centerville Can Help to Make Our Town Safer" or "How Our Country Won the West." (If language is taught as a part of comprehensive units, the teacher needs a check list of language skills and usages appropriate for learning at successive maturity levels so that he may make sure that there are no serious gaps in the language arts curriculum.)

In schools where English is taught as a separate subject, language instruction is likely to be organized in terms of the logical arrangement of the phases of English to be taught—capitalization, enunciation, word structure, correct usage of pronouns, and the like. In considering the adequacy of such organization, the teacher must not lose sight of the fact that English is used all day long, that language skills need to be put to work in all lessons, that in all lessons the children are likely to betray their need for specific language skills, and that language teaching cannot well be divorced completely from the rest of the curriculum. If the contents of the various branches of the curriculum are not specifically related, there should be at least administrative provisions for language instruction that attend to needs that arise in the other subjects.

Do the materials provide for individual differences? A further major consideration in evaluating the organization of the materials of instruction is the type and degree of provision for the individual differences of pupils. These are some of the questions to guide the evaluation of language arts materials:

1. What provision is made for differences in interest?

    a. Is there a multiple listing of topics and activities so that each pupil may choose in the light of his particular interests?

    b. Is there provision for a child's suggesting topics and activities of his own?

2. How are differences in ability and achievement level cared for?

    a. Is there consistent provision for enrichment and more advanced work on the part of the most able pupils?

    b. Is there more simple and gradually advancing development in skills and activities for the slower learners?

    c. Is there considerable practice material for those slower learners who require much repetition if they are to master skills?

    d. Is there a variety of suggestions for encouraging creative expression so that each child can produce in the light of his specialized abilities and interests?

    e. Is it made clear that practice materials are to be used only if practice is needed, so that an individual or a sub-group in the class may use certain exercises while others are engaged in supplementary activities in the way of enrichment or creative expression?

    f. Are there bibliographies that encourage further reading?

It has been shown that evaluation of instruction in the language arts should include an examination of the materials of instruction in terms of timeliness, relative difficulty, the general content (ideas) which the pupils talk and write about, and the organization of the materials to be taught. It is as pupils work with topics of interest and intrinsic value that they learn with enthusiasm, active attention, and a sense of purpose.

Evaluation of Learning Activities

IN THE long run, it is results that count. A language arts program succeeds only to the extent that children gain in proficiency and derive satisfaction from their learning. In the light of the objectives that have been set up, the teacher and his pupils should try to determine how well they are doing, in what ways they are progressing, and in what aspects a different approach may be needed in order to get better results.

EVALUATION OF LISTENING

Measures for evaluating listening must be largely subjective and based on observation. However, the results of carefully planned observation can do much to suggest better ways of teaching and getting improved behavior on the part of listeners.

Attention of the listener. One evidence of the quality of listening is the kind of attention that pupils are paying. If the pupils' eyes are fastened on the speaker, if their facial expressions and emotional responses change in close accord with the ideas and mood of the speaker, they are probably listening well. Many teachers have found the following evaluative measures helpful in determining how well a class in general pays attention (listens) and which pupils need carefully considered guidance if they are to become satisfactory listeners.

1. Have a teacher or supervisor observe the attention of the pupils as you teach. He should have a paper numbered down the left margin, there being as many numbers as there are minutes in the lesson. At the top, head three columns as follows: *Close attention, Partial attention,* and *No attention.* At one-minute intervals, the observer may note the number of pupils in each of the categories. Afterward, the percentage of attention (per minute) in each category may be worked out. While there is a large degree of subjectivity in the results, the teacher still can determine how attentive the class in general is and which parts of a lesson succeeded best in attracting and holding attention, thus getting some idea of what to avoid and what to cultivate in getting pupils to listen. Some teachers have talked over the percentages with their classes and got them interested in trying to improve their listening. (Suggestion: the observer should probably try out making and using a chart like this before doing one for actual evaluation.)

2. The observer concentrates (unobtrusively) on a single pupil who is known to be inattentive. At one-minute intervals he notes what the pupil is doing. For instance, this is the beginning of a record that covered a twenty-minute period.

    a. Watching teacher closely
    b. Ditto
    c. Playing with a marble taken from pocket
    d. Rolling marble from book to book on desk

    e. Tickling neck of pupil in front with a pencil
    f. Watching teacher draw sketch at board, etc.

Such a record furnishes the teacher with evidence of what attracts or fails to hold an individual pupil's attention as the record is compared with the steps in the lesson. It also provides a basis for a conference to help the pupil realize his problem, and experience has shown his awareness will motivate his effort to improve. Each pupil with problems in paying attention should be studied this way.

3. The teacher may test the pupils by reading them a set of directions to be carried out. These should be relatively simple but should involve the pupils in doing a series of acts in definable order so that the test will show whether the respective pupils have followed the sequence. For instance the teacher might say: "Draw five lines across a sheet of paper. On line 1, write your last name. On line 5, write your first name. On the middle line, write the date of your birthday. On line 4, write your mother's first name. On the second line, write your father's age." (There should be a pause between directions.)

In general, the teacher should observe daily the listening behavior of his pupils, make notes to be placed in the individual files of problem pupils or written up as part of anecdotal records, and hold friendly conferences with such children to ascertain why listening is apparently so poor. He may find that some children are hard of hearing and should be seated to better advantage, or possibly referred to the school health office. Or the child may have serious personal problems that absorb his thinking. Or the teacher may be talking "over his pupils' heads" so that they derive little benefit from listening.

Qualities of listening. Early in the year, a few standards for effective listening should be set up and worked on during the lessons of the day. From time to time, an additional standard should be discussed and worked on. Here evaluation may well consist of changing each standard to a question to be used in a check list like the following:

1. Did I put away all materials I do not need in my lesson?
2. Did I look at the speaker?
3. Did I have a question in mind as I listened?
4. Did I find the answer to this question? If not, why not?
5. Did I follow the steps in the explanation so that I can do things in the right order?

A check list should include standards for the following items: sequence of ideas, accuracy, main points, theme, meanings of unfamiliar words from context, contradictions, unsubstantiated statements, evidence of prejudice, obsolescence, and auditory discrimination, which underlies correct spelling.

The teacher should also be familiar with published tests of listening. Some of these are listed in the bibliography at the end of this chapter.

EVALUATION OF SPEECH

Speech should be evaluated according to the objectives or competences which the teacher and pupils have identified and worked toward during a given period of time. Evaluation methods for speech are sometimes objective, sometimes subjective. The evaluation is sometimes done by the teacher, sometimes by the pupils, and sometimes by the child himself.

Review the competences in speech which were identified in Chapter 7 and listed on the Check Sheet, page 133, and the Consonant Chart, page 137. Notice that four areas are specifically mentioned: (1) communication, which includes specific and general items for practice; (2) voice, which is probably best evaluated by pupils and teacher together; (3) speech, which includes seven separate competences and may be evaluated most effectively if separated from the others for emphasis; and (4) articulation, which may be most accurately and objectively evaluated by the teacher who will continue to develop his own skills for accurate listening.

Suggestions for evaluating oral presentation and discussion follow(24):

Organization of ideas. Clarity and organization of ideas may be assessed through the use of questions such as:

1. Was the topic interesting to the listeners?
2. Were the ideas expressed in order?
3. Was the language well chosen for specific meaning, vivid description, etc.?
4. Was each presented idea carefully developed or explained for the listeners?
5. Could my listeners outline my talk?

Mechanics of oral expression. *What* is said should always be emphasized, but *how* it is said needs special attention too. The teacher may develop with the students standards to be emphasized. Stated in question form some of the mechanical criteria might be as follows:

1. Were the sentences kept apart? (few *and's, uh's,* etc.)
2. Did I look at my listeners?
3. Did I talk to them in a conversational tone, neither too loud nor too weak?

4. Did I articulate clearly but naturally?

5. Did I pronounce words correctly?

6. Was I free from annoying mannerisms?

7. Was I poised before my listeners; did I show interest in them and in my subject?

Periodically, the teacher should record and play back the pupils' one-minute talks and short oral reading selections in order to stimulate interest and a desire to improve voice, speech, usage, and the skills of oral reading.

Choice and development of the topic.   On occasion, there may be consideration of the suitability of the topic or of the development of it. For instance, in respect to a presentation at an assembly, there may be reason to discuss such questions as these:

1. Was my story one that would interest the small children who came to the assembly?

2. Was my topic suitable for an assembly held to honor this holiday? Was it suitable at this time of year?

3. Were my language and manner formal enough for this special occasion? Were they too formal for this fun session?

4. What visual aids are best suited to making my ideas clear and persuasive?

For whatever objectives are being stressed, there can be evaluative questions to correspond. Observation based on a check list of such questions is one of the best ways to evaluate oral presentations. As has been suggested, delayed evaluation may well be based on tapes or recordings of the first presentation. On the other hand, such matters as directness, gestures, and poise may be considered on the spot.

Participation in discussion.   As an instrument of evaluation, flow charts are useful in helping pupils become aware of the part they play in group discussion. There are times, of course, when it is right for one person to assume leadership and do most of the talking, as when one member of the group, either the teacher or a student, has information or understandings which others in the group need. But when the group faces a problem, there will frequently be times when each member should feel the responsibility of sharing in the give-and-take of ideas. Such participation should go far beyond the traditional question-and-answer relationship between teacher and pupil. Real communication of ideas presupposes that pupils have interest and experience enough to ask questions of each other, the teacher, or a visiting resource person; to exchange points of view even when there is a conflict of opinions; to listen to others and to respond— in fact, to enter into mature discussion, eliciting information and opinion, toward a solution of a problem or a better understanding of a subject for common concern.

It is not always easy to persuade pupils that such a mature kind of discussion is either desired or desirable. Those used to a more autocratic leadership in the classroom may not find it easy to meet such demanding requirements in group discussion, since they have become used to waiting for a teacher's question and being satisfied by giving a response. They will have to be taught the meaning of group participation. A way to explain intercommunication and make possible a measurement of growth in this group skill is to keep a flow chart from time to time to show the interplay of ideas expressed by members of the group.

In the flow charts, arrows drawn toward the middle indicate contributions to the group as a whole; those drawn toward the margin indicate irrelevant remarks; arrows that extend from pupil to pupil show exchange of ideas that might still be significant to the group as a whole; those connecting teacher and pupils show direct pupil-teacher communication.

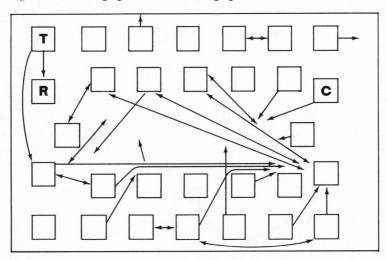

Flow chart showing participation in discussion in a seventh-grade classroom.

This chart shows a double-circle arrangement of a classroom containing thirty pupils. The letter *T* indicates the teacher's seat; *C* indicates the location of the class chairman; *R* shows where an invited resource person is sitting. The single-headed arrows show a one-directional statement or question, and double-headed arrows show an interchange between two persons. It is apparent that, in this classroom situation, the teacher really allowed the chairman to assume the role of leader, that the pupils were free to approach the resource person directly, and that only two pupils made irrelevant remarks. The group dynamics of the situation were apparently good: a wide distribution of response, a democratic atmosphere, and close adherence to the topic of discussion.

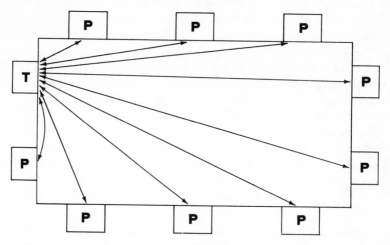

Flow chart showing a completely teacher-dominated discussion.

This chart depicts a situation in which a group of pupils is seated around a table under the direction of a teacher who dominates in a question-answer type of discussion. There is little opportunity for the pupils to challenge or reinforce one another's statement, to interpret, to think independently, or to learn democratic procedures. While few teachers go to such an extreme, still there are classroom situations in which pupils rarely question, challenge, or reinforce one another's statements.

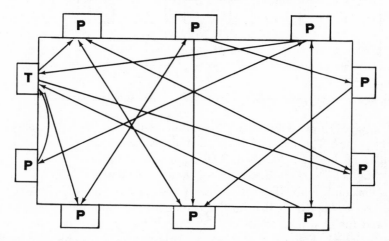

Flow chart showing a democratic group discussion where pupils freely interchange ideas and where the teacher gives considerable guidance.

Quite different is this last flow chart shown. Here there is free interchange between pupil and pupil as well as pupil and teacher. In this situation, the teacher is still needed to guide the discussion, as is shown by the arrows that lead to and from him in a number of instances. Probably the practice of having a pupil chairman, even when a small group is seated around a table, might permit the teacher to play a less prominent role (though he should always be ready to "dip his oar in" whenever the discussion becomes repetitive, argumentative without citing evidence, or too random and non-directive).

By devising check lists and flow charts, teachers can go far in a program of continuous evaluation. The former is directly derived from clearly identified goals of instruction; the latter does much to evaluate classroom climate and to indicate constructive changes that permit and facilitate democratic pupil participation.

EVALUATION OF WRITTEN ENGLISH

The child comes to school with some skill in listening and speaking, but with no skill in writing. The responsibility for his competence in written English, within the limits of his ability and experience, rests entirely with the school. How is his competence measured? Most adults outside the school would judge an individual's written work as a whole. Evaluation in the school, however, must be more analytical. By determining specific weaknesses, a teacher can help a pupil to overcome them; by noting specific strengths, he can build upon them.

Mechanics of writing. Some of the mechanics of writing can be measured objectively; some must be evaluated with a good deal of subjectivity. *Handwriting,* for example, can be judged by established criteria. A check list to guide the teacher or pupil in his judgment would include such items as these: letter formation, spacing between words, spacing between lines, letter size, slant, pressure, and rate of writing. Still more detailed evaluation of letter forms, for example, might include specific points such as these: (1) fullness of letters, as in *m* and *n*; (2) completion of loops, as in *a* and *o*; and (3) parallel loops above or below the line, as in *l* and *h* or *j* and *g*.

A published handwriting scale (1) is available which shows models of handwriting of varying ability arranged in order to show progressive improvement. A pupil's handwriting can be measured somewhat roughly by finding the model in the scale which it most nearly resembles. Similar scales of handwriting can be constructed on the classroom bulletin board from samples of writing done in class.

The *manuscript form* of written work can also be evaluated by comparison with models. Points to include for comparison are (1) margins, (2) paragraph indentation, (3) heading, (4) title, (5) general neatness, and (6) legibility.

Spelling, punctuation, and *capitalization* are usually included as parts of test batteries in language arts. The objectivity of such tests is a desirable factor; they can be scored without the variable of human judgment.

DIRECTIONS: In each pair of words in heavy type in the letter below there is an error in either capitalization or punctuation. You are to decide which one of each pair has the correct capitalization and punctuation. Then mark the answer space at the right that has the same number as the correct form.

SAMPLES: This is 1 mr. Jones.
         2 Mr. Jones. · · · · · · · · · ·

         3 St. Louis, Missouri
         4 St. Louis Missouri

1 654 Magnolia, Avenue
2 654 Magnolia Avenue   1

3 Fort Lyon, 15, Georgia
4 Fort Lyon 15, Georgia   2

5 Sept. 8, 1953
6 Sept 8, 1953   3

1 Dear Dick,
2 Dear Dick — ·   4

Can you come to my 3 birthday
                    4 Birthday · · · · · ·   5

party on 5 saturday at about half.   6
         6 Saturday

past 1 twelve. We will listen.   7
     2 twelve?

to 3 "Treasure Island" on the record.   8
   4 "treasure island"

that you gave me last 5 july.   9
                      6 July.

Mother said, 1 "you may ask.   10
             2 "You

any five boys you 3 wish.   11
                  4 wish."

This excerpt illustrates the way in which the language skills of capitalization and punctuation may be evaluated by standardized tests. (Stanford Achievement Test, Elementary Battery, New York, Harcourt, Brace & World, 1953.)

It is well to remember that tests of this kind measure just what the tests include and no more. A spelling test, for example, measures skill in spelling from dictation or in discovering misspellings in print, as the case may be; it does not measure skill in spelling in daily written work. Experienced teachers know how frequently pupils spell words correctly in a test but misspell the same words when they write. To evaluate competence in spelling one would have to learn not only how well the pupil *can* spell but how well he *does* spell in written work. Attitudes that inspire persistent effort in applying knowledge and skill appear to be an important part of learning but are not easily measured.

Choice of subject, its development and organization. As with oral expression, the evaluation of written work will be concerned with the pupil's choice of topic—whether it is suitable to his level of ability and sufficiently limited in scope to permit adequate development. The teacher must also evaluate the content and organization of the material. Are the main points clearly stated? Are they supported by the necessary facts or reasons? Are the facts correct, complete, and current? Are the reasons sound? Do they cover various viewpoints? Is the material presented effectively? Is it introduced with helpful information or explanation? Is it designed to interest the reader?

Such questions as those above suggest a check list as the most likely form of evaluation. Evaluation of such qualities in writing is subjective but provides useful information when made by a trained reader. The pupils as well as the teachers should know the criteria by which their papers will be graded. Some teachers are reluctant to mark features of written work which do not easily fall into a classification of right or wrong. The result is an overemphasis upon mechanics, and in such case the pupils correctly assume that only the mechanics are important. The evaluation of quality in the thought, organization, and expression of written work is difficult, but it is the surest way to convince pupils that these matters are important.

Some standardized tests attempt to measure these elements in writing by setting up sample compositions with questions on possible revisions or editing. The STEP(17) tests on written communication, grades 4–6 and 7–9, call for judgments of this kind.

Quality of sentences. Sentences in written expression include some elements easily measured objectively and some that must be evaluated subjectively. The *completeness of sentence structure*—its punctuation as a separate and whole unit of expression—may be scored as a part of a punctuation test. However, the seriousness of punctuation errors varies; errors that result in sentence fragments, run-on sentences, or comma faults are more serious because of their effect upon the structure of the written sentence.

Grammatical usage in sentences is often objectively measured by standardized tests or informal check tests. In correcting papers, the teacher may wish to keep an inventory of usage errors that persist after instruction in the writing of some individuals. The record gives evidence of those needing individual or small-group attention. Such an inventory might look like the chart on page 385.

Whether the learning of standard usage carries beyond the exercises in the book and the tests that follow must be a matter of observation. The teacher needs to know whether pupils use the right verb forms in daily written work, or whether they need more instruction; whether they manage the right choice of pronouns; whether they use the correct comparative forms of adjectives and adverbs; whether they use accepted idioms—in all their subjects as well as in their language lessons.

More difficult is the evaluation of *exactness* in expression. Has the pupil chosen the right word to express his thought and feeling? Can he select from several choices the most effective words or phrases? The answers depend in part upon his vocabulary, and vocabulary tests can provide objective evidence on the individual's understanding of word meanings.

The application of the pupil's knowledge of words suggests other factors less easily measured—his interest and effort in expressing himself well; his sensitivity to the situation as he seeks an appropriate word or phrase; his knowledge of his subject matter and his awareness of his reader's understanding. Evaluation of such characteristics is subjective and can best be used with pupils in direct discussion, individually or in a small group, where their specific sentences are considered.

To keep the pupil's papers at hand for comparison and to note gains, the teacher should find a place to keep individual folders of written work. Examples of original paragraphs or compositions, filed for each month of the year, provide the best picture of the pupil's progress in using written language. Only by observing how a pupil assembles correct and adequate facts or thoughtful opinions, how he organizes his ideas, how he expresses them, and in what technical form he presents them for his reader can the English teacher be sure of the pupil's progress.

Summary of Evaluative Techniques

AN EVALUATION of the program in language arts should show for each area of instruction: (1) the achievement of pupils, and (2) their growth and development. A pupil's achievement is his total learning at a given time. His growth is the gain he has made over a period of time. Both can be measured in relative terms, comparing one pupil with others in his group.

The two measurements may reveal quite different standings for the same individual. For example, in the graph below, Pupil 1 starts the year with the advantage of higher achievement and finishes with higher achievement, excelling Pupil 2. On the other hand, Pupil 2, starting at a lower level of achievement, makes a greater gain than Pupil 1.

PUPIL LEARNING FOR THE SCHOOL YEAR

a = achievement at start of the year
b = achievement at the finish
a to b = growth during the year toward c, the desired goal

We have much to learn about how to evaluate growth. Through standard achievement tests given in successive months or years, growth can be measured by comparing scores at the beginning and end of the period tested. These measurements are limited to items that are evaluated objectively in the test and to such periods of time as are determined by the test schedules.

We need means of continuous evaluation so that teachers and pupils can see gains as they occur and can build upon even the small successes that characterize the progress of slow learners. Such evaluation presupposes a knowledge of the stages of growth, which we have not yet defined sufficiently well in most language arts areas.

We need to evaluate in the light of the pupil's capacity to learn and his background of experience. Certainly the normal expectancy should not be the same for all individuals.

Since English is a complex of skills and abilities, attitudes and interests, knowledge and understandings, we need to be able to analyze the pupil's development, to note his strengths and weaknesses. How inadequate is the mark that goes down on a report card as the measure of a pupil's learning! Only when we are specific in evaluation can we or our pupils use the information to redirect energies and make some progress toward desired goals.

The following techniques suggest some of the ways that have been used successfully by teachers or through teacher-pupil cooperation to measure growth and achievement in specific areas of language arts. Many of them have been mentioned elsewhere in the textbook. They are listed here as a convenient summary.

TECHNIQUES FOR THE TEACHER

Among the useful techniques which teachers use for evaluation are these listed below.

Observation. To list observation as an evaluative technique may seem to be stressing the obvious; no one can teach with eyes closed, and the evidence of pupils' development is all around. To merit an important place on a list of evaluative techniques, however, observation must be more than casual. It must be developed as a particular skill, serving a particular purpose. A trained and systematic observer looks for these things:

1. *Evidence of attitudes.* Pupils indicate their attitudes by what they say and do. More important than their words are their actions. What do their facial expressions show—interest or boredom? How prompt are their responses? How involved do they get in their work? How do their voluntary actions correspond to their school behavior? A pupil may say that he likes to read; does he go to the library on his own? Examples of how to observe the specific skill of attention in listening are noted on pages 405–06.

2. *Evidence of skills and abilities.* The objective in teaching skills is to enable pupils to apply them as needed. The teacher in an elementary classroom often has the opportunity to observe how well the skills taught in the language class are applied in other subjects. Every teacher can observe how well a skill taught at one time of the year is applied throughout the rest of the year.

3. *Evidence of knowledge and understanding.* At the appropriate grade level, a teacher may try to develop the understanding that broad statements of fact are of little value unless they can be substantiated by evidence. This is a lesson that must be taught and repeated many times under various circumstances that develop in the classroom. A trained observer will note how well the pupil understands the lesson when he questions unsubstantiated statements or fails to do so, when he controls his own broad statements or fails to do so.

Analysis of daily written work. Evaluation is an essential part of all teaching. The teacher does not wait for a test period to check performance but watches the daily work of pupils. The writing assigned for daily lessons holds the evidence of pupil needs and gains. Analysis of written work can be conducted at times in individual conferences at the pupil's or teacher's desk. When there is not time, marks on the paper can be useful. The analysis must be tempered to the ability of the pupil, that he may find enough to challenge him but not so much that he will be continually frustrated. When pupils write without receiving some analysis of their work, their progress is impeded. They need the teacher's evaluation to direct their next efforts. Some studies indicate that pupils who receive no marginal comments or general marginal comments, like "Excellent" or "Good work, Tommy" or "This is better," made fairly small gains in writing ability. Those who received papers with specific comments which they could interpret and use in revising their papers benefited noticeably.

As has been noted, the easiest factors to find and mark in written work are technical skills and mechanics. These do not represent the total objectives in teaching children to write, however. Despite the extra time required, evaluation of underlying qualities like the following is essential: the suitability of the topic, the adequacy of treatment, the logic of the conclusions, the clarity of the sentences, the effect of the organization.

Analysis of daily oral work. The pupils need the teacher's guidance in their daily speech as with their written work. Constant interruptions to point out poor expression would be devastating to the class. Some teachers keep a note pad at hand and jot down specific criticisms which they deliver to the individual. When the right rapport has been developed, pupils can learn to ask for and benefit from criticism following practice of speech skills.

Frequently the quality of class discussions, oral reports, and the like will be evaluated by teacher and pupil. In addition, specific suggestions for class goals should be clarified and reviewed by the teacher when the need becomes apparent. Evaluation of content and organization, as well as technical speech skills is as important in directing oral work as written.

Inventories and records. The evidence needed for evaluation can sometimes be gathered by direct questioning. An interest inventory may be useful in judging appropriate reading for a pupil; and for such an inventory the teacher can list questions that will reflect degree of interest in many fields. An inventory of individual needs for improving usage is illustrated on page 385. Cumulative reading lists that are kept in each pupil's folder can provide valuable information on extent and quality of required and voluntary reading.

Subjective or essay-type tests. The difficulties in scoring essay tests fairly are well known. Studies show that teachers do not grade papers consistently and that grades range over a wide scale when papers are graded by different teachers or by the same teacher at different times. Despite the weakness of the essay test, its strengths cannot be denied. In a test that requires a paragraph or more to answer each question, the pupil tests his ability to select pertinent information, organize it, and express it.

The subject matter of an essay test can relate directly to what has been taught (not always true of objective tests). In preparing the test, the teacher needs to select questions that cover the most important matters, word the questions clearly to prevent misunderstanding, and limit them specifically to one kind of answer for the sake of comparing results. The length of the tests must be carefully planned for all pupils to complete it.

Walter N. Durost and George A. Prescott(7, pp. 50–51) have these suggestions regarding the grading of subjective tests:

Here the problem is to objectify the scoring as much as possible.
  1. Prepare a scoring key of acceptable responses in advance. List the

points to be covered. If appropriate, categorize acceptable responses as *essential* and *desirable*.

2. Decide in advance on the weight to be given each question, that is, the number of points of score. Inform the pupils of these weightings before they start the test.

3. Score the test without knowledge of the name of the pupil, if possible. This will minimize the "halo" effect. . . .

4. Do not be influenced by handwriting and spelling. Evaluate these separately if you wish, but keep your evaluation of ideas and content separate from them.

5. Score the same question for all pupils at one time, that is, score the first question for all before going on to the second question.

Objective tests, teacher-made. The types of objective tests are familiar. They include true-false, multiple-choice, matching, factual recall, and completion items. The teacher must decide what learnings are to be tested and construct questions that will measure them. Some objective tests aim only at measuring a pupil's recognition, asking the pupil to identify the right answer among several. Some aim to measure recall, requiring memory to make or complete a statement. With proper planning, objective tests can be constructed to test ability to interpret what is read or to observe points of comparison or contrast between ideas or ways of expressing them. Tests can be devised to evaluate a pupil's judgment. The purpose of the test must be clear in the teacher's mind and the test must be constructed for the purpose. No question tests all such abilities at once.

Standardized tests. In standardized tests the teacher finds objective tests prepared by experts. Usually a simplified scoring is possible through a key or by IBM. The advantages are attractive. In choosing a standardized test, a teacher needs to ask the question: Does it test the objectives of the curriculum in this school at this grade level? An analysis of the test items will show how well the test fits the need of a particular school or class.

Since commercial tests are standardized under a set of specific conditions, comparison of test results with test norms can have meaning only if the tests are administered properly. Scoring must be accurate and the interpretation of results demands care. When test results seem not to fit the teacher's judgment of an individual, retesting should be done and the teacher should look outside the test results to find confirmation.

Standardized tests in English cover such subjects as spelling, usage, reading, comprehension, vocabulary, and essay writing. They prove useful in rating skills against a larger group than one classroom provides and help pupils and teacher to measure achievement in the skills tested. They do not pretend to take the place of tests prepared by the teacher to evaluate the work of the classroom.

Many evaluative techniques are teaching techniques, since evaluation is a part of teaching. These listed below can be used by teachers and pupils working cooperatively to evaluate performance and guide further development.

Check lists and standards. Pupils can be helped to establish criteria and use them in evaluating their performance. Before they make oral reports, for example, they formulate standards and list them on a chart called "How to Make an Oral Report." They use the chart in measuring individual performance. Check lists of this kind should not be static. As pupils extend their experience and develop new concepts, they should add new criteria to their lists.

Rating scales. To help children evaluate their own position in relation to their objective, some teachers arrange samples of work (unsigned) to illustrate progressively better skill. A handwriting scale of this kind was described on page 326.

Individual charts or graphs. Pupils can keep individual records of growth in specific skills. In their own notebooks they can chart their voluntary reading, showing month by month how many books they have read and what they are. For example, a chart called "My Reading Road" may show a colored silhouette of an auto for every book read, with the name of book and author written on it.

Class charts. Achievement charts, hung on the classroom wall, may be embarrassing to those who tag along at the end. A different emphasis can be arranged. For example, a chart showing class reading of a limited list of titles available in children's literature may list names of books rather than names of children. A bar graph can move forward an inch after the title of a book every time a pupil finishes reading it. A long bar after a title stimulates other pupils to get the popular books and soon the whole class is clamoring for books that are judged good by their fellows.

Card index files. Some teachers have voluntary reading listed by a dual entry system. Two card index files are kept in alphabetical order—one by book title, on which readers enter their names and a brief comment; the other by pupils' names, on which each pupil lists the books he has read and marks them with a symbol that indicates his rating of the book.

Individual folders for written work. The plan for filing compositions at regular intervals during the year has already been explained. Teachers who use the plan find that the folder produces many kinds of evidence regarding pupil progress. A profile of developing skills in writing is thus made available for both teacher-pupil and teacher-parent conferences.

Paired papers. Growth in language skills is often relatively slow, yet sometimes it is dramatically swift. When the strong purpose and effort of a pupil are combined with good instruction, rapid strides take place. In written work, growth can be shown by pairing two papers of a similar nature. A paragraph written in September can be mounted on a color background with one written in December. Notes identifying specific improvements can be printed on the mat to catch the attention of pupils or visitors. The most radical changes will be noted in the early primary grades. A paper that shows a child's first effort to write his own name or a sentence can be paired with his handwritten copy of a group composition a few months later. The startling improvement of first graders is enough to silence the critics of the schools and make those responsible for such development feel very proud.

The opaque or overhead projector. Devices for showing an individual's work for class study and evaluation are useful. With an opaque projector or the overhead projector, attention can be focused on all or part of a child's work. Evaluation may be concerned with technical skills such as handwriting or spelling, or it may be focused on content or organization. A rapid review of the work of a number of pupils will remove personal embarrassment, or an individual's work may be studied after his name has been blocked out. The projector can save a great deal of time otherwise devoted to copying on the board.

Taped recordings. Some pupils find it almost impossible to listen to themselves speak with any degree of objectivity. They are completely unaware of their own deficiencies in articulation or rate of speech. A tape recording permits them to listen to themselves critically. Only after they have been convinced of their need can they really make steps toward improving.

Disc records. While the tape recordings make a somewhat more faithful record of the voice, discs for making records have their own advantages. Schools can obtain small discs that permit three minutes of recordings. These may even be divided so that a child's speech can be recorded for one or one and a half minutes early in the year and again a few months later. The discs can be identified and filed where they are easy to reach. It is difficult to get comparative performance on tape recordings because of the problem of locating a specific part for comparison.

Individual records of needs. Children can be encouraged to keep a record of their own needs. Thus they may keep a notebook entitled "My Spelling List" in which they enter words they have misspelled. The same kind of list can be made with usage items. Another kind of individual record is a "reading pie." The pupil draws a large circle and marks off the circumference with types of reading, such as history, nature, machines, biography, poetry, mythology, fiction. Other divisions can be designated as the class plans the pie. The balance or lack of balance in the reading list is thus apparent.

Group records. On pages 408–09 three examples of group records may be found in the descriptions of flow charts. The charts record the participation of various members in a group discussion, with arrows indicating who initiated a comment and to whom he directed it.

Evaluative discussion. The devices already mentioned require paper and pencil or machines. One technique of evaluation that requires neither is discussion. After a project (or one of its parts) has been completed, the children can profit from evaluation to see what is being done best and what should be avoided. Some teachers use discussion at the end of the school day to review major work accomplished, attitudes shown, and skills utilized. Through such means they find that ideas are sharpened, motivation increased, and the proper direction for improvement found.

Actually no limitation should be placed upon the right time for evaluative discussion. It serves as the check that prevents scattering of efforts; it is the guide that prevents progress down the wrong path; it constantly reorients a learner to the desired goal. In all learning activities, evaluative discussion is an integral part of the learning.

SUGGESTIONS FOR STUDY AND DISCUSSION

1. What do you think is the difference between measurement and evaluation? What are their roles in determining language power?
2. Develop a set of standards for evaluating oral communication in a grade of your choice.
3. Do the same for written communication.
4. Use your sets of standards in directed observation of language in the grade of your choice.
5. Use recordings of pupils' speech or some of the children's written communication. Make use of the standards you have devised in Suggestions 2 and 3 above in evaluating the pupils' communication.

FOR FURTHER READING

1. APPLEGATE, MAUREE, *Helping Children Write* (Chapter 5). Scranton, Pa., International Textbook, 1949.
2. AYRES, LEONARD P., *Ayres Measuring Scale for Handwriting*. Princeton, N. J., Cooperative Test Division of Educational Testing Service, 1912.
3. BRADFIELD, JAMES M., and H. STEWART MOREDOCK, *Measurement and Evaluation in Education* (Chapter 10). New York, Macmillan, 1957.
4. BUROS, OSCAR KRISEN, *Tests in Print*. Highland Park, N. J., Gryphon, 1961.
5. CUMMINS, ROBERT E., "Evaluating and Grading." *Education* (March 1962), 403–05.

6. DAWSON, MILDRED A., *Outline for Teaching the Language Arts.* New York, Harcourt, Brace & World, 1959. Pamphlet.
7. DUROST, WALTER N., and GEORGE A. PRESCOTT, *Essentials of Measurement for Teachers.* New York, Harcourt, Brace & World, 1962.
8. DUSEL, WILLIAM J., "How Should Student Writing Be Judged?" *English Journal* (May 1957), 263–68, 299.
9. *The English Language Arts* (Chapter 18), Commission on the English Curriculum of the National Council of Teachers of English. New York, Appleton-Century-Crofts, 1952.
10. GREENE, HARRY A., and WALTER T. PETTY, *Developing Language Skills in the Elementary School* (Part IV). Boston, Allyn and Bacon, 1959.
11. —— A. N. JORGENSEN, and J. R. GERBERICH, *Measurement and Evaluation in the Elementary School* (Chapters 15, 16). New York, Longmans, Green, 1953.
12. HATCHETT, ETHEL, and DONALD HUGHES, *Teaching Language Arts in Elementary Schools* (Chapter 15). New York, Ronald, 1956.
13. HERRICK, VIRGIL E., and LELAND B. JACOBS, eds., *Children and the Language Arts* (Chapter 20). Englewood Cliffs, N. J., Prentice-Hall, 1955.
14. KOCLANES, T. A., "Can We Evaluate Compositions?" *English Journal* (April 1961), 252–57, 264.
15. *Language Arts for Today's Children* (Chapter 13), Commission on the English Curriculum of the National Council of Teachers of English. New York, Appleton-Century-Crofts, 1954.
16. LINDVALL, C. M., *Testing and Evaluation: An Introduction.* New York, Harcourt, Brace & World, 1961.
17. ROSS, C. C., and JULIAN C. STANLEY, *Measurement in Today's Schools.* Englewood Cliffs, N. J., Prentice-Hall, 1954.
18. *Sequential Tests of Educational Progress: Writing.* Princeton, N. J., Cooperative Test Division of Educational Testing Service, 1957.
19. SHANE, HAROLD G., and E. T. MCSWAIN, *Evaluation and the Elementary Curriculum* (Chapter 9). New York, Holt, 1958.
20. STRICKLAND, RUTH G., "Evaluating Children's Composition." *Elementary English* (May 1960), 321–30.
21. THOMAS, R. MURRAY, *Judging Student Progress* (Chapter 4). New York, Longmans, Green, 1954.
22. TRAVERS, ROBERT M. W., *Educational Measurement* (Chapter 6). New York, Macmillan, 1955.
23. WRIGHTSTONE, J. WAYNE, JOSEPH JUSTMAN, and IRVING ROBBINS, *Evaluation in Modern Education* (Chapter 14). New York, American Book, 1956.
24. ZOLLINGER, MARIAN, and MILDRED A. DAWSON, *Speech*, Leaflet 11. Champaign, Ill., National Council of Teachers of English. From *English Journal* (November 1958).

Index

T

training lessons, 42, 203, 209, **222–23**, 242, 243, 244, 247, **248–52**, 254, **263–66**, 282, **284–93**
transitional words, 164, 253, 302
transposition for emphasis, 7–8
trips, 20, 63, **195**, **206**, **276**

U

unfinished story, **264–65**, 338, 361
unit teaching, **48–50**, 403
Untermeyer, Louis, 218
usage, word, 11, **13–14**, **15–16**, 41, 43, 45, 46, 176, 253, **295–96**, 308, **377–92**, 394, **413–14**
  aims of instruction of, **379**
  errors in, 52, **384**
  initial stages of instruction of, **380–86**
  inventory of, **130–33**, 383, **385**, 413–14, 417
  methods of instruction of, 51–52, 306, **386–92**
  motivation for, **380–81**
  socio-economic influences on, **11–14**, 64, 128, 188, **377–78**, 380

V

vocabulary
  additions to, 3, **10–11**, 45, 187, 285, 394
  as a common element, **28**
  development of, 40, 41, 42, 44, 45, **61–80**, 175–76, 223–24, **303**, 335, 336
  enrichment of, 40, **66–68**, **76–78**, 95–96, 112, 162–63, 176, 246, 268, 269, 271, 294
  factors affecting growth of, **62–66**, 142
  faulty teaching of, **74–75**
  history of words in, **9–13**, **173–74**, **179–81**

vocabulary—(*Continued*)
  in curricular areas, 30, 44, 69–70, 81, 82, 285, 294, 338
  types of, **61–62**
  variations of, 3, **11–12**, 63, 64, 73, 224
  variety and precision in, 44, 72–74, 76, 77, 90, 96, 176, 246, 253, 257, 279, 282, 283, 294, 300, 302, 303, 310, 313, 414
voice problems, **141**

W

Watts, A. F., 23
Webster, Noah, 333
Wells, Charlotte, 244
Who's Who, 86, 92
Wilt, Miriam, 148
Witty, Paul A., 150
word order (*See* sentences, word order in, *and* syntax.)
word usage (*See* usage, word.)
World Almanac, 86, 92
written language, 3–4, 13, 256–314
  basic motivation for, 26, 284, 306, 308
  basic principles of instruction in, **308–11**
  content of, **413**, 414
  evaluation of, 308, **411–14**, 416–17 (*See also* checking written work and socialized correction.)
  functions of, 26, 298–99, 308
  kinds of compositions in, **266–67**, 276, **279–84**, **357–58**
  practice in, **263–64**, **290–92**, 310
  relation to oral, **30–31**
  stages in learning, 40–41, 42, 44, 45–46, 258–67, 269–72
  technical skills in, 57, **263–64**, 269, 283, **295–96**, 300, **305–07**, 309, **411–13**, 420
  use of standard English in, 31, 414